THE
QUEEN

THE
QUEEN

ANDREW MORTON

Michael O'Mara Books Limited

First published in Great Britain in 2022 by
Michael O'Mara Books Limited
9 Lion Yard
Tremadoc Road
London SW4 7NQ

Copyright © 2022 by Andrew Morton
Published by arrangement with Hachette Book Group, Inc., 1290 Avenue of
the Americas, New York, NY 10114, USA

A CIP catalogue record for this book is available from the British Library.

Papers used by Michael O'Mara Books Limited are natural, recyclable
products made from wood grown in sustainable forests. The manufacturing
processes conform to the environmental regulations of the country of origin.

ISBN: 978-1-78929-448-4 in hardback print format
ISBN: 978-1-78929-464-4 in trade paperback format
ISBN: 978-1-78929-449-1 in ebook format

1 2 3 4 5 6 7 8 9 10
Front cover photograph by Everett Collection Inc/Alamy
Jacket design by Ana Bjezancevic
Designed and typeset by Design23
Printed and bound by CPI Group (UK) Ltd, Croydon, CR0 4YY

www.mombooks.com

*To my mother Kathleen and all those
of the war generation*

CONTENTS

SURFING WITH HER MAJESTY

F OR THOSE OF US FORTUNATE enough to have met Her Majesty the Queen, it's a moment we're unlikely to forget.

I was on my first major tour as a royal correspondent for a British newspaper and I recall watching in wonder as the Royal Yacht *Britannia*, pristine and glowing in the dappled sunshine, slowly sailed into San Diego Bay. It was February 1983, and those few days in the company of the Queen and the Duke of Edinburgh transformed my life.

Britannia was surrounded by a raucous welcoming armada of speedboats, yachts, catamarans, skiffs and canoes. It was a Saturday morning when the yacht docked and the royal party emerged. The Queen's nine-day tour of California, land of surf, sun and starry-eyed dreams, was supposed to be a carefully curated review of the best that The Golden State had to offer, from the artifice of Hollywood to the natural splendour of Yosemite National Park.

However, if the visit had been a Broadway play it would have been named: *The Tour That Goes Wrong.*

In days gone by, when the Royal Family arrived in a new country, with some reluctance they would hold a cocktail party for the press corps who dogged their every move. So, suited and booted, I found myself handing over my gold-embossed invitation card to a waiting Navy officer and was then invited to take a proffered gin and tonic – a measure naval and substantial – on *Britannia's* aft deck.

It took me back to a foggy day in October 1965. I was eleven years old and, proudly dressed in a freshly pressed Scout uniform, I took my place lining the route on the outskirts of Leeds to see the Queen and the Duke of Edinburgh go by on their way to open the brand-new, brutalist Seacroft Civic Centre. As they drove past, the dank, claustrophobic fingers of fog, combined with the bright interior light in their high-domed Rolls-Royce, only served to heighten the effect of two exotic beings dropped in from outer space, alien creatures come to view mundane municipal life. Although I caught just a fleeting glimpse of the Queen and her consort, the memory has always stayed with me.

The Queen has been part of my life forever. Growing up, the Royal Family were like the White Cliffs of Dover: immutable, impregnable, ever present. A necessary part of life, like breathing. Not only did her image appear everywhere, from postage stamps to coins, but it could also be seen looking down disapprovingly from behind the headmaster's desk, just as punishment was being administered. At the Regal Cinema in Cross Gates, we regularly mumbled through the national anthem after watching that week's children's offering – Cliff Richard's 1963 movie *Summer Holiday*, about a group of friends singing and dancing their way across continental Europe on a London double-decker bus, was a favourite.

Viewed through my young eyes, the Queen was not a real

human being. She was a distant, faraway symbol, an occasionally smiling personage who in her Christmas Day broadcast, which we gathered round the telly to watch at three in the afternoon, spoke in barely understandable English.

For me, the only relatable and human element of our Monarch was the fact that she was a few months younger than my mother and both had served in the Second World War: my mother Kathleen in the Land Army and Princess Elizabeth in the Auxiliary Territorial Service (ATS).

On that Saturday in San Diego, I have to confess that my first encounter with Her Majesty was less than memorable. The diminutive lady in a striking blue-and-white outfit, which some fashionistas described as reminiscent of a Cockney Pearly Queen, listened with increased inattention as I went on about the impressive size of the US fleet lying at anchor in the harbour. She agreed politely and promptly moved on.

The next few days, though, did peel back some of the mask of monarchy, revealing a somewhat different character to the stern visage reproduced on Britain's postage stamps. The visit became the very antithesis of a royal programme, where every movement, every meet and greet is timed to the minute. What with gale-force winds, storms at sea, overflowing waterways, noisy IRA sympathizers, washed-out roads and inebriated celebrities, what could possibly go wrong?

It seemed she positively relished it when a meticulously devised schedule was thrown up in the air. Years later, her grandson Prince William made the same observation. 'They love it when things go wrong,' he said. 'They absolutely adore it because obviously everything always has to be right, but when things go wrong around them, they're the first people to laugh.'[1]

On this particular royal visit, the weather proved to be the key disruptor. While the Queen and Prince Philip attended engagements in San Diego and Los Angeles, *Britannia* had sailed up the coast to Long Beach, where the plan had been for the couple to rejoin the royal yacht and cruise a little further north to Santa Barbara. On arrival in Santa Barbara Harbour, they were due to be met by the President and First Lady, Ronald and Nancy Reagan, before heading up to their home – Rancho del Cielo (translated as 'ranch in the sky') north-west of Santa Barbara – for a taco lunch and a horseback ride. Following a tornado over LA, however, the Pacific was far too rough for the royals to travel from Long Beach to Santa Barbara by sea, so they had to go by plane instead.

But even the morning journey from the yacht's berth to the airport proved far from straightforward, as roads in the area had been closed due to flooding. The only way through the rising water was in a high-axled US Navy bus. Not wanting to let people down, the Queen donned a pair of galoshes and climbed into the front seat. Secret Service agents were glad she didn't sit further back as, during their cursory examination, they discovered that the bus had more than its fair share of lewd graffiti scrawled on the rear of several seats.

Further unexpected drama was to come after landing in Santa Barbara. Following handshakes and a brief exchange of pleasantries with the Reagans, the Queen and Prince Philip embarked upon a jouncing 7-mile switchback ride in a four-wheel-drive Chevrolet Suburban, which involved motoring through a steep obstacle course of flooded streams, submerged roads, falling boulders and downed tree limbs to reach their destination. Her Majesty remarked that it was all 'terribly exciting'. Unfortunately, a much-anticipated horseback ride in the scenic Santa Ynez Mountains was cancelled and the tacos were eaten indoors.

After that experience, Reagan later wrote to the Queen somewhat contritely: 'I know your visit to our West Coast became a harrowing, tempest-tossed experience but through it all your unfailing good humor [sic] and graciousness won the hearts of our people.'[2]

A couple of days before the organizational fiasco surrounding the Rancho del Cielo visit, the royal couple had attended a gala dinner alongside a host of Hollywood stars at the sound stage of the M*A*S*H TV show at 20th Century Fox studios in Beverly Hills. Although Frank Sinatra and Perry Como might have sung one duet too many it seems that the Queen enjoyed the entertainment, which included comic George Burns and Dionne Warwick, as well as meeting American stars such as Fred Astaire and James Stewart, and a British contingent comprising the likes of Michael Caine, Roger Moore, Jane Seymour and Elton John.

Five days after the gala event, at a more intimate dinner for about thirty on board the royal yacht in San Francisco Bay, the Queen and Prince Philip hosted the President and First Lady in celebration of the Reagan's thirty-first wedding anniversary. The British Royal Marine Band played the 'Anniversary Waltz' on the pier and later, the Deputy White House Chief of Staff, Michael Deaver, serenaded the party on the piano, singing 'True Love' for the couple. Reagan told the party that when he married Nancy, he promised her 'a lot of things, but not this'.[3] Among the guests at this exclusive gathering was the preacher Billy Graham and his wife Ruth, who had been specially invited by the Queen. It was another insight into her personality, her Christian faith having inspired a long friendship with the charismatic American pastor.

The following day, the royal couple went to Yosemite National Park where they stayed at the exclusive Ahwahnee Hotel which had a spectacular view of a 1,400-foot-high unique rock formation called 'the Royal Arches'.

When the Queen and Prince Philip went for a stroll, they were disconcerted to find members of the American Secret Service following closely behind them. However quickly they walked, the agents were right on their tail. This was not the British way, where bodyguards know to keep their distance.

At first the two royals were irritated. Then they played a game, walking backwards so that the Secret Service agents would have to mimic them. They moved back and forth, and finally everyone started laughing. Hardly the expected behaviour of a Head of State, but another clue to her character, a woman with a fine appreciation of the absurd.

Her Majesty is a person whose whole life has been punctuated by a series of superlatives: the longest reigning, the most travelled and, for a shy person, the most gregarious, as she has met more of her subjects face-to-face than any other sovereign in history. In 2008, when the then French President Nicolas Sarkozy asked her if she ever got bored, she replied honestly: 'Yes, but I don't say so.'[4] In an age of celebrity and artifice, she has always preferred being down to earth and straightforward.

She has regularly appeared on *The Sunday Times* Rich List, but has also enjoyed donning rubber gloves to do the washing up and cleaning after barbecues on her Scottish estate at Balmoral. At her favourite log cabin, a member of staff once suggested that they should install a plaque there that read: 'Queen Elizabeth Swept Here.'[5] Though she has always lived in palaces and castles, she seemed to relish a life more normal.

As a young woman, she had been cast into an extraordinary role. Even as a child she was one of the most talked-about people on the planet, the early clues to who she was and what she became to be found on the top floor of a central London townhouse almost a century ago.

CHAPTER ONE

SHIRLEY TEMPLE 2.0

T HE YOUNG GIRL WITH the furrowed brow and intent expression bent furiously over her book. She carefully turned the pages and then when she spotted her target, she would grab her pen and scribble and scratch out the offending words: 'Dr Simpson.' Scribble. 'Dr Simpson.' Scratch. That he was but a name in one of the books in her nursery was irrelevant as far as the angry ten-year-old girl was concerned.

As Princess Elizabeth went about her solemn, destructive task, her younger sister Margaret played with the snaffles, bridles and saddles of the wooden horses that crowded their nursery. Margaret was focused on her make-believe world, unconcerned about her sister's silent rage concerning a certain Mrs Simpson who, unbidden, had begun to change all their lives. She was also less than interested in the growing crowds that jostled and shoved in the winter gloom to catch a glimpse of the comings and goings to and from 145 Piccadilly, the London home of their parents, the Duke and Duchess of York.

After all, the sisters were used to peering out from their top-floor bedroom, watching people looking at them, both sides wondering what the other was doing. It was a game that would last a lifetime. On this occasion, though, the number of onlookers was greater than normal and the atmosphere inside the stone-fronted townhouse was tense and hurried. The two front doorbells, labelled 'Visitors' and 'House', rang more frequently and as the crowds of the curious and concerned grew, police were drafted in.

The name 'Simpson' had initially been whispered and then became part of disapproving discussions that ended abruptly whenever the girls came within earshot. Much as her parents tried to protect Lilibet – the family's nickname for the princess – and her sister, the older daughter was sensitive to moods and rhythms. She was adept at catching the conversational drift, especially as, since her tenth birthday, she enjoyed the privilege of taking breakfast with her parents – and occasionally her grandmother, Queen Mary. She was able to gather crumbs of information that were denied her younger sister. Not that Elizabeth was old enough to appreciate what was really going on.

She just knew that at the heart of the puzzle was that woman Simpson. The evidence was all around. Her father looked visibly ill, Queen Mary, who was routinely ramrod-straight and imperious, seemed older and somehow shrivelled, while her mother's normally jaunty demeanour had for once deserted her. Nor did it help when, in early December 1936, the Duchess of York came down with a nasty case of flu and was confined to bed.

When Elizabeth asked the three women in her life – her governess Marion Crawford (known as Crawfie), her maid Margaret 'Bobo' MacDonald and nanny Clara Knight (known as Alah) – about what was going on, their responses were evasive and dismissive. Indeed, Crawfie often took the girls for swimming lessons at the Bath Club as a necessary distraction. This down-to-earth triumvirate were the girls' window on the world, their genteel observations and prim prejudices shaping the children's own responses. As far as the princesses were concerned the name 'Wallis Simpson' was taboo in the House of York. So, Elizabeth went through her books, scratching and scribbling in a futile attempt to delete from her world the name of the woman who would change her life, and that of her parents, forever.

A short while after celebrating her tenth birthday, Elizabeth had briefly met Wallis Simpson in the spring of 1936. Not that the American woman made much of an impression. Mrs Simpson had arrived with the princess's Uncle David, the new King Edward VIII, to see her parents at their weekend home, Royal Lodge, in the manicured acres of Windsor Great Park. Her uncle had come to show off the two American interests in his life – a brand-new Buick station wagon and his other fascination, the twice-married lady from Baltimore. After the couple had left, Elizabeth asked her governess Crawfie who that woman was. Was she responsible for the fact that Uncle David rarely came to see them these days? Of all her father's brothers and sisters, he had been the most frequent visitor to 145 Piccadilly, joining the girls for card games of Snap, Happy Families and Racing Demon after tea. He was always fun and took time to play outdoors with his nieces. On one occasion, captured on a home movie from the early 1930s, the then Prince of Wales is seen ushering the Duchess of York and her daughters onto the lawns at Balmoral and teaching them how to perform the Nazi salute – to much hilarity.

While Crawfie's response to Elizabeth's questions about the chic American may well have been non-committal, the Scottish governess found herself rather liking Mrs Simpson, later describing her as a 'smart attractive woman, with that immediate friendliness common to American women'.[1] Her employers did not share this opinion. After spending a convivial hour discussing gardening and taking tea with the Yorks and her paramour, Wallis was left with the distinct impression that 'while the Duke of York was sold on the American station wagon, the Duchess was not sold on [the King's] other American interest'.[2]

On the day, it was the two young princesses who provided the chief talking point, not the American contingent. 'They were both so blonde, so beautifully mannered, so brightly scrubbed, that they might have stepped straight from the pages of a picture book,' recalled Wallis in her memoir, *The Heart Has Its Reasons*.[3] Elizabeth and Margaret were, as children often are, used as the human equivalent of coffee-table books, their presence a neutral conversational diversion, a way of avoiding tricky grown-up issues. By the time they first met with Wallis Simpson, the girls had become practised at being used in this way, impeccably mannered children introduced to the visiting adults to help break the conversational ice.

It was the same in the summer of that fateful year, when they travelled to Scotland to stay at the modest eighteenth-century house called Birkhall Lodge, part of the Balmoral estate that was first purchased by Queen Victoria. The Yorks' principal guest was the Archbishop of Canterbury, Dr Cosmo Gordon Lang, who had accepted their invitation after the King, who traditionally would have invited England's senior Protestant prelate to Balmoral Castle, had seemingly snubbed him in favour of a livelier list of guests. Instead, up the road at the castle, he and Wallis were hosting a jaunty party of aristocrats, Americans and royal relatives, including his second cousin Louis Mountbatten and his younger brother Prince George with his wife Princess Marina.

After tea on the second day of the prelate's visit, Elizabeth, Margaret and their cousin Margaret Rhodes sang songs 'most charmingly'. The Archbishop noted: 'It was strange to think of the destiny which may be awaiting the little Elizabeth, at present second from the throne. She and her lively little sister are certainly most entrancing children.'[4]

The King was not so enamoured. When he heard that the ecumenical head of the Church of England was staying with the Yorks, he suspected his brother of attempting to set up a rival court. Their emerging conflict centred on the Sovereign's wish to marry Wallis once she had divorced her husband, the shipping agent Ernest Simpson. In those days, divorce wasn't just frowned on; it was deemed anathema in the eyes of the Church. As the secular head of the Church of England, the King should have been the last person to marry a divorcee, let alone a soon-to-be twice-divorced American of no standing or status. For his part, Edward VIII threatened to renounce the throne unless he was allowed to wed the woman who had stolen his heart.

Although the British media had kept a lid on the blossoming romance – pictures of the King and Wallis on board the steam yacht *Nahlin* during a summer cruise in the Adriatic had appeared everywhere except in Britain – the potential constitutional crisis was finally made public early in December 1936. It set in motion a series of calamitous events that unintentionally placed Princess Elizabeth at the heart of the drama.

By then, Wallis had secured a decree nisi from her husband but had to wait a further six months for the decree absolute, thus allowing her to marry the King and become his Queen. In spite of a dire warning from his private secretary Alec Hardinge – supported by Prime Minister Stanley Baldwin – that he would cause irrevocable damage to the monarchy and probably provoke a general election if he continued along this path, the King's mind was made up. At a tense meeting on 16 November, he informed the Prime Minister that he intended to marry Mrs Simpson as soon as she was legally free. If the government opposed his plan, he would simply abdicate. He later conveyed his decision to his mother and siblings, who were shocked to the core. Queen Mary even sought the advice of a therapist to verify her conclusion that her eldest son had been bewitched by a skilful sorceress. Baldwin was more sanguine, informing his Cabinet colleagues that the elevation of the Yorks to the positions of King and Queen might prove to be the best solution, as the Duke of York was rather like his much-loved father, George V.

Not that Prince Albert, known as Bertie, would have agreed. He was slowly but surely being wound into a constitutional web that gave him no opportunity of escape. It was the stuff of nightmares. While there was some discussion that Prince George, the Duke of Kent, who was the youngest of the four brothers, could take over the throne as he already had a son, the fickle finger of fate pointed to the second-born, the unfortunate Bertie.

Shy, diffident and cursed with a congenital stammer, as the duke considered the hand he was now being dealt, his immediate thoughts went out to his eldest daughter, whose position would change from third in line to the throne to Heiress Presumptive, a future Queen sentenced to a lifetime of duty and public solitude.

Though he had grave doubts about himself and his own capacity to take on such a great office of State, he quietly admired his firstborn. She had extraordinary character and solid qualities that, as he told the poet Osbert Sitwell, reminded him of Queen Victoria. High praise even from a doting father who was, as Dermot Morrah, royal historian and friend of the duke, observed, 'reluctant to sentence his daughters to the lifetime of unremitting service, without hope of retirement, even in old age, which is inseparable from the highest place of all'.[5]

Princess Elizabeth was rather more matter-of-fact and practical. When it became inevitable that her father was going to succeed his elder brother as King, Princess Margaret asked, 'Does that mean you're going to be Queen?' to which her sister replied, 'Yes, I suppose it does'.[6] Elizabeth didn't refer to it again, except when her father casually mentioned that she would need to learn to ride side-saddle for the occasions when, hopefully in the far-distant future, she would have to appear on horseback at the annual Trooping the Colour ceremony at Horse Guards Parade.

Although she gradually grew resigned to becoming Queen she did, according to her cousin Margaret Rhodes, think that moment would be 'a long way off'.[7] As an insurance policy, she added to her evening prayers the fervent hope that she would have a baby brother who, by dint of his sex, would leapfrog over her and become the heir apparent.

While Princess Elizabeth largely accepted her new station with the phlegmatic unconcern of youth, her father reacted differently. He 'broke down and sobbed like a child'[8] when he visited his mother, Queen Mary, to tell her the abdication was imminent. On Friday 11 December 1936 – the year of three kings – Edward VIII's abdication was announced. It was at Windsor Castle where the now ex-King gave his historic live broadcast containing the memorable passage: 'I have found it impossible to carry the heavy burden of responsibility and to discharge my duties as King as I would wish to do without the help and support of the woman I love.' After praising his younger brother's 'long training in the public affairs' of the country and his 'fine qualities', he also pointed out that he had 'one matchless blessing, enjoyed by so many of you and not bestowed on me – a happy home with his wife and children'.[9]

But no longer so happy for the family in question. While his wife, now Queen Consort, lay confined to her bed with a nasty bout of flu, the new King described the momentous event as 'that dreadful day'. The next day, the hitherto ignored but now central characters in this unfolding drama greeted their altered circumstances with a mixture of excitement and irritated acceptance. When Princess Elizabeth saw an envelope addressed to the Queen, even her calm demeanour was punctured. 'That's Mummy now, isn't it?' she asked, while her younger sister lamented the fact that they had to move into Buckingham Palace. 'You mean forever?' she remarked, incredulously.[10]

On the day of the official proclamation on 12 December 1936, both girls hugged their father, who was dressed in the uniform of Admiral of the Fleet, before he left to attend the Accession Council at St James's Palace. After he had gone, Crawfie explained that when he returned he would be King George VI, and from then on they would have to curtsy to their parents. They had always curtsied to their grandparents, King George V and Queen Mary, so were already more than familiar with this respectful practice.

When he came back at one o'clock, each princess presented him with a beautiful curtsy, the behaviour of his daughters bringing home to him his new station. Crawfie recalled: 'He stood for a moment, touched and taken aback. Then he stooped and kissed them both warmly. After this we had a hilarious lunch.'[11]

By virtue of her father's changed royal status, Elizabeth began to transition into a living symbol of the monarchy; her name mentioned in prayers, her doings and her dogs now the daily fodder for the breakfast newspapers, her life owned by the nation. Along with the Hollywood child star Shirley Temple, she became the most famous face in the world, a subject of wonder and adoration.

Her life as a fairy-tale princess was, in reality, less Walt Disney and more Brothers Grimm. The sisters' new life in Buckingham Palace, a sprawling, echoing place of sinister shadows, scurrying mice, gloomy rooms and portraits with eyes that followed as one tiptoed past, was a mixture of excitement, boredom and isolation. It was a place where childhood nightmares came to life, where the daily round of the royal ratcatcher and his deadly paraphernalia symbolized the gruesome reality behind the perceived regal glamour. Thrown into the circumscribed circle of her sister, governess, maid and nanny, with her parents a distant harassed presence, Elizabeth became an object of fascination for millions.

———•———

Apart from having to settle into a new home, in some ways not much had changed for the Heiress Presumptive. With her glowing ringlets of blonde hair, Elizabeth had been a national symbol all her life. Born on Wednesday 21 April 1926 at 2.40 in the morning, just days before the General Strike that crippled the British economy, she represented, in the midst of national crisis, values of family, continuity and patriotism. Not only was her arrival a welcome diversion from the daily struggle for subsistence in a post-war Britain wracked by dispute and want, it was also somehow medieval, mysterious and rather comical.

Royal custom dating back to the seventeenth century decreed that the Home Secretary be present at a royal birth, lest an imposter be smuggled into the bedchamber. In keeping with tradition, the person who occupied that Cabinet office in 1926, William Joynson-Hicks, whose agitated mind was occupied with thoughts on how to defeat the trade unions in the coming conflict, sat in a nearby room at 17 Bruton Street, the Duke and Duchess of York's London family home, when the birth was imminent.

Once the baby was delivered, the royal obstetrician Sir Henry Simson gave Joynson-Hicks an official document outlining the bare details of the arrival of a 'strong healthy female child'. The certificate was then handed to a special messenger, who hurried to the President of the Privy Council to enable him to make the formal announcement. The Lord Mayor of London was also notified and he duly posted the news on the gates of his residence, Mansion House.

In the official medical bulletin, signed by Simson and the

duchess's personal doctor Walter Jagger, they stated that a consultation had taken place before the confinement and a 'certain line of treatment was successfully adopted', decorously suggesting that the princess had been delivered by Caesarean section.[12]

Though the sleeping infant was, by virtue of the 1701 Act of Settlement, then third in line to the throne behind the Prince of Wales and her father and not expected to reign, her lineage was a rich stew of the royal, the exotic and the common.

While her great-great-grandmother was Queen Victoria, she was also linked, through her grandmother Queen Mary, to dentist Paul Julius von Hugel, who practised in the Argentinian capital of Buenos Aires. On her father's side, the blood of European royalty, notably the German Houses of Saxe-Coburg-Gotha and Hanover predominated, though it was her mother's British heritage that intrigued.

Anthony Wagner, Garter King of Arms from 1961 to 1978, noted that among Elizabeth's many aristocratic ancestors were two dukes, the daughter of a duke, the daughter of a marquess, three earls, the daughter of an earl, one viscount, one baron and some half a dozen country gentlemen. And it was not only the aristocracy who were represented in her bloodline, but also the worlds of commerce and religion.

According to Wagner, her hereditary pedigree included a director of the East India Company, a provincial banker, two daughters of bishops, three clergymen – one related to the first American President, George Washington – an Irish officer and his French mistress, a London toy dealer and a metropolitan plumber, as well as a certain Bryan Hodgson, the landlord of The George coaching inn in Stamford, Lincolnshire.

Though her heritage demonstrated a wide social range, the historically regal names chosen by her doting parents – Elizabeth Alexandra Mary – suggested her future destiny as Queen. Others agreed, the *Daily Graphic* newspaper observing presciently: 'The possibility that in the little stranger to Bruton Street there may be a future Queen of Great Britain (perhaps even a second and resplendent Queen Elizabeth) is sufficiently intriguing.'[13]

With Uncle David only thirty-one in April 1926, and expected to marry and produce an heir, that likelihood seemed remote. Yet there was no doubting the fact that the royal infant had been taken into the nation's bosom. Judging by the excited crowds gathered outside her London home, there was something singularly special about Princess Elizabeth, perhaps a reflection of the fondness felt towards her mother who was held in such high esteem and affection. In an authorized account of the Duchess of York's life, first published in 1927, biographer Lady Cynthia Asquith admitted that she struggled to find anything other than sweet perfection in the character of the new mother.

Early photographs revealed young Elizabeth to be the quintessential bonny baby, with her clear blue eyes, perfect pink and white skin, and a mop of blonde hair. Or as Queen Mary, one of the first visitors to Bruton Street, noted in her diary, she was 'a little darling with lovely complexion & pretty fair hair'.[14]

Without uttering a word, she propelled her parents from the quiet backwaters of royal life to the front pages of newspapers and magazines. She was the Princess Diana of her day, every morsel of information turned into a banquet of gossip and speculation. Newspapers were merely supplying popular demand – weeks after her birth, the pavement outside her London home was packed with so many people that it was sometimes necessary for her to be taken out by the back entrance, concealed in her pram, for her daily breath of fresh air.

On the day of her christening in the chapel at Buckingham Palace on 29 May, such was the crush to see the infant that a number of well-wishers broke through the police cordon outside the royal building. Until order was restored, the lucky few who had surrounded the Yorks' car were able to catch a glimpse of the child who, it was later reported, had cried throughout the ceremony which was conducted by Dr Cosmo Lang, the Archbishop of York.

After a few months, the Yorks moved to 145 Piccadilly near Hyde Park, a four-storey establishment that came complete with a ballroom, electric lift, library, a dining room for thirty, and around seventeen staff, who included a steward, two footmen, the duke's valet and three nurses to attend the new arrival. Yet, in a collective case of myopia, media correspondents lovingly described how the Yorks had rejected the showy and ornate, opting for a life of simplicity, especially in the royal nursery. In this miniature kingdom, neatness, order and a sensible routine reigned. There was much clucking of approval when it was revealed that the princess was only allowed to play with one toy at a time. Ironically, when her parents returned from a six-month tour of Australia in 1927, they brought with them an estimated 3 tonnes of toys for the little girl whom the media now dubbed 'Betty'. Thus the eternal paradox of royalty, or our perception of royalty, evolved: that they were and are different, but also the same as ourselves.

By the time she could walk and talk, the child dubbed the 'world's best-known baby' had appeared on the cover of *Time* magazine above the tagline 'Pincess Lilybet', which was a reference to how she spoke her own name. She featured, too, on Commonwealth postage stamps, boxes of chocolates, tea caddies, tea towels, commemorative mugs and other goods. Songs were sung in her honour, Madame Tussauds installed waxworks of her as a two-year-old and again two years later on a pony, while the Australians named a piece of Antarctica after her. Her only rival in this sea of adulation was her Uncle David, the Prince of Wales, who for many years was a bona fide international pin-up.

Her mother was concerned about the inordinate amount of

attention she received. During a visit to Edinburgh in May 1929, she wrote to Queen Mary: 'It almost frightens me that the people should love her so much. I suppose that it is a good thing, and I hope that she will be worthy of it, poor little darling!'[15]

As the months and years passed by, the contours of the young princess's personality, real and imagined, began to emerge. Frequently described as 'cherubic' or 'angelic', she was portrayed as a sunny, well-behaved girl with an innocent wit and an engaging and endearing temperament.

When the Royal Family gathered at Sandringham for Christmas 1927 and held a party for the estate workers, she was described by the *Westminster Gazette* as 'chattering and laughing and bombarding the guests with crackers handed to her by her mother'.[16] Even Winston Churchill was impressed. On a visit to Balmoral in September 1928, the then Chancellor of the Exchequer wrote to his wife Clemmie: 'She has an air of authority & reflectiveness astonishing in an infant.'[17]

Stories soon circulated about how the unafraid girl had tamed her irascible grandfather, King George V, who was known to strike terror into the hearts of his children and senior staff. When Princess Elizabeth was in his presence, he was like putty in her little hands, the Archbishop of Canterbury recounting an occasion when the Monarch acted in the role of a horse being led round the room by his 'groom' and granddaughter, who clung to his grey beard as he shuffled along the floor on his knees.

'He was fond of his two grandsons, Princess Mary's sons,' recalled Mabell, Countess of Airlie, a former courtier, 'but Lilibet always came first in his affections. He used to play with her – a thing I never saw him do with his own children – and loved to have her with him.'[18]

The fact that she was a cherubic little girl with an unselfconscious and vivid imagination, particularly with regard to horses, made her so appealing and charming to the King. So much so, when she was just four, the doting Monarch gave her a Shetland pony named Peggy.

Indeed, her ability to soothe the troubled brow of the Sovereign – echoes here of the medieval notion of the healing royal touch – became a talking point among the nation in February 1929, when George V travelled to the seaside resort of Bognor on the south coast of England to recover from a near-fatal illness. The two-year-old princess kept the old man amused with her chatter and was widely appreciated for her curative role in helping to effect his recovery. He loved that she began to call him 'Grandpa England' and was always attentive in his company, listening gravely as he extolled the virtues of duty, decency and hard work.

The constant company of doting adults encouraged a certain guileless precocity. When she was about to go for a walk with the Archbishop of Canterbury, Dr Cosmo Lang, in the garden at Sandringham, she is believed to have requested that their conversation did not dwell on God. 'I know all about Him already,' said the nine-year-old, solemnly.[19]

At the age of four, Elizabeth made her first friend outside the immediate Royal Family when she was in Hamilton Gardens, near her 145 Piccadilly home, and saw a girl of about her own age playing. She was called Sonia and was the daughter of George V's radiologist, Dr Harold Graham-Hodgson. 'Will you come and play with me?' asked the young princess, and then together they enjoyed a game of French cricket for an hour under the watchful gaze of their respective nannies. Afterwards, they met virtually every day – until Elizabeth had to move to Buckingham Palace. Even so, for a long time she considered Sonia to be her best friend. She even dedicated an unfinished novel – *The Happy Farm*, written when she was eight – to her. The inscription read: 'To Sonia, My dear little friend and lover of horses.'[20]

Sonia had happy memories of their long acquaintance: 'She was a sweet child and great fun. She always had a great sense of humour and a vivid imagination.'[21] Most games involved horses, but sometimes the two friends imagined they had been invited to a grand ball and would earnestly discuss what they would like to wear. Before the Second World War, they took dance lessons together and in 1946 Elizabeth was guest of honour at Sonia's twenty-first birthday. In spite of Elizabeth's elevation, they stayed in touch and saw each other from time to time at dinner parties or for afternoon tea.

On 21 August 1930, a playmate of a very different kind entered her life when her sister Margaret Rose was born at Glamis Castle, the haunted ancestral home of the Duchess of York's Strathmore family, located north of Dundee in Scotland. Once the formalities were dealt with – the new Home Secretary John Robert Clynes had travelled to the northern redoubt to certify the birth – Elizabeth was introduced to the infant. She was suitably 'enchanted', especially when she realized that it wasn't a perfectly formed dolly, but rather a living, if sound asleep, sister.

Thousands of well-wishers, some driving from Glasgow and Edinburgh, as well as south of the border, joined the celebrations at Glamis Castle where a huge bonfire was lit.[22] As with the birth of Elizabeth just days before the General Strike, Margaret's arrival served as a sunny counterpoint to the dark economic clouds that had blanketed the nation since the effects of the Wall Street Crash the previous autumn had reached the UK.

The temporary feeling of disappointment arising from the birth of a girl rather than a boy served once more to highlight Elizabeth's constitutional position. It led to earnest discussions about the proposition that the Crown could technically be shared between the sisters or that the younger sister could take precedence. It became such a matter for debate that the King ordered a formal investigation into the vexed issue. As common sense suggested, it was officially recognized that Elizabeth had seniority.

The constitutional niceties of being a member of the Royal Family were further brought home to the Duchess of York when it came to the naming of her second child. She had to accept that the final decision would be made by her daughter's grandparents, King George V and Queen Mary, and not the parents. Initially, the Yorks were set on naming their child Ann Margaret, the duchess thinking Ann of York a pretty name. Her in-laws demurred, preferring Margaret Rose; Margaret being a Scottish Queen and family ancestor. The King and Queen prevailed. It would not be the last time that they interfered in the upbringing of the royal princesses. Margaret's mother bit her tongue and busied herself with the new arrival. She was eager to describe the child's personality to friends and family. In a letter to Dr Cosmo Lang, she wrote: 'Daughter No. 2 is really very nice, and I am glad to say that she has got large blue eyes and a will of iron, which is all the equipment that a lady needs! And as long as she can disguise her will, & use her eyes, then all will be well.'[23]

The arrival of Margaret Rose added a new actor to the royal melodrama. Now a neat quartet – 'We four', as the duke repeated endlessly – they represented home, hearth and family. In an age of uncertainty, mass unemployment and poverty, they were the embodiment of an ideal of ordinary, decent, God-fearing folk who lived modestly and sensibly. Even though their London residence was a grandly exclusive townhouse adjacent to Hyde Park, complete with ballroom and electric lift, it was the fact that they preferred a cosy home life to café society which ensured their popularity.

This connection between the nation and the Royal Family was epitomized by the kindness of the people of Wales – the most depressed kingdom of the realm in the early 1930s – who presented Princess Elizabeth with a miniature house called Y Bwthyn Bach

(The Little House) for her sixth birthday. Designed by Edmund Willmott and made using Welsh labour and materials, the two-storey thatched cottage, two-thirds the scale of a normal house, was a magnificent creation that came complete with electricity, running water and a flushing toilet. There were pots and pans, books by Beatrix Potter, food cans and even a gas cooker – all reduced to scale. It was installed at the Royal Lodge, the Yorks' new, if dilapidated, country retreat in the grounds of Windsor Great Park.

The princesses were enthralled with the present, spending hours cleaning, brushing, polishing and 'cooking'. Elizabeth would wrap the silverware in newspaper so that it wouldn't tarnish, while Margaret's great joy was running up and down the stairs, and pulling out the plug in the bathroom and listening to the water gurgle through the pipes. Official palace-sanctioned photographs of the girls standing outside the front door of their cottage, or playing with their beloved corgi dogs in the house garden, gave the watching public a window into their innocent lives, further cementing the generational bond between the Royal Family and their subjects. Assessing the public's covetous fascination with the two princesses, Alan 'Tommy' Lascelles, who at this time was the King's assistant private secretary, described them as the 'Pets of the World'.[24]

The sense that the young princesses were somehow daughters of the wider national family was reinforced by the authorized publication in 1936 – months before the abdication – of a picture book entitled *Our Princesses and Their Dogs*, which lovingly chronicled the eight dogs, including two corgis, owned by the family and the central place they occupied in their daily lives. The book also stands as a heart-warming allegory of the intimate relationship between the monarchy and its people, the book symbolizing that immutable compact, one that was strained but not broken before the year was out.

While the girls' corgis, Dookie and Jane, were constant companions, the animals that ruled Elizabeth's nursery kingdom were her horses: real, inanimate and imagined. Though her corgis became synonymous with her life and reign, her first passion was for the equestrian world, and Anna Sewell's well-thumbed equine classic, *Black Beauty*, was her bedside testament to that love. 'If I am ever Queen, I shall make a law that there must be no riding on Sundays. Horses should have a rest too,' she once pronounced, gravely.[25]

Equine creatures were all-consuming in her young life: from leading her grandfather around the room by his beard and turning a string of Woolworths' pearls into a rein to perform the same manoeuvre on her mother's biographer, Lady Cynthia Asquith, to playing circus horses at Birkhall Lodge in Scotland with her cousin Margaret Rhodes, where it was 'obligatory to neigh'.[26] Later injuries that she sustained, notably when she was thrown against a tree and on another occasion kicked in the jaw, did nothing to dim her enthusiasm. When she was five, she rode to a meet of the Pytchley Hounds on her pony Peggy, her father hoping that she would be 'blooded' if there was a kill. There wasn't.

When Elizabeth's new governess, Scottish-born Marion Crawford, walked into her bedroom at Royal Lodge in October 1933, their first conversation concerned the two abiding interests in her life, namely her horses and her sister Margaret Rose. She had been allowed to stay up late to meet the woman whom she would later call 'Crawfie' and was sitting on her wooden bed driving imaginary horses around the park. For reins, she used cords from her dressing gown which were tied to her bedknobs. 'Have you seen Margaret?' asked the princess. 'I expect she is asleep. She is adorable but very naughty sometimes. Will you teach her too and will you play with us both? Will you let me drive you round the garden?'[27]

For several years Crawfie, as the girls' companion and teacher, played the role of a docile working horse, making deliveries of imaginary groceries and other items to pretend customers in the neighbourhood. During these playtime diversions, she gained an insight into Elizabeth's vivid imagination, especially when the princess delivered the goods herself. As Crawfie recalled: 'Then the most wonderful conversation took place – about the weather, the householders' horses, their dogs, chickens, children and menfolk.'[28]

Crawfie quickly realized that Elizabeth's interest in all matters equine was more than a passion: it verged on an obsession, a first and lasting love. The princess often remarked that 'had she not been who she was, she would like to be a lady living in the country with lots of horses and dogs'.[29] A variation on this childhood wish was to marry a farmer and have lots of cows, horses and children.[30]

She was also very protective of the thirty or so wooden horses that crowded the top-floor nursery, to the extent that when the family was about to move to Buckingham Palace, she decided to leave her favourite horse, Ben, with her friend Sonia for safekeeping. It was delivered to the palace two weeks later after her other horses had been unpacked and lined up in the corridor outside her bedroom.[31]

As she settled into her new life at Buckingham Palace, the highlight of her week was her riding lesson with instructor Horace Smith. She spoke knowledgeably about galling, girths and currying, an indication that her interest in horses extended to both their care and their management.

For Elizabeth, horse riding was a chance to be herself, to enjoy control in a socially acceptable setting. So much of her daily routine was out of her hands: Bobo chose her clothes; Alah picked her menu; Crawfie organized her lessons; her parents, grandparents and the men in suits at Buckingham Palace defined her future. She went through a phase where she would wake several times in the night and ensure that her shoes and clothes were folded and arranged just so. It was a form of control but in another guise.

Her education was a classic example of the continual battle for the heart and mind of the Heiress Presumptive. While her grandfather, King George V, barked at Crawfie, 'For goodness' sake, teach Margaret and Lilibet to write a decent hand, that's all I ask of you,'[32] Queen Mary was much more involved. She vetted the governess's academic timetable, the royal matriarch suggesting more Bible reading and the learning of dynastic history. Most Mondays, the Queen took the girls on educational excursions incognito to places such as the Royal Mint, the Tower of London and the Bank of England, as well as to art galleries. These visits didn't always go to plan. On one occasion, the party was looking around the Harrods department store when a craning crowd gathered to catch a glimpse of the princesses. Elizabeth became excited at the prospect of so many people wanting to see her that her grandmother, not wanting her moment of stardom to go to her head, gently ushered her out by a back door.

It was Queen Mary who led the palace faction, augmented by the royal librarian Owen Morshead, and the formidable Lady Cynthia Colville, the Queen's senior lady-in-waiting, who felt that Elizabeth's education was too ladylike and easy-going. There was little cognizance in her syllabus, such as it was, of her possible future role and responsibilities. According to Lady Cynthia, 'No Bowes-Lyon ever cared anything for things of the mind.' It was a judgement that trusted royal chronicler Dermot Morrah considered a tad harsh, given the fact that the family had produced three female poets in the previous two decades.[33]

The princesses' mother felt very differently. She and the duke were not overly concerned about their daughters' academic education. The last thing they wanted was a pair of 'blue stockings', girls who were too smart for their own good. As Crawfie observed:

'They wanted most for them a really happy childhood, with lots of pleasant memories stored up against the days that might come and, later, happy marriages.'[34]

For her part, the Duchess of York had been brought up on fresh air, a little French and a smattering of German. Her own parents, Lord Glamis (later the 14th Earl of Strathmore and Kinghorne) and his wife, Cecilia Cavendish-Bentinck, had educated their youngest daughter at home with a governess, only sending her to a private day school in London when she was eight. More emphasis was laid on arranging a vase of flowers, sewing, dancing a reel and reciting poetry than learning Greek or Latin. Young Elizabeth Bowes-Lyon was taught to be polite, how to look after visitors, where to cast for salmon, when to pick up dead birds during a shoot and how to handle a shotgun. She was, however, no intellectual slouch. When she finally attended school, she passed the Oxford Local Preliminary Examination when she was just thirteen.

Literature and scripture were her scholastic strengths and so it was no surprise that the duchess insisted on teaching the girls Bible stories in her bedroom every morning. Kindness, courtesy and Christian values mattered. She believed that a decent character, a moral compass and a sensitive awareness of the needs of others was as important, if not more so, than intellectual endeavours. In a letter to her husband she laid out her own strictures, reminding Bertie that his own father had lost the affection of his children because he had so often shouted at him and his brothers.

Stuck in the middle was the hired hand, Marion Crawford, who was only twenty-two, and though a teaching graduate of Moray House Training College in Edinburgh – the future alma mater to *Harry Potter* novelist J. K. Rowling and Olympic cycling gold medallist Sir Chris Hoy – she was out of her depth in the subtle back and forth of palace politics. Indeed, the Yorks had chosen Crawfie precisely because she was young enough to enthusiastically join in with the children's games.

Lessons, which included arithmetic, geography, history, poetry – anything about horses captured Elizabeth's interest – and English grammar, took place only in the morning between 9.30 and 11.00 with an hour's break for elevenses and games, followed by another hour of reading before lunch was served at 1.15 p.m. There were also frequent interruptions for visits to the dentist, hairdresser and dressmaker, Crawfie clearly sensing that education did not come high on the list of the duchess's priorities.

Any attempt to extend the school day by their governess was resisted, as the girls' mother was keen for them to enjoy outside play. Often, their father joined in games of hopscotch, hide-and-seek and Sardines in Hamilton Gardens at the rear of their home. As she grew in confidence, Crawfie took the children further afield, organizing trips on the Underground, boat rides on the River Thames and even, at Elizabeth's insistence, riding on the top deck of a double-decker bus. It quickly became clear to her that the princesses were eager to experience what other children enjoyed as a matter of course.

The girls, as well as Elizabeth's friend Sonia Graham-Hodgson, enjoyed weekly dancing lessons with Marguerite Vacani, during which Elizabeth proved particularly skilful at Scottish country dancing. It was, however, those Hollywood hoofers Fred Astaire and Ginger Rogers who were all the rage. For a time, Elizabeth's favourite was the 1935 hit song, 'Cheek to Cheek'.

They were also enrolled for music lessons with piano teacher Mabel Lander, a graduate of the Viennese School. Elizabeth, sometimes accompanied by her mother, would sing English ballads, African-American spirituals and Scottish airs – 'The Skye Boat Song' was an enduring favourite. When Margaret was old enough to join in, her elder sister was immediately impressed by her ability to pick up a tune by ear.

French classes, which often took place when Crawfie was on holiday, were not so popular. On one occasion, presumably in protest at the dull teaching methods, a bored Elizabeth picked up a silver inkpot and turned it upside down on her blonde locks. Their French mistress duly had an attack of the vapours and left Crawfie to sort out the inky mess.

Music, dance and drawing classes interspersed with occasional French lessons were all very well, but Crawfie felt that Elizabeth and Margaret needed the stimulation and companionship of children their own age. 'In those days we lived in an ivory tower, removed from the real world,' she recalled in her memoir, *The Little Princesses*.[35]

In 1937, Crawfie experienced one of her most satisfying achievements when she first set up a Girl Guide company – and later a Brownie pack – that met at Buckingham Palace every Wednesday. For once, the sisters were able to mingle with their contemporaries. The twenty-strong Guide troop comprised children of palace employees, friends and courtiers. In the Kingfisher patrol of the 1st Buckingham Palace Company, Elizabeth was deputy to her older cousin, Lady Pamela Mountbatten. Because Margaret was too young to be a Guide, she joined the specially created Brownie pack, mixing with up to thirteen others.

It was just as well that they had children of their own age to play with as there was a step change in their lives once they had moved into their rooms at Buckingham Palace in the spring of 1937. When Elizabeth went out and about, she was now accompanied by a detective who had the ability, to the girls' amusement, to seemingly make himself invisible. Elizabeth now spoke of 'the King and Queen' rather than 'Mummy and Daddy', and spent more time curtsying and being curtsied to than she had at 145 Piccadilly. Even the nursery menus were in French – just like those put before her parents. As for the nightly pillow fights and other high jinks that had punctuated their lives at 145 Piccadilly, they were soon a distant memory. The King and Queen were just too busy.

Besides playing skittles in the long corridors of Buckingham Palace, there was one significant perk to being a princess in a palace. Elizabeth discovered that the act of walking in front of the sentries guarding her new home meant that they had to present arms each time. Wandering back and forth in front of a sentry, therefore, became a new game that she never tired of.

Trumping this delight was the excitement surrounding the Coronation, which was scheduled for May 1937. Queen Mary took the event as a didactic opportunity, bringing a panorama of the 1821 Coronation of King George IV into the nursery and proceeding to teach the princesses about the symbolism and meaning of the ceremony. By the end of the lesson, Elizabeth was, according to Crawfie, an expert. Perhaps as enticing as these rites and rituals was the prospect of wearing their beautiful Coronation attire and lightweight coronets designed by their father. 'They came to me very shyly,' recalled Crawfie, 'a little overawed by their own splendour and their first long dresses.'[36]

In her serious motherly way, what concerned eleven-year-old Elizabeth most about the Coronation was whether her little sister, then six, would conduct herself properly. She remembered that when she had been bridesmaid at the wedding of her uncle and aunt, the Duke of Kent and Princess Marina of Greece and Denmark, at Westminster Abbey in November 1934, Margaret was allowed to sit quietly with her mother. However, when Elizabeth first appeared, walking down the aisle and holding the bridal train, Margaret had waved at her, possibly in a mischievous attempt to distract her from her solemn duties. Elizabeth would not be swayed. She gave her sister a stern look and shook her head in order to discourage Margaret from further misbehaviour. The older princess did not want a repeat at the Coronation. In the end, she was happy to report to Crawfie that her sister had behaved beautifully. It was all the more commendable as both girls had been awake most of the night due to the singing and chatter emanating from the waiting crowds outside the palace.

Princess Elizabeth recorded her memories of that historic day in a lined exercise book neatly tied with a piece of pink ribbon, with a touching inscription written in red pencil on the cover. It read: 'The Coronation, 12th May 1937. To Mummy and Papa in memory of their Coronation. From Lilibet by herself.'[37]

She described how she was awakened by the band of the Royal Marines outside her bedroom window and then, wearing a dressing-gown, shoes and an eiderdown, how she and Bobo MacDonald had 'crouched in the window looking onto a cold, misty morning'.[38] After breakfast, they dressed and paraded about in their finery before visiting their parents who were themselves in the midst of dressing for the big day.

After wishing them 'good luck', the princesses and Queen Mary climbed into a glass coach for a 'jolty' ride to Westminster Abbey. Elizabeth was mesmerized by the elaborate choreography of the Coronation and was rather disappointed that her grandmother had not been able to remember much about her own special day. At one point in the proceedings, when the prayers had seemed interminable, Elizabeth looked through the Coronation programme and pointed to the word '*Finis*', the princess and her grandmother smiling at one another as they enjoyed a conspiratorial moment together.

The Coronation was a piece of living history, up close and personal, as well as a vivid and enthralling foretaste of the next stage in Elizabeth's royal education. This began with her attendance at her first Buckingham Palace garden party, followed by Trooping the Colour and finally the ancient royal ceremony of the Order of the Garter, held in St George's Chapel at Windsor Castle.

With no baby brother on the horizon, Elizabeth's on-the-job training intensified. When Joseph P. Kennedy, the new US Ambassador to the Court of St James's, arrived in London with his family in the spring of 1938, they were invited to a weekend stay at Windsor Castle. The King placed his eldest daughter next to him at a luncheon held there in early April. So that she did not feel entirely left out, Margaret accompanied the Kennedys and her family on a walk through Frogmore Gardens. On another occasion, at the end of a State visit made by President Albert Lebrun of France in March 1939, Elizabeth joined her father and the French leader on the drive from Buckingham Palace to Victoria Station, from where the French delegation were set to depart on their return journey.

Somewhat belatedly, the new Queen now realized that her eldest daughter's academic education needed to be broadened. After discussions with, among others, Sir Jasper Ridley, a banker and Fellow of Eton College, it was decided that the princess should study constitutional history with Henry Marten, the Vice-Provost of Eton. Although she was at first apprehensive about her twice-weekly visits to the all-boys college, Elizabeth soon struck up a friendship with the dapper scholar, enjoying this grown-up introduction to politics, history and current affairs. Indeed, political theatre was playing out right in front of her when her parents appeared on the balcony of Buckingham Palace on 30 September 1938, with British Prime Minister Neville Chamberlain and his wife Anne, to celebrate the famous Munich Agreement that notoriously brought 'peace in our time' with the Nazi leader of Germany, Adolf Hitler.

She was indeed growing up. By the age of thirteen, she was, according to Crawfie, 'an enchanting child with the loveliest hair and skin and a long, slim figure'.[39] Not that the Eton boys seemed to notice. If any pupils needed to visit the Vice-Provost's rooms during her lessons or saw her in the corridors, they politely doffed their top hats and went about their business. For a girl who had been gawked at all her life this was a refreshing change, though it is possible that the growing adolescent, seeing boys en masse for the first time, felt that their well-bred indifference was a tad too, well, indifferent.

Apart from her cousins, George and Gerald Lascelles, the sons of Princess Mary, her aunt, Elizabeth had had little to do with boys during her childhood. It is perhaps unsurprising, given her fascination with horses, that her first girlish crush was on Owen, a young groom who had helped to teach her to ride. In her eyes he was the fount of all wisdom and could do no wrong – much to the exasperated amusement of her parents, particularly her father.

The father-daughter bond they shared was particularly significant. 'The King had great pride in her, and she in turn had an inborn desire to do what was expected of her,' observed Crawfie.[40] Theirs was a loving, complex relationship. The King, a reserved, shy man, admired her precocious maturity while gallantly trying to protect her from her lonely future. At times it seemed that he wanted to stop the clock, to keep his daughters as children rather than growing girls.

For her part, her father brought out her mothering nature, especially when he suffered one of his 'gnashes', which were outbursts of temper often caused by his frustrated inability to conquer his persistent stammer. Both girls developed techniques to coax him out of these dark moods. They also learned to keep out of his way and let Mama deal with him.

In the summer of 1939, with the prospect of war hovering over the horizon, the royal party sailed to the Royal Naval College at Dartmouth in south-west England, on board the Royal Yacht *Victoria and Albert*. It was here on 22 July that Elizabeth would meet the young man who would change her life. The omens were not propitious.

Originally, the princesses had been due to attend a service in the chapel following an inspection of the cadets, but as two cadets had contracted mumps, which can cause infertility, it was decided that the girls should spend time at the house of the Captain of the College, Sir Frederick Dalrymple-Hamilton. His two eldest children, nineteen-year-old Christian and seventeen-year-old North, were deputed to keep them occupied. In the midst of playing with a clockwork train on the floor of the nursery, the quartet was joined by a good-looking boy with piercing blue eyes, sharp features, an off-hand manner and the look of a Viking. Enter Prince Philip of Greece and Denmark, the Adonis-like nephew of the King's personal naval aide-de-camp, Lord Louis Mountbatten. The eighteen-year-old prince soon grew bored with the trains and suggested jumping over the nearby tennis net instead. Crawfie thought that 'he showed off a good deal', while her charges had a different perspective, admiring how high he could leap. Even though Elizabeth never took her eyes off him, he paid her little attention. He was simply doing his duty when his Uncle Louis (more commonly known as 'Dickie') had ordered him to keep the girls company. He would have much preferred to have been present at the main event, where the King was inspecting the ranks of aspiring naval officers.

If he had been told by that incorrigible royal matchmaker Lord Mountbatten to befriend Elizabeth, then he made a half-hearted job of it. At lunch the following day, he exhibited a youthful enthusiasm for the extensive menu rather than making small talk with his royal companion. In short order, the hungry cadet, who was used to rather more modest Navy rations, devoured several plates of shrimps, a banana split and anything else in his reach. 'To the little girls, a boy of any kind was always a strange creature out of another world,' noted Crawfie, who was somewhat censorious of his over-confidence in company. 'Lilibet sat, pink-faced, enjoying it all very much. To Margaret, anyone who could eat so many shrimps was a hero.'[41]

He was a strange, exotic creature indeed. After all, royal blood aside, the background and upbringing of Elizabeth and Philip could not have been more different. His was an extraordinary, scarcely believable early life: his grandfather, King George I of Greece, was assassinated; his father, Prince Andrew of Greece and Denmark, was arrested, court-martialled and sentenced to death; his mother, Princess Alice of Battenberg, was forcibly placed in an asylum. Philip was famously born on a dining table in a villa called Mon Repos on the Greek island of Corfu. In December 1922, the eighteen-month-old infant, an orange box for his crib, and the rest of his family escaped the island on board HMS *Calypso*, a British light cruiser vessel, after his father was sent into permanent exile; the death sentence imposed by a military tribunal was commuted following the intervention of King George V.

Following the family's rushed departure from Greece, the young prince led a fairly unsettled life until the age of nine. He saw little of his father, who moved to Monte Carlo with his mistress, and even less of his mother, who was diagnosed with schizophrenia and admitted to an asylum. Between December 1930 and August 1931, his four older sisters had all married and moved to Germany to be with their aristocratic husbands. Philip, who lived for a time with his maternal grandmother Victoria Mountbatten at Kensington Palace and also with his uncle, George Mountbatten, was enrolled at Cheam School in 1930 as a boarder. He then studied at the Schule Schloss Salem in Germany in 1933, before completing his formal education at Gordonstoun in northern Scotland, a newly established school run by Kurt Hahn, a German Jew and founder of the Salem school, who had escaped from his home country.

For all his travails, Philip was remembered as a cheerful, lively fellow with an inquisitive mind and a natural sporting ability. He has no sense of self-pity about those days. 'The family broke up,' he told his biographer Gyles Brandreth. 'My mother was ill, my sisters were married, my father was in the south of France. I just had to get on with it. You do. One does.'[42] At Gordonstoun he was made Guardian or Head Boy in his final term, while at Dartmouth he won the King's Dirk for the best all-round cadet in a term, as well as the Eardley-Howard-Crockett prize for the best cadet in the college.

He certainly caught the eye of the princess and the rest of the royal party, as the *Victoria and Albert* slowly sailed along the estuary pursued by a flotilla of rowboats carrying excited cadets who gave the ship a rousing farewell. As the estuary broadened, some boys still followed in the ship's wake. Finally the King, fearing that one of the cadets might get into trouble, told the Commander of the Royal Yacht, Sir Dudley North, to signal to them to go back. Gradually, all the boys began to return to shore apart from one young blade, who had ignored all entreaties to leave and had kept on rowing. It was Philip, who was being watched intently through the binoculars by Lilibet. Eventually, the young prince realized that no one was impressed by his seaborne bravado and so he turned round to return to college.

Six weeks later, Britain declared war on Germany, and by early January 1940 Philip found himself commissioned as a midshipman and assigned to the battleship HMS *Ramillies*.

The girls first heard the news of the impending conflict when Minister Dr John Lamb preached an emotional sermon at Crathie Kirk near Balmoral, where they were staying in August–September 1939. He told the congregation that peace was over and Britain was once again at war. As they left the service, nervous and excited, Margaret asked Crawfie: 'Who *is* this Hitler, spoiling everything?'[43]

They would soon find out.

CHAPTER TWO

BOMBS AT BEDTIME

S HORTLY AFTER WINSTON CHURCHILL became Britain's
wartime prime minister in May 1940, a Nazi spy parachuted
into England. The Dutch-born agent, who went by the name
of Jan Willem Ter Braak, carried with him a revolver, a radio
transmitter, fake documents and a bundle of cash. His orders were
simple: find and kill Winston Churchill. For a time, Ter Braak
lived with a couple in Cambridge and then, his money running
out and fearing capture, he walked inside an air-raid shelter and
shot himself.[1] This was probably the earliest of at least three plots to
assassinate the British leader, the conspirators sometimes hitting
the wrong target. As Churchill himself noted in his war memoirs:
'The brutality of the Germans was only matched by the stupidity
of their agents.'[2] But he was too dismissive. The German policy of
killing or seizing political leaders and royal Heads of State came
within a whisker of success. George VI, the Queen – whom Hitler
later described as 'the most dangerous woman in Europe' – and
their daughters were key targets for capture and imprisonment.

One plan was for parachutists to drop into the garden of
Buckingham Palace and other royal parks from low-flying aircraft
with the intention of apprehending and holding the King and his

family under 'German protection'. The man behind this scheme, Dr Otto Begus, had almost snared Queen Wilhelmina of the Netherlands during the Nazi invasion of the Low Countries. In May 1940, while troops were parachuting over the Dutch royal residence in The Hague, Begus and his *Kommando* were involved in air-landing missions that led to a number of gliders crashing at the nearby Valkenburg Airport.

Wilhelmina just managed to avoid being caught, leaving behind all of her personal belongings and making her way to the Hook of Holland, where a British destroyer, HMS *Hereward*, was waiting to pick her up along with her family, the Dutch government's gold and diamond reserves, and members of the Dutch government too. The operation, code-named Harpoon Force, was a success, though the vessel was attacked by German Stuka bombers on arrival in the Netherlands and also on departure. Eventually, Wilhelmina arrived safely at Buckingham Palace, where the exhausted Dutch ruler recounted her adventures to the British King and Queen.

King Leopold III, the Belgian monarch, was not so fortunate. On 28 May, about a month before the fall of France, he controversially surrendered his forces to the Nazis after his embattled troops were surrounded. He was imprisoned in his chateau outside Brussels until 1944 and then ultimately sent to Austria. Throughout Europe, other crowned heads were on the run from the Nazi invaders. King Haakon VII of Norway spent several weeks evading capture as he and his son, Crown Prince Olav, were pursued by a hundred-strong squad of crack Nazi paratroopers. Like Queen Wilhelmina, he too was finally rescued, the shattered sovereign and his son clambering on board the British heavy cruiser HMS *Devonshire* and taken to England. Upon arriving at Buckingham Palace, they were so tired after their traumatic escape on 7 June that they fell dead asleep on the floor, the Queen quietly tiptoeing around them lest she disturb their slumbers.

Further south, the Duke and Duchess of Windsor, who were in neutral Portugal, also narrowly avoided being kidnapped. Under a plan code-named Operation Willi, Hitler sent his top spymaster, Walter Schellenberg, to Lisbon to lead a team tasked with seizing the royal couple and spiriting them across the border to General Franco's Spain. In the nick of time, Churchill got wind of the plot and ensured that the couple boarded a ship bound for the Bahamas, where the former British king was appointed as Governor of the islands, albeit reluctantly.

Hitler's stratagem had been based on the thinking that by installing the Duke of Windsor as a puppet king of the soon-to-be conquered England, or holding other European royals as hostages, then their presence could be used as a means of controlling the behaviour of their citizens. This strategy of threatening or coercing national leaders to support the invaders was as old as warfare itself.

In the summer of 1940, with Britain on the ropes – its expeditionary force having been rescued at great cost from the blood-stained beaches of Dunkirk from late May to early June – Hitler was circling for the kill. At some point in August, as the plan to invade Britain, code-named Operation Sea Lion, was being drawn up, Begus, according to his later testimony, received written instructions to report for an important mission.[3] His target this time was the British Royal Family: a specially trained *Kommando* of parachutists, including some from the Dutch mission, was being readied to capture the King, Queen and their daughters, and the emphasis was on taking the royal hostages alive. Parachutists were even briefed on the correct salute and form of address when seizing a member of the Royal Family.

In the grand German scheme, it was Hitler's belief that if the airborne kidnapping attempt had succeeded Britain would have been forced to surrender. Only the failure of the Luftwaffe to triumph over the RAF in the Battle of Britain resulted in the plan being scrapped. Even so, the prospect of German paratroopers landing in the environs of Buckingham Palace, the Tower of London and other royal residences was one taken very seriously by the Royal Family and senior military and political leaders.[4]

The Queen, who was frightened of being captured, practised her shooting skills with a pistol in the gardens of Buckingham Palace and used rats flushed from bombed royal out-buildings as target practice. Her niece Margaret Rhodes later recalled: 'I suppose, quite rightly, she thought if parachutists came down and whisked them away somewhere, she could at least take a parachutist or two with her.'[5]

King George VI, who now always kept a rifle and a pistol in his car when he travelled, personally supervised the removal of the priceless Crown Jewels from the Tower of London to their temporary new home at Windsor Castle, where they were carefully wrapped in cotton wool, put in leather hat-boxes and hidden in the dungeons below the castle.

Behind the brave smiles and the confident, public glad-handing, both the King and Queen felt a sense of impending doom during the most fateful summer since the Spanish Armada had threatened invasion in 1588.

Anticipating the grim, uncertain days that lay ahead, the Queen wrote to her eldest sister Rose, asking if she would look after the princesses if anything happened to the King or herself. Rose gladly agreed, writing in response: 'I do promise you that I will try my very best & will go straight to them should anything happen to you both – which God forbid!'[6]

Though both the King and Queen spoke about going down fighting should the Nazis invade, there was the distressing issue of what to do about their precious daughters. Many of their aristocratic friends had sent their offspring to Canada, while others had opted to evacuate their children to the British countryside. After the declaration of war on 3 September 1939, following Germany's invasion of Poland, the princesses had gone to stay at Birkhall Lodge in the Scottish Highlands – with Balmoral Castle considered a Nazi bombing target – while their parents, along with a skeleton staff, kept Buckingham Palace open.

For the first few months of the so-called 'Phoney War', the girls rode their horses, enjoyed innocent pastimes such as catching falling leaves and making a wish, and learned French under the watchful eye of Georgina Guérin. She later returned to her home country where she would play a leading role in the French Resistance. In addition, Elizabeth continued her history lessons with Henry Marten by post. The war seemed a long way away, though doubtless the girls, sensitive to parental moods, discerned the strain behind the light-hearted banter during the daily six o'clock telephone call. Even the fitting of gas masks seemed little more than a game, Princess Margaret, then nine, treating the rubber object like a strange toy.

Naturally, the Queen wanted to spare her daughters from worry as far as possible, telling their governess to monitor radio broadcasts and newspaper coverage. 'Stick to the usual programme as far as you can, Crawfie,' ordered the King. That was easier said than done, as the girls frequently tuned in to hear the loquacious pro-Nazi broadcaster 'Lord Haw-Haw', the American-born Irishman William Joyce, and his propagandist radio show. Often, they were so appalled by his anti-British invective that they pelted the radio with cushions and books.

In October 1939, the sinking of the *Royal Oak* battleship, which led to the loss of 834 men and boys, brought home to the girls the cruel reality of warfare. 'Crawfie, it can't be,' expostulated Princess Elizabeth. 'All those nice sailors.' It was a confusing and concerning time, especially as their parents were more than 500 miles away in a place where, to their young minds, it seemed that Hitler could easily capture them.

Even though the princesses were staying in the idyllic surroundings of Royal Deeside, the tentacles of war touched everything. Every Thursday, Crawfie organized a sewing club in aid of the war effort, the girls serving refreshments for the roomful of local women. The King's decision to allow Craigowan Lodge on the Balmoral estate to be used to house evacuated children from the tenements of Glasgow certainly widened his daughters' horizons. When the kids arrived, often with their mothers, Crawfie insisted that Elizabeth and Margaret welcomed their visitors and offered them a cheering cup of tea. For the princesses, it was like an encounter with creatures from an alien planet. Many of these youngsters, raised in poverty in the Gorbals district of Glasgow, had never seen a rabbit, a deer or a pony, and never soaked up the silence of rolling hills – nor experienced the pleasures of a hot bath.

Another unusual presence at this time were the Canadian lumberjacks of the Newfoundland Overseas Forestry Unit, who used their expertise to cut a swathe through the Balmoral estate to provide timber for the war effort. Wartime made for odd friendships, and ensured that both girls grew up much faster than they would have been allowed in peacetime. Though the Queen liked to see her daughters in matching outfits, which inevitably made Princess Elizabeth seem younger than her years, the dislocation of their routine, the absence of their parents and the uncertain grind of war made for a childhood cut short.

At the end of 1939, the girls enjoyed a welcome change of scene when the Queen asked Crawfie to bring her daughters to Sandringham for Christmas, even though the flat Norfolk coastline was seen as a possible German invasion site. Indeed, while the princesses were heading south, their near neighbour, the Earl of Leicester, who owned Holkham Hall in Norfolk, sent his daughters Anne and Carey to stay with their great-aunt in Scotland, out of harm's way.

The royal children, though, were different. Their whereabouts on mainland Britain was seen as a litmus test of the resolve of the nation's leaders. If they had been sent to Canada or a neutral country, it would have been a body blow to the UK's morale and resistance. In late May 1940, when Prime Minister Churchill was shown preparatory plans for the evacuation of himself, the government and the Royal Family, he flatly stated that 'no such discussion'[7] should even be permitted. For once, the Queen outdid Churchill's rhetoric with her ringing phrase: 'The children could not go without me, I could not possibly leave the King, and the King would never go!'[8]

Yet the subject was still discussed, despite Churchill's firm stance. In preparation for the potential arrival of the Royal Family following a German invasion, the Canadian government spent $75,000 purchasing Hatley Castle, a forty-roomed Tudor-style mansion on Vancouver Island, as a means of adequately housing the British royals. In a diary entry at the end of May 1940, the Canadian Prime Minister William Mackenzie King wrote that the King and Queen could be arriving shortly, implying that Britain would soon fall and Canada would be the refuge for the defeated government and what was left of the nation's armed forces.[9]

The debate about what to do with the Heiress Presumptive and her sister, independently of their parents, greatly occupied the minds of ministers and the military. It was accepted that George VI and his wife would want to stay with the resistance in Britain. However, if the fight were to continue from Canada, then the Heiress Presumptive should be there as the legitimate Head of the British State in exile. With Churchill refusing to discuss the matter and the nation under imminent threat of invasion, some generals feared that any delay in sending the princesses to Canada, either by ship or air, would place them in unnecessary danger. The government would hear none of it, with ministers alarmed that rumours had begun to circulate which suggested the girls had already departed for North America.

At that time, in the summer of 1940, the princesses and their father and mother were being protected by different military units. In July, Major James Coats MC of the Coldstream Guards was assembling what George VI would later call 'my private army'. Coats, a brilliant skier, skeleton racer, ace shooter, skilled fisherman and, more importantly, friend of the Royal Family, was in charge of the eponymous Coats Mission. Under the code name Operation Rocking Horse, he and his fellow Coldstream Guards were tasked with protecting the King and Queen to 'the last man and the last bullet'. If the royals were in peril of being captured, it was the soldiers' job to ensure a fighting retreat to one of four country houses in Worcestershire, Yorkshire or Shropshire. Specially adapted armoured cars were earmarked for the operation to ferry the couple and anyone from the family to relative safety inland. Only when the country was in danger of complete collapse would they be taken to Canada via Iceland or alternatively sail to the Dominions on a destroyer anchored at the port of Liverpool. Members of the Royal Family were asked to keep a suitcase packed by their bedsides, ready for their possible evacuation. Queen Mary, safely ensconced in Badminton House in Gloucestershire, kept her most precious jewels – rather than clothing and toiletries – in her leather overnight baggage.

The strategy for the Heiress Presumptive and her sister – who had settled at Royal Lodge following their Christmas stay at Sandringham before being moved to Windsor Castle during the desperate days of May 1940 – was somewhat different. Should there be a parachute attempt to kidnap the girls along the lines of Begus's plan, it was up to Lieutenant Mike Tomkin of the 2nd

Northamptonshire Yeomanry to ensure their safety. This company was effectively 'Lizzie's private army'. Such was the importance of their protective mission that, shortly after receiving his orders, Tomkin and his troop found themselves in possession of four of the handful of armoured cars that remained in the country – the retreating British Army having left all of its heavy equipment behind in France and the Low Countries. Two were adapted for the princesses, removing the guns and installing two small armchairs for their comfort.

His troop then began practising, usually at night, the routes that they would take to a selected safe house – known as 'Establishment A', Madresfield Court in Worcestershire was initially earmarked as the base for the Royal Family and government. As a special treat, Tomkin took the two princesses plus Crawfie and a corgi on a drive in one of the adapted cars around Home Park. It was, as far as the girls were concerned, an exciting and enjoyable experience.

Their father's rival private army did not fare so well. One evening, George VI was discussing security with his temporary house guest, King Haakon VII, who asked about what preparations were in place in the event of a much-feared German parachute attack. With a flourish, the King pressed an alarm signal and then invited the Norwegian king to join him and the Queen in the garden to watch what he anticipated would be a rapid response from the designated defence force. Unfortunately, nothing happened. An equerry, who was eventually dispatched to discover what was going on, reported back that after the alarm had sounded, the duty police sergeant had told the officer of the guard that no attack was pending. Somewhat belatedly, after this unexpected bureaucratic error, guardsmen finally began running into the garden. As far as the exiled king was concerned, their behaviour did not inspire confidence.

The King's biographer, John Wheeler-Bennett, takes up the story: 'To the horror of King Haakon, but the vast amusement of the King and Queen, they proceeded to thrash the undergrowth in the manner of beaters at a shoot rather than of men engaged in the pursuit of a dangerous enemy.'[10]

The dire situation facing the country was no laughing matter, of course. Several weeks later, on the evening of 7 September 1940, the code word 'Cromwell' was broadcast, signifying that a German invasion was imminent. Church bells tolled through the night, several bridges were blown up and landmines were laid haphazardly on roads. The warning, which placed the men of the Coats Mission on high alert, marked the effective beginning of the Blitz, with the Luftwaffe sending wave after wave of bombers over key sites in the UK but initially focusing on the nation's capital. London would be the hardest hit, placing the Royal Family firmly on the front line.

Buckingham Palace was targeted in the first attack, though the explosion in the grounds caused little damage. The second attack, on Sunday 8 September, could have been far more serious. A bomb landed near the King's study, but it failed to go off. Having assumed that it was a dud, the Monarch was at his desk on Monday morning, carrying on regardless. However, the bomb exploded later that night while George VI was in bed in another part of the building, causing considerable damage to the north-west corner of the palace, breaking every window and dislodging much plasterwork. It was a lucky escape for the King – and the country.

An even more serious attack took place on 13 September, when a single German bomber flew straight up The Mall and dropped six bombs, two of which landed near the King, who was with his private secretary, Alec Hardinge. 'The whole thing happened in a matter of seconds,' His Majesty wrote later. 'We all wondered why we weren't dead.'[11] It was clear that Buckingham Palace was the target for this daring daylight attack, the King and others suspecting that the pilot was one of his many German relations. In total, the palace received nine direct hits from German bombs.

Thanks to the RAF and its decisive impact in the Battle of Britain, the fear of parachutists landing in the King's garden receded.

In reality, the bombing attacks on Buckingham Palace were a tremendous propaganda victory, which cemented the emotional compact between the Sovereign and his people, and produced a worldwide wave of sympathy for the beleaguered Royal Family, especially in the United States. This patriotic sentiment was expressed in the Queen's ringing phrase: 'I'm glad we've been bombed, now I can look the East End in the face.'[12] (The East End was a poor part of London that had borne the brunt of the damage during the Blitz.)

The sympathetic smiles and handshakes with victims and rescuers alike disguised the increased strain felt by both the King and Queen. She in particular found the air-raid shelter at Buckingham Palace deeply claustrophobic, the nightly bombing terrifying and the fate of herself and her family a constant source of concern. The war was all-consuming, physically and emotionally, and with every passing day there came another reminder of the transitory nature of life. The Queen, whose beloved older brother Fergus Bowes-Lyon was killed during the First World War, felt the suffering of others keenly. Every new dawn brought fresh horrors. In mid-September 1940, for example, during a tour of the bomb-damaged streets of East and West Ham in East London, she visited a school that had been hit. Scores of children who had been waiting to be evacuated were among the dead and injured. 'It does affect me seeing this terrible and senseless destruction. I think that really I mind it much more than being bombed myself,' she wrote to Queen Mary.[13]

At least she and the King were able to see their children most evenings, the couple spending nights at Windsor Castle where a large, reinforced air-raid shelter under Brunswick Tower had been prepared for the Royal Family. In the first few weeks of the

Blitz, Windsor was spared the worst of the bombing, the only excitement being the downing of a German Messerschmitt fighter in the grounds of Windsor Great Park at the end of September. The princesses and their friend Alathea Fitzalan Howard, who lived at Cumberland Lodge within the park grounds, found the German plane in the woods and took souvenirs back to the castle. Most nights the ringing of the alarm bell inside the castle warned of an imminent air raid. Sleep was constantly disrupted by the bombing and retaliatory ground fire. 'We seemed to be living in a sort of dimly lit underworld,' commented Crawfie, who was also dismayed by the lack of central heating.[14]

In the early days, the tardy arrival of the princesses in the air-raid shelter caused anxiety among members of the Royal Household, who were fearful that the girls could be injured or worse if they didn't reach the relative safety of the shelter in time. On one occasion, young Princess Margaret, then ten, was delayed looking for a pair of suitable knickers to wear. After the girls were provided with one-piece siren suits and their 'treasures' put in small suitcases to bring with them, the journey time from their bedroom to the shelter was much improved.

This was just as well, as for two consecutive nights in October 1940 the princesses suffered the unnerving sound of the 'whistle and scream' of bombs amidst the thud, thud, thud of anti-aircraft guns, which were mounted around Windsor Castle. Though the castle was not hit that night, by war's end 300 bombs had exploded in or around it. Alathea Fitzalan Howard, who lived only a short distance from the castle, recorded her own terrifying experience in her diary as several bombs, some delayed-action, exploded nearby in the early hours of 1 October: 'In my bed, I lay and shook with a wild terror I have never known before.' At 9 a.m. later that same morning, an unexploded time bomb went off: 'I lay in speechless horror watching my walls rock violently from side to side.'[15] Doubtless Alathea, who joined the princesses for drawing and dance classes every week, would have regaled them with news of the alarming incidents.

The noise of falling bombs, and the strain and stress of the constant anticipation of another air raid, physically changed the princesses. The Queen noted that her daughters looked careworn and 'different'. 'Though they are so good & composed there is always listening, & occasionally a leap behind the door, and it does become a strain,' she wrote to Queen Mary later in the war.[16]

In the middle of that same month, Princess Elizabeth, then fourteen, made her first-ever radio broadcast, a word-perfect four-minute chat about the trials and tribulations suffered by the children of the Commonwealth, many of whom had left their families behind for the relative safety of life in either the British countryside or the far-flung Dominions. The princess, who endlessly practised her speech, reminded her worldwide audience – special arrangements were made to broadcast her talk in America – that the children at home were 'full of cheerfulness and courage' in spite of having to 'bear our share of the danger and sadness of war'.[17] The broadcast ended with Elizabeth encouraging her sister to join with her in wishing everyone goodnight. Princess Margaret dutifully responded with, 'Goodnight, children.'

As she listened to the broadcast at her temporary home in Scotland, their playmate Anne Coke, from Holkham Hall in Norfolk, remembered thinking that they were 'our heroines ... there were the two princesses, still in England, in as much danger as us all'.[18] And sharing the same privations, too. The King was punctilious in abiding by the rationing and heating rules. When they were older, the girls were told that they should never accept presents, especially such coveted items as nylons. This life of necessary parsimony even affected the normally compliant princesses. On one occasion, when the senior politician Sir Stafford Cripps came to dine, he asked for an omelette, which made a considerable dent in the Royal Family's egg ration. As he tucked in, the children scowled and pulled faces behind his back, knowing that they would have to go without.

Like many in wartime Britain, the girls led a daily life of dramatic contrasts. On the days when Elizabeth met with her history teacher Henry Marten, who would travel to Windsor Castle in his pony and trap, they would sit and discuss British history in one of the nation's most historic buildings, while in the skies above them history was being made during the Battle of Britain.

Though a sure-footed teacher, Marten became rather hesitant when the topic moved firmly on to the British constitution. Given that the decline in the Sovereign's authority went hand in hand with the development of the nation's unwritten constitution, he was worried as to how he should discuss the subject with the future Monarch. When he asked Tommy Lascelles for advice, the King's assistant private secretary told the scholar to 'hide nothing'.[19] For his efforts, in 1945 the King knighted Marten.

Less contentious was the academic assistance of Marie-Antoinette de Bellaigue, known as Toinon, who had replaced Georgina Guérin after she left to become a French Resistance leader. Toinon was hired to make the princesses proficient in spoken French. 'In our general conversations,' she later recalled, 'I endeavoured to give the princesses an awareness of other countries, their way of thought and their customs – sometimes a source of amusement. Queen Elizabeth II has always had from the beginning a positive good judgement. She was her simple self, *très naturelle*. And there was always a strong sense of duty mixed with *joie de vivre* in the pattern of her character.'[20]

Princess Margaret translated her language tuition into the singing of French country and nursery songs. Her clear young voice was often heard ringing out from her room as she accompanied herself on the piano.

Their time in the classroom conferred a sense of routine and normality during the dark days of war. Far from being hidden upstairs with their governess, Crawfie ensured that the girls were introduced to a wider cross section of the population than they ever would have during peacetime.

She was particularly proud of inaugurating a Girl Guide troop at Windsor, which comprised daughters of Royal Household officials as well as local children and youngsters from London's impoverished East End, whose houses had been bombed or who had lost their parents and were living with families on the Windsor estate. There was no standing on ceremony. These young Cockneys, whose accents were as indecipherable as those children from the Gorbals in Glasgow, called Princess Elizabeth by her family-only pet name of 'Lilibet' after hearing Margaret address her in that way.

'Margaret was the livelier one, full of fun and jokes; Elizabeth was more reserved,' recalled Joan Scragg, a member of the Sea Rangers (the next step up from the Girl Guides), in which Elizabeth later enrolled in February 1943 and which Margaret joined in 1945.[21]

Over-familiar or not, everyone mucked in. When the girls went camping in Windsor Great Park, the King would sometimes join them, helping to erect tents and dig latrines. After cook-outs and campfires, the princesses, somewhat dolefully at first, did their fair share of washing dishes and foraging for wood. (Elizabeth enjoyed doing the washing-up so much that regular and enduring Christmas presents were pairs of rubber gloves.)

After spending Christmas at Windsor Castle, towards the end of December 1940 the princesses left the Guide troop behind and travelled with their parents to Appleton House, a retreat regularly used by the Norwegian royal family on the Sandringham estate. Here they mixed and mingled with youthful officers from the Coats Mission, the eager young men soon seen as almost part of the wider Royal Family. They joined them at church, were invited for dinner and tea and went pheasant shooting with the King on the estate's broad acres – though a four-star general objected when his soldiers were used as beaters to flush out pheasants for the guns.

During their winter sojourn, the princesses played hide-and-seek and riotous card games, went on treasure hunts and enjoyed enthusiastic snowball fights with the soldiers. On one occasion, Princess Elizabeth joined the men for a game of ice hockey on the frozen lake near York Cottage, where George V had lived, and she scored a goal.

The Royal Family would return to Appleton House the following Christmas, remaining under the protection of the men of the Coats Mission. One of its members, Temporary Captain Ian Liddell, took responsibility for organizing the Christmas pantomime, *Cinderella*, which was subtitled *So What! and the Severn Twirps*. The royals joined in heartily when 'Old Macdonald Had a Farm' was sung during a performance at West Newton village hall, and Margaret practised the snorts and other farmyard noises for hours afterwards.[22] Sometime later, at a cocktail party for Coats Mission officers and their wives, she sang the song again – farmyard noises included.

Such was the informality between the Royal Family and their military escorts that the men had a collection and bought a box of chocolates for Princess Elizabeth's fifteenth birthday, which was on 21 April 1941.

Upon their return to Windsor Castle, Elizabeth and Margaret entertained officers from the Grenadier Guards, those recuperating from injury as well as airmen on leave. Though their father's preferred service was the Royal Navy, his daughters had a sneaking admiration for the magnificent men in their flying machines, whose airborne heroics had saved the nation from Nazi invaders. Like thousands of children, the princesses had memorized the characteristic sound and silhouette of every plane,

German or British. In April 1941, they were thrilled to receive a model of a Spitfire, fashioned by a Czech pilot from the scrap of a downed Dornier bomber.

Later in the war, the girls endlessly played the 1943 dance favourite 'Coming In on a Wing and a Prayer' on their gramophone, which was all about a missing plane limping back to base after a successful mission. Given their sky-high passion for the RAF, it is not hard to imagine the excitement felt by both princesses when, the following year, they were introduced to a genuine, medal-wearing Battle of Britain fighter pilot who was to be a temporary equerry. He was the highly decorated squadron commander and ace Peter Townsend – as heroic and dashing a figure as the war had ever produced in England. In a letter to Queen Mary in April 1944, the Queen described him as 'charming' and someone who 'fits in beautifully'.[23]

At teas and more formal luncheons in honour of the military men, some of whom were preparing for combat, Elizabeth arranged the seating plan, offered food and opened the conversation. For the princess, who was appointed Colonel of the Grenadier Guards in February 1942 and whose first official public engagement on her sixteenth birthday two months later was an inspection of a regimental parade at Windsor, life at the castle was about keeping conversation bright and light-hearted, leaving dark thoughts of mortality for another day.

In her capacity as Colonel of the Grenadier Guards, she experienced at first hand the prosaic and arbitrary brutality of war, a profound sense of impermanence where she was now able to put faces to the names of those killed in action. Temporary Captain Liddell, for example, who in happier times had organized the 1941 Christmas pantomime at Sandringham, was killed in action a few days before VE Day, his heroism in early April 1945 earning him the Victoria Cross, the highest award for gallantry.

The princess found herself writing to the families of those who never returned, describing the characters of their loved ones and how they were remembered during their time at Windsor Castle. Queen Elizabeth was sensitive to the effect that the war was having on her daughters, aware, as she wrote to her brother David Bowes-Lyon in October 1943, that it was a 'beastly time' for people growing up. 'Lilibet meets young Grenadiers at Windsor, & then they get killed, & it is horrid for someone so young. So many good ones have gone recently.'[24]

One positive side effect of her social leadership role was to force her to confront her chronic shyness head on – with a little advice from her mother.

As Elizabeth's lifelong friend Prudence, Lady Penn recalled: 'Her mother said to her, "When you walk into a room, walk through the middle of the door." She meant, don't go in apologetically, walk like you're in charge. That was very good advice.' [25] Crawfie noted the transition with some satisfaction. From having been 'a rather shy little girl', Elizabeth became 'a very charming young person, able to cope with any situation without awkwardness.'[26] Her governess had also watched her develop into 'an excellent conversationalist'.[27]

The princess, though, was not one for idle chitchat, as Alathea Fitzalan Howard, her best friend during the war, described in a diary entry: 'She's the most ungossipy person I know. Placid and unemotional, she never desires what doesn't come her way; always happy in her own family, she never needs the companionship of outsiders; she never suffers, therefore she never strongly desires.'[28]

The constraints and responsibilities of her position in wartime Britain emphasized and endorsed her stoical, reserved character and her somewhat solemn demeanour, qualities perceptively observed by the American First Lady Eleanor Roosevelt when she visited Britain in October 1942 and stayed in the Queen's rooms at a bombed and freezing-cold Buckingham Palace. On two occasions, Mrs Roosevelt met the sixteen-year-old princess, who had officially entered the adult world after formally signing on at a labour exchange in Windsor in May 1942, and during the First Lady's visit she was strenuously lobbying her reluctant parents to let her face the same hazards as other girls her age.

'If she were anyone's child that I met outside a palace, I would say she was very attractive, quite serious, a child with a good deal of character,' Mrs Roosevelt commented. 'Her questions put to me about life in this country were all serious questions. She has had to think seriously. I don't think they have kept her from seeing the seriousness of the war – after all, practically every window in Buckingham Palace is out!'[29]

The First Lady was introduced to Princess Elizabeth at a time when the King was gradually introducing his daughter to the unique world of a reigning monarch – through the interminable red despatch boxes that contained top-secret Cabinet and Foreign Office documents for the Sovereign's perusal and signature. Unlike previous monarchs, notably Queen Victoria and George V, who very reluctantly allowed their heirs an insight into their destiny, George VI was eager and earnest in the training of his successor. As F. J. Corbitt, who worked at the palace for twenty years as deputy comptroller of supply, later noted: 'I don't think any Sovereign of England has been taught so much in advance about his work by his predecessor as Queen Elizabeth was by her father. It was always a joy to see them together so happy in each other's company.'[30]

The death of their Uncle George, the Duke of Kent, in a plane crash in August 1942, further brought home to the princesses the sudden arbitrary reality of war. His passing marked the first time in more than 450 years that a member of the Royal Family had died on active service. It was all the more shocking as the King and

Queen, who were staying at Balmoral, had organized a Highland ball in his honour for later in that tragic week.

The duke's death, the remorseless toll on the Home Front and overseas fronts, then, in the latter stages of the war, the bombardment of London by deadly flying bombs or 'doodlebugs', which terrified the population more than the Blitz itself, made both the King and Queen aware that if their turn was next, they had better make preparations. In June 1944, days after a flying V1 bomb had achieved a direct hit on the Guards' Chapel near Buckingham Palace, killing 121 civilians and soldiers, and injuring 141 more, many of whom were trapped beneath the rubble, the Queen wrote to her eldest daughter about what to do should she get 'done in' by the Nazis' doodlebug bombs. The tone was typically jaunty and light, but betrayed her serious concerns: 'Let's hope this won't be needed, but I know that you will always do the right thing, & remember to keep your temper & your word & and be loving – sweet – Mummy.'[31]

No one was immune from thoughts of their own mortality. The following month, shortly before leaving on a secret flight to visit the troops in Italy, the King outlined to his wife where she should live if he did not return.

Though Princess Elizabeth's stoical and phlegmatic character matched the 'make do and mend' mood of the times, on the flip side was the growing desire to spread her wings. The princess chafed at the cordon of caution that surrounded her. As family friend Veronica Maclean noted: 'The quiet determination which is part of her character, and which is perhaps a variation of her father's patience and steadfastness, was beginning to emerge.'[32] The teenage princess would be driven – under escort and in a group – into London for dinner or to watch plays and concerts. In May 1944, her first opera was Puccini's *La Bohème*, which was performed by the Sadler's Wells Company at the New Theatre in the West End. On another outing, she attended an event at the Royal Albert Hall to mark the fiftieth anniversary of the Proms.

She and her sister were also enthusiastic members of the weekly meeting of the madrigal choir under the leadership of Dr William H. Harris, the organist at St George's Chapel in Windsor Castle. The choir's genesis began during a musical session when the girls discovered 'My Ladye Nevells Booke', a collection of sixteenth-century virginal music. This expanded into a madrigal choir every week with, at the invitation of Dr Harris, Guards officers and students from Eton joining in. Because of her natural love of music, it was entirely fitting that in May 1943, shortly after her seventeenth birthday, Elizabeth became the President of the Royal College of Music.

Other cultural entertainments were less successful. A poetry recital organized by the Queen's friend, Osbert Sitwell, at Windsor Castle was an unmitigated disaster. One drunk female poet had to be removed from the makeshift stage, the diminutive Walter de la Mare was obscured by the lectern and another bard declaimed his rhyming couplets for so long that he was asked to cut short his reading. It was all too much for the princesses, who were barely able to keep a straight face. Many years later, their mother described the somewhat surreal and unintentionally comic affair to biographer A. N. Wilson.

'We had this rather lugubrious man in a suit, and he read a poem ... I think it was called "The Desert". And first the girls got the giggles, and then I did and then even the King.'

A somewhat perplexed Wilson interjected: '"The Desert", Ma'am? Are you sure it wasn't called "*The Waste Land*"?', referring to the now classic work by T. S. Eliot.

The Queen [Mother] continued: 'That's it. I'm afraid we all giggled. Such a gloomy man, looked as though he worked in a bank, and we didn't understand a word.'

'I believe he DID once work in a bank,' responded Wilson.[33]

More notable than this poetic interlude were the Christmas pantomimes starring the young princesses. While the endlessly dramatic Margaret Rose was a natural on stage, the real revelation was the Heiress Presumptive, who showed a confidence, vigour and command before audiences of 500 or so. Even the cynical Tommy Lascelles was impressed, deeming the 1942 Christmas pantomime, *Sleeping Beauty*, worthy of the West End's Drury Lane theatres. 'The whole thing went with a slickness and confidence that amazed me,' he wrote.[34] He remained captivated the following year, when Princess Elizabeth starred as a 'charming' Aladdin, although the King thought her breeches way too short and somewhat indecorous.

Equally memorable was a ball that George VI organized to celebrate Elizabeth's seventeenth birthday. It was such a success that it did not end until dawn. Towards the end of the war, the King would also give smaller dances in the Bow Room at Buckingham Palace. On one occasion, the Monarch led a conga line through the palace rooms and corridors while the band played on in a now empty room.

One of the guests at these events was Lieutenant Mark Bonham Carter, who had made a daring 400-mile escape from an Italian prisoner-of-war camp in 1943. The grandson of the former British Prime Minister Herbert Asquith recalls twice dancing with the teenage Princess Margaret at Windsor Castle and later reported that she was 'full of character and very tart in her criticisms'.[35] Decades later, in an unusual coincidence, Bonham Carter's actress niece Helena would play Princess Margaret in the popular TV show *The Crown* and also Queen Elizabeth in the 2010 film *The King's Speech*. At the time, the sisters found him highly entertaining thanks to his free-flowing repartee and witty jokes.

He was one of a number of eligible young Guards officers, usually with a stately home lurking somewhere in the family background, who were invited by the King and Queen to Windsor Castle and later in the war to Buckingham Palace to amuse their daughters. The Queen referred to them as 'the Bodyguard'.

Besides Bonham Carter, other eminently suitable young men put in the path of the princesses included Andrew Elphinstone, the son of the Queen's sister, Lady Mary Bowes-Lyon, who became a vicar after the war. Princess Elizabeth thought he would make an ideal husband for some lucky woman. In November 1943, Elizabeth wrote to her cousin Diana Bowes-Lyon: 'I saw Andrew for a moment last week. And the more I see of him, the more I wish he wasn't my first cousin, as he's just the sort of husband any girl would love to have. I don't think one could find anyone nicer.'[36] Andrew felt that he was being left behind in the marriage stakes by his friends and asked the princess outright if she knew anyone that he could marry.

But there were plenty of other potential suitors, including Lord Rupert Nevill, aide-de-camp to Lieutenant-General Sir Brian Horrocks during the Allied advance in 1945, Lord Wyfold and handsome Irish Guards officer Patrick Plunket, who later became temporary equerry to the King. The presence of so many eligible bachelors gave rise to newspaper speculation in America, suggesting that Elizabeth was about to announce her engagement either to Charles Manners, the 10th Duke of Rutland, or Hugh FitzRoy, also known as the Earl of Euston.

Apparently, Manners ruined his chances at a union by making a pass at the princess, which she found greatly offensive. Eminently safe in taxis was Henry Porchester, known as 'Porchie', later the 7th Earl of Carnarvon, whose Highclere House home became rather more famous than the family itself when, years later, it featured as the setting for the long-running saga of aristocratic life, *Downton Abbey*. Porchie, a childhood friend who shared Elizabeth's love of horses, was not a serious threat to win her heart and eventually became her racing manager.

It was, however, South African-born Hugh FitzRoy, the Earl of Euston, who was a descendant of King Charles II and later became the 11th Duke of Grafton, who had unknowingly caused something of a romantic rivalry between Princess Elizabeth and her wartime friend, Alathea Fitzalan Howard. Alathea, two years older than the princess, was utterly infatuated with the earl, who was a regular guest at social events organized by the King and Queen at Windsor Castle. To her chagrin, he was often seated next to Elizabeth at meals or to watch films and they would regularly lead off the dancing at parties. She suspected that the princess's parents were trying to make a match between the earl and their daughter, recording in her diary: 'They're so pointedly nice to him that one wonders if there's anything behind it; he gets on so well with all of them – I'm sure he likes Lilibet better than me.'[37]

Not that Elizabeth was immune from jealousy herself. At one party in 1941, the princess quizzed Alathea about how often she had danced with Euston as, she complained, he had only shared the first one of the evening with her out of obligation. This genteel rivalry came to a natural conclusion in 1943 when the young man was posted to India as the aide-de-camp to Field Marshal Archibald Wavell, the Viceroy of India.

Long before that day, however, the princess and her sister had let Alathea into the secret of the man who genuinely made Elizabeth's heart beat a little faster. In early April 1941, she confided that Prince Philip of Greece and Denmark was the genuine beau – or, as the princess put it, 'boy' – in her life. Her flirtation with the future Duke of Grafton was merely a distraction. Quietly and very privately, Elizabeth was corresponding with the prince and even cut out relevant newspaper articles about the activities of his ship.

Her cousin Margaret Rhodes recalls: 'I've got letters from her saying: "It's so exciting. Mummy says that Philip can come and stay when he gets leave." She never looked at anyone else. She was truly in love from the very beginning.'[38]

Her beau had a good war. His first wartime posting was on board HMS *Ramillies*, escorting convoys of Australian and New Zealand troopships bound for Egypt. At the beginning of his appointment he told his captain, Vice Admiral Harold Baillie-Grohman, that he was in contact with the princess and confided that Louis Mountbatten, his Uncle Dickie, had ideas for him: 'He thinks I could marry Princess Elizabeth.' Somewhat surprised, the captain asked: 'Are you really fond of her?' 'Oh, yes,' replied Philip, 'I write to her every week.'[39] As the sweethearts were only eighteen and thirteen respectively, Baillie-Grohman advised him not to mention his friendship to any of his shipmates. When *Ramillies* arrived in Sydney, Baillie-Grohman, mindful of the possible marital plans for the prince, sent Philip to a remote sheep farm rather than let him spend his leave among the temptations of the big city.

Though the correspondence was platonic, Lady Myra Butter, Philip's cousin, was convinced that it was the intention of his ambitious uncle to engineer a royal marriage and burnish the house of Mountbatten in the process. Myra recalls: 'Philip would never have married her if he hadn't been in love with her, I can tell you that, because I knew his other girlfriends.'[40]

Philip, almost five years older than his royal pen pal, was a popular bachelor, squiring any number of eligible ladies around town. Beautiful Osla Benning, a dark-haired Canadian, was a regular girlfriend. Years later, Osla's daughter Janie Spring described Philip as her mother's first love.[41]

As his cousin Alexandra, the daughter of Princess Alexander of Greece and Denmark, noted wryly: 'Blondes, brunettes and redhead charmers, Philip gallantly and, I think, quite impartially, squired them all.'[42] However, it was to Princess Elizabeth that he dashed off notes about his military life – subject to the censor's pen. He had much to relay.

After deciding to commit to the British Navy rather than the Greek, in early January 1941 he joined the battleship HMS *Valiant* at Alexandria and sailed to Athens, where he took some shore leave and spent some time with his mother Alice, as well as King George II of Greece. One of the guests at a cocktail party attended by Philip was the American-born diarist Henry 'Chips' Channon. He described the young man as 'extraordinarily handsome' and then noted: 'He is to be our Prince Consort and that is why he is serving in our Navy.'[43] Channon implied that Philip's decision to serve in the British Navy would make him more acceptable to the British public should he and Princess Elizabeth marry.

At the time, Philip was more concerned with matters naval than marital. In late March 1941, *Valiant* was part of the three-day Battle of Cape Matapan in the eastern Mediterranean, which saw the prince mentioned in dispatches for his handling of a searchlight to outline targeted Italian warships, swiftly resulting in the sinking of two Italian cruisers. King George II of Greece subsequently awarded Philip the Greek War Cross for his actions.

A few weeks later, he returned to Britain to study for and sit his sub-lieutenant's examination. At various times during the war, while on shore leave in the UK, he was a guest at Windsor Castle, and in October 1941 he regaled the King and company about his adventures in the Mediterranean. His Majesty was impressed by Philip's crisp summary of the Battle of Cape Matapan, which effectively crushed the Italian navy. He later wrote to the prince's grandmother, Victoria, Marchioness of Milford Haven: 'What a charming boy he is, & I am glad he is remaining in my Navy.'[44]

Having passed his sub-lieutenant exam with flying colours, in June 1942 Philip was posted to HMS *Wallace* on the Firth of Forth in Scotland. During his time on board, the crew was tasked with the hazardous job of escorting Merchant Navy ships along Britain's eastern coast from Rosyth down to Sheerness in Kent, and faced the constant threat of attack from German U-boats. By October that same year, the twenty-one-year-old prince had been promoted to first lieutenant, one of the youngest in the Royal Navy.

By July 1943, *Wallace* was situated off the Sicilian coast, where late on 8 July it was attacked in the open waters by the Luftwaffe. After the first wave of enemy planes had departed, it was obvious that further bombardments would follow. The crew only had twenty minutes or so to fashion an escape. Philip had the presence of mind to have a wooden raft thrown overboard with smoke floats attached, to create the impression that the German bombs had hit their target, hence the billowing smoke and debris apparently ablaze on the water. It was hoped that German pilots flying overhead would be duped into thinking that the first bombers had sunk the ship. HMS *Wallace* duly steamed away from the smoking raft and then the captain ordered the engines stopped so that marauding bombers would not see the tell-tale wake. Philip's ruse worked. The next wave of German aircraft flew past *Wallace* and focused their attack on the source of the smoke instead. Years later, crew member Harry Hargreaves recalled: 'Prince Philip saved our lives that night. I suppose there might have been a few survivors, but certainly the ship would have been sunk. He was always very courageous and resourceful and thought very quickly.'[45]

Five months after his heroics in Italian waters, Philip accepted an invitation to stay at Windsor Castle for Christmas 1943. This news delighted Elizabeth. 'Who *do* you think is coming to see us act, Crawfie?' asked an excited and pink-faced princess. 'Philip!'[46]

Earlier in the year, Elizabeth and Philip had enjoyed their first dance together at a private party held at Coppins, the Buckinghamshire home of his cousin, Marina, Duchess of Kent. Although the prince was unable to attend the Christmas dance that the King had organized for his daughters due to a bout of flu, he was well enough to watch one of the pantomime shows, laughing along with the rest of the 500-strong audience at the dreadful puns and the ham acting.

Elizabeth, in the title role of Aladdin, made her entrance by jumping out of a laundry basket. Her tap-dancing skills – she skittered her way through the American hit 'In My Arms' – were widely admired and her dance routine earned general applause, though this was clearly a performance for one particular member of the audience. Crawfie was surprised at her animation and unmistakable sparkle – here was a young woman in love.

Her suitor was no longer the brash and boastful cadet who had jumped the tennis net at Dartmouth Naval College but, to Crawfie's critical eye, a young man who was sober, serious and charming, his wartime exploits clearly tempering and maturing him. He joined the Royal Family for the Christmas Day festivities, playing games of charades, watching film shows and dancing to the gramophone until the early hours. It was time together that both would cherish.

Alathea Fitzalan Howard had watched the evolving romance with quiet satisfaction. She remembered a June day in 1942, when Elizabeth, who normally kept her feelings to herself, wondered aloud if she would ever marry and resolved to run away with the man of her dreams if necessary. Now, eighteen months later, she had seemed to have found a fitting partner. 'He seems so suited to PE [Princess Elizabeth] and I kept wondering today whether he is her future husband,' she noted in her diary entry of 18 December 1943. 'I think it is the most desirable event that could possibly happen. She would like it and, though he could not be in love with her, I believe he is not averse to the idea.'[47]

The following year, when Philip sent Elizabeth a photograph of himself for Christmas, Margaret told Alathea that her sister had 'danced round the room with it for joy'.[48]

The war had changed everyone, whether they were on the front line or not. Elizabeth was no longer a little girl in white ankle socks, but a shapely young woman who knew her own mind. She was branching out.

For her eighteenth birthday in 1944, she received a diamond tiara from her mother and a sapphire-and-diamond bracelet from her father. That year marked a number of firsts in the princess's life: she shot her first stag, caught her first salmon (a sturdy 8-pounder), launched her first ship (HMS *Vanguard* on Clydebank), gave her first public speech as President of the National Society for the Prevention of Cruelty to Children, attended her first official Buckingham Palace dinner and took on the role of Counsellor of State when her father made a top-secret flight to see the troops in Italy.

Elizabeth's elevation drove her sister wild with jealousy and validated her feeling that she was always left out of anything of substance or interest. She had previously railed against the decision to keep her from attending history lessons with Henry Marten. Now her sister had been made a Counsellor of State at eighteen when the normal age was twenty-one.

There was further sisterly envy when, in March 1945, Princess Elizabeth was allowed to join the Auxiliary Territorial Service (ATS) at the rank of second subaltern. Every day, after first learning to drive, she drove her commandant to their base at Camberley, 15 miles from Windsor Castle. Along with the other girls, she learned how to strip an engine, change a tyre, spark plugs and oil, as well as how to read a map and navigate at night. The high point was when the princess, who looked, according to Tommy Lascelles, a 'duck' in her ATS uniform, drove her company commander from Aldershot to the courtyard of Buckingham Palace.

At long last she had been allowed to do her bit, which made her feel that she had earned the right to join in with the wild celebrations following the German surrender on 8 May 1945. The princesses accompanied the King and Queen and war leader Winston Churchill on the balcony of Buckingham Palace to wave to the huge, cheering, delirious crowds.

Elizabeth and Margaret, who had spent a lifetime looking out at the passing parade, pleaded with their parents to allow them to join the celebrating multitude. After some hesitation, their father agreed. The fact that, on this night of all nights, she and her sister had had to beg to be allowed out vividly demonstrates what sheltered lives they led, their every movement, every desire fretted over by the King, the Queen and their courtiers.

The princesses, though, were not allowed out alone, and were escorted by sixteen chaperones, including Group Captain Peter Townsend, Lord Porchester and the King's starchy equerry Captain Harold Campbell, who was dressed in a pinstripe suit, wore a bowler hat and carried a rolled umbrella. He strongly disapproved of the impromptu jaunt, which Elizabeth described as 'one of the most memorable nights of my life'.[49] Perhaps he had a point.

Though Pathé News showed the crowds taking part in cheerful conga lines, the real picture was rather more salacious. Aristocratic Army wife Diana Carnegie was part of the throng and later wrote to her husband James, who was still in Germany, that she and her party had 'stumbled across fucking couples in the dark' as they made their way from the West End to Buckingham Palace.[50]

Years later, the Queen told veteran BBC war correspondent Godfrey Talbot that her overriding emotions that night were 'thrill and relief'. The Queen, who gave a rare interview to commemorate the fortieth anniversary of VE Day, recalled: 'My parents went out on the balcony in response to the huge crowds outside. I think we went on the balcony nearly every hour – six times. And then when the excitement of the floodlights being switched on got through to us, my sister and I realized we couldn't see what the crowds were enjoying ... so we asked my parents if we could go out and see for ourselves.'[51]

She remembered being 'terrified of being recognized' and pulled her uniform cap down over her eyes. But the Grenadier Guards officer with her refused to be seen in 'the company of another officer improperly dressed' and so she had no choice but to adjust her cap and wear it 'normally'.

'We cheered the King and Queen on the balcony and then walked miles through the streets,' Her Majesty recalled. 'I remember lines of unknown people linking arms and walking down Whitehall [the main street of British government], all of us just swept along on a tide of happiness and relief.'[52]

CHAPTER THREE

A WALK IN THE HEATHER

S HE WAS AN UNLIKELY CUPID. Princess Marina of Greece and
Denmark was the chilly beauty who had captured the heart
of King George V's youngest son, the wild and wilful Prince
George. Though she was titled the Duchess of Kent, that most
English of the home counties, she remained resolutely European,
so proud of her Greek and Russian heritage that she never truly
allowed herself to be absorbed into the British Royal Family. She
had contempt for the middle-class American Wallis Simpson,
whom she had met at Balmoral in 1936, and referred to the Queen
and her sister-in-law, the Duchess of Gloucester, as 'those common
little Scottish girls'.[1]

She was less judgemental of her European relations. The
duchess and her husband regularly invited her first cousin, Prince
Philip of Greece and Denmark, the son of her uncle Prince
Andrew, to stay with them at Coppins, their converted farmhouse
in the charming Buckinghamshire village of Iver just a few miles
from Windsor Castle.

Philip stayed with the family during breaks from boarding at

Cheam School in southern England and Gordonstoun in the far north of Scotland, as well as during his attendance at the Royal Naval College in Devon. With his lively mind, positive attitude and energy, the prince proved himself to be an entertaining house guest. When the Duke of Kent was killed in an air crash in August 1942, Philip's sensitive if no-nonsense approach to life was crucial in raising Marina's spirits. After a brief initial collapse, the Duchess of Kent not only took on her husband's former royal duties, but she also trained as a nurse.

Over Easter 1944, the duchess hosted the prince and a 'certain young lady'. The presence of the King and Queen at the gathering indicated a degree of parental approval. Clearly romance was in the air. When Elizabeth drew compliments from Philip for wearing a particular outfit, the next time they were due to meet she made sure she wore a similar style and colour. The historian Sir Steven Runciman, who was a friend and confidant of Princess Marina and also Elizabeth's mother, would later reveal: 'It was Princess Marina, not [Louis] Mountbatten, who was the marriage broker between the Queen and Prince Philip.'[2]

Indeed, in the early months of the royal romance, Lord Mountbatten had had his hands full in the Japanese theatre of war where he was Supreme Allied Commander South East Asia Command. During his occasional visits to London, however, he continued to press the case for his nephew. He wrote to influential figures, including the Independent Member of Parliament Tom Driberg, stressing Philip's Englishness. At times, his chirpy and irrepressible ambition on behalf of the prince exasperated George VI. 'I know you like to get things settled at once, once you have an idea in mind ... but I have come to the conclusion that we are going too fast,' the King told him. He was concerned that his eldest daughter was too young and inexperienced to be content with the first eligible bachelor to cross her path.[3]

Even Philip felt that his uncle's relentless lobbying on his behalf was a double-edged sword. He wrote to him in earnest: 'Please, I beg of you. Not too much advice in an affair of the heart or I shall be forced to do the wooing by proxy.'[4]

Though he had the support of his influential uncle, as well as the steadfast devotion of the princess, Philip's acceptance as the favoured suitor for the hand of the future Queen was by no means assured. The Royal Family and their courtiers were suspicious and wary when this penniless and rather rough interloper, who, some thought, would not be faithful, arrived on the scene. Inevitably, there were all kinds of salty rumours about the flotilla of girls who had crossed the prince's path. Most gossip emanated from Sydney and Melbourne in Australia, where he spent time ashore on arrival in May 1945 while his ship, HMS *Whelp*, underwent a refit. He attended parties and other social gatherings where there was no shortage of attractive young ladies. Two girls in particular who caught his eye were society belle Sue Other-Gee, and singer and model Sandra Jacques. He remained friendly with Other-Gee for many years. She even kept a scrapbook recording their occasional meetings. As for Sandra Jacques, film producer Robin Dalton, who met the prince during the war, recalls that his relationship with her was 'a terrific love affair. A very full love affair.'[5] Just to complicate matters, romantic novelist Barbara Cartland, a great friend of Lord Mountbatten, claimed that, following one intimate liaison with an unnamed woman, Philip fathered a child who was born in Melbourne. However, she always refused to give further details.[6]

Though his title, striking good looks and easy charm ensured that he was a target for a stream of society ladies, those who knew the man, rather than the rakish image, regarded him as a cautious, cagey fellow who kept his feelings to himself. In this regard he was similar in manner to Princess Elizabeth. Even her family described her as 'the cat who walks alone'. His friend and fellow naval officer,

Australian Mike Parker, described Philip as a 'reserved' young man who never really played the field. 'We were young, we had fun, we had a few drinks, we might have gone dancing, but that was it.'[7]

Perhaps the King was looking for a reason, however spurious, to reject his daughter's long-distance suitor. Whether he wanted to admit it or not, George VI was possessive and had found a happiness and completion in family life that had been missing from his own chilly childhood. He also felt his daughter, not yet twenty-one, was too young to make such a life-changing choice. His redoubtable mother, Queen Mary, disagreed. She told her close confidante Lady Airlie: 'She [Elizabeth] would always know her own mind. There's something very steadfast and determined about her.'[8]

The Queen wanted her daughter to be happy, but fretted that Philip, self-confident, independent-minded and ambitious, would find it difficult to accept the junior role in a marital partnership with the future Monarch. She favoured a well-born Guards officer for Elizabeth – preferably a duke, but an earl would do – with a stately home lurking in the family background. Her brother David Bowes-Lyon supported her view. In his eyes a British aristocrat, rather than a foreigner whose sisters were married to Nazi officers, was an infinitely preferable choice.

On this weighty matter, the Queen had the endorsement of the King's influential private secretary, Tommy Lascelles, who was firmly opposed to Princess Elizabeth marrying Prince Philip.[9] According to Edward Ford, the newly appointed assistant private secretary, Lascelles' choice was Hugh FitzRoy, the Earl of Euston, who later became the Duke of Grafton. It seems that Alathea Fitzalan Howard's suspicions, that the King, Queen and their courtiers were quietly and deliberately pushing together Elizabeth and Hugh, upon whom Alathea had developed a huge crush, were well founded.

The earl remained friendly with both the princess and Alathea. He may never have realized the romantic consternation he caused every time he arrived at Windsor Castle during the war. Alathea, too, accepted that it was not meant to be and eventually came to terms with the fact that he was the one who got away. In October 1946, the romantic door was closed for good when he married Ann Fortune Smith, the daughter of Captain Eric Smith, a member of the Smith banking dynasty. At the court of Queen Elizabeth II, from 1953 to 1966 she would serve as Lady of the Bedchamber, and then in 1967 be appointed Mistress of the Robes.

By the time Hugh had married, the princess's own romance was in full swing. Philip had arrived back in Britain in January 1946 after witnessing Japanese leaders formally sign the instrument of surrender on 2 September 1945 in Tokyo Bay aboard the aircraft carrier USS *Missouri*.

On his final voyage, he brought British prisoners of war safely home to England. Then he was tasked with decommissioning HMS *Whelp*. Several months later, he was posted to an officers' training college at Corsham in Wiltshire, around 100 miles west of London, where he was tasked with giving lectures on seamanship to petty officers.

On free weekends or on leave, he scrounged gas coupons – petrol was still rationed – from his fellow officers and drove his small black MG sports car at reckless speeds to central London where he stayed at Chester Street in Belgravia, home of the Mountbattens. Philip also became a regular and welcome visitor to Elizabeth's suite of rooms at Buckingham Palace.

As she later wrote to journalist Betty Shew: 'We first started seeing more of each other when Philip went for a two-year job to the RN Petty Officers' school at Corsham – before that we hardly knew each other. He'd spent weekends with us, and when the school was closed, he spent six weeks at Balmoral – it was great luck his getting a shore job first then! We both love dancing – we have danced at Circo's and Quaglino's as well as at parties.'[10]

During his visits to Buckingham Palace, Crawfie, who acted as chaperone, looked on indulgently as she watched the nascent romance grow and blossom. She liked Philip's breezy and informal manner, but felt that the young couple had too little time alone together, especially as Princess Margaret was always the third wheel. She was a permanent fixture during his visits unless Crawfie came up with a reason to give the couple some privacy.

Philip's presence in Elizabeth's life had an immediate effect. Her circle could not help but notice the changes. She was more confident and humorous, with an ear for a funny anecdote. In February 1946, the princess attended a party in Belgravia hosted by the Grenfell family, during which she impressed Laura Grenfell with her natural conversational style and her sharp observations. She amused fellow guests with her rendition of a sentry losing his hat while presenting arms. Her eye for oft overlooked details and her keen sense of the ridiculous would serve her well in times to come.

Others were equally impressed by the princess's choice of suitor. At a dinner held at the home of the Elphinstone family at Beaconsfield, fellow guest Sir Michael Duff described Prince Philip as 'charming' and argued that he had all the right qualities – handsome, intelligent, and a brave sailor – to be a popular consort to the future Queen. The fact that he only spoke English was, Duff believed, 'admirable and necessary' especially 'when one considers the point of view of the man in the street, who has an innate prejudice against any language but his own'.[11]

It was a shrewd observation, as Philip was seen by some as too continental. Even though his mother was born at Windsor Castle, and he had been educated in England and served courageously in the British Royal Navy, he was often dismissed as 'the Hun' or 'Charlie Kraut' by certain individuals in court circles. This knee-jerk hostility was perhaps understandable: one of his relations, Prince Philipp of Hesse, had been arrested by US forces during the war and been placed under Allied detention, while his deceased brother-in-law, Prince Christoph of Hesse, had been widely (though falsely) suspected of being the mastermind behind a daring daylight bombing raid on Buckingham Palace.

During his first summer back in Britain, he was invited to spend a few weeks at Balmoral. Though not as rigorous as the lessons he taught at Corsham, the Balmoral test was, and continues to be, an important assessment by the Royal Family of a potential bride or groom. Essentially, the intention was to judge, quite informally, the sailor prince and see if he would fit in to a country lifestyle where deer-hunting, grouse-shooting and salmon-fishing are key elements of the royal rounds – along with frequent wardrobe changes.

Philip did not get off to the best of starts. His clothing was as threadbare as his bank balance, his late father Prince Andrew having left him only a few modest items, including several suits, an ivory-handled shaving brush and a gold signet ring on his death in 1944. He had also had to borrow a kilt for his sojourn on the 50,000-acre royal estate. As it was just a wee bit too short, the prince, in attempting to turn a fashion faux pas into a moment of levity, dropped a cute curtsy rather than a neck bow when he greeted the King. George VI, who, like his brothers, was a stickler for the correct attire and formalities, was not amused. Philip's behaviour added to the sense among his detractors at court that this rather unpolished, overly confident young man, without a home, a fortune or a kingdom to bolster his credentials, was little more than a continental carpetbagger.

During his stay, his shooting was as wayward as his dress sense, with the ghillies and beaters describing his marksmanship as 'erratic and poor'.[12] He did, though, hit the target in matters of the heart. This is where it really mattered. Forthright and to the point, he took Elizabeth out for a drive on the estate and then, as they walked alone on the heather, the sound of a distant curlew adding to the sense of solitude, he asked if she would be his bride. The princess, who had inserted images of the prince in her photograph album and had had a framed picture of her bearded Navy beau on her desk for months, accepted on the spot. It was only later that Philip separately sought the formal permission of the King, his consent required under the 1772 Royal Marriages Act, which was passed by Parliament to prevent unsuitable or improper marriages that would diminish the standing of the royal house.

During Philip's six-week stay at Balmoral, the King formed a warm attachment to him. Like any father, he was happy to see his daughter blossom thanks to the prince's love and support. In the dynastic juggling act, this was, caveats aside, deemed to be a good match and George VI willingly gave his permission. But there was one condition.

A royal tour of South Africa, which had been months in the planning, was scheduled for early 1947 and so the King asked the couple to wait until the Royal Family returned in May before making a formal announcement. The palace even issued a statement in early September 1946, denying the rumour that there was an engagement between Elizabeth and Philip. This prevarication left the princess bewildered and crestfallen. She knew her own mind; it was her parents who were being indecisive, using the excuse of the South African tour to test the couple's resolve. In fairness, the prince still needed to become a naturalized British citizen before their future nuptials could be revealed, and that was not going to be a straightforward application.

Reluctantly, Elizabeth and Philip agreed to hold off on the announcement and to continue disguising their feelings for one another in public for just a little longer. Following his stay at Balmoral, the emotionally circumspect prince sent a letter of thanks to the Queen, dated 14 September 1946, which offered a window into his feelings. He wrote: 'I am sure I do not deserve all the good things which have happened to me. To have been spared in the war and seen victory. To have fallen in love completely and unreservedly makes all one's personal and even the world's troubles seem small and petty.'[13]

Although the couple were keeping their betrothal a secret, the public sensed that a romance was blossoming between the heir and the naval officer when they appeared at the wedding of Patricia Mountbatten, Philip's first cousin, to Captain Lord Brabourne at Romsey Abbey in Hampshire in October 1946. Sharp-eyed onlookers noticed that Philip and Elizabeth were probably more than just friends. Not only did he walk with the Royal Family to the church but, at the entrance, he also solicitously helped Princess Elizabeth, who was a bridesmaid, with her fur coat. Over the next few months well-wishers, who read media speculation about the couple, took to asking 'Where's Philip?' whenever Elizabeth appeared in public, much to her embarrassment and irritation.

In late January 1947, just a couple of days before the Royal Family sailed for South Africa on board HMS *Vanguard,* some of those genuinely in the know attended a small dinner party at Chester Street hosted by Lord Mountbatten. Noël Coward serenaded the party and guests toasted Philip and Elizabeth with champagne, except for the King who always drank whisky. The Royal Family would be away for over three months and at least two of those present were counting the days until their return.

—·—

A key member of the travelling party was the journalist Dermot Morrah who, from almost the moment he was born, was a passionate monarchist. When he was four years old, his nanny found him in floods of tears after learning of Queen Victoria's death.

A mathematician, classicist, historian, Fellow of All Souls College who went by the title Arundel Herald of Arms Extraordinary, he became a leader writer for *The Times*, always ready with a high-flown phrase or lofty sentiment. If a Latin simile was required, Dermot was your man. During the Second World War, he came to the notice of the King who, his stammer under control, felt much more comfortable about speaking in public. Frequently, the gentleman journalist was drafted in to prepare, construct and polish His Majesty's utterances.

Morrah was one of the gaggle of correspondents who boarded the air-conditioned White Train in Cape Town, which was to be the Royal Family's home from home for the next few weeks as they visited more than 400 towns and hamlets throughout southern Africa, from South Africa to Southern Rhodesia and Swaziland. During the epic and exhausting 11,000-mile tour, Morrah was frequently called upon to craft speeches for the King.

Although the visit was ostensibly to thank the South Africans for their sacrifice and support during the war, there was an expectation that the sunshine and temperate climate would give George VI, who was visibly gaunt after the tribulations of the conflict, a much-needed tonic. The politics of the visit were important, too. Not only was it hoped that the presence of the Royal Family would bolster the moderate government of General Jan Smuts against racist nationalists, but the palace also considered Princess Elizabeth's planned coming-of-age speech, which was due to be broadcast on her twenty-first birthday, to be the high point of the trip.

Its content would reference the time-honoured values of monarchy –service, loyalty and tradition – while articulating the continued significance of the institution in a rapidly changing world. It was an important address of commitment and connection that needed careful thought and memorable prose as the speech would serve as a manifesto for the post-war monarchy. The King's private secretary, Tommy Lascelles, assigned the delicate task to Morrah, who worked assiduously on a draft throughout the tour. At one point, the precious manuscript went missing somewhere on board the train, but was finally located among the bottles of booze in the bar of the 'Protea' dining car.

The normally gruff Lascelles was mightily impressed by the speech. 'I have been reading drafts for many years now,' he wrote to Morrah on 10 March, 'but I cannot recall one that has so completely satisfied me and left me feeling that no single word should be altered. Moreover, dusty cynic though I am, it moved me greatly. It has the trumpet-ring of the other Elizabeth's Tilbury speech, combined with the immortal simplicity of [Queen] Victoria's "I will be good".'[14]

Others were not so impressed. For once, the King disagreed with his private secretary. According to the BBC radio correspondent Frank Gillard, the Monarch found Morrah's original 'too pompous and full of platitudes'.[15]

As it was likely to be one of the most important royal speeches ever made, it deserved everyone's full attention. One Sunday, following a church service held at the Victoria Falls Hotel, the King, Queen and Princess Elizabeth, as well as Frank Gillard, took deckchairs into the garden and for the next two hours worked on the content, page by page, line by line, the princess reading out passages and changing words here and there to improve clarity and meaning. As Elizabeth would be the one reading this declaration of intent, she was an important voice, both literally and figuratively, in the shaping of the historic speech.

Once everyone was satisfied, the princess rehearsed the finished product under the watchful gaze of Gillard. The radio veteran deemed Elizabeth to be 'composed, confident and extremely cooperative'.[16] The speech was then recorded and filmed in secret under the trees in the hotel garden, the proceedings watched by a curious troop of baboons. On the princess's birthday, 21 April, her words were broadcast as if being delivered live from Government House in Cape Town, with a global audience of more than 200 million tuning in to listen.

She made clear from the opening sentence that her life, which she voluntarily yoked to the growth of the Commonwealth of Nations, would not be an all-white affair: 'On my twenty-first birthday, I welcome the opportunity to speak to all the peoples of the British Commonwealth and Empire, wherever they live, whatever race they come from and whatever language they speak.'

The climax to the seven-minute speech came as she dedicated her life to the service of the Crown and the people. It was an almost nun-like vow which had made Elizabeth tearful when she first read the draft: 'I should like to make that dedication now. It is very simple. I declare before you all that my whole life, whether it be long or short, shall be devoted to your service and to the service of our great imperial family to which we all belong. But I shall not have strength to carry out this resolution alone unless you join in it with me, as I now invite you to do: I know that your support will be unfailingly given. God help me to make good my vow and God bless all of you who are willing to share in it.'[17]

Many around the world paused their daily routine to listen to the princess's speech, which clearly came from the heart. It brought tears to the eyes of the King and Queen as well as Queen Mary, who confided to her diary: 'Of course I wept.'[18] She was not alone. Winston Churchill, a romantic to the tip of his Romeo y Julieta cigar, admitted that he too was moved to tears.

Tory grandee Viscount Templewood, formerly Sir Samuel Hoare, wrote in *The Times*: 'It may well be that the Crown will make possible a Commonwealth of free peoples and many races far more varied than any that may exist today.'[19]

During her radio address, Elizabeth stated that while she was 6,000 miles away from her place of birth, she was certainly not 6,000 miles from home. That was a cute compliment to her South African hosts, but something of a stretch. While the ever-loyal Bobo MacDonald brought her morning calling tray, and her sister and parents gave her private gifts over breakfast, the princess's twenty-first birthday was mostly spent in the company of strangers who, though they wished her well, were not her friends or family. Her coming of age reminded her that in a lifetime of duty, personal happiness and pleasure came a poor second.

For much of the day she nursed a headache. She found herself surrounded by over-eager outsiders, while the man she loved was thousands of miles away.

As the final insult, at the first of two birthday balls hosted in her honour, her dance partner, a clumsy if good-looking rugby player called Nellis Bolus, not only trod on her toes with his size thirteen shoes but also succeeded in dancing her into a fender in front of the ballroom mantelpiece. At the end of the dance, departing revellers recall seeing the two princesses, their shoes off, sitting on the staircase giggling and rubbing their sore feet.[20]

There were, though, glittering compensations. At the second ball, which was held at Government House, General Jan Smuts presented her with a beautiful necklace of twenty-one flawless, brilliant-cut diamonds with fifty-two facets. She would forever refer to them as 'my best diamonds'.[21]

Though her birthday speech was a personal triumph, the opening sentiments of inclusion and racial integration fell on stony ground, at least in South Africa. Within a year, the National Party was in power and the cruel apartheid system was voted into law. An informal policy of racial segregation was already in effect when the tour began. It infuriated the King that he was prevented from personally pinning medals on black ex-servicemen or shaking the hands of chiefs or elders at gatherings. During walkabouts and open-car tours, while members of the indigenous black population were on one side of the road, the whites were on the other. It was an eye-opening experience for the princess. Already learning to see beyond official bromides, during the tour Elizabeth began to appreciate the reality of life in South Africa and understand why her father was frustrated by the way he was controlled by the tour organizers.

She wrote to Queen Mary: 'The Zulus nowadays are a broken people, not at all what one expects to see after hearing about the "huge Zulus" [of British military folklore]. The Union Government has been very ruthless with them, which is sad, and removed a lot of their customs.'[22]

As the tour progressed, the King, far from feeling relaxed and revived, became increasingly tetchy. Even Smuts was alarmed by his deteriorating health and his frequent uncontrolled outbursts of temper. During what his family called his 'gnashes', the King was notorious among his entourage for kicking wastepaper baskets and twisting bath sponges to destruction. On one occasion, the White Train stopped on a remote bay by the Indian Ocean so that the King could go for a swim on his own. He was described as 'the loneliest man in the world' by the British journalist James Cameron.[23] Far from the trip to South Africa being a rest cure, when the King returned to Britain he was 17 pounds lighter and looked much frailer.

If the rigours of the seemingly endless tour and the constant pain in his legs distracted him, it was his family who provided support and consolation. As the King's equerry Peter Townsend observed: 'A perpetual current of it [affection] flows between them, between father and mother, between sister and sister, between parents and their daughters and back again.' He mused, somewhat optimistically given the hostility of the National Party to the tour, that the love within the Royal Family had an impact across the globe. 'Then it [affection] radiated outwards to the ends of the world, touching thousands of millions of hearts who sent, rolling back, a massive wave of love to the Royal Family.'[24]

This romantic image perhaps expressed the courtier's own feelings towards the Royal Family – and one member of it in particular. It was on this visit to South Africa, the land he described as a 'paradise', that Townsend, then still married with two young boys, fell in love with Princess Margaret who was almost sixteen years his junior.

Theirs was a love affair that began in plain sight of the rest of the family, their courtiers and the accompanying media. Every morning and evening, the princesses, accompanied by Townsend and assistant private secretary Michael Adeane, went riding through the rolling countryside or along the seashore. 'We sped in the cool air, across the sands or across the veldt,' wrote Townsend. 'Those were the most glorious moments of the day.' It was during these exhilarating and much-anticipated daily rituals that the sixteen-year-old princess, as she admitted years later, fell 'madly in love'[25] with her riding companion.

In her sensible way, her elder sister would have initially dismissed her sister's mooning over the married RAF group captain as a juvenile crush. Only later would she be obliged to take their burgeoning relationship more seriously.

Elizabeth was the great success of the tour, the princess seen as sensible, solicitous towards others, a skilful conversationalist with a well-developed sense of fun and a briskly business-like attitude to bread-and-butter royal engagements. Her 'let's get on with it' approach was often at variance with her mother's dilatory, if more theatrical, style.

She developed a habit of jabbing the Queen on her Achilles heel with her parasol to hurry her along if the schedule was in danger of overrunning. Nor was Elizabeth – known by some as 'the colonel' – averse to putting her father on a 'charge' if he were being too difficult. In short, she was a courtier's dream. Yet, and this was mentioned time and again, she was always solicitous with regard to the well-being of others. Elizabeth's chief cheerleader, Dermot Morrah, described watching her scrambling up a granite hillside in her stocking feet because she had handed over her own pair of shoes to her mother after hers had been damaged during the trip to Southern Rhodesia.[26] Tommy Lascelles wrote to his wife about the 'remarkable' development of Princess Elizabeth: 'She has come on in the most surprising way and all in the right direction.'[27]

It was George VI who struck a poignant and knowing observation about his beloved daughter during a visit to Cecil Rhodes' grave when a government minister asked him if the princess should be accompanied. With a brief shake of his head, the King watched her walk away from the monument and said: 'There she goes, Elizabeth, poor lonely girl, she will be lonely all her life.'[28]

As they left Cape Town bound for Portsmouth on 24 April, Princess Elizabeth would perhaps have little imagined that she would not return to South Africa for nearly half a century. However, the vibrant colours, endless skies and the banquet of exotic food left an indelible impression on her. It was a nation, as the princess concluded, where some lived like kings.

Thoughts doubtless returned to her much-missed beau as HMS *Vanguard* made its way steadily back to the UK. As the vessel approached the south-coast port on 11 May, Elizabeth was seen doing a jig of glee on deck, knowing that the announcement of her engagement could not be much further delayed. Her father, recognizing his daughter's stalwart patience on this important matter of the heart, later wrote to her: 'I was rather afraid that you had thought I was being hard-hearted about it. I was so anxious for you to come to South Africa as you knew. Our family, us four, the "Royal Family" must remain together ...'[29]

On their return home, the Royal Family realized that the trials and tribulations of their long tour abroad were as nothing compared to the catastrophic weather conditions that the people of Britain had experienced while they were away. In the worst winter in memory, the country had suffered dreadful flooding, towering snowdrifts, transport chaos, dwindling coal supplies and food rationing worse than during the war.

At the naval training base in Corsham, Prince Philip had taken to wearing a heavy greatcoat in the freezing classroom where he delivered his lectures by candlelight. Before the royal party had left for South Africa, he had accepted that the King was right to ask them to delay revealing their engagement. Now he was eager to end the secrecy.

He had not been idle while Elizabeth was away. The prince had been all too aware that his exotic surname and family background was a potential cause for criticism. In February, in order to deflect these concerns, he had taken the oath of allegiance and become a naturalized British subject. No longer Prince Philip of Greece and Denmark, on 28 February he became known as plain Lieutenant Mountbatten RN. It had been a close-run thing and the matter needed all of Louis Mountbatten's legendary string-pulling to encourage an indifferent Court and civil service to thread the administrative needle and formally make his nephew a British citizen.

However, it would be another two frustrating months before news of the engagement was made public. The King and Queen still had their doubts, with the Queen expressing her ambivalence to Tommy Lascelles. She wrote: 'One can only pray that she has made the right decision, I <u>think</u> she has – but he is untried as yet.'[30]

Finally, on 9 July, their engagement was officially announced. It was a brief pick-me-up for a nation on its knees, a country where rationing was so severe that some concerned folk from the Dominions had sent food parcels to help out. Britain may have won the war but was rapidly losing the peace. This was the age of austerity, a pervasive attitude that cast a long shadow over the planning for the wedding, which was officially set for 20 November 1947.

If the Royal Family and their courtiers had their reservations about the untested prince, as the wedding day approached Philip too had doubts about the prospects of marrying the future Queen. A week after the engagement was announced, he and Elizabeth travelled to Edinburgh where she was given the freedom of the city. As the princess made her acceptance speech, he dutifully stood two steps behind her. It was to be his default public position in the years ahead.

Over breakfast at Kensington Palace on the morning of the royal nuptials, the prince confided in his cousin Patricia Mountbatten: 'I don't know if I'm being very brave or very stupid going ahead with this wedding.'[31] In an attempt to reassure him, she replied: 'I am quite sure you are being very brave.'

As she later recalled: 'We were well aware that he wasn't just taking on the immediate family: he was taking on all the outer aspects of the Court life. He was very well aware, I think, that there were going to be difficulties.'[32] For her part, Queen Wilhelmina of the Netherlands was a little more candid regarding the realities of Philip's new circumstances, warning him that he would be 'entering the royal cage'.[33]

During his first Balmoral visit as the princess's fiancé, he had a taste of what he was up against. Many fellow guests, who included the Queen's brother David Bowes-Lyon, Lord Eldon and Lord Salisbury, had been doubtful about the match. The prince, knowing he was in hostile territory, was perhaps more combative and 'chipper' than usual. Courtiers who ran the rule over the couple concluded that she was in love with him, but they were not too sure about her controversial husband-to-be. They felt that he was too offhand towards the princess for their liking. For his part, Philip found the courtiers, particularly that gnarled and grizzly palace infighter Tommy Lascelles, patronizing and dismissive.

As the wedding day approached, he concluded that he was simply seen as a cipher, albeit a dashing one. All the major decisions about the event were taken out of his hands. Even though Philip had fought loyally during the war, the King deemed it too soon to invite his sisters, each of whom had married German royals who had gone on to join the Nazi party. 'So soon after the war you couldn't have the Hun,' Lady Pamela Hicks later commented bluntly.[34] It was a disappointment to both the prince and his three surviving sisters, but he completely understood the King's reasoning. On the big day itself, Philip's dubious family connections were forgotten in the euphoria surrounding the momentous occasion.

When Princess Elizabeth looked out from her second-floor bedroom window, she was amazed by the scene that greeted her. In the dawn November light she saw hundreds of people lining The Mall, some lying on mattresses and blankets now sodden with the rain that had fallen during the night. At Kensington Palace, where Philip Mountbatten RN had spent his last night as a bachelor, he seemed remarkably relaxed for a man who had just given up smoking – at the urging of his fiancée. He decided to wear his somewhat careworn Navy uniform, a move admired by the Queen and her friends. Though he wore a pair of darned socks at his wedding, on joining the Royal Family he found himself in possession of enough funds to buy himself a few new pairs when his £11 a week Navy pay (approximately £450 in today's money) was augmented by the granting of an annual allowance of £10,000 from the Civil List. His bride was awarded £50,000 by the government, with a further sum of £50,000 made available for the restoration of Clarence House, which had been bombed during the war and was now earmarked as their London residence.

That wasn't the only bounty the naval officer received. The day before the royal nuptials the King had made him a Knight of the Garter, and on the wedding day itself, he awarded Philip the titles of the Duke of Edinburgh, Earl of Merioneth and Baron Greenwich. Once again, Dermot Morrah had come to the rescue. When George VI was agonizing about what his future son-in-law should be called, Morrah compiled a list of appropriate names and ranked them in order of historical relevance and suitability. Several found favour with the Sovereign.

By contrast with the groom's modest preparations, his bride and her eight bridesmaids were being fussed over by couturier Norman Hartnell and his team. It took them two hours to fit the princess into her duchess satin and ivory silk wedding dress, a creation that had taken a team of 350 dressmakers seven weeks to make. The dress, with its theme of rebirth and renewal, had even been discussed in Cabinet, when the Labour Prime Minister Clement Attlee had expressed concern that the silk may have come from a country recently at war with Britain. Hartnell tartly pointed out that the silkworms were from Nationalist China, then an ally of Great Britain.[35]

Inside the palace, as the princess was carefully eased into her wedding dress, there was subdued panic. First the bride's bouquet went missing, only to be discovered in a cool cupboard after a footman recalled he had left it there to keep it looking fresh. Then, as the princess's veil was fitted, the frame of the sun-ray tiara, which had been lent to the bride by the Queen, snapped off.

Fortunately, the Crown Jeweller was on hand. He was escorted by police to his workshop to make the necessary repairs. Finally, Elizabeth's double string of pearls given to her by the King and Queen were declared lost. Luckily, a courtier remembered that the absent pearls were on display with the other 2,583 gifts at St James's Palace. So the princess's private secretary, Jock Colville, commandeered the official limousine used by King Haakon VII of Norway, intending to race directly to St James's. However, the crowds were so huge that he couldn't get through by road and had to run there on foot, where, after a tricky conversation with police who were guarding the wedding gifts, he was able to retrieve the precious piece of jewellery.[36]

As the drama took place backstage, Westminster Abbey itself saw the largest gathering of royalty since before the outbreak of war in 1939. Crown Princess Juliana of the Netherlands scanned the other royals, many looking distinctly down-at-heel, and commented: 'Everyone's jewellery is so dirty.'[37] Besides Philip's sisters, there were three other telling omissions from the guest list – the Duke and Duchess of Windsor and the Princess Royal, the King's sister Mary. Her absence was attributed to two key reasons: firstly, she was still in a state of grief over the death of her husband, who had passed away six months previously, and because her own wedding had taken place at the Abbey she would have found the occasion too hard to bear; secondly, being very close to her eldest brother, she felt that the Windsors' exclusion was unfair and un-Christian. It was the first public example of a pattern that would continue for the rest of their lives, the duke and his American wife exiled from the land he had once briefly ruled.

By contrast, his friend Winston Churchill, who had played a telling role in the abdication crisis, was treated as the all-conquering hero. He deliberately arrived late and almost stole the show as everyone in the congregation, including royalty, rose to their feet in acknowledgement of his past contribution to securing victory, liberation and peace in Europe. As the former war leader had predicted, the royal wedding was 'a flash of colour on the hard road we have to travel', as more than 200 million listeners tuned into the radio broadcast and thousands lined the streets leading to Westminster Abbey.[38] For many, it was a chance to escape grinding austerity and soul-destroying drabness just for a day. For others, it was a renewal of the ancient compact between the public and the Royal Family, a chance for the nation to pat itself on the back and celebrate an eternal ceremony that speaks of commitment, love and hope.

The star of the show arrived to a fanfare and the hymn 'Praise My Soul, the King of Heaven', as Elizabeth and her father walked slowly down the red carpet – which was secondhand during the era of austerity – to the High Altar where Philip and his cousin and best man, David Mountbatten, the Marquess of Milford Haven, were waiting.

'I was so proud and thrilled at having you so close to me on our long walk in Westminster Abbey', the King later wrote to his daughter. 'But when I handed your hand to the Archbishop, I felt that I had lost something very precious.'[39]

At the wedding breakfast, Philip made a short speech, saying, 'I am proud. Proud of my country and of my wife', while the new bride wished for nothing more than that 'Philip and I should be as happy as my father and mother have been, and Queen Mary and King George before them.'[40]

Acknowledging that 'we four' were now 'we five', the latest arrival to the House of Windsor wrote tenderly to the Queen to reassure her that her daughter was in good hands: 'Lilibet is the only "thing" in this world which is absolutely real to me and my ambition is to weld the two of us into a new combined existence that will not only be able to withstand the shocks directed at us, but will also have a positive existence for the good.'[41] Perhaps the suspicious courtiers had misread the royal romantic.

Though 'blissfully happy', Elizabeth considered the first few days of her honeymoon, which were spent at the Mountbattens' Broadlands estate in Hampshire, to be rather taxing due to the unbearable lack of privacy. In particular, she described their attendance at Romsey Abbey on the first Sunday of their stay as a most 'vulgar and disgraceful affair',[42] as their every movement was monitored by the press and the public. Curious crowds arrived on foot or by car to watch them. Those who couldn't get inside the place of worship climbed on gravestones or propped ladders up against the walls in order to peer through the windows. One family even brought a sideboard to use as a makeshift stand from which to view the royal newly-weds at prayer.

Royalty as celebrity, monarchy as circus. It was a sign of things to come.

CHAPTER FOUR

THE BAREFOOT PRINCESS

MARRIAGE CHANGED ELIZABETH. She seemed more womanly, more assured and more confident. The family dynamic had altered. Her world now centred around her husband and less so her parents and sister. Nonetheless, in the early days, the princess's instinctive reaction to a troubling decision was often to consult her mother first and her husband second. It was a difficult habit to give up and one which the Queen continued to encourage, believing that Philip challenged her authority as the family matriarch. The prince bided his time.

History professor Jane Ridley has argued that the Queen viewed him as 'rather an enemy', describing the early years of the relationship between Philip and the Queen as 'a tug-of-war and a tussle' for the ear of Princess Elizabeth.[1] As forthright and tactless as he could be, however, the prince was in no hurry to clash with his formidable mother-in-law. It was perhaps inevitable that in any close family, royal or non-royal, the arrival of a newcomer will upset the existing power balance.

In their day-to-day life Philip ruled the roost domestically, choosing menus, giving orders to staff, placing furniture and organizing private engagements. For her part, Elizabeth consulted with her private secretary Jock Colville on matters of State, royal engagements, official signatures and the like. Philip kept his nose out of such things, just as he avoided conflict with the third wheel in the marriage, his wife's companion and dresser Bobo MacDonald, who was in attendance during the first part of their honeymoon at Broadlands and again when they went north of the border to Birkhall on the Balmoral estate.

The dour Scot, who dressed just like her mistress, was the guiding hand behind the princess's daily wardrobe. She kept an inventory of her handbags, hats, dresses and shoes, and ensured that every item coordinated and fitted correctly. She was the one who brought the princess her calling tray with a cup of tea every morning and, more importantly, passed on the palace gossip. Her presence occasionally grated, but for the most part Philip held his peace.

In the meantime, the princess was excitedly plotting her departure from Buckingham Palace and starting married life in a place they could call their own. While Clarence House underwent extensive renovations over the next eighteen months, the couple lived at Kensington Palace briefly before returning to Elizabeth's suite of rooms at Buckingham Palace, but there was also the matter of their country residence. Initially, the plan had been to settle into Sunninghill Park, a rambling country house on the boundary of Windsor Great Park near Ascot in Berkshire. For a young woman who wanted to be surrounded by dogs, horses and eventually children, the early nineteenth-century country house estate set in 665 acres was ideal. Three months before their wedding, however, the rambling pile, which had been invaded by squatters, caught fire and burned down. Arson was initially suspected, but after an investigation the police concluded that the fire had begun during repairs. Instead, a lease was successfully secured on Windlesham

Moor, a country manor set in more than 50 acres in leafy Surrey, for weekend getaways.

Back in their interim London home, from their separate bedrooms the couple would exchange jolly banter while being dressed by, in Philip's case, his valet John Dean, and the ever-present Bobo took care of the princess. Privacy-wise, the newly-weds were under constant scrutiny, watched by silent footmen, judged by knowing courtiers and minded by their police bodyguards. Even so, compared to life as a twenty-first-century royal, it was a relatively relaxed state of affairs. Prince Philip was able to walk unhampered along The Mall to the Admiralty, where he had a desk job working for the Director of Operations. He was often able to take a break during the day to oversee the works at Clarence House. It was Philip who was responsible for the installation of the latest gadgets, including washing machines, televisions, an intercom system and an electric trouser press, but the princess also joined in, busying herself by mixing the paints for the green walls of the Adam-style dining room.

Her private secretary Jock Colville was active too, trying to mix and match the newly-weds, who were still royal apprentices after all, with a swatch of different events that would help them to gain a better insight into the workings of modern Britain. So the couple attended a debate in the House of Commons, visited a juvenile court and had dinner, hosted by Prime Minister Clement Attlee, with young politicians and their spouses.

But it was not all serious matters of State. On 28 February 1948, the family went en masse to the London Palladium to watch the American entertainer Danny Kaye. For the first time, the Royal Family sat in the front row of the stalls rather than the royal box. The King joined in with a singalong and was the one to call out to the comic in a skit about missing his tea break. The royals loved Kaye's zany, often improvised routines. Over the decades, the comedian became a regular and welcome visitor to various royal homes. Elizabeth's delight in seeing Kaye perform even inspired the American poet Delmore Schwartz to write the poem 'Vaudeville for a Princess', which featured the telling subtitle 'Suggested by Princess Elizabeth's Admiration of Danny Kaye'.

On their first overseas tour together, in May 1948 the couple visited Paris, which gave the princess the chance to put all those French conversation lessons to good use. While they enjoyed watching the horse races at Longchamp and danced at a fashionable nightspot, the princess was nursing a secret. She was in the early stages of pregnancy and prone to morning sickness. On several occasions during the visit, she only just managed to maintain her composure. Most spectators thought that her indisposition was due to her depth of feeling.

In the meantime, the couple had appointed a comptroller and treasurer, Lieutenant-General Sir Frederick 'Boy' Browning, a decorated military man known as 'the father of the British airborne forces', who was also the husband of novelist Daphne du Maurier. One of his first jobs had been to arrange the renting of Windlesham Moor, where Philip had turned the tennis court into a cricket pitch and organized matches with friends and locals during the summer. The couple had eight staff when they were in residence, including a footman whose job was to bring the corgis their food on a silver tray at 4.30 p.m. precisely.

Regular weekend visitors were Philip's great naval friend Mike Parker and his wife Eileen, who, like the princess, was pregnant but with her second child. Though the two wives did not know one another at all well, they had a common topic of conversation – babies.

Mrs Parker recalled that the princess often spoke about the dreams and ambitions she had for her children, wanting their lives to be less restricted than hers had been. The word 'normal' was frequently used – as it would be by future generations of royal mothers. As Eileen explained: 'She longed for them to be brought up under what she called "normal" circumstances. "I would like them to be able to lead ordinary lives", she used to say.' The princess also revealed that her idea of happiness was 'to live quietly in the country with her children, dogs and horses'.[2] Her ambition would be something of a pipe dream.

No sooner had the palace alluded to her pregnancy on 4 June, by issuing a bulletin stating that she would 'undertake no public engagements after the end of June', than she and her husband were showered with layettes, bootees, blankets and toys sent by well-wishers. When the time came to give up her royal duties, the princess spent her days in the then traditional way of mothers-to-be, namely organizing the nursery and developing a craving for her favourite chocolate cake.

Elizabeth insisted on having the baby in her own rooms at Buckingham Palace and was relieved when the Home Secretary, James Chuter Ede, made it clear that a presence of a senior government minister at the birth was no longer required. Neither, it seemed, was her husband, who played squash with Mike Parker in the palace courts as the princess, attended by four doctors, was in labour. When it was all over, the prince was interrupted by Tommy Lascelles with the news that, as of 9.14 p.m. on 14 November 1948, he was now the father of a baby boy. They named him Charles Philip Arthur George.

As the new parents celebrated with flowers and champagne, a cloud hung over the palace. The King, increasingly irascible and fragile, had been struggling with a worrying medical complaint. Throughout his daughter's pregnancy, he had been suffering from wrenching cramps in his feet that made standing – part and parcel of his job – agonizing. Not wishing to cause a fuss, the stoical Sovereign had soldiered on until the pain had become too much to bear. He had relied on the remedies prescribed by his homeopathic doctor, Sir John Weir, but this dubious course of treatment was suspected of delaying more conventional investigation. On 30 October – two weeks before the birth of his first grandchild – doctors established that George VI was indeed seriously ill. Once he had given himself up to the ministrations of the orthodox medical fraternity, the King, exhausted and distressed, slept for two days straight.

After further tests he was diagnosed as suffering from Buerger's disease, a chronic inflammation of arteries and veins in the arms and legs which reduces the flow of blood to the hands and feet. There was such a severe danger of gangrene in his right leg that surgeons even discussed amputation.

During these anxious few days secrecy and evasion was the order of the day to ensure that nothing would upset the heavily pregnant princess.

No word of the King's condition became public before she had given birth. Two days later, on 16 November, the Monarch accepted that a long-anticipated tour of Australia and New Zealand would have to be postponed. He also gave permission to release a medical bulletin and announced that he was cancelling all engagements for the foreseeable future. He was, however, sufficiently well to attend the christening of Prince Charles on 15 December. Besides other members of the Royal Family, also present at the ceremony was Elizabeth's former governess, Marion Crawford, accompanied by her husband George Buthlay, whom she had married in September 1947.

As the Buthlays watched the Archbishop of Canterbury, Geoffrey Fisher, pour water from the River Jordan over the infant's head in the Music Room at Buckingham Palace, they were devising a stratagem that would rupture the lifelong relationship between Crawfie and Elizabeth: Mrs Buthlay was planning to write a memoir about her time with the princesses and their parents. It was an incendiary idea, especially as it soon became abundantly clear that the Royal Family were wholly opposed to former or existing members of the Household writing or talking about their experiences.

She initially asked the Queen for permission to commit details about her courtly life to paper, with a view to future publication, but in a letter sent to Marion Buthlay in April 1949, the Queen made the family position clear: 'I do feel, most definitely, that you should not write and sign articles about the children, as people in positions of confidence with us must be utterly oyster.'[3] The message was unequivocal: stay silent.

When she defied her erstwhile employer and went ahead with a series of articles in the American magazine *Ladies' Home Journal*, and then published her memoir in 1950, members of the Royal Family were furious and shocked. Even though her book, *The Little Princesses*, was anodyne and highly complimentary, depicting Elizabeth, Margaret and their parents as a virtuous family who extolled wholesome fireside values of duty, love and fidelity, Crawfie was deemed to have betrayed their trust. Princess Margaret felt sick and her sister was deeply upset by the perceived betrayal committed by their old governess.

Elizabeth accused her of having 'snaked', that is to say having deceived the family, and advised any ladies-in-waiting who received letters from Mrs Buthlay to hold them with a long pair of tongs. It was not what she had written that concerned the Royal Family – the woman had conjured up a world which was human yet dignified, and where love, duty and obedience were the currency of everyday life – but her deliberate act of disloyalty. In a six-page letter to Lady Nancy Astor, the Queen lamented that 'our late and completely trusted governess' had 'gone off her head'.[4] The phrase 'to do a Crawfie' became a term used to describe any member of royal staff who subsequently sold stories about their time in service.

This unhappy episode vividly illustrated a Royal Family trait: at any sign of danger, its members immediately circled the wagons. Cross one and, as Crawfie found to her cost, you cross them all. There was no going back, the one-time royal employee was cast into the outer darkness forever. Shortly after *The Little Princesses* was published, she vacated her grace-and-favour home, Nottingham Cottage, within the grounds of Kensington Palace and moved to Aberdeen, just a few yards from the road to Balmoral. She longed for a reconciliation but it never came. In her later years, she twice tried to take her own life. On one occasion she left a note that read: 'The world has passed me by and I can't bear those I love to pass me by on the road.'[5]

That said, the former governess should have anticipated the stern and unforgiving reaction of the young woman whom she had loved and adored as if she were her own child. When Jock Colville, who was Elizabeth's private secretary for two years before a third spell working for Winston Churchill, asked the princess if it might be possible for him to write about his experiences in her office, he was given short shrift. His request cast a pall over the remaining months of his secondment to the Royal Family in 1949.

Just as Elizabeth was completely loyal to her family and the institution, so she expected absolute trustworthiness from those with whom she worked. The long-term effect of the Crawfie affair was to place a distance between the princess and those in her employ, no matter how steadfast they had been. At times of crisis, members of the Royal Family instinctively withdrew into themselves.

If the Crawford affair marked the end of childhood innocence, so the ailing King's incapacity – he underwent a significant spinal operation in March 1949 to improve the circulation in his legs – firmly propelled the twenty-two-year-old princess into the front line of the monarchy. During his slow recovery, it was Princess Elizabeth who grew in stature, taking over many of his formal duties. In June, the King was driven in an open carriage to observe the Trooping the Colour ceremony while his eldest daughter led the parade on horseback.

Though endlessly concerned about her father, the princess was beginning to lead the life of an independent married woman, a process that accelerated when the couple finally moved from Buckingham Palace to Clarence House the following month. Earlier in the year, when Elizabeth celebrated her twenty-third birthday, she went to the fashionable Café de Paris on Coventry Street near Leicester Square after watching Laurence Olivier and Vivien Leigh in a production of *The School for Scandal*. The two glamorous thespians were then invited to join the royal party for an evening of tango, quick-step and samba, before the group later moved on to a nightclub. At a ball held at Windsor Castle that summer, the royal newly-weds stole the show. Henry 'Chips' Channon commented that they 'looked like characters out of a fairy tale'.[6]

In July, at another ball that was hosted by the American ambassador Lewis W. Douglas, whose daughter Sharman was a close friend of Princess Margaret, the couple arrived in fancy dress – Elizabeth as an Edwardian parlour maid and her husband as a waiter. Determined to make an impact, nineteen-year-old Margaret came as a Parisian can-can girl, complete with lace knickers and black stockings. In her thank-you note she told Sharman: 'I was feeling so over-excited by the time our Can-Can was due that I could hardly breathe.'[7] That didn't stop the 'ecstatic' royal from putting on her costume and repeating her routine for her mother when she got home to Buckingham Palace.

Improvements in the King's condition coincided with the end of Philip's sojourn ashore. He was appointed first lieutenant and second-in-command of the destroyer HMS *Chequers*, which was based in Malta, and he left for the island in mid-October 1949. Elizabeth joined him a month later with the King's blessing.

Malta was a place that had become dear to George VI's heart in the days of the Second World War. In April 1942, during the brutal siege of Malta, in honour of the country's 'brave people' he awarded the entire island the George Cross 'to bear witness to a heroism and devotion that will long be famous in history'. In June 1943, he also paid a personal visit to the island. The Queen, who had a photograph of her husband arriving at Malta displayed on her bedroom dressing table, later recalled: 'The King was so determined to get to Malta somehow, to try and convey his gratitude and admiration to the brave citizens for their courage and tenacity under endless attacks.'[8]

The feeling was entirely mutual as, on Elizabeth's arrival in November, thousands thronged the streets to catch a glimpse of the King's eldest daughter and their future Queen. Such was the fascination with and adoration of the princess that Mabel Strickland, the owner of the *Times of Malta* newspaper, wrote an article asking the public to leave the royal couple alone on private occasions.

Princess Elizabeth, who came to the island on her second wedding anniversary, 20 November, hardly had a chance to join her husband to celebrate before she was plunged into a round of engagements. During her six-week stay, she visited Malta's cathedrals, the national library, the dockyard, the Mediterranean fleet, an industrial exhibition, numerous hospitals, presided over the annual children's toy tea at the Palace and unveiled an updated war memorial commemorating the dead of two world wars.

For all the formality and protocol – Prime Minister Paul Boffa and Archbishop Michael Gonzi were a seemingly constant presence – this was one of the happiest periods of her life. Malta was where her second child, Princess Anne, was conceived and where she and her naval husband were able to spend time alone, exploring the many inlets and coves on board a cruiser aptly named *The Eden*. To keep seasickness at bay, she would always bring along a supply of *galletti* (Maltese wafer biscuits), which would help to ease her stomach when needed. She and the duke found time to go dancing on board his ship at an officers' mess shindig and also visited the Phoenicia Hotel where the band leader would play her favourite tune, 'People Will Say We're in Love' from *Oklahoma!*, the Rodgers and Hammerstein musical.

For most of her first stay in Malta, Elizabeth and Philip lived at Villa Guardamangia, a sandstone property with commanding views of the harbour at Pietà, whose then residents were Philip's uncle and aunt, Louis and Edwina Mountbatten. In fact, the couple kindly gave up their own rooms in the rambling establishment to ensure that their esteemed visitors had the best suite in the house.

One of Philip's former Navy colleagues from his Corsham days, Lieutenant Bill O'Brien, was also stationed in Malta as commander of the frigate HMS *Venus*. Three years previously, he had graciously given the prince his petrol-ration coupons so that Philip could drive to London to court the princess. Bill and his wife Rita became regular guests at the dinner parties hosted by the royal couple at Villa Guardamangia.

Another fixture in Elizabeth's life was Mabel Strickland, the colourful, controversial newspaper proprietor who brought the princess into her circle and helped her to organize guest lists for social events. After Elizabeth and Philip moved into the villa, Mabel was invited to their first dinner party. Fellow attendee Vice Admiral Guy Grantham, who eventually became the Governor and Commander-in-Chief of Malta, recalled: 'We had a local dish as a second course, and we were using gold-plated fish knives and forks – and the first thing that happened was that one of the knives used by the ADC [aide-de-camp] snapped off. The princess told him not to worry, [saying] "It was a wedding present", but before we had finished the course another couple of handles had gone too! This amused the princess frightfully.'⁹

The atmosphere at the villa was warm and friendly, and Edwina Mountbatten enjoyed coddling the young mother: 'It's lovely seeing her so radiant and leading a more or less human and normal existence for once.'¹⁰ But as a reminder of the responsibilities to come, on one occasion Philip got an earful from his uncle when he kept his wife out late, which caused them to miss the start of a dinner party hosted by the Mountbattens. He summoned the prince to his office where he told him, 'Don't you dare do it again. Remember, she is the Queen of tomorrow and please never forget that.'¹¹

This turned out to be one in a series of clashes between two hard-driving men who liked to have their own way. After several weeks of brusque, offhand behaviour displayed by Philip towards his Uncle Dickie, the two of them finally sat down for a heart-to-heart to resolve their issues. The prince admitted that he was trying to resist his dominating uncle's influence in the only way he knew how – by fighting back. In response Mountbatten agreed to ease off. Once the grievances had been aired, the two men resumed their previously friendly and affectionate relationship.

Mountbatten was desperate to be liked and admired by the future Queen and so he was thrilled when he discovered that she found him rather good company. He told his sister Patricia: 'Lilibet is quite enchanting and I've lost whatever of my heart is left to spare entirely to her. She dances quite divinely and always wants a samba when we dance together.'¹²

The dancing had to come to an end just after Christmas, when it was time for Prince Philip to resume his naval duties on board HMS *Chequers*, heading for the Red Sea in the light of tribal clashes in Eritrea. As the princess witnessed her husband's departure, it was a salutary rite of passage experienced by all Navy wives, including Edwina Mountbatten, who felt a surge of sympathy for the young woman standing on the docks watching her man sail away. Not long afterwards, Elizabeth boarded a Vickers Viking plane and returned home.

'Lilibeth has left with a tear in her eyes and a lump in her throat,' Edwina informed Jawaharlal Nehru, India's first prime minister, with whom she shared a long and intimate romance. 'Putting her into the Viking when she left was, I thought, rather like putting a bird back into a very small cage and I felt sad and nearly tearful myself.'[13]

The princess's only consolation was that she would be reunited with her son, who had spent Christmas with his grandparents at Sandringham. She stayed at the Norfolk retreat for the next few weeks, helping to entertain the numerous visitors who had been invited to a 'dine and sleep', effectively spending the night after dinner. It was a way of efficiently hosting important guests, such as politicians and diplomats, as Sandringham was well off the beaten track. During such a visit in February 1950, Cynthia Gladwyn, the wife of Sir Gladwyn Jebb, the UK's Ambassador to the United Nations, observed the contrast between Elizabeth's youth and her exalted position. She noted that she had 'a most charming mixture in her expression of eagerness to please and yet a serious awareness of her rank and responsibility. Her charming diffidence was very appealing, for a touch of genuine gravity was always the traditional barrier which separated royalty from the common herd, warning them that no liberty should be taken. But all this with a sweet smile, a very pretty soft voice and a certain gaucherie in her walk, showing her still to be a young girl.'[14]

In late March, Elizabeth left for Malta to be reunited with her husband once again. The princess spent part of her twenty-fourth birthday watching her husband and Lord Mountbatten playing a competitive game of polo. These were happy days for the pregnant princess who, according to Philip's friend Mike Parker, spent only 10 per cent of her time being a royal. For the rest she 'mucked in' with other naval wives, organizing tea parties and other social events.[15] For the most part she was left alone, the islanders heeding the urgings of Mabel Strickland and others to respect her privacy.

All too soon, though, that carefree spring and early summer came to an end as the princess left for Clarence House where thousands of curious onlookers gathered to catch a glimpse of her before she gave birth to her second child. On 15 August 1950, the waiting multitude were rewarded for their noisy patience when it was announced that a girl had been born. Normally in robust health, Elizabeth spent longer than expected recovering from the birth, her doctors advising her to cancel public engagements for the next three months.

In late November, five weeks after her daughter Anne Elizabeth Alice Louise was christened, the princess returned to Malta to spend Christmas with her husband, leaving the children behind at Sandringham with her sister and parents – as well as a small platoon of nurses and nannies. When she arrived, Philip was eager to show her around his new 'baby'.

In September, shortly after the birth of his daughter, the twenty-nine-year-old prince had been given command of the anti-submarine frigate HMS *Magpie*, just two months after being promoted to lieutenant-commander. Clearly, his naval career was on the up.

Not long after joining him in Malta, she and the duke sailed to Athens on an official visit to the Greek royal family, Philip's cousin King Paul and his wife Queen Frederika. Elizabeth made the journey on board HMS *Surprise,* the Commander-in-Chief's despatch vessel, while the prince remained on *Magpie.* During the voyage, the royal couple exchanged humorous signals which are still preserved in the Navy log. One famous example was: *Surprise* to *Magpie*: 'Princess full of beans.' The reply from *Magpie* to *Surprise* was: 'Can't you give her something better for breakfast?' Others related to Biblical texts, the princess on one occasion signalling 'Isaiah 33:23', which features the words 'Thy tacklings are loosed'. Her husband rapidly responded with 'I Samuel 15:14', which includes the question 'What meaneth then this bleating of the sheep ...?'[16]

Their highly successful visit, which was sanctioned by the Foreign Office, was the perfect union of Philip's naval and Elizabeth's royal duties.

Back at Villa Guardamangia, where the couple were in residence once again – this time without Uncle Dickie interfering, as the Mountbattens had returned to London earlier in the year – the princess probably enjoyed her most pleasant stay in Malta, especially when her sister Margaret arrived to join in the fun. In a memo to her staff, Elizabeth made it clear that she wanted a life that was sunny side up. 'I sincerely hope that full cooperation will exist between all members of the staff as to create a happy atmosphere at the Villa Guardamangia.'[17] Tony Grech, the son of her maid Jessie, took to calling her 'Auntie Liz'. He was not the only one. Long after she had left Malta, she sent Christmas cards to her Maltese staff and later invited all of them to celebrate her twenty-fifth wedding anniversary at Westminster Abbey and Buckingham Palace.

While Philip raced his yacht *Coweslip* across the bay or spent time improving his polo skills aboard a wooden practice horse, the princess went riding herself, drove around the island in her Daimler with her lady-in-waiting or detective for company, or visited other Navy wives for tea and sandwiches. She is also remembered for trying local dishes like rabbit pâté, pastizzi (traditional savoury pastries), lampuki pie (made from the lampuki fish) or hobz malti, a type of local sourdough bread.

On one occasion in April 1951, the royal couple visited the tiny island of Gozo, where the princess unveiled a war monument in Victoria and also a plaque at the local hospital. Together, they watched lace-making in Sannat and were later taken to the site of a new reservoir.[18] Though a plaque in Sannat now commemorates the visit, at the time it only attracted polite local interest.

The precious time spent in Malta allowed the princess to live a life that was barely imaginable in England and it was an experience that she always looked back on with affection and gratitude. Even in January 1975, almost a month after Malta became a republic, she was waxing lyrical about the place. 'I have been thinking so much about Malta and the happy times we had there as a naval family – something I shall never forget,' she wrote to Mabel Strickland, who sent her an annual gift of avocados, oranges, lemons and other exotic fruits from her garden.[19]

It was hard to give up such a contented berth. But by the summer of 1951, it became clear that the couple had no choice. Both the Royal Navy and the Royal Family were full-time commitments and something had to give. Philip was forced to accept the inevitable when he was eventually put on indefinite leave in July 1951. Looking wistfully at his Navy whites, he told his valet John Dean: 'It will be a long time before I want those again.'[20]

A bout of influenza, which had caused the ailing King to cancel a visit to Northern Ireland in May 1951, rather sealed Philip's fate. As the Sovereign recuperated, the Queen and the princesses took on his duties, Elizabeth once again representing her father at Trooping the Colour in June. During the summer George VI's condition deteriorated, news which cast a pall over Princess Margaret's twenty-first birthday celebrations at Balmoral in August. Then, on 22 September, seven doctors issued a brief but dramatic bulletin advising that the state of the Monarch's left lung was concerning and it was recommended that an operation should soon be performed. Elizabeth and Philip, who had been due to sail to Canada for a tour of North America, postponed their departure temporarily to be in London during George VI's surgery on 23 September.

The news was not good. After the operation, the King's surgeons informed the Queen and Elizabeth that there was evidence of cancer in the excised lung. This significant detail was not shared with the patient. While the Monarch began his slow and painful recovery, he was adamant that the royal tour of North America should continue as planned.

So, on 7 October, the prince and princess dutifully boarded a plane for the seventeen-hour journey to Montreal. It was the first time that an heir to the throne had made a long-distance flight, and such was the concern that Royal Navy ships took up strategic positions across the Atlantic route in case an emergency arose. Black clothes of mourning had been packed in their luggage, as well as a sealed envelope containing the draft Accession Declaration, so that they were fully prepared if the King passed away during their trip.

Their arrival in Montreal was a far cry from those halcyon days of untroubled anonymity in Malta. A friendly but boisterous crowd of around 15,000 welcomed the royal couple and so numerous was the legion of photographers that Princess Elizabeth's fur coat was peppered with glass from exploding flashbulbs. The pace on the thirty-three-day visit was relentless and exhausting, and the princess was so unnerved by the good-natured mayhem which accompanied their every move that a muscle in her right cheek twitched constantly. She also reverted to her default pose of polite but contained interest. As a result, critics complained that she was too distant and formal.

These sentiments surprised Elizabeth, who noted that her ceaseless smiling had in fact resulted in an aching jaw. It would not be the only time that people mistook her impassive demeanour for aloofness, even though it was simply a mask she wore to keep her natural emotions in check. She would not be able to escape these serial misconceptions throughout her future reign. As her former private secretary Lord Martin Charteris, who knew her for fifty years, observed, the key to her character was that she was actually afraid of her emotions because they were very strong and she always tried to keep them under iron control.[21]

When Elizabeth and Philip returned from their overseas trip in November, the princess was reassured by her father's weight gain and that he was considering going shooting, albeit with a light gun. She agreed with the plan for him to travel to South Africa in March 1952, to enjoy the winter sunshine and hopefully regain his strength. He was still so weak that, when he recorded his Christmas message, he was only able to manage a single sentence at a time.

As a result of the King's continuing poor health, it was decided that the Duke and Duchess of Edinburgh would finally embark upon the oft-postponed trip to Australia and New Zealand in his place, leaving on Thursday 31 January with a stopover in Kenya. The last evening that the Royal Family spent together before the tour was at the Theatre Royal Drury Lane, where they saw a performance of *South Pacific* by Rodgers and Hammerstein.

On the day of the royal couple's departure, George VI ignored his doctors and travelled from Sandringham to see them off from London Airport (now Heathrow). Despite the windy conditions, the King stood hatless for thirty minutes on the airport tarmac to say goodbye to his much-loved daughter. 'He is like that,' she later acknowledged. 'He never thinks of himself.'[22]

Although the King was seen conversing with Churchill and other members of the official group, there was no denying that he looked haggard and strained. Consequently, the nation was upset and saddened when images of the British Sovereign were published. 'I felt with foreboding that this would be the last time he was to see his daughter, and that he thought so himself,[23] recalled the Colonial Secretary, Lord Chandos. Others thought the same.

Indeed, around Christmas 1951, after the Australian Minister for External Affairs Richard Casey had met Princess Elizabeth, he told his wife Maie: 'I am not sure that Elizabeth doesn't know that practically at any moment she may become Queen of us all. She has such a serious demeanour that I think she was warned or has some instinctive knowledge that at any time she might have this burden thrust upon her.' When he shared this impression with Churchill, the Prime Minister replied: 'Yes, there is too much care on that young brow.'[24]

Back at Sandringham, on Tuesday 5 February the King was in exuberant spirits and went shooting on a bitterly cold but blue-skied day. During dinner that night, his racing manager Charles Moore regaled him with tales of his adventures spent in Kenya at the Treetops Hotel in the Aberdare Forest, a place where, at that precise moment, Elizabeth and Philip would have been sitting in a small cabin in the branches of a huge fig tree, giving them the perfect vantage point from which to observe elephants, rhinos and other large game in the moonlight.

That evening, George VI retired early. The next day, 6 February, at 7.15 a.m. his under-valet James MacDonald entered the King's room with his morning tea, but was unable to rouse him. The fifty-six-year-old Sovereign was dead. Later investigations revealed that the cause of death was a coronary thrombosis, a blood clot that had reached his heart.

The Queen was informed and immediately went to her husband's bedroom. He looked so peaceful that at first she thought he was merely sleeping deeply, but then she realized what had happened. She gave him a gentle kiss on the forehead. Then she went to tell Princess Margaret the terrible news before putting into motion the mechanics of 'Hyde Park Corner', the code word used to inform senior courtiers at Buckingham Palace, as well as top government officials, that the King had passed away.

In Kenya that morning, the sky shimmered with a pale-blue light and the surrounding atmosphere was vibrant and seemingly tinged with magic. Elizabeth regarded the iridescent landscape in wonder, and as she did so a majestic eagle circled overhead for a while before dropping down a few feet, as though it was saluting her, and then flying away. Mike Parker, Philip's equerry, also witnessed the unusual scene, the memory of which would stay with him for quite some time.

Without communication of any kind having yet reached her, Elizabeth was blithely unaware of the drama unfolding at Sandringham. The previous evening, the small group of people accompanying the royal couple, their faces illuminated by kerosene lamps, had listened intently as the princess had spoken proudly of her father and his determined efforts to regain his health. She recalled the moment he had put a walking stick to his shoulder and said: 'I believe I could shoot now.'[25] His daughter hoped that the King's forthcoming visit to South Africa would do him good and that he would have made a full recovery by the time she returned home from the tour of Australia and New Zealand.

After breakfast, the party returned to Sagana Lodge, the cabin given to the couple as a wedding present by the Kenyan people. Here Elizabeth sat at her desk, writing a letter to her parents about the excitements of the night before. Philip was having a rest before a planned trout-fishing trip. Along the corridor, Mike Parker took a phone call that left him shocked to the core. It was from the princess's private secretary, Martin Charteris, who had been at the Outspan Hotel in Nyeri when he was informed by a journalist about wire reports from London announcing the King's death.

Parker's first instinct was to wake Prince Philip. Instead, he waited in his room quietly, listening to a shortwave radio for more information. Once he was doubly certain, he broke the news to Philip. The prince looked as if the world had dropped on his shoulders as he absorbed the full import of George VI's passing. After taking a moment to compose himself, he went into his wife's room and led her out into the garden. There, in the dappled sunlight against the calming backdrop of a gently flowing stream, she was told of her father's death and accepted that she was now Queen.

Her response revealed the extraordinary calibre of the young woman, aged only twenty-five, who had inherited the throne. She seemed almost prepared for this dread event as her reaction was quite matter-of-fact and business-like. There were no tears or any emotional outburst as the full significance of losing her beloved father began to sink in and she started to accept the inevitability of her destiny. Certainly she was pale, almost translucent, very tense and strained, but those who travelled with her remember the new Sovereign as being remarkably contained, clear-sighted and in control.

Some days later, hunter Jim Corbett, who had accompanied Elizabeth during her stay at Treetops, summarized the unique circumstances when he wrote in the visitors' book: 'For the first time in the history of the world, a young girl climbed into a tree one day a Princess and, after having what she described as her most thrilling experience, she climbed down from the tree the next day a Queen.'[26]

When Elizabeth reappeared at Sagana Lodge, Philip's cousin and her lady-in-waiting, Lady Pamela Mountbatten, approached her with a warm hug and asked, 'What can one say?' The Monarch simply shrugged and replied: 'It's one of those things.'[27] Moments later, Lady Pamela gave a deep curtsy, realizing that the woman before her was no longer just her friend but also her Sovereign.

For the next few hours, Elizabeth's lifetime of training kicked into action as she busied herself with her new and onerous responsibilities. Her own emotions were completely put to one side, subordinated entirely to her duty. She remained dry-eyed and focused on the job in hand. In the words of Edward Windley, the then provincial commissioner of Central Province in Kenya: 'She was very pale. She was like ice; just like ice.' Asked how she responded when she heard the news of her father's death, he replied: 'She took it like a queen.'[28]

When her private secretary Martin Charteris arrived at Sagana Lodge still wearing his sports jacket, she looked up from her desk and declared: 'Australia must be told.'[29] Then she wrote a note to the Governor-General of Australia, Sir William McKell, expressing her regret for the postponement of the forthcoming tour. As part of the procedural formality, Charteris had to ask by which name she wished to be known, to which she replied, 'My own name, Elizabeth, of course.'[30] To underline her decision, she signed some photographs of herself and her family with her new signature: 'Elizabeth R.'[31]

Though time was of the essence – thunderstorms were gathering near the airport at Nanyuki – she insisted in thanking all the assembled lodge staff. The couple's chauffeur, James Cosma A. Gabatha, knelt to kiss her feet when she said goodbye.

As her mourning clothes were on board the SS *Gothic*, which was moored at Mombasa harbour, she left Sagana Lodge in her day clothes, namely a floral dress and white gloves, as well as a black armband that was always carried in the official royal bag. The Queen was pleased to note that the covey of photographers had agreed to her request, conveyed by Charteris, not to take pictures and had instead placed their cameras on the ground as a mark of respect.

On the drive to Nanyuki, the royal couple marvelled at how many villagers lined the side of the road with their heads bowed in respect. Clearly the bush telegraph had been working overtime.

When she climbed the aircraft steps, she paused at the top for a long time, as if drinking in the electric, primal atmosphere of this rugged land. Writer John Hartley described the moment: 'She stood in the gathering darkness, unmoving and totally removed. Everyone and everything were silently poised, waiting breathlessly and listening.'[32]

Then it was down to business. During the lengthy flight back to London, they were in sporadic radio communication with the government and the palace. Prime Minister Winston Churchill sent a message of condolence on behalf of the Cabinet. Her mother too sent a telegram, which read: 'All my thoughts and prayers are with you, Mummy.'[33] On the long journey home, the Queen had plenty of time to review the draft of a speech she was due to make to the Privy Council the following day.

By the time they reached London Airport, the Queen was tightly controlled, composed and rested, all set to face the official welcoming party. With her mourning-wear left behind on board SS *Gothic*, she waited before disembarking in order to change into a black dress and veil that had been brought to her from Clarence House. When she was at last ready to meet Prime Minister Churchill and several other politicians, she took a final look out of the aircraft window before descending the steps.

During their tenure at Clarence House, the royal couple had eschewed the outsized and cumbersome royal Rolls-Royces and Daimlers for a more modern and modest fleet of Austin Princess cars. As they taxied along the runway, the Queen looked out at the row of black official Daimlers and Rolls-Royces waiting for her. 'Ah, they've sent those hearses,' she remarked.[34] Her sense of entombment was complete.

CHAPTER FIVE

CROWNING GLORY

AS QUEEN ELIZABETH II was driven along the silent streets of London on her return to Clarence House, a new kind of blackout was in progress. Men were in black suits and women wore black dresses or at the very least black armbands. On fashionable Bond Street, a haberdasher dressed his window display with black lingerie. Avuncular historian John Wheeler-Bennett, who became George VI's official biographer, recalled how 'the people of England made no secret of the depth and sincerity of their sorrow. I saw many in tears.'[1]

Elizabeth, however, had no time for sentiment. When she arrived at Clarence House her grandmother, Queen Mary, was waiting for her. She stood erect and dignified as the new Sovereign entered the reception hall. Then the old Queen, who had witnessed five reigns – from Victoria to her second son – curtsied and kissed the young Queen's hand. It was such a powerful moment of family intimacy and royal symbolism that Queen Mary's lady-in-waiting, Lady Cynthia Colville, struggled to keep her composure. Not so the unflappable royal, who reminded her granddaughter that her dress was too short for official Court mourning.[2]

On 8 February, the Queen and Prince Philip, in his capacity as

Privy Counsellor, attended her first meeting of the Privy Council as Monarch, comprising some 175 dignitaries, at St James's Palace where the Queen took her Oath of Accession. After proclaiming herself Queen Elizabeth II, she told the council: 'My heart is too full for me to say more to you today than I shall always work, as my father did throughout his reign, to advance the happiness and prosperity of my peoples, spread as they are all the world over.'[3]

While Prime Minister Churchill confided to his joint principal private secretary Jock Colville that the new Queen was 'only a child',[4] he gave her a rousing oration in a packed House of Commons: 'With the new reign we must all feel our contact with the future. A fair and youthful figure – princess, wife and mother – is the heir to all our traditions and glories never greater than in her father's days, and to all our perplexities and dangers never greater in peacetime than now. She is also heir to all our united strength and loyalty.'[5]

With the initial formalities dealt with, the new Queen drove to Sandringham to help comfort her grieving mother and sister and to bid a private farewell to her father. On arrival at the 20,000-acre estate in Norfolk, she immediately went to the King's bedroom, where his body lay in a simply carved oak coffin that had been crafted from a single tree. She quietly affirmed that she would follow in his footsteps and make him proud. It would not be easy. Beyond the teachings of Sir Henry Marten in constitutional history and the limited insights her father had given her, she did not feel wholly prepared for her role, though perhaps being the same age as the first Queen Elizabeth when she ascended the throne in 1558 provided some comfort.

In those first few turbulent days with no father to guide her, she relied on the support of her husband as well as her experienced and forthright private secretary Tommy Lascelles, and of course Mr Churchill. She placed her personal doubts to one side, knowing that she had to be the strong member of the remaining trio for the sake of her mother and sister who had, as she later acknowledged, 'the biggest grief to bear, for their future must seem very blank, while I have a job and family to think of'.[6]

The King and Queen had been an emblem of hope and unity during the war. They were a partnership – Queen Elizabeth, now the Queen Mother, had been as dependent on her husband's 'wisdom, his integrity, his courage' as he had relied on her confidence and support.[7] Now she was alone. She felt worthless and empty, her sense of loss 'beyond description'.[8]

Elizabeth's sister was equally despairing. The King, second-born himself, had always had a soft spot for his youngest daughter, calling Margaret his 'joy' and Elizabeth his 'pride'. An indulgent father, a convivial friend and wise counsellor, he had been the centre of her universe. In return, she had been the one able to calm him when, in his later ailing years, he had given in to angry 'gnashes'. Margaret explained 'the awful sense of being in a black hole' as she tried to come to terms with his death, the first time she had lost someone really close.[9] She wrote to her friend Veronica Maclean, thanking for her 'support at this time of anguish': 'One is happy to think that he is safe in Heaven, away from everything that can hurt or harm him, and soon we will feel him nearer to us than he has ever been.'[10] Even her faith – Margaret, like her sister, knew and reflected upon her Bible – could not help her through the dark nights of the soul. Instead, feeling 'tunnel-visioned', she turned to sedatives, hard liquor and cigarettes, and lost a worrying amount of weight.

Elizabeth felt guilty and helpless but had no choice but to soldier on, aware too that the sailor in her life was grieving as well. While Philip certainly mourned the loss of his father-in-law, he was also bidding farewell to his naval career at the very moment that it was really taking off. Though he had taken sabbaticals to accompany the princess on overseas visits, he had assumed that he had another twenty years or so in the Navy before retiring from the service. According to his cousin, Pamela Mountbatten, the couple had planned their life based on the expectation that Elizabeth would not accede to the throne until they were in their fifties.[11] Just over four years after their wedding day was simply too soon for Philip to give up on all his naval ambitions. Now he was his wife's subject, obliged forever to walk two paces behind her in public.

She may have been the one to wear the crown, but she was not head of the household. That was Philip's dominion. While it had been that way from the beginning of their marriage, it became even more pronounced when she became Sovereign. Not only was he in command of their domestic world, but as the children grew older he would be the first parent with whom they would discuss personal matters. 'He was the boss man,' a former close aide told me. 'She left all the decisions about family and home to him. Anything royal, symbolized by the red boxes, was her department and he kept out.'[12]

Before George VI's funeral on 15 February, it was the new Queen, not her consort, who had an awkward meeting with the black sheep of the family, the Duke of Windsor. Little effort had been made by the palace to inform the duke, who was in New York, of his brother's death and he only learned of his passing as a result of media enquiries. He sailed to England alone on the RMS *Queen Mary* as he realized that his wife would doubtless endure a chilly reception from those who now ruled his former kingdom. His main purpose was to ensure that the £10,000 a year income (around £300,000 in 2021) he had been receiving from his brother would continue. A week after the funeral, still waiting to hear the verdict on his royal monies, he wrote to Wallis: 'It's hell to be even this much dependent on these ice-veined bitches.'[13]

Ultimately, though, he would be grievously disappointed. In one of her first acts as Monarch, his niece would cut his allowance completely, dealing a bitter blow to the duke, who had expected a little leniency from her. Not that he would be forced to live in penury, having made over a million pounds for his memoir *A King's Story*, which was published in 1951.

To no one's surprise, George VI's death did not end the duke's exile nor the family feud, which would continue almost until the day he died. However, on a bitterly cold winter's day, the former king did accompany the funeral cortège to Westminster Abbey and was carefully attentive as Dr Geoffrey Fisher, the Archbishop of Canterbury, described his brother as having 'made two perfect marriages – one to the Queen and the other to his people'.[14] One mourner remarked how the funeral was 'a great tribute to him and it's a great tribute to us. Because George VI *is* us. He is us and we are him. He is the British people, all that is best in us, and we all know it'.[15]

With silenced dockyard crane jibs dipped, flags at half-mast, transport at a standstill and sporting fixtures suspended, there was no doubt as to the extent of national mourning. At the head of his coffin, his eldest daughter left a wreath of white flowers. Its intimate and loving inscription read simply: 'To Papa, from Lilibet.' Her sister's words were similarly modest: 'Darling Papa, from his ever-loving Margaret'.[16]

From then on, whenever she was in doubt the new Queen would refer to how her father had done things. If it was good enough for him then it was good enough for her. She sensed his presence as she pondered the many difficult decisions she faced as Sovereign. In any case, change was not part of her emotional lexicon. Her motto then and for some time to come was: 'Safety first.'

One of the first decisions she made was to appoint her dour, traditional but loyal maid Bobo MacDonald as her official dresser.

As the iconography of royal fashion and styling essentially defines a reign, it was arguably a more important appointment than that of a private secretary. It certainly described her in the public imagination: a tight helmet hairdo, intimidating handbag, twin set, pearls and white gloves. It was only after the retirement of Bobo and the arrival of Angela Kelly in 1994 that the Queen's clothes became more sophisticated and imaginative.

Even though everyone still carried identity cards and, more than six years after the war's end, sweets and eggs remained rationed, change was in the air with excited chatter about a 'New Elizabethan Age'. The nation was in vigorous dialogue with itself about its past and the future. It was more than just a nostalgic look back to the glory days of Elizabeth I and the Tudor dynasty, but an embrace of the new, the playful and vibrant, as symbolized by the Festival of Britain which, though originally opened in May 1951, had caught the appetite for change and challenge.

The left-leaning *New Statesman* magazine hoped that the young Monarch, described as 'capable, energetic and sensibly progressive' would 'seize the opportunity to sweep away the old order at Court and substitute a way of life that matches the times they live in'.[17] As Buckingham Palace was still a place where footmen and other servants wore powdered wigs, and it took fifteen minutes for a pot of tea to arrive from the kitchens to the royal apartments, it was asking a lot.

While Britain was a nation on the cusp of profound social change, it was also a country at war yet again, this time in the Korean conflict of 1950–53. Early in her reign, Elizabeth invested fusilier Private Bill Speakman with the Victoria Cross, the highest military award for gallantry, for his part in saving his comrades' lives and dispatching the enemy during an audacious attack against Chinese fighters in Korea. It was a reminder that Britain had over 80,000 men fighting on the Korean Peninsula. Recalling his investiture at Buckingham Palace, Speakman remarked: 'It was a wonderful moment. I think she was nervous and I was very nervous!'[18]

She was learning on the job and having to make swift progress. Her courtiers were impressed by her dedication, attention to detail and her brisk no-nonsense approach. Practical rather than poetic, she read documents more quickly and thoroughly than her father had, and she retained information more accurately. She was balanced, detached and cool under pressure, her attitude reminiscent of the far-flung British colonial administrators who had held together the greatest empire the world had or has ever seen. Self-controlled, cautious and conscientious, she was keen to ensure that she got everything right.

In the early months, the chief problem she faced was that there weren't enough hours in the day to fulfil all her duties, and her schedule was so jam-packed that her role of mother was neglected. 'Why isn't Mummy going to play with us tonight?' Charles and Anne would protest.[19] One solution was to delay her Tuesday audience with the Prime Minister by an hour, so that she could spend time with and bathe the toddlers before leaving them in the care of their strict Scottish nanny, Helen Lightbody, who became known as 'No-Nonsense Lightbody' because of her stern ways.

The Queen soon learned that hers was a very solitary position, continuously in demand but always alone. Her corgis were her faithful companions and could be employed as a useful diversion if conversations became too difficult. She needed Dookie and company for her initial meeting with Churchill, three times her age and an esteemed war leader. Would he take her seriously? Little did either realize during their first tentative official rendezvous that they would become good friends and confidants.

With hindsight, Churchill was the perfect first prime minister for Elizabeth, as his shrewdness, experience and understanding of the role of the Sovereign in relation to government proved invaluable. As a dedicated monarchist, he became her willing and enthusiastic mentor. His wife Clementine once described him as 'the last believer in the divine right of kings'.[20]

When a former courtier, Sir Richard Molyneux, asked Elizabeth whether her relationship with the Prime Minister could be compared to that of the 'over-indulgent' Lord Melbourne and Queen Victoria, she replied: 'On the contrary, I sometimes find him very obstinate.'[21] Churchill was the authoritative yet devoted father figure that the young Queen needed. The watery gleam in his eye suggested that he might even have been somewhat infatuated with her. His joint principal private secretary Jock Colville described him as being 'madly in love' with the Queen, the Prime Minister stretching out his weekly audiences from the regulation thirty minutes to an hour and a half.[22]. He found her cautious, astute and, in the best sense of the word, conservative. While courtiers could not hear what was said, Tommy Lascelles noted in his diary that their conversations were often 'punctuated by peals of laughter, and Winston generally came out wiping his eyes. "She's *en grande beauty ce soir*," he said one evening in his schoolboy French.'[23] The much younger woman, unschooled in government, would accept his advice, while he came to respect her judgement.

Elizabeth's first crisis was not long in presenting itself. As was to be the case throughout her reign, it concerned her family: on this occasion, the family name was the source of the problem. Two days after her father's funeral, the editor of *Debrett's* – the bible of the aristocracy – had written that because Philip had taken the name Mountbatten as his surname, the royal house was now the House of Mountbatten rather than the House of Windsor. Churchill and his ministers made it clear that this 'appalling fact' had to be amended.[24] But it was not so simple. The issue went to the heart of the relationship between Elizabeth and Philip.

As the wife of Philip Mountbatten, it was tradition that she indeed took his name. What was more, he expected it. However, as with so many aspects of the institution, Britain's monarchy is literally a law unto itself. Members of the Royal Family can be known both by the name of the royal house or a surname, which is not always the same. Until 1917, the British Royal Family did not have an official surname and could only use the name of the house or dynasty to which they belonged. Hence Henry VIII or Henry Tudor, he of six wives' fame.

This all changed during the First World War. With anti-German feeling at its height, King George V changed the name of the dynasty from Saxe-Coburg-Gotha, which was Germanic in origin, to Windsor in order to appear more British. At a meeting of the Privy Council on 17 July 1917, George V declared that all male descendants of Queen Victoria would bear the name of Windsor. Therefore, because the new Queen came from the female line, it was argued by Lord Mountbatten and Prince Philip that the family name should reflect his surname as well.

The matter came to a head at a dinner party held at Broadlands, during which Lord Mountbatten had reportedly boasted that since George VI's death the 'House of Mountbatten now reigned'. When this piece of gossip was passed on to Queen Mary, she was horrified. The steely-eyed matriarch contacted Churchill and convinced him – not that he needed much convincing – of the necessity of continuing the House of Windsor. She insisted that the Prime Minister should formally ask the Queen to confirm the continuation of the House of Windsor now and in the future. This also applied to the royal offspring.

In spite of her husband's furious protests, the Monarch took the government's formal advice, as she was obliged to do, and, at a meeting of the Privy Council at Clarence House on 9 April 1952, signed an Order in Council confirming the ascendancy of the House of Windsor.

At a time when she needed Prince Philip's support, she found herself living with a morose, resentful man who had exclaimed that he was nothing more than 'an amoeba – a bloody amoeba' as he was the only husband in the land not able to confer his surname upon his children.[25] For such an alpha male it was a bitter pill to swallow. Even after the announcement he continued a rearguard action, and sent a memo to Churchill arguing that the royal house be called 'Edinburgh-Mountbatten'. Queen Mary's view was typically robust. 'What the devil does that damned fool Edinburgh think that the family name has got to do with him?'[26] That 'damned fool Edinburgh', though, would not let the matter drop.

Precedent was on his side as Queen Victoria had taken Prince Albert's surname when they married. His opponent, the Prime Minister, also relied on British history. He and Queen Mary argued that the name 'Windsor' had been created by George V in 1917 not only to disassociate the monarchy from its German origins at a time of conflict, but also to convey native grit and stoicism in the face of a redoubtable enemy.

The Queen, as Sovereign and wife, was put in a difficult position, with her implacable grandmother, mother and Churchill on one side ranged against her husband and his uncle on the other. This rancorous family debate was, as politician Rab Butler recalled, the only time he had seen the Queen close to tears. In the end, much as Philip and Lord Mountbatten might seethe, Churchill and all the queens would prevail.

Churchill had already bested Philip on one contentious issue and it was not long before he was to usurp his domestic authority again. This time, the argument concerned where the Royal Family should live. Clarence House had been their home since July 1949, a place where they had invested time and energy making it their own. They had chosen the soft furnishings, mixed the paint colours and picked the curtains. Philip's interest in technology ensured that their residence had boasted the latest labour-saving devices, including a wardrobe that could eject the required shirt or jacket at the touch of a button. For a young man who had led a rootless existence, the chance to build a home for his wife and family had been naturally appealing.

During lunch one day, it was suggested that they stay at Clarence House and use Buckingham Palace as an office. The idea made practical sense, especially as Queen Elizabeth the Queen Mother and Princess Margaret were still living at Buckingham Palace and the former, at least, was showing no inclination to move out. She had been mistress of the grand property since 1936 and clearly wished to stay on for as long as possible.

Discussions about a move from Buckingham Palace were awkward and emotional. On at least one occasion the Queen Mother uncharacteristically burst into tears. Elizabeth was highly sensitive to her mother's profound personal loss, as well as to her sudden demotion in the Court hierarchy. For the first few months of her reign, Her Majesty had selflessly taken the junior role, even though their regal positions were now reversed. At Sunday church services, for instance, the Sovereign encouraged her to sit in the Monarch's seat. A courtier recalled that there was an 'awkwardness about precedence' in terms of 'the Queen not wanting to go in front of her mother and the Queen Mother [being] used to going first'.[27] Elizabeth knew that her widowed mother was keen to remain at Buckingham Palace and, for the sake of family happiness and unity, the young woman went along with the proposal. However, Churchill and the Queen's crusty but knowledgeable private secretary Tommy Lascelles would have none of it: 'The flagpole [at Buckingham Palace] flies the Queen's Standard and that's where she must be,' Churchill decreed.[28]

Philip reacted badly. He remained in his room, depressed and gloomy, dreading the move from Clarence House.[29] It was easier for Elizabeth to accept Churchill's edict as she was simply moving back to her former home, albeit in the grander surroundings of the Belgian Suite. The prince, on the other hand, would be moving from the only home he had ever known, as well as giving up the last remaining realm in his life over which he still had control. 'It was bloody difficult for him. In the Navy, he was in command of his own ship – literally,' Mike Parker explained. 'At Clarence House, it was very much his show. When we got to Buckingham Palace, all that changed.'[30]

The move, in May 1952, while the surname battle was at its height, was as bad as Philip predicted. Being under the constant scrutiny of a swathe of courtiers, he recollected that there were 'plenty of people telling me what *not* to do: "You mustn't interfere with this;" "Keep out."'[31] In a reference to his previous role as a ship's captain, he recalled wistfully: 'People used to come to me and ask me what to do.'[32] Now he was ignored.

Churchill had fallen out with Lord Mountbatten over his unnecessarily hasty handling of Indian independence, which Churchill called a 'shameful flight' and a 'premature hurried scuttle'.[33] The premature partition resulted in a genocidal bloodbath when Pakistan and India came into being with new borders. The Prime Minister seemed to take out his antagonism towards Mountbatten by blocking the viscount's nephew's every suggestion. He once told an aide that, while he wished Philip no ill, he neither liked nor trusted him and hoped he would not do harm to the country.

As the prince's cousin Pamela Mountbatten recalled: 'Prince Philip was completely excluded and unwelcome at Buckingham Palace. Everybody closed ranks. Churchill made him feel totally apart from the whole thing.' Although the Duke of Edinburgh had never expected to be King, he had certainly not anticipated being so brutally and cruelly sidelined.[34] In a matter of months, Philip had lost his career, his name, his paternal naming rights, his home and his authority as a husband. As a pitiful consolation, he bought himself an electric frying pan so that he could fry his eggs and bacon in the morning without waiting for his breakfast to be brought up from the kitchens.

The Queen, who as Lascelles had noted was unusually sensitive to others, could see that her husband was struggling. She had married a dynamic, ambitious naval officer, not a man who felt sorry for himself. It was clear that he needed to stop brooding and be put to work on a project.

Initially, she asked him to oversee the construction and design development of the new royal yacht, which was being built in Scotland at the John Brown & Co. shipyard in Clydebank. It was the perfect job for the former commander with an interest in design and an eye for detail. He liaised with Sir Hugh Casson, who had been commissioned to lay out the interiors of the royal apartments on board the 412-foot yacht, which the Queen would later name *Britannia* at its launch on 16 April 1953.

While Philip's work on the royal yacht channelled his love of architecture and technology, the Queen's request that he chair the committee responsible for organizing the Coronation, which was due to take place on 2 June 1953, four days before the famed Derby horse race at Epsom, plunged him once more into conflict with the Establishment. This time it included his wife. The Queen was completely opposed to the Coronation being televised. The prince thought otherwise. Her point of view was supported by the Queen Mother, Churchill, Lascelles and the Archbishop of Canterbury. But Philip, as a man of science and innovation – in 1953 he became the first royal to fly in a helicopter – supported the opening up of this most significant royal ceremony to the common man using the new technology of the day.

His wife's objections were both practical and personal. She recognized that the Coronation was a profound and sacred moment in history, when an ordinary mortal is transformed into a potent symbol in accordance with a centuries-old tradition. But she was also concerned that television coverage would mean that if anything went wrong millions would witness her blushing embarrassment.

She vividly remembered her father's memories of his own Coronation in 1937, which had been beset by numerous mishaps: a priest fainted and in so doing held up the procession; the oversized Bible proved too heavy to carry and had to be replaced; a bishop accidentally covered the words of the oath when the nervous King was about to read it; another bishop stood on George VI's robe as he tried to stand; and, lastly, the crown appeared to have been handed to the Archbishop of Canterbury the wrong way round, which created a tense moment of hesitation before its placement on the Monarch's head. His experience made for an amusing story – albeit after the event. It had seemed funny until she had to accept her own dread destiny.

Philip, a man of progressive temperament, was convinced that opening the Coronation to the people via the medium of television was the simplest and surest way of maintaining the monarchy. He turned the argument of Victorian constitutionalist Walter Bagehot on its head, as he argued that 'daylight should be let in on magic'. In spite of his sound reasoning, though, the old guard won out. On 20 October 1952, it was formally announced that the Coronation would be broadcast live on radio alone. The mass media and politicians immediately attacked the decision, blaming the men in grey rather than the Queen. 'Truly astonishing,' declared the *Daily Express*. 'The people will be denied the climax of a wonderful and magnificent occasion in British history.'[35] In the face of overwhelming criticism, however, intense discussions took place in government resulting in a change of heart that same month. On 8 December, the U-turn was officially confirmed when it was declared that the ceremony would now be televised.

The new Queen was praised for her somewhat falsely perceived role as the 'people's queen', as the public was under the impression that she had stood firm against the *ancien régime* that had sought to exclude her subjects from her big day. It was an early example of collective projection. Her Majesty was cautious rather than progressive, cleaving to the past and precedent, just like her father. It was her husband who was the agent for change in their partnership. It would not be a complete victory for people power, though, as Elizabeth insisted that there should be no close-ups of her face and that the sacred act of communion and anointing would not be filmed by the cameras.

Not long after the television debate had finally been resolved, in December Margaret arranged a private meeting with her sister in the Belgian Suite. Another crisis was in the making. After dropping an abbreviated curtsy, she joined her sister over tea and explained her deep feelings for Peter Townsend – the King's former equerry who had since been made comptroller of the Queen Mother's Household – who was almost sixteen years her senior, a father of two young boys and about to be divorced. Though his age and existing family may have been frowned upon, it was the delicate issue of divorce that presented the greatest obstacle. After all, just sixteen years previously their Uncle David, Edward VIII, had abdicated the throne so that he could marry the twice-divorced American Wallis Simpson. The unprecedented situation had rocked the monarchy and changed the trajectory of both their lives. Under the Royal Marriages Act of 1772, twenty-two-year-old Margaret, being third in line to the throne behind Charles and Anne, had to obtain the Sovereign's permission before she could marry. Upon reaching the age of twenty-five she could wed whomsoever she wished – though still dependent upon the verdict of the Privy Council. Marriage to a divorcee, as Margaret knew full well, was a serious no-no in the eyes of both the Church and the State.

The Queen, who is a great noticer of social nuance, was seemingly unsurprised by her sister's admission. Perhaps Margaret and her war hero lover had not been as careful as they thought. Elizabeth's response was muted and sympathetic, but ultimately non-committal. She was acting both as her sister, who naturally wanted Margaret to be happy, but also as her Queen, who had obligations to the institution of monarchy. Having been placed in an extremely difficult position by Margaret, she would have no choice but to accept the formal advice of her government.

Some days later, she invited Margaret and her lover to dine with her and Prince Philip at Buckingham Palace to discuss the matter in a less formal setting. Philip seemed to find what Townsend described as a 'poignant situation' most amusing, cracking jokes and making merry throughout supper. While the irony of the late King's daughter falling in love with a divorcee only a matter of years after the abdication was lost on no one, the loving couple felt that, given the Queen's benign reaction, there was hope that they could one day fulfil their dream and get married. After all, they had secretly played out their romance for more than five years, ever since the tour of South Africa in 1947.

Over time, what had begun as indulgent friendship gradually blossomed into a full-blown love affair. People had noticed. During a week-long visit to Balmoral in August 1950, young socialite Lady Jane Vane-Tempest-Stewart observed their social interplay and concluded they were in love. On her return to London, she told her mother of her suspicions only to receive short shrift: 'Don't be so romantic and ridiculous. He's the King's servant. She can't be in love with the King's servant, that would be utterly wrong.'[36] Back then, of course, not only was he a servant, but he was also still married – though in name only.

The death of George VI in February 1952 had brought the couple closer, Townsend's sympathetic presence helping to fill the void left in Princess Margaret's life. But whatever hopes they had harboured about eventually being accepted as a married couple were brutally dashed by Tommy Lascelles during a bruising encounter in his office late in 1952. He bluntly told Townsend that he was either 'mad or bad' for even contemplating such a match.[37]

As confusing as this was for the romantic protagonists, the back and forth continued during the Christmas break at Sandringham in Norfolk, where Lascelles had further discussions with the Queen, her sister and Prince Philip about the Townsend affair. They came to no definitive conclusions, although the Queen did ask Margaret to wait until after the Coronation in June before taking any further steps. Her policy of 'delay, delay, delay' was to become a mantra during her reign, a mindset that was epitomized by her habit of taking her dogs for a long walk rather than face an awkward encounter.

Everyone agreed, however, that the Coronation must come first. It was an all-consuming event. In the months leading up to it, arguably the most important day in the reign of the Sovereign, the Queen was concerned to ensure that the televised ceremony went with 'balletic' precision. No fainting clergymen wanted here.

In the White Drawing Room at Buckingham Palace, she rehearsed her lines endlessly. She would practise walking down a makeshift aisle, sometimes with several sheets tied to her shoulder to act as robes. She spent time listening to recordings of the 1937 Coronation and also put the St Edward's Crown on when doing her daily tasks, just to get used to the feel of bearing a 5-pound weight.[38] Other times she walked, unembarrassed, with a bag of flour on her head as a substitute crown. The young Queen even had a private word with Michael Ramsey, the Bishop of Durham, and begged him not to wiggle his eyebrows during the ceremony because, if he did, she could well succumb to a fit of giggles.

With the pitfalls of her father's Coronation in mind, no detail was too small to escape her notice. She had a shortened length of pile made for the carpet in Westminster Abbey to ensure that her heels and train would not get stuck, she arranged for two silver stars to be secured on the crown so that the Archbishop of Canterbury could tell the front from the back, and had armrests installed in the Gold State Coach so that she could appear to be freely holding the weighty orb and sceptre for the 5-mile procession around London. She carefully scrutinized the guest list, chose the flowers, floral hangings and colour scheme for the Abbey, examined numerous Coronation stamp designs and, though not a vain woman, studied dozens of photographs of herself to judge the best type of make-up and lipstick colour for her television appearance.

Even her husband was brought to heel. At a rehearsal at the Abbey, Prince Philip made a hash of swearing the oath of allegiance to the new Queen. He knelt, mumbled his words, gave an air kiss and backed off rapidly. 'Come back, Philip, and do it properly,' she said patiently.[39] Although the preparations seemingly had every contingency covered, her dressmaker Norman Hartnell had sewed a little, sequinned four-leaf clover in her gown just for luck.

On 24 March 1953, preparations paused for a time following the death of the Queen's grandmother, Queen Mary. She was eighty-five and as dutiful in death as she was in life. At the end she had insisted that the forthcoming Coronation celebrations should not be halted or delayed due to Court mourning. Queen Mary may not have been the most outwardly affectionate grandmother, but she had showed her love and devotion in more practical ways. She taught Elizabeth the secret of good posture, and how high heels and large hats help royal women to assert themselves. She also advised her that the best way of dealing with overly intimate questions or inappropriate remarks was to keep smiling at the presumptuous individual as if hearing nothing and then gracefully move on.

By contrast Princess Margaret, like the Duke of Windsor, shed few tears for the chilly matriarch. She never forgave her grandmother for the constant criticism of her short, rather plump, figure, especially when she was an adolescent, as well as the disapproval of the princess's love of singing, dancing and lively company.

On Coronation Day, however, Queen Mary would have very much approved of the patriotic sing-songs that erupted spontaneously among the milling crowds around Buckingham Palace as they waited expectantly in the chill and rain for a glimpse of their Sovereign. The universal feeling was that her reign would usher in a new Elizabethan era of dynamism, abundance and hope. 'All this – and Everest too!' announced the *Daily Express* front page on 2 June 1953, after news that Edmund Hillary and Sherpa Tenzing, part of a British expedition, had scaled the world's highest mountain at the end of May, just in time for the big day.[40] There was clearly something in the air. At a luncheon with Commonwealth leaders on the eve of the Coronation, the Queen appeared exultant and triumphant. She later confided to a friend: 'Extraordinary thing, I no longer feel anxious or worried. I don't know what it is – but I have lost all my timidity.'[41]

On the day itself, her high spirits were much in evidence. When a lady-in-waiting asked her if she was feeling nervous, she is said to have replied, straight-faced, 'Of course I am, but I really do think Aureole will win' – a tongue-in-cheek reference to her horse, which was due to run in the Epsom Derby the following Saturday.[42]

The Queen was serenely composed as she and Prince Philip rolled along in the opulent but uncomfortable Gold State Coach for the brief journey – which she later recalled as 'horrible' due to the carriage's lack of suspension combined with the weight of her heavy crown – to Westminster Abbey. Before she made her grand entrance, the Queen, with a beaming smile on her face, looked at her maids of honour and said, 'Ready, girls?'[43] With that, she moved forward, never looking back, primed for a ceremony of consecration and coronation that would last for nearly three hours.

It was the thirty-eighth Coronation for reigning monarchs to be held at Westminster Abbey, and while the arcane ritual still conveyed an aura of magic and authority, the Queen's youth and femininity suggested the promise of new beginnings, as well as a requiem for the old aristocratic order. 'She was consecrated, and that makes her Queen. It is the most solemn thing that has ever happened in her life,' Canon John Andrew later observed. 'She cannot abdicate. She is there until death.'[44] His thinking was based on the solemn oath she had taken before the nation and also before God. It was a nun-like vow of service.

The Royal Family's favourite journalist, Dermot Morrah, observed that 'the sense of spiritual exultation that radiated from her was tangible'.[45] As the St Edward's Crown came down upon her head – the right way round this time – the Queen felt the weight of monarchy being placed on her. But she held herself high and, ever since then, the crown has remained firmly in place.

The long coach procession back to Buckingham Palace in the Gold State Coach surrounded by exultant crowds was every bit as moving and profound as the intimate ceremony. 'The sound reached fever pitch, so loud it felt as if the whole nation was entering into one massive long cheer,' recalled one of the maids of honour, Anne Glenconner.[46]

Queen Elizabeth II returned to the palace, her eyes shining with relief and jubilation. The wife of a palace courtier recalled the 'extraordinary impact' which the crowded streets and cheering people had had on her: 'She [the Queen] said that she had never guessed it would be like that, the feeling of elation and joy, of being carried forward on a great wave.'[47]

Huge numbers of people had watched the ceremony in black and white as they crouched around television screens. More than 27 million people across the UK, twice the BBC estimate, had tuned in, endorsing Prince Philip's democratic instincts.

Once back in the Green Room at Buckingham Palace, the Queen and her maids of honour fell on to the sofa with a sigh of glee and relief before trooping off for some Coronation Chicken – cold, cooked chicken in a creamy curry-flavoured sauce, a dish invented specially for the occasion. As they reviewed the day, they acknowledged a few minor hiccups. Elizabeth forgot to curtsy at the North Pillar of the Abbey, preventing the rest of her maids from doing the same. When she went to sign the text of the Oath, she found there was no ink. 'Pretend you're signing,' the Lord Chamberlain whispered in her ear. Even though the Queen had ordered a gold rug with a shallow pile, it was laid the wrong way which caused her mantle to get stuck. Fortunately, the Archbishop of Canterbury was alert to the situation when the Queen hissed: 'Get me started.'[48]

Her husband, after his halting performance during rehearsal, was faultless, kneeling before her and pledging to be her 'leige man of life and limb'.[49] He kissed her cheek so firmly that she had to steady the crown. Back at the palace he was at his most officious, bossing everyone around for the photographs. Eventually, an exasperated Cecil Beaton put down his camera and said: 'Sir, if you would like to take the photographs, please do.'[50] The Queen and Queen Mother looked on, horrified, and the duke, realizing he had gone too far, retreated.

As the camera clicked and everyone chatted excitedly about

the events of the day, Prince Charles, then four, saw his mother's crown and made a beeline for it. The little boy got as far as picking it up, but an alert lady-in-waiting managed to grab it before any harm came to either the prince or the royal headgear.

His time would come. One day.

CHAPTER SIX

HEARTS AND CORONETS

EVERY NEW GENERATION of the House of Windsor walks with a shadow. The good royal versus the naughty royal. The royal rebel and the sensible prince. Or princess. Harry the wild child, William the straight shooter. Diana the demure, Fergie the roustabout. Nonconformist Meghan, level-headed Catherine. Once that narrative is shaped, it becomes accepted wisdom. Yet this endless exercise in perceived character contrasts merely disguises as much as it reveals.

In her day, Princess Elizabeth was a competent singer and actress who enjoyed concerts and dancing. In social situations she was able to winkle out the amusing and unusual, or weave a funny story around a royal encounter. On one occasion, she kept a member of the Privy Council in fits of laughter as she performed the contortions of a wrestler she had watched during a televised bout. Yet these qualities were often overlooked because her younger sister was more overtly theatrical, eagerly joining Hollywood stars in singing around the piano late into the night, the blue-grey plume from her cigarette holder giving her sitting room the feeling and odour of a downtown nightclub.

Margaret was 'a girl of unusual intense beauty' who was

'capable of an astonishing power of expression' as observed by her lover Peter Townsend, who described the royal comedienne as both 'coquettish' and 'sophisticated'.[1] It was a description that, by and large, stuck – even though in pictures of the sisters, Elizabeth was taller and slimmer with more open, welcoming features. Her younger sister often seemed as if she were only present at public occasions by force. She was the royal bachelor girl who was catnip for the gossip columnists, linked to thirty-one different suitors by the time she was twenty-one. Her public image was that of the excitable young girl out for a good time in the nightclubs of Mayfair in central London, surrounded by a coterie of the frivolous sons and daughters of the aristocracy.

Though very different from her sister, Margaret was also similar in so many ways. Romantically, they both fell for the first man they met and ignored the wishes of their parents, particularly their mother, to find happiness with a duke or an earl. Elizabeth was just thirteen when she first met Prince Philip, and Margaret was only sixteen when she realized that she had fallen for Group Captain Townsend.

Her parents had no inkling of the secrets hidden deep in Margaret's heart. They made sure she mixed with the 'right sort' of men who would not be overawed by her class or position. Even Tommy Lascelles joined in the romantic guessing game. After watching Johnny Dalkeith, later the 9th Duke of Buccleuch, making 'cow eyes' at the princess as she celebrated her twenty-first birthday at Balmoral in 1951, he gave him the thumbs-up, telling Townsend that the young aristocrat was the chosen one. Townsend smiled inwardly, knowing where Margaret's true feelings lay.

These emotions were expressed perhaps unconsciously as Group Captain Townsend stood outside Westminster Abbey at the end of the Coronation ceremony. Margaret, looking sparkling, ravishing and pink-cheeked from the excitement of the day, came up to him and casually smoothed his lapel, brushing a little fluff from his immaculately pressed sky-blue RAF uniform. It was a moment of tenderness and routine familiarity caught by the cameras. The following day, this affectionate gesture received the same front-page coverage in several New York and continental newspapers as the Coronation itself.

Although the British media focused on the unique and profound ceremony, in the offices of national newspapers the wheels had been set in motion regarding other royal matters. Just as the palace feared, the story was about to become public. The Queen agreed for Lascelles to travel to Chartwell, Churchill's country home, to alert the Prime Minister. Once briefed, Churchill's initial reaction was, according to his joint principal private secretary Jock Colville, typically romantic. 'What a delightful match! A lovely young lady married to a gallant young airman, safe from the perils and horrors of war!' His redoubtable wife Clementine immediately put her foot down: 'Winston, if you are going to begin the Abdication all over again, I'm going to leave! I shall take a flat and go and live in Brighton.'[2] An ironic remark, given that their own son Randolph was divorced and remarried, and three members of Churchill's Cabinet had also been divorced.

Clemmie was perhaps overstating the situation – Margaret was third in line to the throne with no realistic chance of ever becoming queen, and Townsend, though divorced, was a bona fide war hero who was liked and admired by his adopted family. Once the romance became public, he rapidly assumed the status of a folk hero. The Crown was not in existential peril as it had been during the abdication of Edward VIII, but the conflict between the couple and the Church of England, which would not countenance divorce or allow divorced couples to marry in church, remained.

Two weeks after the Coronation, *The People* newspaper backed into the story with the headline: 'They Must Deny It Now.' They pointed to the 'scandalous' and 'utterly untrue' rumours of the love affair between the princess and a divorcee named Group Captain Peter Townsend. The newspaper editorialized that it was 'quite unthinkable' for a royal princess to even 'contemplate a marriage with a man who has been through the divorce courts'.[3] When she heard the news, the Duchess of Windsor, who blamed the Queen Mother for exiling her and the duke from Britain, could barely contain her delight. She telephoned one of her friends in Paris and gloated: 'So now it's happened to her own daughter.'

For the most part, the man in the street wished them well. They were an attractive couple; she a beautiful princess, he a gallant fighter pilot who had helped to save Britain in its darkest hour. A poll in the *Daily Mirror* attracted more than 70,000 responses on the subject of whether they should be allowed to marry. Almost 97 per cent were in support of the union.[4] Though Churchill's first instincts reflected popular opinion, that viewpoint was no match for precedent, the law, the Church and Tommy Lascelles. The latter had already advised the Queen that Townsend should leave and take an appointment abroad, preferably in a distant location, in order to dilute and contain the scandal. But it was not advice that she was at all keen to hear.

She was having to cast judgement on her shadow self, a sister who, for all her faults and foibles, she loved and supported in the same way that Margaret had come to her aid when doubting Thomases at the palace had wrinkled their noses at the arrival of Prince Philip. The sisterly bond remained strong. During Ascot week in June, they were seen cheerfully racing one another on horseback along the Royal Mile, riding neck and neck, and both laughing as Margaret rode out the winner.

They were both aware that whatever their personal feelings, the monarchy was bigger than either of them and the Queen must be guided by her ministers. It was her 'get out of jail free' card that spared her from a jolting and potentially acrimonious confrontation with Margaret. Though the princess would later complain, somewhat disingenuously, that she was unaware of the consequences should she marry Townsend, it seems that Lascelles had, with the Queen's agreement, been punctilious in fully briefing her about her options. Indeed, she even sent him a note of thanks after he explained that, under the Royal Marriages Act of 1772, if she wished to marry without the Queen's permission she would have to wait until she was twenty-five, and even then obtain dispensation from both the House of Commons and the House of Lords. He further pointed out that she would lose her position in the line of succession and of course be obliged to marry in a civil ceremony. In the worst-case scenario, she would also have to relinquish her title, her Civil List payment and possibly live abroad as plain Mrs Townsend. As her friend and biographer Christopher Warwick observed: 'We now know that far from keeping her in the dark, Lascelles clearly outlined the obstacles to her.'[5]

On 16 June 1953, at his weekly audience with the Queen, Churchill advised her that, for the well-being of the nation and the Crown, Group Captain Townsend should be posted overseas without delay. The royal lovers should not be permitted to see one another for at least a year. It was one of the most difficult decisions she had had to make, weighing the happiness of her sister against the prerogatives of the Crown.

As the wheels were set in motion, the Queen asked for one concession, that Townsend could remain in Britain until the Queen Mother and Princess Margaret had returned from a visit to Southern Rhodesia (modern-day Zimbabwe) in July. With that agreement in place, Lascelles summoned Townsend and abruptly informed him that he would be leaving the country for a period of two years and that he had the choice of postings in either Brussels, Johannesburg or Singapore. Townsend was utterly stunned by the turn of events. One moment he was enjoying dinner with the Queen and the Duke of Edinburgh, the next he was facing exile. After regaining his composure, he opted for the post of air attaché in Brussels, which would at least keep him near to his two boys who were at a boarding school in Kent.

After Princess Margaret and her mother left for Africa on 30 June, the Queen asked Townsend to accompany the royal party on a three-day visit to Belfast in Northern Ireland early in July. Townsend saw it as her way of ensuring that he was still seen as part of the wider Royal Family. Unfortunately, the Queen's press secretary Commander Richard Colville (a cousin of Jock Colville) announced Townsend's imminent move to Brussels during the trip, which resulted in him unwittingly receiving more media attention than the Queen.

Upon their return to London, the Queen deliberately sought out Townsend after she had alighted from the plane. She wished him good luck and shook his hand – a move that was seen by many as a gesture of friendship and goodwill. However, Colville's premature pronouncement would lead to Townsend's departure from Britain being accelerated, the newly appointed attaché sent to Brussels before Margaret's return from Africa. When she heard the news, Margaret broke down and wept, and Townsend needed all his soothing influence over a scratchy telephone line to calm her down. Not surprisingly, she completed the rest of the tour in low spirits. Ultimately, the couple would not see each other again until the following year.

In the meantime, the Queen had to endure a sorrowful parting of her own. She and Prince Philip spent the summer at Balmoral on holiday with their two children before undertaking the much-delayed visit to Australia, New Zealand and various Commonwealth nations. It was not the happiest of holidays in Scotland. The weather was miserable, Charles was confined to bed with an ear infection and his sister had come down with a fever. Princess Margaret, glum and missing her lover, was moody and overcast. Understandably, the Queen, who was out of sorts at the prospect of not seeing Charles and Anne for half a year, was not as sympathetic to her sister as she might have been.

In the royal couple's absence, the Queen Mother and Margaret would be supervising their children's education. Charles would later trace his parents' route on their tour of the Commonwealth with the aid of a globe in the palace classroom. It offered scant consolation when the prince celebrated his fifth birthday and Christmas with the Queen and Prince Philip on the other side of the world. For the most part communication was by letter, as the time difference and technical difficulties made phone conversations something of an ordeal.

The six-month tour, which began in November 1953, was truly a marathon but brought great happiness to thousands. In Australia, such was the wild delirium that more than three-quarters of the population turned out on the streets for a glimpse of the Queen and her consort as they passed by. During the tour, the royal couple travelled 43,000 miles, Her Majesty gave 102 speeches and was personally introduced to more than 13,000 people. Constantly on parade, they developed into a smooth double act, with Philip making the jokes and the Sovereign accepting the flowers – and the plaudits. This façade was punctured only once on the lengthy visit, when an Australian camera crew captured a royally undignified scene on film. The unexpected insight into their marriage occurred on the shores of the O'Shannassy Reservoir in Victoria, where they were staying in a luxury chalet during a rare weekend off duty.

They had agreed to a brief filming session for an official documentary about the tour entitled *The Queen in Australia*. Outside their chalet, cameraman Loch Townsend and his deputy waited patiently for Elizabeth and Philip to emerge, so that they could be filmed admiring kangaroos and other indigenous wildlife. Suddenly, the chalet door flew open and out came a distinctively ruffled prince followed by an irate Queen, who threw a pair of tennis shoes and a tennis racquet at the rapidly disappearing figure.[6] She shouted at her husband to come back, then dragged him into the chalet and slammed the door. All this was captured on film.

As Townsend and his crew debated their next move, they were confronted by the Queen's press secretary, Commander Colville, who firmly requested that they hand the film over. They duly obeyed his command. Shortly afterwards the Monarch, now smiling calmly, emerged from the chalet and apologized for the domestic altercation. 'I'm sorry for that little interlude but, as you know, it happens in every marriage. Now, what would you like me to do?'[7] Then she posed for the camera. While we shall never know the background to the row, the incident indicated that beneath the composed, controlled image the couple enjoyed a rumbustious, sparky relationship – and that Philip did not entirely rule the roost.

Ironically, although the visit was a tremendous success, once again critics complained that the Queen didn't smile enough. The narrative of a distant Sovereign was beginning to take shape. She was ruled by her head, while her wilful younger sister was ruled by her heart. Or was she? As Margaret's twenty-fifth birthday approached in August 1955, the world wanted to know if she would give up her royal status for the love of a divorced war hero. It was a seductive story. When she celebrated her birthday at Balmoral Castle, the estate was surrounded by around 300 journalists and photographers, all waiting for some kind of signal from the beleaguered inhabitants. 'Please make up your mind!' urged the *Daily Mirror*.[8]

The princess, though, was not quite the romantic of popular imagination. Six days before her birthday, she had written to the new Prime Minister Anthony Eden, himself a divorcee, to inform him that she had no intention of seeing Townsend before October, when he had annual leave, and only then would she be in a position to make up her mind as to whether or not she wanted to marry him. She explained:

'But it is only by seeing him in this way that I feel I can properly decide whether I can marry him or not. At the end of October or early November I very much hope to be in a position to tell you and the other Commonwealth prime ministers what I intend to do. The Queen of course knows I am writing to you about this, but of course no one else does, and as everything is so uncertain I know you will regard it certainly as a confidence.'[9]

This letter, which lay undiscovered until 2009, recasts the orthodox view that Margaret sacrificed her romance on the altar of duty and monarchy. As her biographer Christopher Warwick argued: 'Here you've got a very determined and confident young woman in control of the situation, telling the Prime Minister that she has not decided and is wavering, which is at odds with what the public was led to believe and certainly with what she told me.'[10]

While the limitations of her royal position hemmed her in, it was the Church that had perhaps played the dominant role in her eventual decision. As a committed Christian, she found the idea of being prevented from marrying inside the Church of England deeply distressing. At the same time that she was ruminating upon her future, a rangy, blond farmer's son from North Carolina with a passion for hamburgers and the word of God came into her life. He made a deep and lasting impression, and not just on the conflicted princess but on the whole Royal Family.

The charismatic Christian crusader Billy Graham first visited London in March 1954. By the time of his departure in May, he had preached to more than 2 million Britons, his services producing the largest outdoor gatherings since the Coronation, including an audience of over 120,000 at Wembley Stadium. When he returned in May 1955, just three months before Margaret turned twenty-five, he and his wife Ruth were asked to join the Queen Mother and the princess for coffee at Clarence House. That successful first meeting resulted in an invitation to preach before the Queen at Windsor Castle. He accepted and busily prepared a punchy sermon from Acts 27:25: 'Wherefore, sirs, be of good cheer: for I believe God, that it shall be even as it was told me.'

After giving his sermon, he and his wife were invited for luncheon at Windsor. On entering the castle, Graham heartily shook the hand of the butler who was reaching to take his hat. It was a rather clumsy beginning to what would become a long-lasting friendship between the Queen, Princess Margaret, the Queen Mother and the American preacher.

Over the years he sent the Sovereign regular reports of his ministries, especially if he was preaching in a Commonwealth country. As his son Franklin Graham observed: 'There's no question, she's very devout in her faith and very strong in her faith. Her faith has been consistent not just with conversations with my father, but throughout her life.'[11]

Their relationship, which continued until Graham's death in 2018, was anchored not just in their shared religious beliefs, but because of their distinct yet similar stations in life. Both were eternally yoked to organizations that were demanding of their every breath: Graham with his allegiance to the word of God, the Queen to the monarchy. It was both a calling and a confinement, Graham describing the life led by himself and his wife as akin to being prisoners.

Marshall Frady's biography of Billy Graham revealed the occasion when Graham and the Queen were looking out of a window in one of her homes, perhaps Buckingham Palace, observing the huge crowd standing outside who were peering up at the royal edifice: 'I asked Queen Elizabeth if she ever felt sometimes she would like to be able to just go down and join them. She said, "With all my heart." I said to her, "That's just the way I feel."'[12] The little girl who looked out at the passing parade from her bedroom window at 145 Piccadilly had not changed much. Just as the world was curious about her life, she remained intent on knowing about theirs.

So the arrival of Billy Graham that fateful summer would remind both sisters of the role that faith played in resolving their conflict. Ultimately, though, it was Anthony Eden who teased a pathway through the secular and spiritual jungle on behalf of the princess. When he arrived at Balmoral in early October 1955 for the Prime Minister's customary autumn visit, he was able to inform the Queen and her sister that, after reviewing the situation, Margaret would only have to give up her right of succession (and that of any children she may have) but not her title or her Civil List monies, nor have to go into exile. In fact, should she decide to marry Townsend, he could be conferred with his own title and receive a Civil List allowance. Of course conflict with the Church of England would remain, but the State now stood aside from her decision.

This was all very different to the dire prognostications of Tommy Lascelles and Winston Churchill. There were potential pitfalls – but for the Queen and the monarchy. An unsigned Downing Street memorandum suggested that the Crown could sustain some damage if the match went ahead, as there would be objectors among the wider population which could have an effect on the institution, but it would not be ruinous. Eden encouraged Margaret to make up her mind sooner rather than later, in order to end the uncertainty for all concerned, namely herself, her sister and the monarchy. He made it clear in a letter to other Commonwealth leaders that the Queen did not wish to stand in the way of her sister's happiness.[13] With Townsend now on leave and preparing to see Margaret, the Queen gave her licence to meet him discreetly at Clarence House and at the homes of known friends.

From mid-October, the couple spent the next few days wining and dining with one another, wooing and testing the water. Townsend, though, seems to have been kept in the dark about Eden's revision of the penalties that they would face if they married. There is no indication in either his memoir, *Time and Chance,* nor in subsequent interviews that he had the faintest idea that Margaret would only have to surrender her position in the line of succession and marry in a civil ceremony. He laboured under the impression that she would have to give up everything – and Margaret did little, if anything, to correct that view during their time together. He was very much on the outside looking in.

Just as Eden had anticipated, with public hysteria building to a crescendo the Princess Meg question had to be resolved one way or another. As Townsend admitted in his memoir: 'Everyone was by now impatient, and critical of a situation which was fast becoming ridiculous.' The two people at the centre of this maelstrom were 'exhausted, mentally, emotionally and physically'.[14] Decisions had to be taken.

She spent the weekend of 22/23 October in an emotional reckoning with the Queen Mother, her sister and brother-in-law at Windsor Castle. Tensions were running high. Margaret had barely spoken to her mother, who was greatly distressed by the entire affair. At one point she had queried where Margaret and Peter would live should they marry. This earned the crushing reply from Prince Philip that it was still possible to buy houses.[15] The Queen Mother's response was to leave the room, slamming the door as she went.

The tension within the Royal Family mirrored the uproar without. After spending just a few days in Townsend's company, Margaret had come to the conclusion that she no longer felt as strongly about him as she had done before their long parting. Ultimately, the choice was hers. The Queen had put no pressure on her. If anything, Her Majesty had been prepared to accept criticism of the Crown for the sake of Margaret's happiness. Her sister, however, chose faith and family. Townsend himself, though not in possession of the full facts, independently reached the same decision.

After a restless night's sleep, he jotted down what would become the spine of her public statement. When she read his draft at Clarence House, she was in complete agreement. He recalled: 'For a few moments we looked at each other; there was a wonderful tenderness in her eyes which reflected, I suppose, the look in mine. We had reached the end of the road. Our feelings for one another were unchanged, but they had incurred for us a burden so great that we decided, together, to lay it down. As we did so, we both had a feeling of unimaginable relief. We were liberated at last from this monstrous problem.'[16]

After speaking with Dr Geoffrey Fisher, the Archbishop of Canterbury, Margaret released her statement on 31 October 1955: 'I would like it to be known that I have decided not to marry Group Captain Peter Townsend. I have been aware that, subject to my renouncing my rights of succession, it might have been possible for me to contract a civil marriage. But, mindful of the Church's teaching that Christian marriage is indissoluble, and conscious of my duty to the Commonwealth, I have resolved to put these considerations before any others. I have reached this decision entirely alone, and in doing so I have been strengthened by the unfailing support and devotion of Group Captain Townsend. I am deeply grateful for the concern of all those who have constantly prayed for my happiness.'

She received more than 6,000 letters of support, from lamenting her decision to give up her relationship to congratulating her for accepting the strictures of the Church. As family friend Veronica Maclean observed: 'It was the first time that Queen Elizabeth, a very private person, had to face up to a personal dilemma in the full glare of the public's gaze and it had been an unpleasant, painful experience for her and for the whole family.'[17]

Though still in the early years of her life as the Queen, Elizabeth had handled the family crisis with care. She had adhered to the formal advice of her ministers while giving her sister as much latitude as she was able. While the Sovereign did not want to be the one to stand in the way of Margaret's happiness, this was the abiding narrative in the popular imagination. It was only the release of letters and government papers some fifty years after the event that showed how much Margaret enjoyed the support of her older sister.

Just a few months later, the Queen herself needed her sibling to stand by her when her own marriage came under scrutiny. It all arose out of the best of intentions. She had seen how her energetic husband had been frustrated by the solemn pace of change at Court and so had encouraged him to sail to Australia on board the Royal Yacht *Britannia* to open the 1956 Olympic Games in Melbourne. As she perceptively remarked: 'There's nothing worse than to fence a man in and stop him from doing what he wants.'[18]

With a visit to Antarctica on the schedule as well as to other remote corners of the Commonwealth, the four-month voyage was a unique chance to put the yacht, whose construction and design development he had overseen, through its paces. Certainly, with a crew of 240 and a twenty-six-piece Royal Marine band, nothing could evade scrutiny aboard the vessel. Yet this famous journey would end up placing the royal marriage firmly under the international microscope.

Though the Queen affectionately mentioned his absence in her Christmas broadcast, and the duke made an informative forty-minute documentary about his travels, the fact that he was voluntarily away from his family for so long sparked a spate of rumours that resulted in a rare official comment about their marriage. The American weekly *Time* reported in February 1957 that 'the [rumour] mongering winds were howling louder around Buckingham Palace than they had since the day of Wallis Warfield Simpson and Edward VIII'.[19]

The gales of speculation began with unsubstantiated stories about wild parties taking place on the royal yacht. Given the large number of people on board, it was unlikely that any ship-based shenanigans would have gone unnoticed. It was the departure of Philip's equerry, Mike Parker, at Gibraltar in early February that really created a hurricane of innuendo. During the voyage, Parker's wife Eileen had filed for divorce and her lawyer had helpfully tipped off a Sunday tabloid as *Britannia* completed the last leg of the journey. Though it was rumoured that Parker was being punished by the palace for leading the prince astray, in fact, in the light of the Townsend affair, he had decided to leave the ship's company early in order to save Philip or the Royal Family from any embarrassment. Philip was furious that one of his oldest and most loyal friends had had his private life plastered all over the tabloids.

Parker's decision was juxtaposed with stories in the American media about the Queen and Prince Philip in a 'rift' over an unnamed party girl whom he had met regularly at the home of a society photographer, believed to be his friend Baron Nahum (who went by the professional name of 'Baron'). This was an old story that had gained new 'legs' courtesy of the prince's long absence.

During the late 1940s, he joined the all-male Thursday Club, which was a weekly social gathering often held at Wheeler's fish restaurant in Soho, central London, that Baron would preside over. It was an eclectic group that included newspapermen, actors, artists and the odd politician who liked ripe conversation, white wine, practical jokes and oysters. With brilliant raconteurs present, such as actors Peter Ustinov, James Robertson Justice and David Niven, no one stood on ceremony.

Besides organizing the Thursday Club, Baron was notorious for late-night parties held at his Mayfair flat. It was also Baron who first got the prince into hot water after a night out that didn't end until dawn. The photographer was infatuated with the celebrity singer and actress Pat Kirkwood, and, one evening in 1948, he took the prince and his equerry to her dressing room after she had finished her performance in the musical *Starlight Roof*. The quartet went for dinner and then out dancing at the Milroy nightclub. When Philip took to the dance floor with the glamorous actress, there was a palpable hush among the other partygoers. Tongues wagged and word later reached George VI, who was outraged that his son-in-law had been so indiscreet.

Even though Kirkwood always vigorously denied rumours of an affair with Philip – there was talk that she had been given a Rolls-Royce by the prince – her brief association with the Queen's consort would follow her to the grave.

As the marriage of the Queen and the prince came under the media microscope, Kirkwood's name was therefore prominent in the list of Philip's potential paramours. And so too was vivacious nightclub owner Hélène Cordet. He had known the former Hélène Foufounis since he was about three years old and had spent holidays with her at her parents' villa in Le Touquet in northern France. When she had two children while separated from her husband and refused to name the father, Philip's name was in the frame, especially when he agreed to be godfather to both of them. In fact, the actual father was a French fighter pilot. In Philip's defence, Cordet riskily argued: 'Of course he likes women. What the hell can he do to have a decent reputation? If he doesn't look at women, they say he likes men. He likes women. So what? It's a good thing.'[20]

Over the years, the prince has been linked variously to the novelist Daphne du Maurier (whose husband Sir Frederick 'Boy' Browning was his comptroller), the actresses Merle Oberon and Anna Massey, TV celebrity Katie Boyle and Susan Barrantes, the mother of Sarah, Duchess of York.

The Queen's dismay at the marital headlines was reflected in her decision to authorize her press officer, Commander Richard Colville, to issue an official statement denying the scurrilous stories. 'It is quite untrue that there is any rift between the Queen and the Duke' was the official palace line.[21]

The topic of infidelity continued to haunt the prince for the rest of his days. When I first started royal reporting in 1982, within a year I was told that Prince Philip had secret families in Wales, Norfolk, Germany and Melbourne. More recently, when a female journalist summoned up the courage to ask him about the rumours, his response was typically robust: 'Have you ever stopped to think that for the past forty years I have never moved anywhere without a policeman accompanying me? So how the hell could I get away with anything like that?'[22] Of course that didn't stop his eldest son Charles from conducting a lengthy affair with Camilla Parker Bowles, who later became his second wife.

It was a sign of just how seriously the story of a royal estrangement was taken that, in late February, when the Queen flew to Lisbon in Portugal to be reunited with her husband before they embarked on a State visit to England's oldest ally, there were 150 members of the media waiting on the airport tarmac, eagerly watching their every move.

During the 1956–57 voyage, the prince had grown a splendid full beard but had shaved it off shortly before his arrival in Portugal. When Philip boarded the royal plane to greet the Queen in Lisbon, to his surprise the royal entourage, including his wife, were all sporting false ginger whiskers. They apparently hadn't got

After more than a decade of war and grinding austerity, the prospect of a young and glamorous new Monarch lifted the spirits of a weary nation. For the Queen and Prince Philip, their new duties and responsibilities exacted a high price. The Queen placed duty before family, while her husband resigned from his promising career in the Royal Navy. Here she is in 1953, at a concert in central London organized by the governments of Australia and New Zealand, prior to a tour of both nations that the royal couple undertook between December 1953 and April 1954. Prince Charles and Princess Anne were left behind for the duration of the visit.

Left: Princess Elizabeth, an enchanting curly-haired blonde, with her parents, then the Duke and Duchess of York. Only Hollywood child star Shirley Temple could match the royal infant for international appeal. Her winsome features appeared on stamps, plates, mugs and tea towels.

Right: A rare picture of eight-year-old Princess Elizabeth and her sister Margaret, then four, with other children at a fancy-dress party. Elizabeth is dressed as a Tudor lady, Margaret as a fairy. For most of their day-to-day lives, the sisters were in the company of adults who controlled every aspect of their welfare.

Left: After the shock of the abdication in 1936, when King Edward VIII gave up the throne to marry the twice-divorced American Wallis Simpson, the Windsors were keen to re-establish themselves as models of home, hearth and humble family life. Here are what the new King, George VI, called 'we four' posing for happy family snaps with their dogs in the setting of Y Bwthyn Bach or 'The Little House', a miniature cottage given to Elizabeth by the people of Wales.

Above: For his Coronation, King George VI designed lightweight coronets and gowns for his daughters. Margaret, however, complained that her train was shorter than that of her elder sister. On the morning of the Coronation, Elizabeth looked out of her bedroom window at Buckingham Palace at the crowds who had waited all night to watch the ancient ceremony.

Below: The King and his daughters out riding in Windsor Great Park. Ever since she was a little girl, Elizabeth was fascinated by horses. She not only enjoyed riding them, but also became involved in their management and care. Those in the racing community believe that if she hadn't become Queen she would have made an excellent trainer.

Left: The Second World War changed the lives of most; none more so than that of the future Queen. It was vital for morale that the country knew that Princess Elizabeth and her sister remained in England rather than seek safety in Canada or elsewhere. In 1940, with Britain on the ropes, the princess, with Margaret by her side, made her first broadcast to the nation's children, speaking with words of good cheer to those forced to leave their homes and families in the cities and move to the countryside or abroad.

Right: After months of badgering her parents to let her do her bit for the war effort, in early 1945 the King and Queen finally allowed Princess Elizabeth to join the ATS (Auxiliary Territorial Service). She learned to drive lorries, change tyres and perform mechanical repairs. The princess showed off her skills when she drove a truck through central London to Buckingham Palace.

Left: This was the moment when sharp-eyed journalists realized that Princess Elizabeth was dating handsome Navy lieutenant, Prince Philip of Greece, when he helped her off with her fur coat prior to the wedding of Lord Brabourne and Patricia Mountbatten at Romsey Abbey, Hampshire in October 1946.

Left: On her 21st birthday, 21 April 1947, Princess Elizabeth gave the most important address of her life when she dedicated her future, 'whether it be long or short', to the service of the nation and the Commonwealth. Many listening to the radio broadcast, relayed from Cape Town in South Africa, were moved to tears by her simple humility.

Right: Princess Elizabeth and the newly minted Duke of Edinburgh celebrate their wedding day on 20 November 1947. The duke soon realized that he had not just married a princess, he had taken on a dynasty. In the early years he found the going difficult.

Left: Princess Elizabeth cradles baby Prince Charles, who was born on 14 November 1948, after his christening at Buckingham Palace shortly before Christmas. The happy event was overshadowed by general concern regarding the King's health.

Above: The royal couple dancing reels at the Phoenicia Hotel in Valletta, Malta, the Mediterranean island where Philip was stationed in 1949. Princess Elizabeth was able to lead a relatively normal life away from the shadow of the palace. She handled money for the first time, went to the hairdresser on her own and drove or sailed around the island unnoticed. It was one of the happiest periods of her life.

Below left: Bareheaded, the King sees off his eldest daughter from London Airport before she and Prince Philip head to Australia via Kenya on a much-delayed royal visit. George VI died in his sleep at Sandringham days later, on 6 February 1952.
Below right: Elizabeth, now Queen, returns to the UK to be greeted by Prime Minister Winston Churchill and other senior politicians.

Left: During the three-hour Coronation, the Queen, now wearing St Edward's Crown, accepts the formal declaration of loyalty from her husband. Initially the Queen had opposed the televising of this historic event, but in the end she gave in to popular demand.

Right: The newly crowned Queen Elizabeth II waves to the crowds from the balcony of Buckingham Palace, alongside Prince Philip and three of her six maids of honour. It was hoped that the new reign would herald a dynamic Elizabethan age of change, innovation and reform.

Left: Princess Margaret inspects the troops followed by her secret lover Group Captain Peter Townsend (far left), a war ace who held the post of comptroller inside the Royal Household. Her sister's affair with a divorced man would present the Queen with an early problem that tested her character in full measure.

Above: The Queen, shortly before giving her first live televised Christmas address in 1957. The event came at a time of mounting criticism of the 'tweedy sort' who made up the Queen's court. Her critics, though, were very much in the minority as the broadcast attracted a substantial audience of 16.5 million viewers in a nation where television ownership was still rather low. With the success of the first broadcast, the Queen's Christmas message became a festive must-watch.

the memo that he had returned to his usual clean-shaven state. But it broke the ice, a continuation of the practical jokes that the couple often played on one another. During their tour of Canada in 1951, for instance, he left a booby-trapped tin of nuts for his wife to open, and on another occasion he chased her down a corridor wearing a set of joke false teeth.

Princess Margaret summed up the feelings of the Royal Family in a letter to her American friend Sharman Douglas: 'I see the fine old press in your country tried to make out the Queen wasn't getting on with my b-in-l [brother-in-law]. So of course the stinking Press here repeated it all sheep-like, like the nasty cowards they are. However, all is well & he's terribly well & full of fascinating stories of his journeys & it's very nice indeed to have him home again. The children are thrilled.'[23]

Others noted that far from being estranged, the couple had become a close team who worked instinctively together. At least that was the conclusion of Cynthia Gladwyn, the wife of the British ambassador to France, who entertained the royals during a State visit to Paris and Lille in April 1957. She wrote in her diary: 'Prince Philip is handsome and informal, creating an easy democratic atmosphere in the wake of the Queen. This informality makes him very popular. He shines out as a breezy sailor who has known what it is like not to be royalty. He handles a difficult position in a remarkably successful way, and I cannot think that any other person, whom the Queen might have married, would have done as well.'[24]

Not everyone felt the same way. Since the Coronation, Princess Margaret and Prince Philip had been in the media firing line. Now it was the Queen's turn. Criticism of her style and personality came from an unlikely quarter; namely one of her own – a member of the House of Lords. In a trenchant article published in August 1957, Lord Altrincham took the Sovereign and her 'tweedy set' of courtiers to task. Writing in his own periodical, *National and English Review*, he referred to her speaking style as 'a pain in the neck', described her personality as like that of a 'priggish schoolgirl' and called her speeches 'prim little sermons'. Altrincham wrote dismissively: 'Like her mother she [the Queen] appears to be unable to string even a few sentences together without a written text.'[25]

His attack echoed those of other artists and intellectuals who gave the 'New Elizabethan age' short shrift. The playwright John Osborne, who was one of the so-called 'Angry Young Men' of the 1950s, referred to the monarchy as 'a gold filling in a mouth full of decay'.[26] Well known for his loquacity, the TV personality Malcolm Muggeridge dismissed the passion for the Royal Family as a kind of 'ersatz religion'.[27] As a result, the BBC banned him from appearing on its channel.

It was, though, Lord Altrincham who created the greatest stir. Such was the national uproar that after leaving a television studio in central London, he was punched in the face by an incensed sixty-four-year-old member of the League of Empire Loyalists pressure group.

Some of Altrincham's own jabs hit home, notably his criticism of the presentation of debutantes at Court. This outdated ritual was indeed scrapped, but the Queen delayed her decision by a year so as not to seem to have been pushed around by the errant peer.

Of course, what all three men were saying was that the institution of the monarchy was behind the rapidly changing times and that the Queen, artificially buoyed by the worship she had received during and after the Coronation, was encircled by a coterie of men who did not remotely represent modern Britain. As a result, this prevented her authentic personality from shining through, stifled as it was by sonorous platitudes and outdated ritual.

In a letter to *Ladies' Home Journal* publishers Bruce and Beatrice Gould, Lord Altrincham, who gave up his peerage years later, conveyed his sentiments on the subject: 'For the sake of the institution and for that matter of the Queen herself, changes are long overdue, and I hope the recent controversy may have helped to force the pace. Certainly I had given up all hope of achieving results by argument behind the scenes.'[28]

This debate, which was given so much prominence and weight, was a way of obliquely approaching Britain's precipitous military and political decline and fall in the modern world. The monarchy served as the lightning rod for the calamity that was the Suez Crisis. When Altrincham wrote his infamous article, the nation was still licking its self-inflicted wounds.

The debacle had taken place in October 1956 when Israel, Britain and France tried to take control of the Suez Canal waterway which had been nationalized by the Egyptian President, Gamal Abdel Nasser. Although the invasion was condemned by the United Nations, fellow Commonwealth countries and, most importantly, the United States, the triumvirate went ahead with military action against the nationalist leader. Prime Minister Eden, in power for less than two years, ignored the warnings from US President Dwight D. Eisenhower and paid the price, resigning in ignominy after being forced to withdraw his troops. Internationally, Suez signalled the end of Britain's position as a major world power, while domestically it gave licence to question and criticize hitherto inviolable institutions such as the monarchy.

The tectonic plates in society were shifting, but not quite as fast as some had hoped. While the religion of royalty had its critics, they were few in number. After the Altrincham episode, the Queen addressed the criticism in her own way. Although she was shy in front of the television cameras, she agreed to give her first-ever live Christmas broadcast, during which she acknowledged that it was inevitable that she would be seen as a rather remote figure. 'I very much hope that this new medium will make my Christmas message more personal and direct,' she said from the Long Library

SECRETS, SCANDALS
AND SPIES

W HILE THE DAWNING OF a new Elizabethan age proved
to be something of a chimera, the Queen and her
husband initiated a quiet revolution inside the House
of Windsor. For the first time in history, they decided to send their
children to school rather than have them taught by tutors within
palace gates.

Their decision did not meet with wholesale approval. The
Queen Mother, who had effectively been mother and father to
Charles and Anne while their parents were away on their many
travels, lobbied for them to be educated at Buckingham Palace.
The Monarch and Prince Philip, however, were resolute. As he
explained on American television in 1956: 'The Queen and I want
Charles to go to school with other boys of his generation and
learn to live with other children, and to absorb from childhood
the discipline imposed by education and others.'[1]

It was a genuine break from the past, a step change that the
Sovereign had long dreamed about. She had often talked about
her children being able to lead relatively 'normal' and unrestricted

lives. This unique trial to integrate young royals with other boys and girls began in November 1956 when Prince Charles was enrolled at Hill House, a small private school in Knightsbridge, just a five-minute drive from the palace. In the first few days, it was an experiment that seemed doomed to failure as the young prince, who was on the cusp of his eighth birthday, ran a noisy gauntlet of photographers and curious onlookers when he arrived at the school. This was not what Her Majesty had hoped for.

After three days of this mayhem, the Queen kept Prince Charles at home and ordered her press secretary, Commander Colville, to contact every newspaper editor and ask them to call off the dogs. The ploy worked. This editorial compact was the first of many future informal agreements between Fleet Street and Buckingham Palace that allowed royal children to go to school without undue harassment.

Not that Prince Charles saw it that way. He agreed with his grandmother, and craved the protection and certainty of life behind the palace gates, safe in the hands of his devoted nannies. When he was in the presence of other children, the prince was so afraid of their company that he would cling to Nanny Lightbody for support. She was his surrogate mother, the first to wake and feed him in the morning, and the one to kiss him goodnight.

As a toddler, he had played in the nursery until he was taken downstairs to spend thirty minutes with his mother or his father. While it was a distant parenting style, it was one that other members of the aristocracy and the upper classes found familiar. When Princess Elizabeth was in Malta with her husband between 1949 and 1951, it scarcely raised an eyebrow that Charles and his sister were left behind at Buckingham Palace and Sandringham for weeks at a time, cared for by the triumvirate of Nanny Lightbody, the Queen Mother and Princess Margaret – as well as a small army of nursery staff.

In the informal agreement that the Queen and Philip made at the beginning of their marriage, the prince took control of important family matters and she embraced affairs of State, taking on the regal obligations of her ailing father, George VI. Neither parent had expected the King to die so young and it meant that the new Queen was plunged into her royal duties, which allowed for very little time for her children. She constantly had to choose between red boxes and bath-time. Duty always triumphed. Godfrey Talbot, a royal correspondent of the period, recalled: 'She immediately had to take over the responsibilities of State. She had been trained since the cradle by her father that duty came before everything, including family. She reluctantly had to abandon her children and they virtually didn't see their parents for months on end.'[2]

Charles, a shy, sensitive, solitary and rather overweight boy, worshipped his mother but from afar. As his father ruled the roost domestically, it meant that he and his sister Anne spent much more time with Philip – when he was available. As a youngster, Anne, innately determined and competitive, more readily responded to her father's blandishments, while Charles wilted under Philip's tirades. The duke's method of teaching his children to swim, for example, was to throw them into the Buckingham Palace pool. Anne surfaced, all giggles, whereas Charles spluttered and choked, terrified.

While Charles would later describe his father as a bully – a criticism that his siblings rejected and told him so – there was method in Philip's tough and aggressive behaviour. In his own way he was trying to find one sport or activity that his children, especially Charles, would master and give them confidence as they grew and developed. Lady Kennard, a family friend, described Philip as a 'wonderful parent'. 'He played with his children, he read them stories, he took them fishing, he was very involved,' she recalled.[3] Eventually, though, Charles would join his siblings in praising Prince Philip's parenting skills. 'My father was marvellous at arranging silly games,' he said in a 2021 tribute programme that celebrated Philip's life. 'There was lots of chasing around and mad things.'[4]

Though Charles initially had difficulties with this robust parenting style, Anne thrived. Put her on a horse and she purred, the princess becoming the first-ever member of the Royal Family to compete in the Olympics when she rode for the British equestrian team at the 1976 Games in Montreal. While Anne was something of a tomboy growing up, her elder brother struggled. He was neither sporty nor especially horsey. Everything seemed designed to humiliate and belittle him.

When he first started lessons in the palace nursery he was diligent and persevering, but was baffled by the basics of mathematics, found English a chore and floundered with dates in elementary history, much as he loved the subject. Charles was a 'trier' who seemed happiest experimenting with a brush and a box of paints. His modest academic ability, retiring nature and unathletic appearance and ability did not help him fit into Hill House, and so he didn't have an easy time there. But if he thought that Hill House was difficult, his next school was his worst nightmare.

In 1957, he was enrolled as a boarder at Cheam School, his father's alma mater. Philip had survived and excelled, becoming school cricket captain and the first-team football goalkeeper. Not so his eldest son, who was utterly miserable and homesick. Timid and sensitive, he found it difficult to make friends or to join in, and invariably found himself on the periphery of any activity. These were among the most wretched years of his life. Even though the Queen supported her husband completely and wholeheartedly in this project, she did have to steel herself when, at the end of the Balmoral holidays, Charles would plead with her not to return to the house of 'misery'. Much as she sympathized with her son's plight, she believed that his boarding-school experiences would provide good training for the ups and downs of his future position.

But nor did it help when, in late July 1958, Her Majesty decided for no apparent reason to declare that her son was now 'Prince of Wales, Earl of Chester and Knight Companion of the Most Noble Order of the Garter'. The plump pupil blushed bright red and wished the earth could swallow him up as he watched the announcement on television with his classmates. As the Queen's biographer, Sarah Bradford, observed: 'Nobody had even thought of warning him about it beforehand, which seems an extraordinary lack of sensitivity on Elizabeth's part.'[5]

While the Monarch took a benign though imperturbable view of her son's education, she showed little interest in her daughter's academic progress. Anne was given lessons in the nursery by a governess, Catherine Peebles, and even though her schoolroom was just above the Queen's rooms at Buckingham Palace, her mother never came to see how she was faring. Instead, it was Princess Margaret who reviewed her niece's work, discussed her curriculum with her tutor and even tested Anne herself. What she considered to be her own inadequate education had always rankled, so Margaret was pleased when, in 1963, Princess Anne became the first daughter of a reigning sovereign to attend a boarding school when she enrolled at Benenden, an all-girls' school in Kent.

While Anne recalled her 'pleasant' schooldays, her brother memorably referred to his senior school, Gordonstoun on the northern Scottish coast, as 'Colditz with kilts'.[6] He had wanted to go to Eton, the public boys' school near Windsor Castle. In this ambition he was supported by the Queen Mother, who gamely lobbied her daughter and son-in-law. Her arguments fell on deaf ears, though, as Philip argued that Eton was too close to London, meaning that Charles would inevitably be hounded by the media. So Gordonstoun it was. In spite of his early misgivings, eventually Charles made the best of his time there. He joined the theatre group and was made the school's Guardian – or Head Boy – just like his father.

Charles never really got over the detached parenting of his childhood. His official biographer Jonathan Dimbleby described the Queen as 'cold' – a sentiment with which Charles's siblings strongly disagreed. More tactfully, a friend explained the Sovereign's parenting skills this way: 'Motherhood is not the Queen's long suit. She likes getting on with her job and she is extremely busy.'[7]

This long-running narrative of parental distance first started following the release of news footage of the famous reunion on board the Royal Yacht *Britannia* in the port of Tobruk in Libya in May 1954, towards the end of the Queen and Prince Philip's six-month post-Coronation tour of the Commonwealth. When the royal couple first saw their children on deck, Charles and Anne solemnly and politely shook their hands. At least they recognized their parents – there was a fear that after such a long absence they wouldn't know who they were.

Though the private welcome below deck was much more affectionate, this muted maternal display would come to define the Queen's cool approach to motherhood. Much later, her emotional reticence would be seen as a stark contrast to the natural impulses of Princess Diana who, during a similar reunion halfway through a tour of Canada in October 1991, ran down *Britannia*'s deck and scooped her two boys into her arms – right in front of the cameras. But others who have known the Queen for years take a different tack. They view her as a woman of powerful emotions who has been forced to keep herself under iron control because of the relentless demands of her position. Or, as writer James Pope-Hennessy put it: 'One feels that the spring is wound up very tight.'[8]

There have been numerous occasions where she had had to subsume her strong maternal instincts in favour of the Crown. But at times of family crisis, notably her sister's marital breakdown and the death of Diana, Princess of Wales, her first thoughts were always for the well-being of the royal children.

During her teenage and adult years, she spoke often of her somewhat conventional ambition to be a lady living in the country surrounded by dogs, horses and children. It was no idle pipe dream. Her father George VI was a knowledgeable horseman, but his eldest daughter took it to quite another level. She has earned the respect of the racing community because she is an acknowledged authority on the breeding and rearing of racehorses. In 1954 and 1957 she was Britain's Champion Owner of flat racing, the first reigning monarch to enjoy this success twice. 'If she had been a normal person, she probably would have become a trainer, she loves it so much,' observed trainer Ian Balding.[9]

At Balmoral she breeds Highland ponies and at Hampton Court her interest is in Fell ponies. As a breeder of gundogs, she has over the years won numerous prizes for her professional handling in competitive trials. When she gave her brother-in-law Antony Armstrong-Jones (later Lord Snowdon) a black Labrador as a present, he immediately recognized what a special gift it was.

Over the years, dogs and horses helped to keep her sane. They responded to her for who she was as a caring human being, not for being Queen. In a world where she was regularly surrounded by people she barely knew, animals gave her a sense of normality and this helps to explain why, even into her nineties, the Queen would ride out every day, accompanied only by a groom and a detective. It was a chance to be alone, at least for a short while.

Just as she was sincere in her enthusiasm for dogs and horses, so too was she serious about having more children, now that she and Philip had evolved into a professional working couple who were able to cope with the demands of 'the job'. Though the watching world was surprised when she fell pregnant in the spring of 1959, she and Philip had discussed the issue around two years earlier, after he returned from his controversial 1956–57 Commonwealth tour.

The arrival of Prince Andrew Albert Christian Edward in the Belgian Suite at Buckingham Palace on 19 February 1960 was the first child born to a reigning monarch for more than a hundred years. His predecessor was Princess Beatrice, the fifth daughter and youngest child of Queen Victoria and Prince Albert. Both of Prince Andrew's parents were thrilled by the new arrival, particularly Prince Philip, as their third child was named after his father.

There were considerable advantages to having a child later in her reign. No longer the monarchical ingénue, the Queen felt able to spend more time with her baby son, to the point where his big sister Princess Anne thought that he was being spoiled – at least in comparison to her upbringing. His mother taught him the alphabet, how to tell the time, and gave him riding lessons on Mr Dinkum, his first pony. Sometimes she would work at her desk in her study while Andrew played on the floor. If the Queen told his nanny, Mabel Anderson, to leave her to look after the toddler, there was always a page and a footman present to help out. Where diary engagements permitted, the Sovereign would take charge at bath-time while Prince Philip read or made up a bedtime story. Andrew grew to be a boisterous, noisy boy, racing along the corridors with a football or stick. In spite – or perhaps because of – his energetic antics he has always been referred to as the Queen's favourite child, the son who could do no wrong. Prince Philip called Andrew 'The Boss' after he had arrived at an evening engagement sporting a black eye.[10] He later explained that it was the result of a bedtime boxing match with his second son that had got out of hand.

The birth of Andrew also helped to heal a long-standing marital wound. For years Philip had resented the fact that his children did not bear his surname, Mountbatten. Since the Coronation, there had been back and forth discussions between the various parties to resolve this vexatious matter. In January 1960, shortly before Prime Minister Harold Macmillan left for South Africa, where he gave his famous 'Wind of Change' speech, he came to Sandringham to discuss the issue with the Queen. He recognized that she wanted to placate her husband and resolve the ongoing matter of the family name. 'The Queen only wishes (properly enough) to do something to please her husband – with whom she is desperately in love,' Macmillan noted in his diary. 'What upsets me is the prince's almost brutal attitude to her in all this.'[11]

Philip finally got his wish and, eleven days before Andrew's birth, Buckingham Palace issued a proclamation that in future certain members of the royal dynasty would bear the surname Mountbatten-Windsor. The royal house, however, would still be called Windsor.

It was a happy time domestically for the Queen. She was nursing her third child, her husband was content and her sister, normally so unlucky in love, had finally found the man of her dreams and accepted his proposal of marriage. Although the photographer Antony Armstrong-Jones did not come from the serried ranks of the aristocracy – as the princess's parents would have wished – he was eminently acceptable. Not only was he courteous and charming, but he also seemed to make Margaret happy. He even got on with Prince Philip, who tended to be dismissive of photographers as a breed. 'If he hasn't got what he wants by now, he's an even worse photographer than I thought' was his regular – and disconcerting – complaint at formal photo sessions.[12]

When the Old Etonian travelled to Sandringham in December 1959 to ask the Queen for her formal permission to marry Princess Margaret, she gave it with the caveat that the engagement announcement should be delayed until after the birth of her third child. And so, on the evening of 26 February, the news was formally proclaimed, the announcement sending shock waves through the shires and among European royalty, who felt that the freelance photographer was not *ebenbürtig*, that is to say neither equal in rank nor birth to the princess. His newspaper colleagues were equally nonplussed as they never had an inkling that one of their own was about to join the Royal Family.

Yet the general response by the Queen and the rest of the Windsors to this new suitor was welcoming. There was collective guilt among them with regard to Margaret previously relinquishing the love of her life in Peter Townsend, so there was a willingness to tolerate any sensible marital pick. Throughout her reign, the Queen rarely interfered with or commented on the partners chosen by members of her family. Unlike some mothers she was quite passive, content to watch the romantic drama play out. There was no sense of the Sovereign encouraging her offspring to marry the rich and the titled. Modestly well-to-do commoners were the typical choices – apart from Lady Diana Spencer, the daughter of an earl.

However, with regard to her sister's match, the Queen would not have been so accommodating had she been aware that, several months before the wedding, the society photographer was conducting a three-way affair with his first choice of best man, the inventor Jeremy Fry, and Fry's wife Camilla. She became pregnant with Armstrong-Jones's child and gave birth to a daughter named Polly while the newest member of the Royal Family was on honeymoon on board *Britannia*.

Though in smart circles the photographer divided opinion, for the most part the British public were thrilled that Princess Margaret, so often a loser in love, had found happiness at last – and with a man who represented, along with celebrity hairdressers and models, the most 'with it' profession of the Swinging Sixties. For the first time, a royal wedding was televised live and more than 300 million viewers across the world tuned in to watch a lavish spectacle, which featured twenty wedding cakes, a 60-foot floral arch and a dress made from more than 30 metres of fabric by the Royal Family's favourite designer, Norman Hartnell.

During the service at Westminster Abbey on 6 May 1960, it was noted that the Queen looked less than enthusiastic about the happy occasion. 'Everyone has commented on the black depression on the Queen's face,' observed the publisher Sir Rupert Hart-Davis, 'and the rustic mind likes to invent the causes of it as jealousy, snobbery, etc.'[13] Other royal watchers made similar comments, including Kenneth Rose who described her as 'a sulking Queen Victoria throughout the entire service.'[14]

As the Queen recognized early on in her life, she has the kind of face that looks angry when she is trying not to smile. On this day she could at least say farewell to one long-standing family difficulty – her sister. She may have looked severe to onlookers, but inside she was doubtless quietly rejoicing.

Once the Queen had waved goodbye to Margaret, as the princess and her new husband boarded *Britannia*, which had been anchored in the Port of London, it was back to her role as CEO of Great Britain Inc. For all the talk of the Swinging Sixties and sexual equality, there were few working mothers who held high-ranking positions. The Queen was one of that rare breed. In the era made famous by the TV series *Mad Men* – about the chauvinism and sexual prejudice in a Manhattan advertising agency – even the Monarch was given few concessions in her role as mother and executive.

When she was at the palace, she was able to spend time with her third child, but she still missed many of the key points of her baby son's life – notably his first birthday. That year, in 1961, she embarked on a gruelling schedule of visits abroad that took in Cyprus, India, Pakistan, Nepal, Iran, Italy, Vatican City, Ghana, Liberia, Sierra Leone and lastly Gambia. Her frequent absences were something her older children had simply become accustomed to.

'I miss them when I'm away for long,' the Queen told scientist Niels Bohr in 1957, 'but they understand why I have to go.'[15] Anne would later echo her mother's remark, saying that *her* children accepted the demands on her time, while also acknowledging the Queen's own love and support: 'I don't think that any of us, for a second, thought she didn't care for us in exactly the same way as any mother did.'[16]

Aside from all the smiling and glad-handing, her overseas trips were exceptionally important in serving as a visible arm of the UK's foreign policy. Her presence undoubtedly helped to cement allegiances, particularly among those countries that were once part of the British Empire but now played a role inside the Commonwealth of Nations.

In November 1961, the Queen and Prince Philip were scheduled to make a much-delayed visit to Ghana, the former British colony and the first sub-Saharan nation to gain independence in 1957. Under the socialist rule of President Kwame Nkrumah, Ghana was edging towards the Soviet sphere of influence. With the country riven by factional violence – there were explosions in the capital Accra just five days before the Queen's arrival – the engagement hung in the balance. Prime Minister Macmillan and even Winston Churchill were worried about the Queen's safety.

After much soul-searching, Macmillan sanctioned the trip on the grounds that to cancel would give Nkrumah an excuse to leave the Commonwealth and align with the Soviet Union. The Queen agreed, firm in her resolve: 'How silly I should look if I was scared to visit Ghana and then Khrushchev [the Soviet leader] went and had a good reception. I am not a film star. I am the Head of the Commonwealth – and I am paid to face any risks that may be involved. Nor do I say this lightly. Do not forget that I have three children.'[17]

Her attitude reflected her settled view that she didn't want to be treated any differently because she was a woman and a mother. She was firmly backed by the Queen Mother, for whom the spirit of the Blitz was second nature. 'I am sure that if one listened to all the faint hearts, one would never go anywhere,' she wrote in a letter to her daughter.[18]

It proved to be the right decision and – given the febrile atmosphere – a brave one. The Queen demonstrated her serious commitment to the Commonwealth, an organization nurtured during her reign, as well as her robust response to the prospect of personal danger. The tour was such a triumph that the Accra *Evening News* trumpeted, somewhat optimistically, that the Queen was 'the world's greatest Socialist Monarch in history!'.[19]

Her deft diplomacy culminated at a State banquet on 18 November, where the bejewelled Sovereign and President Nkrumah, all smiles, danced together. The picture of the dancing Queen went around the world and for once she succeeded in knocking her glamorous younger sister off the front pages. Not only was the photograph a symbolic demonstration of the altered relationship between Britain and the former colony, but it underlined that although the Monarch's authority was much reduced, she still had global reach and influence.

This Cold War warrior in ermine had a close encounter of a rather different kind shortly before her trip to Ghana when, in July 1961, she met the first man in space, cosmonaut Yuri Gagarin. Once again realpolitik was at play – and the Queen was drafted in at short notice to do her bit. Gagarin's Soviet masters had sent him on a worldwide goodwill mission in order to extol the virtues of Communism. The tour's success had alarmed British ministers so much that when Gagarin arrived in London to a tumultuous reception, it was thought prudent to invite him to 10 Downing Street to meet Prime Minister Macmillan and to Buckingham Palace for breakfast with the Queen.

After the initial introductions, the clearly nervous Soviet visitor took his seat next to the Queen and then, to her utter astonishment, put his hand forward and stroked her leg just above the knee. The Queen followed her grandmother's sage advice and kept smiling while sipping her coffee. He later explained, through interpreters, that he touched her leg to make sure that she was real and not some animated doll.

The former foundryman also struggled with the rules of dining etiquette, baffled by which cutlery he should use. The Queen responded kindly and reassuringly: 'My dear Mr Gagarin, I was born and brought up in this palace, but believe me, I still don't know in which order I should use all these forks and knives.'[20]

One Cold War couple who knew their way around the table settings for a formal dinner were American President John F. Kennedy and his sophisticated First Lady, Jacqueline. They came to dinner at Buckingham Palace at the end of a whirlwind European tour in early June and received a rapturous welcome. However, the rapport between the First Lady and the Queen was not quite as intimate as Her Majesty's future close encounter with the Soviet cosmonaut would be. Mrs Kennedy later complained that she found the Queen rather 'heavy going'. When writer Gore Vidal passed on the remark to Princess Margaret, she exclaimed loyally, 'But that's what she's there for.'[21]

During a later visit, in March 1962, when the First Lady was returning from Pakistan after a successful official trip, the two women bonded over lunch. If the Queen had heard about some of Mrs Kennedy's previous remarks – the First Lady had criticized her clothes and 'flat' hairstyle – she never showed it. The chilly emotional temperature warmed up once they discovered their mutual love of horses – during her stay in Pakistan President Muhammad Ayub Khan had presented the First Lady with a ten-year-old bay gelding called Sardar, which she called her 'favourite treasure.'[22] Like many others before and after her, Jackie Kennedy saw the Queen's face light up and become more animated when equine matters were the topic of conversation.

While they were never going to be best friends, the Queen and the First Lady shared many characteristics besides a love of horses. Both had married extrovert, aggressive alpha-male husbands, while they were quite private and shy women who found themselves in positions where they had to mask their personalities with a calm reserve. When President Kennedy was assassinated on 22 November 1963, the Queen was unable to console or pay her sympathies to the grieving widow in person as she was about five months pregnant with her fourth child. Doctors advised her not to travel to the funeral, which took place in Washington DC, so Prince Philip went in her stead.

—·—

Just over two weeks before Kennedy's assassination, the Liverpool-based pop sensation, The Beatles, sang at the Royal Variety Performance in front of Princess Margaret, her husband Lord Snowdon and the Queen Mother, who was standing in for the pregnant Sovereign.

Before playing their final song, John Lennon asked those in the cheaper seats to clap their hands. 'And the rest of you,' he said, looking pointedly at the royal box, 'if you'd just rattle your jewellery.'[23] Irreverent, iconoclastic and home-grown, they represented the zeitgeist of the 1960s, the quartet going on to become rock-and-roll royalty.

The arrival of The Beatles and other bands, the explosion of satire with shows like *That Was The Week That Was*, and the glamorization of creative professions contributed to the sense that the times really were a'changin'. Even the Queen and her consort were daringly modern with the birth of Prince Edward Antony Richard Louis. He was delivered in the Belgian Suite at Buckingham Palace on 10 March 1964, and for the first time in four occasions Prince Philip was present – a move encouraged by their birthing expert Betty Parsons. Barely a week later, Elizabeth was writing to her old friend Mabel Strickland in Malta: 'The baby is flourishing and is a great joy to us all, especially to Andrew, who is fascinated by him.'[24]

The tectonic plates were genuinely shifting in society. Britain's ruling class was under consistent attack, its decline epitomized by the Profumo scandal. This centred on war minister John Profumo, who had an affair with a call girl named Christine Keeler while she was also sleeping with a Soviet spy named Eugene Ivanov. Eventually, the minister's extra-marital liaison became public knowledge. In a statement to the House of Commons, Profumo lied and formally denied any involvement with Keeler, but once the truth emerged he resigned in disgrace.

The tentacles of the affair spread throughout high society as Keeler's amateur pimp, Stephen Ward, was a well-known osteopath and portrait artist who rented a cottage on Lord Astor's Cliveden estate, where riotous naked pool parties regularly took place. Moreover, Ward, who was a member of the infamous Thursday Club, had made drawings of Prince Philip and other members of the Royal Family. Though the media worked valiantly to link the prince with the sexual shenanigans at Cliveden, there was lots of smoke but no fire. Prime Minister Macmillan wrote a painful apology to the Queen for the behaviour of his minister and others. 'I had, of course, no idea of the strange underworld in which other people, alas, besides Mr Profumo, have allowed themselves to be entrapped.'[25]

While the Queen sympathized with his plight, it wasn't long before the inexorable tide of scandal came lapping at the red-carpeted corridors of Buckingham Palace once again. It flowed from the most unlikely of sources, concerning as it did the long-serving Surveyor of the Queen's Pictures, the noted art historian Sir Anthony Blunt. Her Majesty had never been close to Blunt, who had been appointed to his position by her father. He was a chilly ascetic who was perfectly proper, but one could sense the contempt in his eyes. Blunt found Court life dreary and told friends that the Royal Family's idea of a cultural evening was playing indoor golf with a piece of coal on a precious Aubusson carpet. He only accepted a knighthood in 1956 to please his mother. As his biographer Miranda Carter noted: 'Blunt's social mode, polite but distant, was not unlike the Queen's polite unreadability.'[26]

Sometime after the birth of Prince Edward in 1964, the Monarch's private secretary Sir Michael Adeane delivered the jaw-dropping news that MI5, acting on information from the FBI in the USA, had unmasked Blunt as a Soviet spy: before and during the Second World War, he had been sending information to Moscow. When Adeane briefed the Queen, he emphasized that Downing Street had advised that she do nothing and leave him in place. Blunt had been granted immunity from prosecution on the proviso that he agreed to cooperate and tell the authorities everything he knew. There were also concerns that any publicity would severely damage relations between British intelligence and the Americans, which were already at a low ebb thanks to the Profumo scandal and the unmasking of the so-called Cambridge spy ring, of which Blunt was a member. His fellow spies – Guy Burgess, Donald Maclean and Kim Philby – had all been discovered and had fled to Russia.

Though preserving Anglo-American relations was top-priority, there was also suspicion that keeping the status quo would save the embattled government further embarrassment. Little if any thought had been given to protecting the good name of the House of Windsor when, inevitably, the presence of a traitor at Buckingham Palace was later revealed.

Over the years, the Queen has shown herself a doughty defender of the institution, always ready to prod her ministers should she feel the monarchy's authority was under threat. Though Blunt was not unmasked until November 1979, when Prime Minister Margaret Thatcher revealed the truth in the House of Commons, courtiers have subsequently questioned why he remained in his post until his retirement in 1972, his knighthood intact. It was said that the Queen Mother, who never liked Blunt because of his atheism, would have presented a stouter defence of the monarchy.

'The Queen Mother, whose judgement was usually less good,' wouldn't have worn it for a moment, but the Queen did,' recalled one senior royal official.[27] Another former adviser remarked: 'I'm amazed that the decision to keep Blunt didn't do the monarchy more damage when the facts eventually became public in 1979. I do know that we spun it with great difficulty.'[28]

Though forced to take the formal advice from Downing Street, there was a feeling that the Queen was too passive in accepting the official line and that, as the custodian of the institution, she should have insisted that, at the very least, Blunt was removed from his prestigious role.

Several years later, the affair would provide the inspiration for a brilliant play by Alan Bennett, *A Question of Attribution*, which focused on the delicate philosophical duel between the Sovereign and her surveyor about truth, image and reality.

—·—

By the mid-1960s, no longer the ingénue of the early years of her reign, the Queen was comfortable and experienced, more relaxed in her position as both Monarch and mother. She gave a telling insight into her world when she allowed Pathé cameras to film her and her family as they walked through the grounds of Frogmore

House, Windsor, in Easter 1965, the Queen pushing the pram containing baby Edward. Though the commentary pointed up the frequent absences that were necessary because of her demanding job, it was clear that she was very much enjoying the days and hours with her youngest two children. She had brought forward her Tuesday evening prime ministerial audiences so that she could bathe Edward, and insisted on blocking out time in her diary so she could spend time with Andrew. She told a friend that it was 'such fun' to have a baby in the house and the main theme of her Christmas broadcast in 1965 was 'the family', which she described as 'the focal point of our existence'.

The image of a modern mother only went so far though – there was still a platoon of nannies, nurses and other staff to care for the infants. If not backward-looking, the Queen was seen as upholding tradition, the perception being that she was a dragging anchor as the Swinging Sixties, democratic and daring, sailed on. When Prime Minister Harold Macmillan resigned in October 1963, he suggested that the Queen call for a member of the House of Lords, namely the then Foreign Secretary Alec Douglas-Home, who was the 14th Earl of Home and a Scottish landowner, rather than Macmillan's deputy, Rab Butler.

The move was a public relations disaster. The Earl of Home was a card-carrying member of the 'tweedy' set criticized years earlier by Lord Altrincham. With his weak chin, speech that sounded like he was gargling with a mouthful of marbles and Old Etonian background, Sir Alec Douglas-Home, as he became after relinquishing his hereditary peerage to become Prime Minister, was a satirist's dream.

Conversely, the Queen felt very comfortable with the new Prime Minister who had a family tree that stretched back to the fifteenth century and who owned grouse moors near to her own estate. As a courtier confided: 'She loved Alec. He was an old friend. They talked about dogs and shooting together. They were both Scottish landowners, the same kind of people, like old schoolfriends.'[29]

A decade after Altrincham, the Queen still surrounded herself with land-owning aristocrats, all men naturally, whose conservative outlook bolstered her own natural caution. Her long-serving press officer Commander Richard Colville, for example, thought the media were 'little better than a communicable disease'.[30] His basic rule, one that he had adhered to during his twenty years of service, was that anything which did not appear in the august Court Circular – the venerable record of daily royal business – was not to be filmed, photographed or even discussed. This approach was comforting for a monarch who was shy in front of the cameras and had an ingrained wariness of personal disclosure. It was, though, out of step with the rapidly changing times.

The growing gulf between the Sovereign and her subjects was highlighted when, by a slender majority, the Labour leader Harold Wilson won the October 1964 general election, which had been called amid growing industrial unrest. Their first encounter inspired neither trust nor confidence. Her new Prime Minister was a pipe-smoking former Oxford University don from Yorkshire, the son of a works chemist and a schoolteacher. He was a far cry from the urbane Tory landowners and aristocrats who had come before him. For their first meeting at Buckingham Palace, Prime Minister Wilson brought along his political secretary Marcia Williams as well as his wife Mary, his father Herbert and his two sons, Robin and Giles.

It was an unpromising beginning. While Wilson met the Queen, the family and his secretary waited outside, watched over by Household staff. As Marcia Williams, later Lady Falkender, recalled: 'A number of anonymous Palace individuals chatted to us while the audience took place. As I recall it, the conversation centred on horses. Perhaps it was assumed that everybody was interested in horses, though my knowledge of them is minimal and the Wilson family's less.'[31]

Nor did things go well in the traditional thirty-minute briefing conversation between the Sovereign and her first minister. He arrived unprepared and fluffed a question. She responded sharply, and both withdrew from this initial encounter ruffled and annoyed. It was going to be a steep learning curve.

————•——

Three months into Wilson's tenure as British Prime Minister, the death of Winston Churchill on 24 January 1965 showed how far the nation had changed. Churchill had been born in Blenheim Palace with a lineage of dukes and knights in his family. His pram and rattle had been saved for posterity. At his weekly audiences with the Queen, the elder statesman spent as much time discussing their mutual love of the turf as affairs of State. Wilson's origins could not have been more different. He came into this world at 4 Warneford Road, a small terraced house in the mill town of Huddersfield in West Yorkshire. When wartime Prime Minister Churchill offered only 'blood, toil, tears and sweat' to his beleaguered people, Wilson was able to promise 'the white heat of technology'.[32]

At St Paul's Cathedral, where Churchill's State funeral took place, the Queen responded to the enormity of the event by waiving the precedent that she always arrives last. Instead, she awaited the arrival of the great man. Her simple act of humility, a Sovereign standing aside for her subject, served to make the farewell even more poignant. Nicholas Soames, Churchill's grandson, observed: 'It is absolutely exceptional if not unique for the Queen to grant precedence to anyone. For her to arrive before the coffin and before my grandfather was a beautiful and very touching gesture.'[33]

Churchill's death marked the end of an era and the passing of perhaps Britain's greatest statesman and leader, a man whose loyalty and counsel had been invaluable during Elizabeth's early years on the throne. As actor John Lithgow, who studied the former premier's life before playing him in the TV series *The Crown,* observed: 'Churchill's relationship with the Queen follows a beautiful trajectory ... She's this completely untutored Queen who, arguably because of his instructions, gradually realizes her role and sense of her own power, eventually coming to overrule and discipline him. His last audience with her in 1955 is extremely moving, when age and infirmity force him to step down.'[34]

While numerous men of stature advised kings and queens during their reigns – Cardinal Thomas Wolsey and Henry VIII, William Cecil and Queen Elizabeth I, Lord Melbourne and Queen Victoria – Churchill played a unique role in helping to shape an entire royal dynasty.

CHAPTER EIGHT

A FAMILY AFFAIR

T 9.15 ON A CLEAR blue-skied morning on 21 October 1966, the mining village of Aberfan in South Wales was devastated when a man-made mountain of coal waste collapsed and slammed into a primary school and nearby houses, killing 116 children and twenty-eight adults. It was one of the worst peacetime disasters in British history, a national tragedy of epic proportions. The village looked like a scene from hell as frantic parents, some just using their bare hands, dug in the mud in a futile attempt to rescue their infants. Elsewhere, stunned survivors stood or sat, their eyes and faces blank with shock.

Prime Minister Harold Wilson was one of the first dignitaries to reach the village, having assessed, correctly, that this was a calamity where both consolation and prompt action were required. But while the Queen hesitated about travelling to Aberfan, her brother-in-law showed no such reticence. Without waiting to consult officials, Princess Margaret's husband Lord Snowdon packed a bag and grabbed a shovel before catching a train to Wales.

For a time he became consoler-in-chief, visiting the bereaved and sitting in silence with them as they struggled to comprehend the tragic deaths of their young sons and daughters. He went to local hospitals, talked to doctors, nurses and survivors, and tried to keep up flagging spirits. Prince Philip arrived the next day, bringing with him the sympathies of the nation.

At a moment of national grief, the Queen held back, preferring to wait on events rather than acting on instinct. This was part of her temperamental make-up and it normally served her well. Though she did not want to hamper recovery work or intrude into intense private grief, at the time it was seen by some of her advisers as an opportunity missed. As a courtier told historian Ben Pimlott: 'She regrets that now – she would say it was a mistake, that she should have gone at once.'[1]

Eight days after the disaster, when recovery work was complete, the Queen did visit the devastated village where she was greeted by a young girl with a posy of flowers for her. The card's stark message read: 'From the remaining children of Aberfan.'[2] She came as the Monarch but also as a mother, and the attendant media and watching villagers appreciated her presence in that light.

As she walked slowly through the largely silent crowd and witnessed the full extent of the carnage, reporters noted that she looked pale and that tears pricked her eyes. During her tour, she went to the home of Councillor Jim Williams, seven of whose relatives had perished in the disaster. As she spoke to those who had lost loved ones, a meeting that had been scheduled for an hour stretched to two and a half.

While they derived considerable comfort from the Queen's presence, neither the villagers nor media were privy to the internal debate among her advisers about whether she should have gone there sooner. Her hesitation, some insiders believed, originated from her recognition that, unlike her more theatrical mother, she was not a touchy-feely person. That did not mean that she didn't care any the less, but she didn't show her feelings in obvious ways. She was, as veteran royal correspondent Grania Forbes observed, 'very tightly wrapped'.[3] One courtier noted that the Queen did not have 'outward humanity', the instinctive rapport with strangers which was exhibited years later by Princess Diana and thereafter by her youngest son, Prince Harry. Over the years, the Queen has visited Aberfan on several occasions, which has been interpreted by some as atonement for what she acknowledged as an initial excess of caution.

This overwhelming tragedy came at a time when enquiring minds inside the palace were considering ways of recasting the monarchy for modern times. The sheen of glamour and glitter of the Coronation was well worn and the Queen, by then in her early forties, was seen as middle-aged, dull and remote, as was the institution over which she presided. To use the parlance of the day it was 'square'. That, of course, was no bad thing. In a rapidly changing Britain, where the abolition of the death penalty and the legalization of homosexuality and abortion were all under intense discussion, the monarchy was a security blanket of certainty and stability.

With the prospect of Prince Charles's investiture as Prince of Wales looming in July 1969, thoughts turned to how best to showcase the monarchy to take advantage of the arcane spectacle. Fortuitously, there had been a changing of the old guard at Buckingham Palace, with the affable Australian William Heseltine taking over from the dead hand of Commander Colville in 1968. The new press secretary argued that there was nothing between the dull prose of the Court Circular and the gleeful exaggerations of the tabloid press to explain and illustrate the work of the monarchy and its relevance to the modern world.

Even with Princess Margaret and her photographer husband adding glamour and contemporary lustre to the Crown, the Queen recognized that the crowds were dwindling and interest was waning. Just as television had turbo-charged the monarchy during the Coronation, Heseltine suggested it was time to approach that magic box in the corner of the sitting room once again, to give the monarchy a much-needed jolt. He was supported by Lord Mountbatten's son-in-law, the noted film-maker John Brabourne, and by Mountbatten himself. Prince Philip had long been an exponent of the virtues of television. Not only did he make the argument – against his wife's wishes – to employ the medium at the Coronation, in the intervening years he had made or featured in several documentaries himself.

Philip, the eternal modernizer, argued that a carefully controlled, fly-on-the-wall television documentary would open the world's eyes to the normal way that the royals lived. It would document their official life and the remorseless call of duty, while also pulling back the curtain to give viewers an edited glimpse into their private world. Princess Anne thought it was a 'rotten idea'.[4] Initially, the Queen too was not keen. Not only did she feel self-conscious in front of the cameras, which is why she delayed televising her Christmas broadcast until 1957, but, mindful of the words of Walter Bagehot, she was reluctant to let too much daylight in on the magic of monarchy. Eventually, though, she agreed, on the proviso that an advisory committee chaired by Philip would give her ultimate editorial control.

Whatever her reservations, she felt that something must be done to arrest the slow drip, drip, drip of waning popularity. This then was the genesis of the show that arguably changed the monarchy forever. Filmed over twelve months between June 1968 and May 1969, Brabourne's central problem was to encourage the Queen to be more natural when the cameras were whirring. Ultimately, he succeeded, the Sovereign steadily relaxing and becoming more herself over time.

As the film was titled *Royal Family*, part of the idea was to show the Queen as wife and mother, as well as Monarch and Head of

State. During a stay at Balmoral, she was filmed taking Edward for an ice cream, joining in with a barbecue picnic and chatting over the breakfast table. More formally, she was shown entertaining the British Olympic team at a drinks reception, receiving Prime Minister Harold Wilson at his weekly audience and welcoming US President Richard Nixon to lunch.

She came across as even-tempered and quite serious, but always ready to see the funny, wry side of a situation, such as American ambassador Walter Annenberg's agonizing circumlocution when describing building work at the embassy in London. Moments such as the Queen and Prince Charles exchanging affectionate smiles while preparing a barbecue salad truly gave a sense that the 110-minute film was unrehearsed and authentic.

Scriptwriter Antony Jay, who was later made a Commander of the Royal Victorian Order for personal services to the Royal Family, gave the film an intellectual underpinning with his crisp summary of the value of the monarchy and its relevance to modern times. The Queen's very existence, he argued, was a bulwark against over-ambitious generals and politicians. 'The strength of the monarchy does not lie in the power it gives to the Sovereign, but in the power it denies to anyone else,' he wrote.[5]

Worldwide response to the TV show was extraordinary and unprecedented. It was watched by over 350 million people, including 23 million in Britain, more than half the adult population. But while it brought the Royal Family closer to their public and showed them as three-dimensional human beings, critics felt that the exercise had been a huge mistake by making them seem too ordinary and accessible. The broadcaster and naturalist David Attenborough, since knighted, told director Richard Cawston at the time: 'You're killing the monarchy, you know, with this film you're making. The whole institution depends on mystique and the tribal chief in his hut. If any member of the tribe ever sees inside the hut, then the whole system of tribal chiefdom is damaged and the tribe eventually disintegrates.'⁶

On the other hand, the audience was delighted to be invited into the headman's hut to take a guided tour. They eagerly anticipated a sequel, though the Queen, who was happy with the documentary, was in no mood to turn her family – or herself – into cast members of a television soap opera. She felt the film, which was broadcast ten days before the investiture, had fulfilled its principal function, namely to whet the public's appetite for the colourful ceremony, scheduled for 1 July 1969.

If the TV programme showed a family at work and play, the investiture described a dynasty with roots dating back centuries. Everyone at the palace strained to ensure that the much-anticipated event went off without a hitch. With bomb threats having been issued from radical Welsh nationalists, nerves were on edge. Though the investiture was designed as a kind of Coronation, it had no place in the constitution and little precedent in history. Only two of the previous twenty-one Princes of Wales had had a similar celebration, including a teenage Edward VIII. It was a ritual with modern antecedents masquerading as ancient ceremonial. Given that it had been sixteen years since the Coronation, courtiers were anxious to bring a little razzle-dazzle back to the venerable institution of the monarchy.

The Queen asked Lord Snowdon to take on the task of recreating the spirit of the previous investiture, which was held in 1911 when the current Duke of Windsor was crowned Prince of Wales. Though he had a tiny budget of £50,000 – the equivalent of around £875,000 today – Snowdon, whose family were Welsh, was thrilled at the challenge he had been given of interpreting the ancient and the modern, and moulding it into dramatic harmony with Caernarfon Castle, a massive medieval fortress that was to be used as a backdrop to dramatize Prince Charles's coming-of-age. He was careful to show the Queen and Prince Philip his designs, including sketches for the thrones and the Perspex canopy to shield the modern dais made from Welsh slate for the crowning ceremony.

The race to provide a spectacle fit for the Queen was played out against escalating violence by Welsh nationalists, who made death threats to officials and attacked public buildings with petrol bombs. Uncharacteristically, the Queen, who was normally phlegmatic in the face of danger, told Prime Minister Wilson that she feared for her son's safety and asked whether the ceremony should be cancelled. Wilson assured her that he would do everything in his power to ensure the occasion took place without incident. All police were issued with firearms although, fearing the worst, the BBC pre-recorded a full-length TV obituary of Prince Charles. On the royal train, the Queen Mother jokingly told her grandson that the event was going ahead but he was going to be replaced by a stunt double. Her jovial remark did little to dissipate the tension.

'Charles,' Lord Snowdon told writer Gyles Brandreth, 'was shit scared.'[7] With justification. On the eve of the big day, two activists were killed by the bomb they were intending to plant on the railway track over which Charles would travel on the journey to Caernarfon Castle. They were immediately dubbed the Abergele Martyrs. Half an hour before the event was due to start, there was another loud bang near the castle. The bejewelled and uniformed audience, already settled in their seats, tried to pretend they hadn't heard it.

As the clock ticked towards the start of the ceremony, the guests fell silent. Among the crowd of 4,000 dignitaries were foreign royalty, ambassadors, politicians and local Welsh gentry – as well as a handful of modern-day druids clad in nylon capes, who were dressed in the style of ancient Celtic priests.

Then it was showtime. Heart in mouth, the royal party made its way into the castle and all was well. The investiture played out precisely as planned. There was no repetition of the clownish antics of the dress rehearsal, during which Prince Charles's oversized crown had slipped down over his forehead obscuring half his face, causing the Queen and her son to try to stifle their giggles.

The actual ceremony, though, was both moving and believable, the most affecting moment when the Prince of Wales knelt before the Queen and, after placing his hands between hers, swore: 'I, Charles, Prince of Wales, do become your liege man of life and limb and of earthly worship, and faith and truth I will bear unto thee to live and die against all manner of folks.' It was an echo of Prince Philip's own oath of allegiance during the Coronation.

More than 500 million people worldwide watched the event, a magnetic combination of the feudal and the modern, the symbolic and the familial. The Queen was thrilled with Snowdon's creative vision and awarded him the Knight Grand Cross of the Royal Victorian Order in the 1969 Investiture Honours. In a long, handwritten letter, she admitted that she was initially sceptical that his dramatic vision would work, but was admiring of his 'spectacular and breathtaking' achievement.[8]

The success of the *Royal Family* documentary and the investiture had a real impact. The Queen personally noted the increased size and enthusiasm of the crowds, anecdotal evidence matched by favourable opinion-poll findings. And so, with a positive wind at her back, the dawn of the 1970s marked another way point in the measured modernizing of the monarchy.

During a visit to the New Zealand city of Wellington in March 1970, the royal car came to a halt and the Queen, Prince Philip, Princess Anne and Prince Charles all emerged and started shaking hands and making small talk – 'Have you been waiting long?' –

with the somewhat startled crowds. Thus began the 'walkabout', the name derived from the Aboriginal Australian term 'to go wandering'. A little piece of history was made as the Queen became the first sovereign since Charles II, more than three centuries previously, to mingle with her people. Back in Britain, she successfully repeated the trick during visits to Coventry and Manchester. 'There was a clear policy of making her much more accessible,' observed the BBC's royal correspondent Ronald Allison. 'Suddenly, the lady on the schoolroom wall, on the postage stamp, was a real person.'[9]

But a real person who also cost the taxpayer a lot of money. It was not some radical politician who first raised the sensitive issue regarding the cost of the monarchy but Prince Philip, four months after the investiture, during a conversation with American journalists on the NBC television programme *Meet the Press* in November 1969.

He told the surprised TV inquisitors that the Royal Family were about to go into the red, and went on to explain that they had already sold their private yacht *Bloodhound*, that they may have to move into smaller premises and he might have to give up polo. It was a classic example of what the duke himself called 'dontopedalogy' – putting one's foot in one's mouth – as he was wildly mistaken if he thought he would find any sympathy from the British public. The country, on the brink of a tumultuous decade of industrial action and political radicalism, which culminated in the miners' strike and the imposition of the three-day working week, was angry and hostile.

Though the Queen's response is not recorded, she cannot have been happy that her husband had exploded this sensitive issue in such a blunt, headline-grabbing manner. Although she lived in palaces, castles and stately homes, had the world's finest collection of jewellery and travelled on board a royal yacht that came complete with a twenty-six-piece Royal Marine band, she carefully projected an image of frugality and modesty. She was a monarch who turned off lights to conserve electricity, sent her eldest son to look for a lost dog leash with the ringing rebuke that 'dog leads cost money' and stored her morning breakfast cereal in a plastic Tupperware container. Less welcome was the story that she was the world's richest woman – an unwanted accolade that her senior advisers insisted was way wide of the mark.

In May 1971, against this sensitive financial landscape, lawmakers set up a Select Committee to review the Civil List, a fixed annual allowance that covered costs generated by the running of the monarchy, including payment of staff salaries and maintaining the upkeep of the Royal Households. Inflation had eaten into the original Civil List, which made it difficult to balance the royal books. Hence the genesis of Prince Philip's provocative comments. However, politicians were in a fighting mood. Firebrand Labour Member of Parliament Willie Hamilton described the request for greater royal funding as, 'the most brazenly insensitive pay claim made in the last two hundred years'.[10]

Ultimately, the Royal Family got the raise they required, but it was a surprisingly confrontational process. During its review, the inquiry inadvertently illuminated the relationship between the Queen and her mother, after lawmakers pointedly asked why the Queen Mother's personal allowance had increased even though, at seventy-one, she was well past retirement age and undertook far fewer engagements than in previous years. It was a question that perplexed even long-serving royal courtiers.

The issue of the Queen, the Queen Mother and their financial relationship began in earnest following the death of George VI. As Queen Consort, Elizabeth had grown used to being the star of the show, but after the King's passing she struggled to accept second billing. Her eldest daughter, who was the reluctant agent of her demotion, felt guilty about her mother's unhappiness and as a result found it difficult to deny her anything, especially when it concerned the royal coffers.

At the beginning of the reign, there was much internal correspondence about the Queen Mother's desire to live in the palatial splendour of Marlborough House, the home of Queen Mary who had died shortly before the Coronation. A review of royal finances concluded, much to the Queen Mother's disappointment, that it was too expensive to renovate this imposing Grade I listed mansion for her sole use. Over the years, however, her daughter indulged her in other ways.

She restored several properties for the Queen Mother's benefit, namely Clarence House in central London and the Castle of Mey, a desolate pile in the far north of Scotland which the Queen Mother had bought on a whim in 1952. The Sovereign also expanded her mother's home of Birkhall on the Balmoral estate and confirmed her continued occupancy of Royal Lodge, the country house in the middle of Windsor Great Park which she and her husband, as the Duke and Duchess of York, were given in 1931 by George V.

Even years after the King's death, the Queen just couldn't say no to her mother's extravagances. She always felt that it was such a tragedy to have been widowed at the young age of fifty-one. As a result, the Queen Mother was granted the equivalent of an open chequebook, which she used to the full. 'She had none of the usual Scottish carefulness,' recalled former assistant private secretary Sir Edward Ford. 'She didn't seem to know anything about money.'[11]

With half a dozen or so limousines and a staff comprising, among others, three chauffeurs, five chefs and numerous pages, footmen and butlers, the Queen Mother was cocooned in an Edwardian time warp of excess and indulgence. Admonishment came there none. The most the Queen could muster was a plaintive note saying 'Oh dear, Mummy!' after she had spent a small fortune on new bloodstock for her stables.[12] When it was finally reported in public that she had a staff of fifty and an overdraft of £4 million, most observers, including Prince Charles, thought the figure way too low.

Just as during Princess Margaret's romantic vacillation regarding Group Captain Peter Townsend, the Queen was prepared to accept a degree of short-term criticism of the Crown in exchange for her sister's ultimate happiness, she was also willing to endure some public censure of her mother's finances if it kept her content and avoided personal confrontation.

The Queen Mother was the unseen power behind the throne, a matriarchal figure who wielded enormous influence. Beneath the twinkly, somewhat exaggerated, personality was a strong-willed, deeply conservative woman who enjoyed the ear of her daughter in daily phone calls which in themselves were a kind of vaudeville act, as the operator intoned: 'Your Majesty, Her Majesty, Your Majesty.' What is more, the Queen listened and took note of what she said. As exasperating as she might be at times, the Sovereign usually found it easier to go along with her mother's wishes than oppose her will.

Drinks before lunch at Royal Lodge after Sunday morning service was the usual time for the Queen Mother to buttonhole her eldest daughter. 'Her mindset was pre-war,' argued a former private secretary, suggesting that the monarchy would have modernized much sooner but for her interference.[13] Courtiers soon realized that the Queen had to be firmly convinced of a course of action in case she was waylaid by her mother, whose views, however old-fashioned, had to be taken into account. Although at heart the Queen was also a traditionalist, who regularly followed the precedents set by her late father, the Queen Mother was always around to reinforce this viewpoint, particularly with regard to family matters. She was not always successful, though, notably concerning the schooling of the Queen's children.

Even if she failed to convince her daughter, she invariably found a willing ally in the heir to the throne. Prince Charles doted on her, seeing her as his surrogate mother, while she thought of him as the son she never had and spoilt him accordingly. As historian Graham Turner observed: 'Although she was deeply fond of her mother, the Queen often felt thoroughly irritated at the Queen Mother's indulgence of Charles's foibles and resented the fact that she too often gave him a soft ride when a gentle word of reproof might have helped him more.'[14] During his twenties, the Prince of Wales imitated the grand comfort of his grandmother with an indulgent lifestyle that included a valet whose duties included ironing the prince's money for the church collection and squeezing the royal toothpaste onto the royal toothbrush each night. Charles had a love of high living that neither his mother nor father could understand.

Although the Queen Mother had lost out in her contention that her grandchildren should be educated in the palace, where her voice was heard loudest was in relation to the Duke and Duchess of Windsor. It was the Queen Mother's fixed view that her husband's life had been cut short because of the stresses and strains of his unwanted position as King. That he was a heavy smoker who died of lung cancer had seemingly little to do with it. Her stern attitude had thus ensured that, since the 1936 abdication, the duke and duchess had enjoyed only very occasional contact with members of the Royal Family.

The Queen had briefly and reluctantly visited the couple at the London Clinic in 1965, where he was recovering from an eye operation, during which they discussed their funeral arrangements. Her uncle informed her that he had bought a burial plot in Baltimore for them both if the Royal Family insisted on the original arrangement, that he be buried alone at Frogmore in the grounds of Windsor Castle. The prospect of a former King of England and his wife being interred outside the country was a proposal that the Sovereign could not countenance – whatever her mother might say. After some back and forth it was agreed that, in death, Wallis Simpson would be allowed to lie next to her ducal husband at Frogmore. The only other occasion that the Windsors mingled with the Royal Family was when the Queen invited them to the unveiling of a plaque in memory of Queen Mary at Marlborough House in 1967. Apart from that, there was silence.

From time to time, a brave courtier would suggest inviting the Windsors to a social function such as Royal Ascot, but the Queen, knowing what her mother would say, quickly blocked any such proposal. Even Prince Charles lobbied his grandmother to invite them to Windsor for the weekend, but he too dropped the idea when he realized how difficult she would find a prolonged encounter with a man whom she blamed for her husband's premature death.

In May 1972, with the ex-King's health rapidly deteriorating, the Queen did agree to a death-bed meeting with him during a State visit to France. There was more than a touch of the macabre about this fifteen-minute encounter. The purpose behind the trip across the English Channel was to ensure Britain's smooth entry into the Common Market or European Economic Community, the precursor to the European Union. Nothing could be allowed to overshadow this diplomatic triumph for Prime Minister Edward Heath – and that included the dying royal. The duke's physician, Dr Jean Thin, was summoned to Paris and bluntly informed by the British ambassador, Christopher Soames, that he could die before or after the State visit but not during. That would be politically disastrous. As a result, Soames would call the French doctor every evening at six o'clock for a medical update.

Fortunately, when the time came, the Duke of Windsor was well enough to see the Queen, and insisted on getting dressed and receiving her in his home on the western edge of Paris. When she arrived he stood and bowed, leaving the doctors worried that his various drips – the 'damned rigging' as he called it – would come apart. The Queen was deeply moved, not only by her uncle's gallantry but also by his remarkable similarity in looks to her own father. It brought back a cascade of memories which, according to one observer, left her with 'tears in her eyes'.[15]

He died nine days later on 28 May 1972 and his body was returned to Britain, where he lay in state for two days in St George's Chapel at Windsor Castle. More than 60,000 people filed past his coffin to pay their respects. The funeral service itself left the Queen with a tricky question of protocol. It was due to take place two days after the annual Trooping the Colour parade, so the question was raised as to whether the popular and time-honoured event should be cancelled. If he had been a reigning monarch that would, of course, have been the case, but as a private citizen living abroad, Court mourning was no longer appropriate.

In the event, the Queen insisted that her uncle's passing should be marked. Knowing that the duke loved the skirl of the bagpipes and was a keen practitioner himself, Trooping the Colour went ahead on 3 June and included an Act of Remembrance in the form of a minute's silence and a bagpipe lament.

The funeral service itself, which took place in St George's Chapel on 5 June, lasted just half an hour. In spite of its brevity, Prince Charles described the ceremony as 'simple, dignified to perfection, colourful and wonderfully British'.[16] However, the achingly thin Duchess of Windsor was nervy and disorientated throughout. It got to the point where the Queen, who was seated beside her, showed 'a motherly and nanny-like tenderness and kept putting her hand on the Duchess's arm or glove' according to the Countess of Avon, wife of the former Prime Minister Sir Anthony Eden.[17] It was a rare sign of affection in public.

That said, later that same year she spoke with humour and feeling about her long marriage when the royal couple celebrated their silver wedding anniversary with a Service of Thanksgiving at Westminster Abbey, followed by lunch at the Guildhall in central London. In her speech, she told her audience: 'If I am asked what I think about family life after twenty-five years of marriage, I can answer with equal simplicity and conviction, I am for it.'[18]

For all the platitudes, theirs remained a sparky marriage, with plenty of fireworks along the way. The Queen realized long ago that Philip's flashes of temper came and went like a summer rainstorm. Whenever he said to her 'You're talking rubbish', which he did on numerous occasions, she either ignored him or smartly changed the subject. During one altercation on board the Royal Yacht *Britannia*, she told her private secretary Martin Charteris: 'I'm simply not going to appear until Philip is in a better temper.'[19] Whatever their disagreements, at the end of the day they still climbed into the same king-sized bed at Buckingham Palace.

Despite the Queen's ringing public endorsement of her marriage, it still failed to stop the persistent rumours about Philip and his alleged extra-marital affairs. Ever since the 'party girl' rumpus in the mid-1950s, which had prompted an official denial, there had been continual speculation that Philip had not been faithful. Evidence, though, was circumstantial. His office was staffed by pretty girls, he always made a beeline for the most attractive female in the room at private and even public functions, and he enjoyed flirting with good-looking women on the dance floor. Though biographer Sarah Bradford did once break cover and suggested that he had affairs, she later backtracked.

Sacha, Duchess of Abercorn, almost twenty-five years his junior, was in the frame for a time, as was Lady Penny Romsey who was his carriage driving partner. Sacha Abercorn conceded she had a passionate friendship for more than twenty years, but it wasn't a full relationship. She was his intellectual 'playmate' who had bonded with him through a shared interest in the Swiss psychiatrist Carl Jung. 'When I see the tabloids,' he once grumbled to Lady Mountbatten, 'I think I might as well have done it.'[20]

The Queen always gave him the latitude to be himself and, in common with many men, he enjoyed the company of pretty and interesting members of the opposite sex. As Michael Mann, the former Dean of Windsor, observed: 'He is attracted by very good-looking women, but I don't think he's ever fallen in love with anyone else since they married.'[21]

While Prince Philip was enjoying himself at a party, she always knew that she could rely on her great friend, Patrick Plunket, to keep her entertained. She had known Plunket, often described as the brother she never had, since the war. He was guaranteed to make any party go with a swing. Plunket, who became Deputy Master of the Household, brought this zest for life to organizing the Queen's social life, be it weekend shooting parties or grand balls at Windsor. During such gatherings, he would always keep an eye out for his boss to make sure that she was being properly looked after. If Prince Philip was dancing with some attractive guest and the Queen was looking a little lonely, he would whisk her onto the dance floor and keep her amused.

Her Majesty and Plunket would even go to the cinema together, dine at discreet Italian restaurants and watch her favourite TV programmes in her apartment at Buckingham Palace. As his cousin Lady Annabel Goldsmith recalled: 'He adored her from the outset. They enjoyed a very special connection. He was the one member of her staff who could talk to her on equal terms.'[22]

When he died prematurely in 1975, a sign of her closeness to him was that, in a break with tradition, she attended both his funeral and memorial service. She was also involved in the writing of his obituary in *The Times*. Later, she had a memorial pavilion built in his honour in Windsor Great Park. Months after his death she still keenly felt his loss.

Theirs was a very royal marriage; Philip and Elizabeth were from a generation that expected loyalty, if not fidelity. She was prepared to forgive him almost anything because he had been such a supportive and steadfast consort. Her sister, however, was not as fortunate in her choice of marital partner. The lengthy disintegration of her marriage to photographer Lord Snowdon involved not just the warring couple but also the Queen, who had to navigate the best course for the monarchy.

As Snowdon himself pointed out, in the beginning all went swimmingly. They were glamorous, modern and hard-working, the very symbols of the Swinging Sixties as they raced round London on his motorbike or in his Mini. Together they wrote speeches, learned to water-ski and travelled the world. They also had two much-loved children: a son, David, was born in November 1961 and Sarah came along in May 1964. Eventually, though, things started to unravel.

After a few years Snowdon, as his close friends had predicted, tired of the straitjacket of royal life. He abandoned his role as royal consort to pursue his photographic career. Possessive and lonely, Margaret would track him down, only for him to pull further away. While the princess could be imperious, having been raised to expect deference, Snowdon became cruel and mocking towards her, leaving malicious notes in various places for her to find. They both took lovers and in the early 1970s began leading separate lives. In public, they were all smiles and maintained an impeccable display of togetherness. Snowdon, though, refused Margaret's demand that he move out of Kensington Palace and agree to a formal separation. Instead, the couple suffered several more years of dramatic and bitter scenes, many in front of embarrassed friends, servants and members of the family.

The breakdown of Margaret's marriage was deeply upsetting and troubling for the Queen and the Queen Mother. The Queen loved her sister, but was also very fond of her brother-in-law. She appreciated his creative abilities as well as his efforts on behalf of the monarchy, particularly his stewardship of Prince Charles's investiture in Wales. The Queen Mother, who had an eye for a good photograph and painting, admired his talent as a documentary-maker and a photographer. In turn, his behaviour towards them was always cheerful, charming and correct without being obsequious. They knew from lifelong experience that Margaret could be capricious, domineering and downright rude, and so, as even-handed as they tried to be, their sympathies tended towards Snowdon.

Or, more accurately, their concerns lay with the couple's children. Both the Sovereign and her mother worried about the impact on David and Sarah, and the Queen paid particular attention to her young niece. She brought Sarah to Balmoral on holiday and would take her horse riding, watching from the sidelines when she took part in gymkhanas.

As much as she indulged her sister, even the Monarch was taken aback when, in the summer of 1973, she heard that Margaret had taken up with a rather aimless young man named Roddy Llewellyn. He was seventeen years her junior, which made him just a year older than the Sovereign's future son-in-law, Captain Mark Phillips, who was betrothed to Princess Anne. Llewellyn's arrival, the archetypal 'toy boy' of popular imagination, complicated an already fraught situation and drove a wedge between the sisters. The Queen believed that if news of Margaret's behaviour became public, it would have a devastating effect on the monarchy and open the institution up for ridicule. 'How can we get her out of the gutter?' she is said to have lamented to an unnamed courtier.[23] Other reports had the Monarch referring to Margaret's 'guttersnipe life',[24] a sign of the uncharacteristic divide between the sisters.

In spite of the brewing behind-the-scenes drama, Princess Margaret and Lord Snowdon were all smiles at the wedding of Princess Anne and Olympic gold-medal-winning equestrian Captain Mark Phillips at Westminster Abbey in November 1973, which was a televised spectacular with an estimated worldwide audience of 500 million. Although the Queen may have had reservations about Anne's choice of husband – Prince Charles called him 'Fog' because he considered him to be wet and thick – she readily gave her permission to the marriage. Drily, she suggested that, given the couple's enthusiasm for all things equine, their children would be four-legged.

Horses were very much on her mind around this time as she had, for once, hit a winning streak. Jockey Joe Mercer received a grateful note from the Queen, the owner of the three-year-old filly Highclere, after winning the 1,000 Guineas at Newmarket in May 1974. She wrote: 'For once I don't remember much about the race owing to the excitement, but I do know that a homebred Guineas winner has given me more pleasure than anything for a long time.'[25]

But Highclere wasn't finished and went on to triumph in the Prix de Diane, the French equivalent of the Oaks, at Chantilly Racecourse, north of Paris, the following month. After the race, winning jockey Joe Mercer and trainer Dick Hern flew back to London on a private plane. They were polishing off a bottle of champagne when the pilot was diverted to Heathrow Airport in West London. The Queen had invited the rather bedraggled duo to dinner at Windsor Castle. When they arrived by limousine, Her Majesty was standing outside in the rain waiting to greet them. 'Come in, my warriors,' she said, and led them into dinner with her, Princess Margaret, Prince Philip and Lord Mountbatten.[26] Pride of place on the centre of the table was the gold Prix de Diane cup that was presented to the winning owner. As racing writer Sean Smith observed: 'It was a privileged peep into the Queen's private world of simply relaxing family enjoyment.'[27]

Appearances, though, were deceptive. The absence of Lord Snowdon from this royal gathering was noticeable. At this time the Sovereign had been encouraging her sister and her husband to try to resolve their differences – at least for the sake of their children. She soon realized, however, that matters were too far gone for a cosmetic makeover and was forced to deal with a sibling whose life was rapidly unravelling. This emotional messiness was new territory for the Sovereign. Such was Margaret's parlous medical state that the princess cancelled all royal engagements in November 1974. On one occasion she phoned a friend, who happened to be hosting a social event at home, and threatened suicide: 'If you don't come over, I'll throw myself out of the window.' Her friend rang the Queen, who calmly replied: 'Carry on with your house party. Her bedroom is on the ground floor.'[28]

Her sister's ill health, both mental and physical, was of continued concern for the Monarch. Though Margaret's ladies-in-waiting were keeping an eye on her behaviour, they could only recommend a course of treatment, while her sister could command. In the end, a lady-in-waiting finally contacted Her Majesty and asked her to intervene. Consequently, she delayed her engagements and drove to Kensington Palace to see her sister. 'I feel exactly like the night nurse taking over from the day nurse,' she remarked drily, before taking Margaret for a quiet weekend at Windsor Castle.[29]

The situation had become increasingly untenable. In late November 1975, Lord Snowdon wrote an anguished letter to the Queen stating that he could no longer tolerate living at Kensington Palace. 'The atmosphere is appalling for all concerned – the children, the staff, the few remaining loyal friends and she and I both.'[30]

His letter genuinely shocked his sister-in-law, who had to admit that her sporadic efforts at counselling had come to naught. All that now remained was to oversee the practicalities of when the separation should be made public. It was eventually decided that, in the interests of the children, the news be announced during Easter 1976 at a time when they would be on holiday and could spend time with their parents. Everyone concerned now faced the sad fact that Margaret was about to become the first member of the Royal Family to divorce since Henry VIII and Anne of Cleves in 1540.

Any hopes that the split could be managed by the palace were shattered, though, when the *News of the World* published pictures of the princess, clad in a swimsuit, and her 'tanned toy boy' Roddy Llewellyn, on holiday together in Mustique in February 1976. She was now seen as the adulterer in the failed relationship, while her hard-working professional photographer husband was cast as the injured and innocent party. Though this was a grotesquely unfair narrative, it was one that stuck. Even the Queen and Queen Mother felt that Margaret had not done enough to try to save her marriage. 'They didn't realize the depths of Margaret's despair,' observed her friend and biographer Christopher Warwick. 'They remembered her as the trickster, the prankster, the little girl getting things her way. There was a feeling it was mainly her fault.'[31]

There was also concern that the acrimonious break-up could overshadow the fast-approaching Silver Jubilee celebrations the following year. The Queen worried that no one would turn up to see them – or her. With the economy in freefall, inflation rampant and unemployment figures rising, the first signs were not hopeful. Local councils reported few applications to stage street parties, the demand for souvenirs, no matter how tacky, was weak and events were cancelled.

She need not have worried, though, as the welcoming crowds

during an initial eleven-day tour of Scottish cities in May 1977 suggested that her jubilee was, after all, going to be well received. A million people filled The Mall to see the Queen and Prince Philip ride in the Gold State Coach from Buckingham Palace to St Paul's Cathedral for a Service of Thanksgiving on 7 June. This was followed by hundreds of local parades and thousands of neighbourhood street parties. The proliferation of red, white and blue bunting and Union flags was reminiscent of Britain's wartime victory celebrations in 1945.

Over three months, she visited thirty-six counties in the UK and Northern Ireland, and witnessed millions of people taking to the streets to greet the passing royal parade. Her Majesty was genuinely touched by the reception. 'I am simply amazed, I had no idea,' she said repeatedly, overheard at the time by a courtier.[32]

Her visit to Northern Ireland, though, proved more challenging than hoped. Riven by sectarian conflict – the Protestant majority wanted to continue the centuries-old union with mainland Britain, while the Catholic minority wanted to become part of Ireland – before the Queen and Prince Philip arrived there were arson attacks and explosions, as well as violent street demonstrations. On the eve of her two-day tour in early August, a young demonstrator and a British soldier were shot dead. When she arrived, 32,000 troops and police were on duty, with the Provisional wing of the Irish Republican Army vowing that the British would pay dearly for the 'Queen's champagne parties on a few acres of Irish soil'.[33]

Such was the security surrounding the brief visit – her time on Northern Irish soil was limited to less than six hours at a cost of millions of pounds in security – that the Queen spent much of the time on board the Royal Yacht *Britannia* and was whisked away to a highly regulated public engagement at Hillsborough Castle by helicopter, the first time in her reign she had used this form of transport, which she considered dangerous. This was a sign, if any more were needed, of the concern for the Queen's safety. She was, a British minister later confided, very anxious and 'terribly, terribly tense'. When she had completed her last engagement at the University of Ulster, he recalled that Prince Philip patted her hand and said: 'There now, it's over. Unless they sink the *Britannia*, we're safe.'[34]

If that was the low point, the crowning personal glory of the Silver Jubilee celebrations was when the Queen received a phone call on 15 November 1977 informing her of the birth of her first grandchild, Peter Phillips, the son of Princess Anne. With regard to high points of the Silver Jubilee year, it was a close-run thing as 1977 also saw Dunfermline, her greatest-ever racehorse, win two of the five British Classics races: the Oaks and the St Leger. The arrival of her grandson edged it, though. Indeed, such was her joy that she uncharacteristically delayed an investiture in the ballroom at Buckingham Palace for ten minutes so that she could call Prince Philip, who was in Germany. He had always been close to his straightforward daughter, and admired her gung-ho spirit and robust independence.

Three and a half years later, Zara was born and Anne signalled that she was going to raise her children very differently from her mother. No governesses, palaces or titles for these two. They were brought up in the country on a working farm, Gatcombe Park in Gloucestershire which the Queen had purchased in 1976, and went to the local nursery. Anne was able to juggle motherhood with an exacting role as the hands-on president of the charity Save the Children, a position she had accepted in 1970.

The Queen and Prince Philip left Anne, fourth in line to the throne, very much to her own devices, proud of the way she had managed to combine domestic and working life. She was a successful product of her parents' philosophy of 'sink or swim'. Their offspring were expected to set up their own administrative offices, choose charities that reflected their interests and, perhaps most importantly, use their own judgement to find a partner. As a former private secretary observed: 'They got the message that they were expected to overcome their difficulties for themselves and get on with it.'[35] As the Queen and Prince Philip were away so often, it was a policy born out of necessity and belief. It enjoyed mixed results, particularly with their eldest son and heir.

While the royal couple's dispassionate style of parenting had worked for Princess Anne, she had neither the responsibilities nor expectations that came with being the heir to the throne. Charles had a much more public and tortuous journey, particularly when it came to his eventual choice of consort, where breeding and background were as important as romantic attachment.

As numerous courtiers have since observed, perhaps with the certainty of hindsight, if the Queen had shown as much diligence about the choice of royal brides, particularly the future Queen, as she had about the breeding of her horses, the House of Windsor may not have been in such a mess. Unlike Queen Victoria, who told her children who and when they were going to marry, giving them no opportunity for discussion, the reigning Sovereign and her consort had allowed their own sons and daughter almost complete latitude.

Not that parental interference was a sure-fire way of guaranteeing marital success, of course. When the previous Prince of Wales, later Edward VIII, fell in love with Lady Rosemary Leveson-Gower, the daughter of a controversial aristocratic family, he was told by George V and Queen Mary that she was not suitable, as there was a strain of mental illness and chronic disreputable behaviour that tainted her close relations. If he had been allowed to marry her, the course of the House of Windsor would have been very different.

The detached approach of the Queen and Prince Philip

gave others, notably the dynastically ambitious Lord Louis Mountbatten, the opportunity to interfere in the torrid love life of Prince Charles. In a letter to the prince, written shortly after Princess Anne's wedding, Mountbatten advised him to 'sow his wild oats' before marrying an unsullied virgin.[36] Of course, the virgin he had in mind was a member of his own family, his granddaughter Amanda Knatchbull, who was almost nine years the prince's junior.

If Elizabeth and Philip shied away from matchmaking in their eldest son's love life, Mountbatten showed no such hesitation. He encouraged Charles to join Amanda and her family on holiday, and they spent weekends together at Broadlands, the Mountbatten family seat, as well as at Balmoral and Sandringham. As they were second cousins, their budding romance passed mainly unnoticed. She was part of the aristocratic family furniture that surrounded the prince. In any case, the media were much more interested in the many glamorous young women he was seen with at public and private events. Eventually, his behaviour as an erstwhile royal Lothario became so obvious that Prince Philip, rather than the Queen, broke cover and wrote an admonishing note to his son for 'parading' his paramours before the public.[37]

Whatever the public and private efforts the prince made towards finding a consort, his heart belonged to another woman, married mother of two Camilla Parker Bowles, whose husband Andrew was a major in a Household regiment, the Blues and Royals. Charles had dated her before she married, but she remained the one that got away. His continued pursuit of a married woman, however, offended many of his fellow officers. After discreet conversations between the palace and the regiment, senior royal officials formally informed the Queen that the Blues and Royals were 'unhappy' that her son was sleeping with a major's wife.[38]

The Queen made no comment nor, crucially, did she speak

to her son about his behaviour. Such a confrontation would, according to courtiers, have been totally out of character. Much rather an hour with her red boxes, which acted as the Monarch's security blanket, than address such an intimate family issue. In the end, she did act by putting out the word that Mrs Parker Bowles was not to be invited to any royal events, and that included Charles's thirtieth birthday party at Buckingham Palace in 1978. The Queen Mother followed suit.

In fairness, Mrs Parker Bowles was, the Queen hoped, but a temporary sideshow. As far as Charles's parents were concerned, the main romantic focus of his life was his quiet pursuit of the young Amanda, a girl they all knew and liked. Dickie Mountbatten, who was eager to cement his family's royal connections, gave the Queen regular updates on the progress of the relationship. His zeal to make a match between Amanda and the future King extended to lobbying to have his granddaughter and himself added to a two-week tour of India, which the prince was due to undertake in early 1980, but both the Queen and Prince Philip expressed their doubts. Philip thought that Dickie would steal the limelight from his son, while the Queen was concerned about Amanda. She thought that her presence would merely excite wild press speculation about a possible engagement. If the relationship came to naught, the young woman would be publicly humiliated. Amanda's father John Brabourne agreed.

In the event, the couple took matters into their own hands. Sometime in the summer of 1979, Charles did propose to Amanda. She refused his suit and diplomatically explained that, although they were great friends and would remain so, royal life was not for her.

There the matter rested, at least for the time being. Everyone expected the indefatigable Dickie to try to revive the romance, but tragically it was not to be. In late August 1979, while he and his family were on holiday in Classiebawn Castle, his summer home on the north-west coast of Ireland, his boat *Shadow V* was blown up by the Irish Republican Army, the militant wing of the Catholic cause to unify Ireland, during a fishing trip. Of the seven people on board, only three survived: Mountbatten's daughter and son-in-law, Patricia and John Brabourne, and their fourteen-year-old son Timothy were seriously injured; Dickie, Timothy's twin brother Nicholas, John's elderly mother Doreen and a local boy named Paul Maxwell all died.

The Queen was at Balmoral when she heard the horrific news. The Brabournes were among her closest friends. She had been a bridesmaid at the wedding of her childhood friend Patricia, whose husband John had been the guiding hand behind the tremendously successful *Royal Family* documentary. With Mountbatten's death, the Queen had lost a living link to her father and his royal generation. She had known him all her life. He had been the family's éminence grise; adviser and meddler-in-chief. A former courtier described their relationship in these terms: 'The Queen's attitude was that he was her Uncle Dickie and she was very, very fond of him, but sometimes she wished he'd shut up. Once she said: "I always say yes, yes, yes to Dickie, but I don't listen to him".[39]

Prince Charles was devastated. 'I have lost someone infinitely special in my life,' he wrote later.[40] His great-uncle had been his friend, mentor, benefactor and surrogate parent, and now he was gone.

As with Margaret's divorce, the Queen's first thoughts were for the children. When she was told that Patricia was confined to her hospital bed as she recovered from her injuries, she invited Timothy and his sister Amanda to stay at Balmoral. Years later, Timothy could still remember the warm glow of the Queen's welcome. He recalled the feeling of a 'mother duck gathering up her lost young ... [her] default setting of love and care ... wrapping us up in a sort of motherliness'.[41]

This then was the human side of the Sovereign, the Queen as family matriarch and consoler-in-chief.

CHAPTER NINE

THEN ALONG CAME DIANA

T HE QUEEN WAS HARD-WORKING, prudent and abstemious. She weighed around 8 stone, ate sparingly and enjoyed good British fare: Welsh lamb, Scottish salmon, game from Sandringham and freshly churned butter from the dairy at Windsor Castle. Excess was never on the menu – either for herself or the monarchy.

She explained her rigorous dietary routine to US President Jimmy Carter when he visited Buckingham Palace in May 1977. As he recalled: 'She pointed out that her waist had to be watched very closely because she had [to wear] seven different tunics, her uniforms ... for the seven different guard troops, during the course of a year and that she couldn't afford to change the costumes and had to wear the same size for a number of years.'[1] The Queen, who is one of the world's wealthiest women, meant of course that she couldn't afford the time and upheaval involved in having these elaborate costumes altered every year.

It was not only her formal regalia that caused her to watch her weight. As the most travelled monarchy in history, she recognized that planning for her visits took place months, sometimes years, in advance. She may be being fitted for gowns and dresses that would not see the light of day for quite some time. Hence the careful diet to avoid unnecessary alterations. If her wardrobe was a metaphor for her reign – steady, unchanging and predictable – so too was her daily routine. It had the cosy familiarity of a well-worn shoe, a shoe that a member of her staff would first break in.

At eight in the morning, her personal maid arrives with a calling tray bearing a pot of Earl Grey tea, before running her bath to a depth of 7 inches and a temperature of 22°C – tested by thermometer. Her clothes are laid out, her hairdresser is waiting and her personal piper plays beneath her windows at nine o'clock sharp.[2] Then, her day continues with a modest breakfast of cereal followed by a ten o'clock meeting with her private secretary, at which matters of State are discussed and correspondence considered, especially those memos and letters in the famous red boxes. Even late into her reign, when most people her age have retired, the Queen is kept busy with the nation's business. This may include a greeting or farewell to an ambassador, an investiture or a lunch with charity and business heads.

If she is off duty, she eats a light lunch, finds time to walk her dogs and settles down to afternoon tea at five o'clock, during which members of her staff or her family may join her. It's here where she picks up the latest chatter about the doings of her family and the palace staff. 'A good gossip is a wonderful tonic,' she once remarked, when she was kept up to date with all the 'scandal' by a loyal cohort led by her dresser Bobo MacDonald.[3] In her day, Princess Diana was a regular visitor and often brought William and Harry along to see 'Gan gan'.

At six o'clock in the evening a drinks tray appears, then at quarter past eight it's dinner time. This regularity has always meant that everyone knows where they stand, from the footman to the chef, resulting in few, if any, surprises.

If Queen Victoria were ever to return, she would find that little much has changed since her day. There is still the Order of the Garter ceremony, the State Opening of Parliament, the reception for the diplomatic corps, Christmas at Sandringham, Easter at Windsor and the much-relished summer holiday at Balmoral, the Queen's 50,000-acre estate which hugs the River Dee in the Scottish Highlands. This was perhaps the last royal kingdom, the one place where the Queen was ruler of all she surveyed.

At this Scottish seat the rhythms and routines are unchanging – apart from the daily wardrobe. The Queen has always liked the familiarity of the place, thankful that she can sleep in the same bed for six weeks continuously as she enjoys what she has called her 'hibernation'. It is a place where she is at her most secure and relaxed, surrounded by her beloved dogs and horses. House guests have tended to be friends of long-standing, or her and Philip's Hanoverian relations who were close enough to call her by the family name of 'Lilibet'. They were and are people who are familiar with the form and the codes, and who know how to treat her as Queen, blood relation or lifelong friend. Even her staff are old Balmoral hands who understand when to keep themselves scarce and when to provide attention.

As the torrent of red boxes slows to a trickle, the Queen spends her days riding, roaming around the estate, checking on improvement works, walking or, in the evening, star-gazing. It is a place where she has always been able to commune with her God through nature.

Visitors are often surprised at how much she does herself, from feeding her dogs and horses to mucking them out. It was a trait noticed early on by her first riding master, Horace Smith. He recalled: 'Princess Elizabeth's progress was very far above the average. She was very conscientious and anxious to improve her horsemanship, and her standard of riding, considering the small number of lessons that she had, soon became very high.'[4]

For most of her life she has stuck to a familiar daily routine during her Balmoral visits. After dealing with State business with her private secretary, until her mid-nineties she used to go riding. Her chosen horse was taken out earlier by a groom to ensure it was not too high-spirited. Afterwards, she may have joined the shooting party for a picnic lunch. Though she liked a brisk daily walk, these were much curtailed in her later years. Following afternoon tea, she changes for dinner, the fourth wardrobe variation in a day. Dinners are formal affairs, with ladies wearing long dresses and the men in black tie or kilts, the Queen's piper marching round the table at the end of the meal.

The pipes are not for show. She actually listens carefully and appreciates the art. On one occasion, during a dinner at her official Edinburgh residence, the Palace of Holyroodhouse, she asked a regular guest, the former Lord Provost of Edinburgh Eric Milligan, to listen to the pipes and tell her if he could hear anything off key. Milligan answered in the negative. The Queen was quietly jubilant, going on to explain that her piper had lost a finger in a bomb explosion during a tour of duty in Iraq and had offered to stand down if he couldn't manage the correct phrasing.[5] She wouldn't hear of it and insisted he play on, thus her faith in her piper proved fully justified.

That decision would have been of immense relief to the Queen's piper, as the Balmoral retreat is seen as a busman's holiday for those members of staff who accompany the Royal Family there. Duties are light and time off plentiful, plus they enjoy frequent and informal day-to-day contact with the family without the presence of many of the Royal Household – essentially, the managerial class – being present.

The Ghillies' Ball is the much-anticipated climax to the Royal

Family's Scottish holiday. It brings royalty and staff together in a blend of jovial informality, good manners and earthy tradition. During Queen Victoria's day, the balls were drunken affairs which saw servants collapsing in the ballroom and the diminutive Sovereign whisked off her feet by kilted ghillies as the pipes whirled and skirled into the early hours. Until recently the Queen chose her dancing partner, which made for a nervous evening for those who hadn't practised their Highland dancing. Mischievously, she often chose someone known for having two left feet – her Scotland Yard bodyguards were favourite targets. If he was a novice, she would indicate to the band leader to slow the pace. She takes the Highland reels very seriously. On one occasion, she was discussing a new dance and, to the surprise of the company, slipped off her shoes and manipulated her stocking feet in order to get into the correct position.

Picnics are another social ritual with traps for the unwary. Most evenings, the Queen and her family and guests enjoy a picnic in one of the shooting lodges on the estate. They are not rough and ready affairs, with boiled eggs and blankets spread out on the heather, but rather grand experiences. Acknowledging the elaborate nature of such occasions, Princess Margaret once observed: 'You can't possibly have a picnic without your butler.'[6] The Windsor picnic arrives in a specially made mobile kitchen, designed by Prince Philip, and towed by a Land Rover. Every table setting has its special place and the Queen carefully supervises the whole event.

Princess Margaret's former lady-in-waiting Lady Glenconner, who was a seasoned house guest, likes to tell the story of the time that she and her husband Colin started clearing up at the end of the meal. As they carried the crockery back to the mobile kitchen, Princess Anne asked what on earth they were doing. She advised fiercely that if they didn't put things back properly 'the Queen will be bloody angry with you'.[7]

Gulp. Even Lady Glenconner, one-time debutante of the year, scion of Holkham Hall and chat-show star, admitted that she got sweaty-palmed at the very idea of HMQ being 'bloody angry'. It is a chilling family trait: one minute fooling around, the next glaring and grand. Of course, Princess Margaret was the worst offender, but they all have that ability to turn it on and off in a heartbeat. A sure-fire way to get a glimpse of the Windsor glare is, in conversation with Prince Charles, Prince William or any of the family, to refer to the Queen as 'your mother' or 'your grandmother'. Way too chummy and lacking in respect.

As Lady Glenconner was an old Balmoral hand and had attended numerous barbecues over the years, there may be an element of exaggeration in her descriptions of the expected reactions of both Princess Anne and the Queen in order to season the yarn. What is true is that Her Majesty liked to take charge of the precise placement of dining utensils in the custom-made Land Rover.[8] This obsessive attention to detail is reminiscent of the childhood stories of the young princess carefully lining up her shoes several times each evening before she went to bed.

However, it is unusual for the Sovereign to be 'bloody angry'. Her response to a faux pas or an internal palace cock-up is far more measured and modulated. She learned from an early age that a full-blown regal rebuke can make even the stoutest heart quail. When her father George VI was in the midst of one of his 'gnashes', his outbursts of uncontrolled anger, courtiers would be left ashen-faced and trembling.

A sharp look, a raised eyebrow or a quizzical 'Are you sure?' tend to be the regal lexicon of reproof. The Queen is so controlled that when she does, very occasionally, lose her temper, those present remember the moment for the rest of their lives.

—·—

It was during one of her walks on her Scottish estate, early in August 1979, that she first encountered Lady Diana Spencer. The Queen was somewhat perplexed as she half remembered her, but had assigned the third daughter of Earl Spencer – one of her equerries from the early years of her reign – as being part of the Sandringham quadrant of her life.

This was undoubtedly because Diana had grown up on the Queen's 20,000-acre Norfolk estate, at a property known as Park House. As a little girl, she was invited over to play with Andrew and Edward and, during the Christmas holidays, to watch films. If she was mentioned at all it was as a playmate and, later, as a possible girlfriend for Prince Andrew, who was of a similar age.

During their conversation, the winsome, rosy-cheeked eighteen-year-old explained that she was staying with her newly married sister Jane and her husband, the Queen's assistant private secretary Robert Fellowes. She described Balmoral as 'magical', a sentiment that found favour with the Monarch.

The following year, in early September, the Queen met Diana at Balmoral under quite different circumstances. This time she was a guest of Prince Charles. Everyone on the estate knew what that meant. Diana was undergoing what was colloquially known as 'the Balmoral test' to see if she was suitable royal bride material. Could she divine the elusive Windsor country code or at least be a willing pupil? Those older and wiser than her had tried and failed. Some had not even bothered. Prince Charles's one-time girlfriend Anna 'Whiplash' Wallace, a Scottish heiress whose nickname derived from her fiery temper, refused at the first fence, later revealing that the idea of even going to the Windsor family seat was 'too tedious for words'.

For others, the possible marital commitment implied by joining the Royal Family at Balmoral was an attachment too far. Lady Jane Wellesley, the daughter of the Queen's friend the 8th

Duke of Wellington, bridled at the very idea of sacrificing her life on the altar of monarchy. 'Do you honestly believe I want to be Queen?' she once said, when cornered by inquisitive reporters.[9]

The bookies' favourite had been Amanda Knatchbull, Mountbatten's granddaughter, who was even given a blank cheque by the ambitious patriarch to improve her wardrobe. Amanda, like a lengthening list of eligible young ladies, eventually decided that a lifetime of sacrifice for the House of Windsor was not what she had been put on this earth for.

Others, like Sabrina Guinness, had accepted the invitation to Balmoral but then failed to crack the code. Even though her previous escorts included Jack Nicholson, Mick Jagger and David Bowie, she found herself in an intimidating world. When she joined the Royal Family for drinks, she moved to take a seat in a high-backed chair, only to be told firmly by the Queen: 'Don't sit there – that's Queen Victoria's chair.'[10] She never recovered her equilibrium after being admonished by the Head of State. On a different occasion, another member of the Royal Family delivered a similar reproof to a friend of the then Lady Diana Spencer and, according to others, the same happened to Tony Blair when he and Cherie arrived for the Prime Minister's traditional autumn weekend.

This routine has the feeling of a long-running family in-joke, the Windsors' equivalent of sitting on an embarrassingly placed whoopee cushion or skidding on a banana skin. Their sense of humour is somewhat Teutonic in the sense of laughing at another's misfortune or *Schadenfreude*. The younger royals at this time, in particular Prince Andrew, hailed from the bread-roll-throwing academy of schoolboy humour. It is a kind of bullying, as the recipient, unless a very close friend, is uncertain how to react – throw one back or take it on the chin?

By contrast, Her Majesty's wit is on the dry side, like her evening

Martini. She and her husband would smile conspiratorially at one another when things went wrong on a royal tour, the classic example being their visit to California in 1983.

Unintentional irony always tickles the regal funny bone. There is a story, possibly apocryphal, that during a regal visit to a coastal town, the mayor, resplendent in his gold chains of office, proudly showed the Sovereign around wooden cabinets in the council chamber that displayed local treasures. In one was a splendid mayoral chain embellished with gold and diamonds. When the Queen asked what it was, the mayor replied that it was a unique chain of office that was only brought out for very special occasions.[11] She needed all of Queen Mary's self-control not to burst out laughing.

Given her ingrained awareness of how those not in the immediate family can sometimes react to her presence, her admonishment of Charles's girlfriend for sitting on Queen Victoria's chair uncharacteristically jars. She has a well-deserved reputation of being a careful and thoughtful hostess, inspecting bedrooms before guests arrive and thinking of suitable books and flowers to place in their rooms. At pre-dinner drinks she is usually at her most relaxed, solicitous and humorous, such as the time when Princess Margaret was chatting to thriller writer Denys Rhodes and she asked him how he was getting on with his latest book. 'It's nearly finished,' he replied, 'but I desperately need a title.' At which point, a voice behind called out gaily, 'And I cannot think of a reason for giving you one.'[12] It was the Queen, most amused with herself at this bon mot.

So why did she embarrass Sabrina Guinness? The most benign explanation is that it was a social reflex, that she has said it so often over the years that there is an assumption that everyone knew what to expect. Or it was an unexpected lapse in someone who is constantly attuned to the sensitivities of others. Alternatively, she disapproved of Charles's cosmopolitan girlfriend, with her rock-and-roll lovers, and so this was one way of making her feelings known.

Fortunately, Diana did not get the Queen Victoria chair treatment. During that fateful visit in September 1980, the Queen expressed her satisfaction with her eldest son's choice of guest. The Spencers were well known to the Royal Family, in fact Charles had briefly dated Diana's elder sister Sarah in 1977. For her part, Lady Diana Spencer was jolly and jaunty, and she joined in. Even when she fell into a bog during a long tramp, she came up laughing. She had a dry sense of humour rather like, well, that of Her Majesty. Diana knew the form, fitted in and, to Prince Philip's relief, wasn't a stranger. 'She is one of us,' the Queen acknowledged in a letter to a friend. 'I am very fond of all three of the Spencer girls'.[13]

But that wasn't quite the whole story – Diana told me years later that before she arrived at Balmoral, she was 'terrified – shitting bricks'. Fortunately, though, she did not convey such feelings of nervousness to her fellow guests, who admired her guile when she accompanied Prince Charles on a fishing expedition on the banks of the River Dee. Every summer, photographers patrolled along the A93 road on the public side of the Dee, hoping for a glimpse of Charles with his latest squeeze. Award-winning photographer Ken Lennox, who has been taking pictures of the Royal Family in Deeside for decades, spotted the prince and noticed that there was a girl lurking nearby. By the time he had got himself into position to take a photo, the young lady in question had spotted him and very calmly walked away up the bank out of sight. When Lennox next located her, he could see that she was standing behind a tree and was using her compact mirror to watch him. In this curious cat-and-mouse game, Diana proved herself to be no ordinary quarry.

Once he had discovered her name, though, the hunt was on, and on 8 September *The Sun* newspaper splashed with the headline:

'He's in love again.' Within days, there wasn't a man, woman or child in Britain who didn't know that Lady Diana Spencer was a polite, if rather bashful, nursery-school teacher whose father was the 8th Earl Spencer and whose family home was Althorp House in Northamptonshire.

An earl's daughter at last. The Queen Mother was delighted, especially as Diana's grandmother – Ruth, Lady Fermoy – was one of her ladies-in-waiting. The Queen and Prince Philip also felt that Diana ticked all the boxes: white, Anglo-Saxon, Protestant, aristocratic and without a known past. Her uncle, Lord Fermoy, trumpeted that she had never had a lover. The royal couple were also hopeful that this development would bring to an end their eldest son's dangerous entanglement with the wife of Major Andrew Parker Bowles.

All seemed to be going swimmingly in Charles's latest courtship. While Diana was caught up in the excitement of it all, however, members of her family sounded notes of caution. Her grandmother articulated her concerns: 'Darling, you must understand that their sense of humour and lifestyle are very different and I don't think it will suit you.'[14] It was a diplomatic way of saying that she had doubts about Diana and her suitability as Charles's wife and consort, but also a warning that, even though she may be a member of the aristocracy, there was still a social and cultural divide between royalty and the upper classes.

There was also the looming presence of Mrs Parker Bowles, which was a matter of concern for both Diana and the Queen. In November 1980, Bob Edwards, editor of the *Sunday Mirror*, ran a story suggesting that Lady Diana had secretly joined Prince Charles on board the royal train in a siding at Holt, Wiltshire. Acting on the personal instructions of the Queen, the palace denounced the story and demanded a retraction. Edwards refused, quoting an 'impeccable source'.[15] Diana knew that she hadn't been on the royal train, but had a pretty good idea who had been: Camilla Parker Bowles. The scales were beginning to fall from her eyes. Unbeknownst to the Queen and her Court, another ultimately calamitous narrative was developing.

During what turned out to be a fevered Christmas and New Year at Sandringham, the influx of national and international media was such that the Queen herself felt under siege. She could not even ride out without being photographed. It was so frustrating that at one point she snapped, shouting at photographers to go away. It was a measure of her impotence and anger that her holiday was being interrupted in this unruly manner. The cause of the Queen's unease was the innocent presence of Lady Diana Spencer in the house party – again at the invitation of Her Majesty – in early January 1981. As Diana later told me: 'The Queen was fed up.'

For his part, the Prince of Wales was indecisive and confused about his marital future. This was nothing new. His romantic prevarication towards the former Camilla Shand was now a matter of profound regret. As he pondered his next move, his circle of friends weighed in on Diana's suitability. The endorsement was hardly enthusiastic. Princess Anne thought the third Spencer daughter a 'silly girl'[16] – perhaps in retaliation for Charles's own dismissal of her choice of husband, whom he referred to as 'Fog' – while Lord Mountbatten's grandson Norton Romsey and his wife Penny felt that Diana was in love with the position rather than the man.

Years later, when I was researching my biography, *Diana: Her True Story*, which was written with the complete participation and enthusiastic support of the late princess, I asked Diana and her best friend Carolyn Bartholomew that very question: position or man? Both, speaking at different times, unhesitatingly responded with 'man'. While Diana was certain in her mind about her love for Prince Charles, he was unsure. It was such a huge commitment.

The Queen was more matter-of-fact. She thought that Diana's supportive, positive nature and girlish high spirits would make an ideal foil for her often disconsolate, melancholic son. The young nursery assistant would, she thought, make a perfect companion and helpmate. At the same time, after her encounter with the scruffy ranks of the mass media in her own backyard, the Sovereign sympathized with Diana's new situation. Every time she left her shared apartment in Coleherne Court, Earls Court, she was tailed by a phalanx of photographers. Her Majesty accepted, even if her son did not, that this state of affairs couldn't continue for much longer. It was damaging both to the reputation of the Crown and Lady Diana. In part, the situation was one of Prince Charles's own making, as he had suggested in a magazine interview that thirty was a good age to marry. From the moment he celebrated that significant birthday in the autumn of 1978, the marital starting gun was fired, with every girl he so much as looked at considered a future queen.

During the siege of Sandringham, the Queen spoke to Prince Philip and he, as was his custom, dealt with the matter by writing a letter. This was not unusual, as all the royal children have received letters of some sort or other from 'Pa'. It is a traditional way the family have of broaching delicate or emotional matters. In what he considered to be a sympathetic and understanding missive, the Duke of Edinburgh outlined the issues facing both sides. The relationship had gone far enough. It should either be ended for the sake of the reputation of an innocent girl or the prince should ask for her hand in marriage. In short, stop dithering.

When the full disaster of his marriage unfolded, Charles would later tell friends that his father had bullied him into marriage, that the letter was an ultimatum. But even his own circle didn't interpret it that way. They felt that Prince Philip was simply asking him to make a decision one way or another. Charles, used to the duke's bombastic nature, read between the lines and concluded that his father, speaking also on behalf of his mother, wanted him to get on with it.

Ultimately, the letter did have the desired effect of provoking his eldest son into action. While he was away on a skiing trip in early 1981, Charles phoned Diana and said that he wanted to see her on his return as he had something important to say to her. It was arranged that she would come over to Windsor Castle on Friday 6 February.

Diana arrived at the castle around five o'clock in the afternoon and there, in the nursery, she was asked by Prince Charles if she would marry him. The setting for this life-changing moment was a bare, unremarkable room with worn green carpet and matching coloured walls adorned with ancient family photographs. Hardly the stuff of a fairy-tale romance. Not a rose or a flickering candle in sight. Even the gruff Prince Philip had managed a proposal at Balmoral 'beside some well-loved loch, the white clouds overhead and curlew crying'.[17]

Diana takes up the story: 'I laughed. I remember thinking, "This is a joke," and I said: "Yeah, OK," and laughed. He was deadly serious. He said: "You do realize that one day you will be Queen." And a voice said to me inside: "You won't be Queen, but you'll have a tough role." So I thought "OK," so I said: "Yes." I said: "I love you so much, I love you so much." He said: "Whatever love means." He said it then.' Then Prince Charles rang the Queen.[18]

'Whatever love means' – three words that came to haunt him, especially as he repeated practically the same equivocal phrase during the engagement interview, before the world's media, on 24 February 1981. Then, he said: 'Whatever "in love" means.' His ambivalence was unnerving for the princess-to-be.

Watching on unnoticed from an upper-floor window at Buckingham Palace, Her Majesty observed the couple as they paraded in front of the attendant media in the palace gardens. It was a moment of quiet triumph. After so many years of prevarication by her son, at last he had chosen a girl who had the pedigree, personality and popularity to support and nurture the future king. Finally, the kingdom seemed secure.

At this moment of triumph, though, shadowy forces were plotting to assassinate the Head of State. The success, as the Provisional IRA saw it, of Mountbatten's murder eighteen months previously had encouraged them to aim higher. This time, it was the Queen who was in the cross hairs of their murderous campaign. As the palace planners started preparing for the wedding of the year, the IRA began organizing their next deadly attack.

On 9 May, just over eleven weeks before the royal wedding, the Queen was due to open Sullom Voe oil and gas terminal on the Shetland Islands. One of Europe's largest building projects, Sullom Voe's construction had cost £1.2 billion and employed more than 6,000 workers between 1975 and 1981.[19] Unfortunately, though, at least one of the site's employees was a member of the Provisional IRA.

When the Queen was due to open the facility, over in Northern Ireland tensions were running high. The IRA hunger striker Bobby Sands had died at the Maze prison on 5 May, and consequently there was an upsurge in IRA activity alongside rioting in nationalist areas. Meanwhile, on the Shetland Islands, the IRA contact at Sullom Voe received a parcel sent over from Ireland that contained 7 pounds of gelignite and a twelve-day timer device. A second bomb was also due to arrive, but had been delayed in the post. The IRA operative, concerned that the other explosive had been intercepted by security services, hid the first bomb in a power station, set the timer and then fled back to his home nation.

Just after midday, as the Queen readied herself to give her speech and the band began to play the national anthems of both

Norway and Great Britain, there was a sharp bang from the power station about 500 yards away, the noise mainly masked by the music. Fortunately, the bomb had only partially detonated, and BP, the site's operator, was able to claim that the small explosion was just an electrical fault. If the postal service had been more efficient, and the second bomb had arrived when it was supposed to, then the Queen, Prince Philip, King Olav V of Norway and many others could have been the victims of one of the most heinous events in history.

Given the confusion surrounding the 'non explosion', the incident received little attention in the press, much to the fury of the IRA, who felt obliged to release two statements claiming responsibility. The second declared: 'Had we managed to place Saturday's bomb close enough to the British Queen, she would now be dead'.[20] Their claims were overshadowed by the attempted assassination of Pope John Paul II four days later, and the happier news that the Queen had become a grandmother for the second time following the birth of Zara Phillips, the daughter of Princess Anne and Captain Mark Phillips, on 15 May.

Just a month later, the Queen faced another assault, this time with the world watching. As she rode along The Mall on her nineteen-year-old Canadian mare Burmese, during the annual Trooping the Colour parade, six shots rang out from the crowd. A gun had been fired by seventeen-year-old Marcus Sarjeant, who was quickly wrestled to the ground by at least one guardsman, a police officer and a St John's Ambulance volunteer. Amidst a flurry of activity, the Queen, who had seen her assailant for a split second before he started shooting, was a study in calm. After many years of riding, she was able to soothe her startled mount, who was more alarmed by the horsemen of the Household Cavalry riding towards her than by the initial gunshots which, it later transpired, were blanks fired from a starting pistol.

Her Majesty, who was riding side-saddle, continued the ceremony without demur, smiling at the crowd and occasionally patting Burmese with her left hand. Lady Diana Spencer, who was attending her first Trooping as Charles's fiancée, recalled that everyone around the Queen marvelled at her sangfroid. She seemed utterly unruffled by the experience, the Sovereign airily dismissing the danger she had just faced. Prince Charles later commented that his mother was 'made of strong stuff'.[21] It took a lot to unsettle her equilibrium.

There was, too, a sense of fatalism about her behaviour. Unlike other Heads of State, she always made it clear that she wanted security kept to a minimum. Her personal protection officer knew to maintain a discreet, unobtrusive presence. It was many years into her reign, for example, before she accepted the need for police outriders to stop traffic, as she didn't want to inconvenience fellow road users. She was backed to the hilt by Prince Philip, who had little time for the cocoon of security. There is also a streak of obduracy in her make-up. She is the Queen and it has always been her choice as to whether or not she will wear a hard hat while out riding. Well into her nineties, she insisted on a Hermès scarf as her only protection.[22] Safety campaigners were worried, but as far as the Monarch was concerned she didn't want to mess up her hair in case she had to be on public parade shortly after her morning ride.

—·—

After the engagement was announced, the Queen went out of her way to make Diana feel welcome. She had deputed several courtiers, notably her lady-in-waiting Susan Hussey and Charles's assistant private secretary Oliver Everett, to show her the ropes. When Charles was away on overseas visits, the Sovereign took the future princess under her wing. She installed Diana in the principal guest room at Windsor Castle and the couple dined together frequently and walked her pack of dogs around the grounds. By then, Diana was suffering from the eating disorder bulimia nervosa, a condition of bingeing and forced vomiting.

Though her wedding-dress-makers David and Elizabeth Emanuel, and her close friends, particularly Carolyn Bartholomew, noticed her rapid weight loss, the Queen seemed not to have seen the warning signs. At the time, eating disorders were surrounded by ignorance and it would have been remarkable if the Monarch had even been aware of this condition. Even if she had spotted that Diana had been losing weight, she would have instinctively put it down to the nerves felt by many brides, particularly one whose wedding day was about to be broadcast worldwide. Although she was busy, 'The Queen made a big fuss over Diana,' according to a former courtier, setting aside as much time for her as possible.[23]

In the run-up to the wedding, Diana was based at Buckingham Palace where the Sovereign frequently invited her to join her for lunch or dinner. However Diana, nursing the secret shame of an eating disorder, made endless excuses to avoid Her Majesty's company. She did not wish to alert the Monarch to her condition. Although her future mother-in-law thought this behaviour was perplexing, she again put it down to nerves. For her part, Diana found the Queen friendly but intimidating. 'I kept myself to myself,' she recalled. 'I didn't knock on her door and ask her advice because I knew the answers myself.'[24]

Around this same time, Diana would often go down to the kitchens to while away a few minutes in idle conversation. Barefoot, wearing jeans and a sweater, she helped with the washing-up and on one occasion even buttered the toast of a junior footman. Her excursions behind the green baize door irritated several chefs, who felt she was spying on them. Eventually, the Queen tactfully asked her to stop these visits as it was upsetting the equilibrium that exists between upstairs and downstairs. What she didn't realize was that Diana went to the kitchens so that she could gorge on packets of cereal and cream. Then she would make herself sick afterwards.

With preparations for the royal nuptials moving along apace, the Queen was fully and enthusiastically invested in her son's marriage. Not only did she pay £28,000 for Diana's oval sapphire-and-diamond engagement ring, she also footed the bill for the opulent gala ball held at Buckingham Palace in the week of the wedding, where the extensive guest list included the US First Lady Nancy Reagan, together with all the crowned heads of Europe. The splendid, extravagant affair was a personal triumph for the Queen. It was certainly a night to remember, though the grand event was set against a backdrop of high and mounting unemployment, riots in deprived areas of London and Liverpool, and a government, led by Prime Minister Margaret Thatcher that preached and practised austerity and low taxes.

While the juxtaposition of two very different Britains was striking – particularly to foreign television crews – on the wedding day itself, 29 July 1981, the focus was on other things, chiefly: Diana's meringue of a dress and its record-breaking 25-foot train; the romantic contention of the Archbishop of Canterbury, Dr Robert Runcie, that the event was 'the stuff of which fairy tales are made'; and the enthusiastic crowds that lined the route from St Paul's Cathedral to Buckingham Palace to watch the horse-drawn parade.[25] It was only later that the most senior member of the Church of England admitted to doubts, the prelate believing that the couple were ill-suited and that the marriage would not last.

Inside the Cathedral, there were others who were equally concerned about the marriage's foundation, including the bride herself. One of her abiding memories was spotting Camilla Parker Bowles, who was wearing a grey outfit with a matching pillbox hat, and hoping that the relationship with Charles was now at an end. It was a sentiment which would have found an echo with the Queen, who had edged towards tackling her son on the subject only to be told by the Prince of Wales, according to a rumour recorded in historian Hugo Vickers' diary: 'My marriage and my sex life have nothing to do with each other.'[26]

For all the doubts, everything seemed well when the newly-weds returned to Balmoral from their Mediterranean honeymoon on board the Royal Yacht *Britannia*. They were healthy, suntanned and all smiles as they greeted family and staff, who formed a guard of honour along the castle drive. 'It was a glorious afternoon,' recalled a member of staff. 'We cheered and we clapped and everything seemed so cheerful and bright.'[27]

It was, however, an illusion; the truth about their honeymoon emerging over time in hints and whispers. The princess, who was suffering from a combination of exhaustion, bulimia and jealousy, still worried that her husband's heart belonged to another, and with good cause. On one occasion during their holiday, photographs of Camilla fell out of his diary, and on another he wore cufflinks with 'C' intertwined with 'C', a gift from Mrs Parker Bowles, which was the prelude to a serious row.

Back on home soil, and smiling brightly during a media photo call by the banks of the River Dee, the princess, in a response to a question about married life, said that she could 'highly recommend' it.[28] During their extended stay at the castle, the couple went for long walks together or he would take out his easel and paints while Diana practised her embroidery. On other days, Charles read to her from the works of his friend, the South African philosopher Laurens van der Post, or from Carl Jung. To add to this scene of romantic tranquility, the prince would give his bride love notes or *billets-doux*.

Diana, though, was anything but content. She found her

revised status and the family dynamic difficult to come to terms with. It was only years later that she expressed her true feelings. She told me: 'All the guests at Balmoral … just stared at me the whole time [and] treated me like glass. As far as I was concerned I was Diana, the only difference was people called me "Ma'am" now, "Your Royal Highness", and they curtsied.'[29]

For her part she felt an outsider, her husband always deferring to the Queen or Queen Mother rather than taking her needs into account. The early signs that all was not well with the royal fairy tale was when Diana chose to stay in her room rather than join the rest of the family for picnics or barbecues. Her resolute refusal to join in irritated the Queen, not only because of the discourtesy to her as host but also because it interrupted the smooth running of the castle, as it meant changing staff rotas so that someone was available to be at Diana's disposal.

It was Princess Margaret who came to the rescue, suggesting to her sister that Diana was having difficulties adjusting to her role and that she should give her time. 'Let her do what she likes,' said Margaret. 'Leave her alone and she will be all right.'[30]

But the issues that Diana faced involved much more than being given some breathing space. The princess had been overtaken by what she later called 'the dark ages' of her life: she was consumed with jealousy, whether warranted or not, regarding Charles and Camilla; her bulimia was rampant; and she suffered wild mood swings. Nor did it help that it was one of the wettest and windiest Balmoral holidays on record. Eventually, she agreed to seek professional counselling and advice from specialists in London.

The general conclusion was that she needed time and space to adjust to the drastic change in her circumstances. She had made a similar diagnosis herself, based on intuition. Drugs were prescribed but she refused them. Instead, she and Charles moved out of Balmoral Castle to Craigowan Lodge, a small stone cottage on the estate. She invited friends, including her former flatmate Carolyn Bartholomew, to stay.

At the end of October, she was able to announce that she was expecting her first child. The Queen and the rest of the family were delighted, their happiness tempered by hope that motherhood would end Diana's 'little local difficulties'.

CHAPTER TEN

MARRIAGES UNDER THE MICROSCOPE

E VERYONE FROM THE QUEEN downwards was taken aback by the intense and continuing interest in the Princess of Wales. Her Majesty and her advisers thought that, once the excitement of the wedding had dissipated, the princess would fade into the background and Prince Charles would renew his position in the royal limelight. But it just didn't happen. Even newspaper and magazine editors were surprised by the public's reaction to the latest addition to the Royal Family. No matter how flimsy the story or grainy the image of the future Queen, Diana sold and kept on selling, the princess seen as the golden goose who laid the circulation eggs. As she succinctly put it: 'One minute I was nobody, the next minute I was Princess of Wales, mother, media toy, member of this family, you name it, and it was too much for one person at that time.'[1]

The consequences were ominous. Diana, suffering badly from bulimia and morning sickness, found herself followed every time she left Balmoral, Kensington Palace or Highgrove. A visit to the shops or the gym became an unpleasant obstacle course as she navigated her way past the numerous photographers who harassed her.

By instinct and convention, the Queen held back from interfering in the marriages of her children. However, seeing the daily trial by media endured by the pregnant princess, the Sovereign felt that she could address that particular problem. She tended to agree with her daughter-in-law, who emphasized that she needed 'time and space' to come to terms with her new royal role. The Queen's press secretary Michael Shea was asked to organize a pre-Christmas cocktail party for newspaper, TV and wire services editors. Only Kelvin MacKenzie, editor of *The Sun*, the most aggressive of the tabloids, refused the invitation to the gathering.

At the event, Shea told the assembled throng that Diana had become 'despondent' about the fact that she could not leave her front door without being followed by photographers.[2] He asked for restraint, and the Monarch herself, in an unusual show of support and concern for her daughter-in-law, appeared and spoke to various groups of editors to reinforce that message, though it was hardly a mutual appreciation society. Barry Askew, editor of the now defunct *News of the World*, told Her Majesty that if the princess wanted privacy she should send a servant to buy sweets from the shops instead of going herself. The Queen tartly responded: 'That's the most pompous thing I have ever heard, Mr Askew.'[3]

The irony of the Sovereign, who rarely visited shops, criticizing the Sunday editor's insensitive comment was lost in the general and gleeful condemnation of the hapless Askew, who, shortly afterwards, was sacked.

Within a matter of weeks, Her Majesty's personal appeal to the media was in tatters. In February 1982, two tabloids, *The Sun* and the *Daily Star*, published pictures of Diana, then five months pregnant, running through the surf in a bikini on the island of Windermere in The Bahamas, where she and her husband were enjoying a holiday in the sun. The prince and princess were livid, while the Queen described the intrusion as 'the blackest day in the history of British journalism'.[4] The honeymoon between the Royal Family and the media, such as it was, was very firmly over. Though both newspapers affected contrition, the plain facts were that photographs of the princess, especially a princess in a bikini, sold like hot cakes. The Monarch and her advisers were in direct conflict with the immutable laws of the market.

Thankfully, the ever-eager media had not got wind of the real drama that was taking place beneath the Queen's roof. With every passing day, it became clearer that the marriage of the Prince and Princess of Wales, the future King and Queen, was not working. A tearful confrontation between the royal couple at Sandringham in January 1982, several weeks before they had headed off for their holiday in the sun, exposed the growing divide.

They had a blazing row about Charles and his indifferent behaviour towards his young wife. What took place next shocked the Sovereign and those present. Diana, according to her account, threw herself down the steps at the North End staircase which leads to the Queen Mother's rooms. Even though she was in tears, Charles accused her of crying wolf and stalked out of the house to go riding. As she lay in a crumpled heap, Her Majesty was one of the first to arrive on the scene. Diana later told me: 'The Queen comes out, absolutely horrified, shaking – she was so frightened.'[5] Her immediate concern was that Diana could possibly suffer a miscarriage.

Others who were present recall a less dramatic encounter. They remember that Diana seemed to trip as she was walking down the stairs and ended up at the bottom of the staircase by the corgis' food bowls, which the Queen Mother was replenishing at the time. The Monarch and other members of the family were alerted to the incident by the Queen's page. When they arrived, Diana was dusting herself off, said that she was absolutely fine and apologized for causing a fuss. As a precaution she was examined by a doctor to confirm that all was well with the princess and her unborn child.

Even if the Queen had taken her at her word, and it was a trip rather than a deliberate, self-inflicted fall, Charles's indifference and Diana's emotional behaviour were causes for alarm. She was in a predicament. The Sovereign couldn't force the couple to love or even like one another. She had played that card with the calamitous marriage of her sister Princess Margaret and Lord Snowdon. That had ended in the first divorce in the Royal Family since Henry VIII. The difference was that the Snowdons' marriage went wrong after a few years, not a few months. Her plan of action for her son and daughter-in-law was to be patient and show understanding. As far as she was concerned, this marriage could not conceivably end in the divorce courts.

———

In March 1982, the arrival of a group of Argentinian scrap-metal workers on the isolated and inhospitable British island of South Georgia in the South Atlantic put an end to these concerns – at least for the time being. Ostensibly, the party had landed to demolish an old whaling station, though diplomatic sources suspected that they were a provocative advance party sent at the behest of the ruling military junta in Argentina, a nation that had long claimed ownership of this remote territory, as well as the larger Falkland Islands which lay some miles west. Matters quickly escalated and the islands, to which a small contingent of Royal Marines had been sent, were overrun by massed Argentine forces. Prime

Minister Margaret Thatcher vowed to retake the British colony and mustered a task force to reassert Britain's dominion.

The hastily assembled naval armada included Sub-Lieutenant Prince Andrew, who was a Sea King helicopter pilot based on board the aircraft carrier HMS *Invincible*. On Thursday 1 April, Thatcher travelled to Windsor Castle to warn Her Majesty about the potential conflict in the South Atlantic and the government's intention to defend Britain's sovereign territory. When the issue of Prince Andrew and his role in the conflict was raised, the Queen, speaking on behalf of her son and her husband, who saw active service during the Second World War, insisted that Andrew be treated like any other naval officer.

According to one report, the prince threatened to resign his commission if *Invincible* sailed without him. Shortly after the mini summit, Buckingham Palace released a short statement to clarify the Queen's view on the matter: 'Prince Andrew is a serving officer and there is no question in her mind that he should go.' On 5 April, the prince and his fellow officers sailed off to an uncertain and dangerous future in the South Atlantic.

What neither he, the Queen nor Mrs Thatcher realized at the time was that the Argentinian junta considered the capture or death of Prince Andrew and the sinking of *Invincible* as their primary war aim. At a meeting of the Argentinian chiefs of staff in Buenos Aires, Admiral Jorge Anaya explained to his colleagues: 'This is an easy war to win. All we have to do is sink one ship – the *Invincible* – and Britain will crumble.'[6] His plan was to launch an audacious air raid and concentrate the entire Argentinian air force on the British aircraft carrier.

Prince Andrew's role was already inherently dangerous. Not only was his 820 Naval Air Squadron involved in search-and-rescue, submarine reconnaissance and airborne supply, his Sea King was also assigned the role of an 'Exocet decoy'. The Argentine air force was armed with French-made Exocet missiles and the theory was that when one was launched at the *Invincible* from an enemy jet, the helicopter would attract the projectile away from the ship. Once it was spotted heading for the Sea King, the helicopter would soar upwards and the Exocet fly harmlessly underneath before falling into the water. At least that was the theory. In reality, the Sea King would be sacrificed to save the aircraft carrier. It was such a terrifying assignment that years later, when he gave an interview to the BBC's *Newsnight* programme regarding his friendship with convicted paedophile Jeffrey Epstein, Prince Andrew admitted that the adrenaline rush he suffered while under fire in the Falklands conflict left him unable to sweat.

The 'frightening' incident that prompted this condition came during the much-heralded attack on HMS *Invincible*. Instead of hitting the aircraft carrier, the assault, which took place on 25 May, ended with the sinking of the 695-foot container ship, the SS *Atlantic Conveyor*, and the death of twelve crew members. In Buenos Aires, after interviewing the returning pilots, the junta falsely claimed that they had sunk *Invincible* and issued a doctored photograph to the world media. Like any parents, the Queen and her husband were concerned and worried about their son, especially knowing the precarious position of the task force.

The next day, 26 May 1982, at the opening of Kielder Water in Northumberland, the UK's largest artificial lake, the Queen told the crowds: 'Before I begin, I would like to say one thing. Our thoughts today are with those who are in the South Atlantic, and our prayers are for their success and a safe return to their homes and loved ones.'[7] Days later, Her Majesty was shaken once more by further claims from Argentinian officials and media that her son was wounded and in enemy hands and that *Invincible* was a blazing hulk. Even Princess Anne made a rare visit to her local church in Gloucestershire to join a prayer service for the well-being of the fighting men in the South Atlantic.

British forces ultimately prevailed and, following the Argentinian surrender on 14 June, Andrew took the opportunity to visit the Falkland Islands' capital, Port Stanley, where he spoke to his 'surprised' mother using one of the few satellite phones.[8]

He spent another three months at sea before his return home, and during that time he suffered a demotion to third in line to the throne after his sister-in-law gave birth to Prince William on 21 June. One of the first visitors was the Queen, who inspected the mite at St Mary's Hospital in central London. 'Thank goodness he hasn't [got] ears like his father,' was Her Majesty's droll observation.[9] Her eldest son's ears were so prominent that not only were they subject of caricature, but the prince had considered an operation to pin them back.

In a truly momentous summer, newspaper cartoonists struggled to depict an episode in the Queen's life that was as comic as it was bizarre. In the early morning of 9 July, Michael Fagan, an unemployed painter and decorator with mental health issues, broke into Buckingham Palace and, after a series of flukes, managed to find his way into the Monarch's bedroom at around 7.15 a.m. Her Majesty, who was startled awake, twice rang for the police for help and, in an effort to placate her unexpected visitor, listened intently as he told her about his marital and financial issues. This was the Queen behaving not as figurehead but as mother figure.

This was the second time in a month that Fagan had gained entry to the palace undetected and, if nothing else, his incursion showed the wholly inadequate security system that was in place. On the second occasion he specifically wanted to see the Queen, in his mind an idealized maternal symbol, to help sort out the mess that he found himself in. He later told me: 'I wanted her to be the woman I could communicate with, who would understand me and my everyday aspirations. I wanted her to know me. This woman is the pinnacle of our society, the summit of our dreams. We are tribal animals and the Queen is the head of the tribe. I wanted to speak to our chieftain.'[10]

The Queen recognizes her mythical status, and once remarked that she accepted that she was seen as a Jungian archetype, a concept developed by the psychologist Carl Jung whereby society projects its dreams of ideas such as motherhood, justice and leadership onto the figure of the monarch.

During his self-imposed quest, Fagan had walked from his home in Islington, North London, to the perimeter of Buckingham Palace. He easily scaled the wall, got through an open window and before long found himself in the Throne Room. By sheer luck, he accidentally pressed a hidden handle in the dado rail which opened a secret door leading to the Queen's private apartments.

His good fortune continued. Normally, a policeman would have been sitting outside Her Majesty's bedroom, but he had gone off duty at 6 a.m. and the Queen's footman, Paul Whybrew, had just taken the royal corgis for their early morning walk. By a million to one chance, the Monarch was alone and unguarded and, after quietly opening a door, Fagan found himself in her bedroom. He hid behind the curtains as he assessed the person in the bed, thinking at first that the small figure must be a child. He pulled the curtains aside to get a better look. The shaft of light woke the Queen, who saw not her female maid but a barefoot Fagan, in jeans and T-shirt, clutching part of a broken glass ashtray which had cut his thumb.

She pressed the alarm bell and then, as was later recorded in the official Dellow report, made the first of two calls to the palace telephonist to send police to her bedroom. As the Sovereign waited for them to arrive she reacted in textbook style, remaining calm and collected while she engaged the intruder in polite conversation. She listened to Fagan's tale of woe and in turn chatted about her own children, noting that Prince Charles was about Fagan's age.

Six minutes later, the Queen made a second call, coolly asking why there had been no response. Then she used the pretext of Fagan's craving for a cigarette to summon a maid, Elizabeth Andrew, to her bedroom. When she saw Fagan sitting on the edge of Her Majesty's bed, the startled housemaid uttered the immortal phrase: 'Bloody hell, Ma'am. What's he doing here?'[11] Afterwards, her broad Northern accent became part of the Queen's own comic repartee.

Fagan's version, which has admittedly varied over time, is somewhat different. According to him, there was no conversation. Instead, Her Majesty grabbed the white telephone, asked for help and then shouted 'Get out, get out', before she jumped out of bed, ran across the room and out of the door. The confrontation was all over in seconds, with Fagan left alone and crying by the empty bed. A few minutes later, he was ushered into a pantry by the footman, who had just returned from walking the dogs.

Whybrew recalls the Queen asking: 'Can you give this man a drink?' The footman, astonished by his employer's calm demeanour, took an unprotesting Fagan into the page's vestibule and poured him a Famous Grouse whisky. As he did so, he heard the Sovereign screaming down the phone, demanding to know why the police hadn't arrived. 'I have never heard the Queen so angry,' he later told colleagues.[12]

The subsequent inquiry revealed a whole catalogue of blunders, from non-functioning exterior cameras and other detection devices not working properly on the palace perimeter to the duty police officer deciding to change into a smarter uniform after being summoned by the Monarch rather than getting to her immediately.

The Queen was as annoyed that her domestic affairs had become a matter of consuming public interest as she was that security had allowed Fagan all the way into the royal bedroom.

'Give her a cuddle, Philip' pleaded the *Daily Mirror*, as the nation gleefully discussed the separate sleeping arrangements of the Sovereign and her consort.[13] The reality was that the royal couple did share the same bed but, by ill luck, Prince Philip had stayed in his own quarters that night as he had an early appointment the following morning.

He was furious at the incompetence of the police and highly complimentary of his wife's bravery. She dismissed the plaudits and told friends that the entire event was too surreal to be taken seriously. There were further unhappy consequences. Michael Rauch, a male prostitute, read about the Fagan story and visited the offices of *The Sun* newspaper to tell them about his own affair with the Queen's bodyguard, Commander Michael Trestrail. The officer, nicknamed Aquarius because one of his duties involved carrying the Queen's Malvern water, promptly resigned.[14]

It was a deeply distressing time. Ten days after her encounter with Michael Fagan, her childhood friend and Prince Philip's private secretary Lord Rupert Nevill passed away, but worse was to come. On 20 July, the Provisional IRA planted bombs in Hyde Park and at a bandstand in Regent's Park that led to numerous deaths and injuries among the soldiers and horses of the Blues and Royals and the Royal Green Jackets from the Queen's Household Cavalry. The blast in Hyde Park at 10.43 a.m. killed four Blues and Royals soldiers and wounded more than twenty others. Seven horses died immediately or had to be put down later having sustained too serious injuries. One horse, Sefton, survived an eight-hour operation to remove nails and other pieces of shrapnel from his bloodied frame.

Just over two hours after the initial attack, a second bomb hidden in a Regent's Park bandstand, where musicians from the Royal Green Jackets were playing, killed seven bandsmen and wounded several others, including civilians. That night the Queen was heard repeating 'The poor horses, my poor soldiers' as the horrors of the day sank in.[15]

Although Her Majesty affected to make light of the Fagan incident, this was, according to friends, a difficult and disconcerting period that unsettled her famous equilibrium for several months. 'She said she met so many dotty people that one more made no difference,' recalled her cousin and friend Margaret Rhodes, who thought she was putting on a brave face to hide the shock.[16] Her instincts proved correct, as the Sovereign, feeling overwhelmed, decided for the first time in her life that she needed medical advice and counselling. She asked Betty Parsons, a no-nonsense childbirth guru who had taught her breathing exercises before the birth of Prince Edward, to come to the palace to give her instruction in how to improve her peace of mind. Using techniques similar to those in yoga, Parsons taught her to 'drop her shoulders, inhale slowly and deeply, and empty her mind of all thoughts.'[17] Following this advice helped to restore a much-needed sense of calm in the heart of the Monarch.

Her Majesty was further cheered when, on 17 September, Prince Andrew returned to Portsmouth on board HMS *Invincible* after 166 continuous days at sea. The prince sauntered down the gangway, a red rose between his teeth, to be met by his parents who were clearly delighted, like many other families, that he had come home safe and sound. He was now celebrated as a bona fide war hero and one of the world's most eligible bachelors.

During his leave, the Queen gladly gave the go-ahead for her second son and a party of friends – which included US actor Kathleen 'Koo' Stark whom he had been quietly dating for a while – to stay at Princess Margaret's clifftop retreat on the tiny island of Mustique. As luck would have it, a Fleet Street photographer and his girlfriend were on the same British Airways flight to Barbados as the royal party. He discovered that Andrew and Koo were travelling together under the name 'Mr and Mrs Cambridge'. At the time, no one could be sure whether the prince had secretly married the American. When it was later discovered that Koo had appeared in a tepidly erotic rite of passage movie called *Emily*, there was a global hue and cry orchestrated not just by the newspapers, but also by British lawmakers, who were horrified that the Queen's son could have married a 'soft-porn star'[18] – a description that was disgracefully wide of the mark.

There was such international media hysteria around capturing the first picture of the lovebirds together in paradise that one cameraman from an American supermarket tabloid considered hiring a submarine and taking photos of the couple through the periscope. Headlines which suggested that the Queen was 'furious' at Andrew's choice of partner were far from true. She had met Koo previously when the American was invited to Balmoral and, like Diana and other members of the family, had found the actor polite, bright and conversationally adept. Her only comment when their romance became public was: 'Oh, I do wish they would call you Kathleen and Andrew.'

In her own way the Queen, who could see that Kathleen was good news for her son, tried to change the narrative about the couple. She showed support for Andrew's choice of partner when, according to Stark, she invited the couple for a picnic tea where they would be seen by the paparazzi. She recalled: 'Her Majesty made a point of snapping open the *News of the World* [featuring the front-page headline: 'Queen Bans Koo']. Her actions spoke volumes as she poured tea.'[19] In 1983, the Queen even took the unusual step of launching legal action against *The Sun* newspaper (and a former employee) over claims that Andrew's girlfriend had regularly stayed overnight at Buckingham Palace. She was ultimately successful and received an out-of-court settlement.

Perhaps inevitably, the couple went their separate ways, though they stayed friends. But for an ill-judged choice early in her acting career, it is likely that Kathleen Stark would have been the first American actor to marry a member of the British Royal Family ahead of Meghan Markle.

Meanwhile, the Queen's only daughter was working through some tricky marital issues. The official release of photographs of Princess Anne and Captain Mark Phillips to celebrate his thirty-four birthday was seen by those in the know as another attempt to alter perceptions surrounding the royal couple. They had been beset by rumours about the state of their marriage, especially after stories emerged in the tabloids that Anne's bodyguard, Peter Cross, had been removed from royal protection duties and transferred back to the uniformed branch after becoming 'over-familiar' with his charge. Even after he was removed from royal duties, Cross and the princess kept in contact by phone or used safe houses. She used the code word 'Mrs Wallis', presumably a reference to Wallis Simpson, when she called.

How far the Queen was privy to her daughter's behaviour is a matter of debate. As affairs are usually conducted in secret, it is doubtful that Anne would have confided in her mother. Her Majesty may well have been aware, though, of the bigger, more concerning picture that her daughter's marriage was in trouble.

Equally worrying was the negative narrative about Diana that was snowballing in the popular press. A fairy-tale princess no more, she was accused of being a 'fiend' and a 'monster' by influential gossip columnist Nigel Dempster, and deemed responsible for a wave of staff departures, including Charles's bodyguard, valet, private secretary and others. Diana, stung by this criticism, told the royal reporter James Whitaker: 'I don't just sack people.'[20]

The Queen showed her confidence in her daughter-in-law and agreed to Diana's request, previously turned down by Her Majesty's private secretary Sir Philip Moore and Prince Charles, that she should represent the family and the monarchy at the funeral of Princess Grace of Monaco, who was killed in a car accident in September 1982. Her demure and dignified manner during the emotional ceremony convinced the Sovereign that her policy of quiet understanding of and support for the Princess of Wales was paying dividends.

The real turning point was the royal couple's highly successful six-week tour of Australia and New Zealand in March and April 1983. The gruelling visit – they took more than fifty flights during their time away – demonstrated to the Queen that Diana had the stamina and sparkle to make these visits a success. However, a green-eyed monster lurked beneath the surface. As the tour gathered momentum, Prince Charles became increasingly jealous of his wife's popularity. During walkabouts, the crowd groaned if Charles went to their side of the street and cheered only if Diana came to shake hands. Though he made light of it in speeches, privately it rankled. It was but another indication of their growing estrangement.

For a while, at least, the scudding storm clouds in the Waleses' relationship would give way to a shaft of sunshine when Diana discovered that she was pregnant with her second child. A new life and a new beginning was always a source of pleasure for the Queen, a sense of history in the making. Prince Harry was born on 15 September 1984 and with his arrival the Queen hoped that the teething troubles of the couple's marriage could be put behind them.

—·—

Eighteen months later, a major milestone beckoned in the life of the Sovereign. To mark the occasion of her upcoming sixtieth birthday, she invited Prince Andrew, a keen amateur photographer, to take her photo and the result was a relaxed, smiling mother, arms crossed and dressed in a twinset. She was more mumsy than monarch.

To commemorate this significant birthday, postage stamps were issued, laudatory documentaries edited and a short musical was commissioned by Prince Edward. The high point on the day itself was the 'Fanfare for Elizabeth' gala at the Royal Opera House that featured an eight-minute-long ballet entitled *Nursery Suite*, choreographed by Frederick Ashton, which reflected the happy childhood of the Queen and her sister. Princess Margaret, knowing the character of her no-nonsense sibling, had warned him not to make the work too whimsical, and the resulting production proved a triumph. Margaret would later reveal that she, the Queen and their mother all ended up in 'floods of tears' after watching this affectionate portrait, many sunny memories doubtless triggered by this dance to the music of time.[21]

Indeed, contrary to popular belief, the Queen was not immune to tears. Just over a week later, on 29 April, the Princess of Wales described her astonishment as her mother-in-law wept during the burial of the Duchess of Windsor, a woman she had met infrequently and barely knew. Diana surmised that it was the passing of a somewhat tragic figure, who had lived her last years as a bed-bound recluse, that had sparked the emotion, Her Majesty's tears perhaps of remembrance and regret. This brief outburst was enough to shock Diana, though, who later told author Ingrid Seward: 'We were at the graveside, Charles and me and the Queen, and when she started crying I said to myself, "I can't believe this is really happening."' She added that the Queen had been 'incredibly kind' to the duchess in her final years, particularly with regard to paying all her bills.[22] From that day onwards, Diana never saw the Monarch cry again in private or public.

However, she was perfectly entitled to shed tears of joy three months later, on a sunny day in July 1986, when she looked on as a beaming Prince Andrew watched Sarah Ferguson, soon-to-be Her Royal Highness the Duchess of York, walk down the aisle of Westminster Abbey on their wedding day. Their marriage was a source of satisfaction for both the Queen and Prince Philip following a period of uncertainty and concern surrounding their middle son's private life.

After his romance with Koo Stark had ended, Prince Andrew had garnered a reputation as a playboy prince with a roving eye. One of his casual girlfriends had sold her story about late-night sexual exploits under a palm tree on a sandy beach in the Caribbean. Her disclosures coincided with Princess Anne's detective lover, Peter Cross, selling his story to a Sunday tabloid in September 1985. The Monarch and her consort could do little about the policeman's allegations other than ride out the storm, but with Andrew they were prompted into action. A few admonishing words from a stern Philip seemed to do the trick. Thereafter, the prince began to date the 'right sort of girl'. Sarah definitely fell into that category.

The daughter of Major Ronald Ferguson, who was Prince Charles's polo manager, she was a familiar face in royal circles. Ginger-haired and freckle-faced, she was ebullient, energetic and game for a laugh. During the week of Royal Ascot in June 1985, she was invited to stay at Windsor Castle as a guest of her friend, the Princess of Wales. It was over lunch that Sarah and the prince first bonded, Andrew feeding her chocolate profiteroles despite her protestations that she was dieting. As he later recalled during their engagement interview: 'There are always humble beginnings; it's got to start somewhere.'[23]

Though Sarah had had boyfriends and clearly had a 'past', no one inside the Royal Family seemed especially worried. She was clearly one of them. The Queen Mother liked her at once. 'She is so English,' she commented. In a letter to the Queen, dated 10 April 1986, she complimented the bride-to-be on how well she had fitted in during the Easter break at Windsor. 'She is such a cheerful person, and seems to be so thankful & pleased to be part of a united family, & is truly devoted to darling Andrew. It seems most hopeful which is a comfort.'[24]

Unspoken but understood was the implication that their union would not be hopeless, unlike that of the Prince and Princess of Wales. By July 1986, they were living separate lives – 'us both having tried' as he would later declare on prime-time television[25] – with Charles back together with Mrs Parker Bowles and Diana finding comfort in the arms of her bodyguard Barry Mannakee and, later, Army officer James Hewitt. During Andrew and Sarah's wedding ceremony, the princess looked unusually distracted. It was because she had just learned that, following a complaint from a fellow protection officer, Mannakee had been moved from her detail.

It was the Queen's hope that jolly, jaunty, endlessly upbeat Fergie would jolt Diana out of her sullen moods and help her to join in with the rest of the clan. The duchess went carriage driving with Prince Philip who described her as a 'great asset', horse riding with the Queen, and regularly joined her mother-in-law for lunch at Buckingham Palace.[26] Thus, she provided a stark contrast to Diana.

The arrival of Fergie did indeed mark a change in Diana's behaviour, though it was not one that the Queen ultimately welcomed. It began on Andrew's stag night, when Diana, Fergie and several friends dressed as policewomen, intending to 'arrest' the prince at the private house where his party was taking place. When that petered out, they ended up in Annabel's nightclub where they drank mimosas. One customer asked Diana if she wanted another drink, to which she replied, 'I don't drink on duty.'[27] But clearly she did, as there was already a glass in front of her.

Once the story got out, her mother-in-law was deeply annoyed that the future Queen of England had been spotted roaming around London dressed as a police officer, which was technically a criminal offence. When she spoke to the princess about it, Diana defended her behaviour as being no more than light-hearted fun. She made it clear that she had not intended to demean either the Queen or the monarchy. Not wanting a confrontation, the Monarch accepted her benign explanation.

The general silliness, though, continued: Fergie encouraged Diana to join her in a can-can at Windsor Castle later that year; early in 1987 they pushed and shoved one another at a photo call on the ski slopes of Klosters, earning a rebuke from Prince Charles; and a few months later, at Royal Ascot, the duo were photographed prodding the rear of their friend Lulu Blacker with their rolled umbrellas. Diana was even criticized for wearing red leather trousers at a David Bowie concert.

The watching world chorused its disapproval. 'Far too much frivolity,' sniffed the *Daily Express*, while other commentators accused the women of behaving like actresses in a soap opera.[28] With her poor fashion choices, greedy enjoyment of royal life – champagne-fuelled parties in her quarters at Buckingham Palace were regular events – and her blatant freeloading, the Duchess of York was singled out for especial criticism. It was not long before she was dubbed 'Freebie Fergie' and described as 'vulgar' by palace insiders. The tide was beginning to turn.

Ironically, the event that ignited a critical firestorm and marked a step change in public attitudes towards the Royal Family was organized by the Queen's youngest child, Prince Edward. On completing his degree at the University of Cambridge, he had joined the Royal Marines. After only a few months, he realized that he had made the wrong choice and, much to the disappointment of the Queen, Prince Philip and the Queen Mother, he resigned his commission. During his college days he had enjoyed acting and decided to make his mark in the theatre world.

In early 1987, before embarking on this new career, he began organizing a TV game show called *It's A Royal Knockout,* with the aim of raising money for four charities. He roped in three other royals – the Duke and Duchess of York as well as Princess Anne – who would join him as captains of four teams that comprised assorted celebrities from home and abroad, including *Superman* actor Christopher Reeve, singer Meat Loaf and film star John Travolta. The plan was for the team members, all decked out in Tudor-style fancy dress, to compete in a series of slapstick games.[29] While the intent was benign, Prince Charles thought that this meshing of pantomime and monarchy was a disaster waiting to happen. He refused to take part and forbade his wife from getting involved. Initially, Diana was resentful at missing out, but she would later have cause to thank her husband for stopping her from making a fool of herself.

Charles spoke to his mother and counselled against giving his younger brother permission to continue. When the Queen was first approached, her instincts were in line with those of her eldest son. She was supported by her senior managerial staff who felt the show, filmed in June 1987, would open the Royal Family up to ridicule. However, Edward secured a face-to-face meeting with his mother and with a combination of youthful enthusiasm and emphasis on the charity contribution, convinced her to change her mind. The royal children and their partners knew all too well that a personal meeting with the Monarch often derailed advice from courtiers.

For once, Prince Charles's instincts proved spot on. Reaction to the show was wholly negative, being seen as puerile slapstick that demeaned the Royal Family. The Queen Mother was so incensed that she summoned Andrew, Edward and Anne and read them the riot act, accusing them of, in one evening, destroying the reputation of the monarchy that she and the late King had spent a lifetime building up. The Queen's reaction was rather more benign. Even though the programme had been made for altruistic reasons, she agreed that it was turning the Royal Family into a soap opera.

The internal post-mortem was matched by a sea change in the attitude of the media and the public. It was felt that the younger royals were frivolous, irrelevant and did little to justify taxpayers' largesse at a time of mass unemployment and growing social division. The decision by the Sovereign to spend £3.5 million on the construction and furnishing of Sunninghill Park – a sprawling ranch-style house dubbed 'SouthYork' after Southfork in the TV show *Dallas* – for the Duke and Duchess of York seemed to suggest that she was out of touch with the mood of her people. Even though there were plenty of smaller and more appropriate 'grace and favour' houses that could have served the royal couple, the Monarch once again gave in, her generosity outweighing her judgement. As one courtier observed: 'The Queen is tight in her own financial affairs, but she has been very extravagant with her children, she has indulged them terribly financially.'[30]

The immature behaviour of the younger royals formed but a part of a swelling chorus of disapproval of the Royal Family, which began just before Andrew and Sarah's wedding. On this occasion, the Queen herself was placed under a critical microscope. Just three days before the royal nuptials, *The Sunday Times* informed its readers that Her Majesty found Mrs Thatcher's style of government 'uncaring, confrontational and divisive'.[31]

Although Thatcher saw the Queen for an audience every week for eleven and a half years, the two women, though cordial, were never close. Thatcher's official biographer Charles Moore described the Prime Minister as 'too nervous' during these meetings for them to be productive.[32]

For the first time, the story, quoting anonymous sources, addressed the constitutional elephant in the room – that the Monarch, who was by instinct and training conciliatory and compromising, was alarmed by the contentious style of the Prime

Minister who had deliberately fostered strikes, particularly in the coal industry, in order to crush the trade unions. Under her tenure, the North had suffered while the South had prospered. In the political shorthand of the time, the Queen was a 'wet' and Mrs Thatcher was a 'dry'. Whatever the Sovereign might think of her government's policies, though, it was not her place to articulate a view one way or the other. To do so was a constitutional no-no and for thirty-four years she had been, as her mother would say, 'utterly oyster' in her political views.

The hunt was on for the 'anonymous source' who turned out to be Her Majesty's press secretary Michael Shea. He vehemently denied making the statement ascribed to him, but the damage was done and a few months later he had left royal employment. The episode jolted the hitherto seamlessly secret relationship between the Monarch and her Prime Minister, the Queen taking the unusual step of phoning Mrs Thatcher to apologize. While Mrs Thatcher worried that the story might affect her grass-roots support, others, of the dry persuasion, felt that a less than even-handed monarch was also a dispensable one.

Her husband's behaviour hardly helped matters. A few months later, in October 1986, the Queen and Prince Philip flew to China on their first-ever State visit to the country. During the tour, the prince firmly put his foot in his mouth when he told a group of British exchange students that they would go 'slitty-eyed' if they stayed in China much longer. Not only was the off-the-cuff remark blatantly racist, it was also insulting to their hosts. They chose to ignore the remark. Not so the British media who dubbed the Queen's husband 'the Great Wally of China'.[33] Until his death in 2021, it remained top of the list of his many 'gaffes'.

In the midst of this largely self-inflicted bombardment of negative headlines, one member of the family managed to evade the fallout in the press. Princess Diana was forgiven any Fergie-inspired daftness after she shook hands, ungloved, with an AIDS patient at the Middlesex Hospital in London in April 1987. At a time when AIDS was dubbed 'the gay plague' with no cure in sight, her behaviour gained international headlines and widespread approval.

When it eventually emerged that the Queen and her advisers had counselled caution, Diana's courage and steadfastness was seen as a positive counterpoint to the self-indulgent silliness of the other royals, a view that became more pronounced after the airing of the *It's A Royal Knockout* show two months later. The emerging consensus was that Diana was different and she cared for the man and woman in the street.

This narrative of a family out of touch with modern realities was amplified during the latter part of the 1980s after a series of disasters, notably the Zeebrugge ferry sinking in March 1987, the Piper Alpha explosion in July 1988 and the Lockerbie air crash in December 1988. Though the Monarch sent Andrew as her representative to the air crash close to the border of England and Scotland, his insensitive remarks suggesting that the American passengers had suffered more than those killed on the ground led to renewed calls for the Queen herself to visit these scenes. It seemed that not much had changed since Aberfan. She later admitted to her then deputy private secretary Robert Fellowes that she should have taken his earlier advice and gone there in person.[34]

At the memorial service for the Lockerbie victims on 4 January 1989, it did not escape notice that Her Majesty was not represented by any member of the Royal Family. 'Where were the royals?' asked *The Sun*, helpfully showing pictures of various family members out riding, skiing and sunbathing.

This negative image was conflated with the debate about the introduction of the poll tax. As the measure taxed individuals rather than property, it disproportionately affected poorer sections of society while providing the wealthier with substantial savings.

The implementation of the new tax provoked widespread rioting and effectively ended Prime Minister Thatcher's career. During this time of social uproar, it was revealed that Prince Charles's butler paid as much poll tax as his master, while the prince saved thousands of pounds on his privately owned properties. The same was true for other members of the Royal Family. It was also pointed out that, during this time of national belt-tightening, the Queen paid no tax on her private income.

A leader in *The Sunday Times,* penned by its editor Andrew Neil, argued that now was the time for the Monarch to pay tax and that unproductive junior members of the Royal Family should be taken off the payroll.[35]

Not only did Elizabeth find herself criticized for her tax privileges, she also found herself blundering in the world of horse racing in which she had an impeccable reputation and enjoyed unrivalled respect and admiration. The saga had begun back in 1982 when the Queen, acting on the advice of her racing manager Lord Carnarvon, bought the racing stables at West Ilsley with funds from the sale of her filly, Height of Fashion, to Sheikh Hamdan al Maktoum of the Dubai royal family.

One of the trainers using the facility was the highly respected Major Dick Hern, who had worked for the Sovereign since 1966. He lived in a nearby rectory which Her Majesty had also bought using her Height of Fashion monies. In December 1984, following a hunting accident in which he broke his neck, the major became confined to a wheelchair, but he still continued training and produced several notable winners. In the summer of 1988, he had open heart surgery and was still recovering in hospital when, in August, Lord Carnarvon told him that he had two weeks to leave the stables and that he would also have to vacate his home.

The racing world was horrified at the treatment of this popular figure. Such was the concern that fellow trainer Ian Balding tracked down the Queen's deputy private secretary Robert Fellowes while he was on holiday in The Bahamas, and warned him that unless the Monarch revised the arrangements for Major Hern, she was in danger of having her horses booed in the winners' enclosure. What shocked horse-racing fans the most was Her Majesty's seemingly hard-hearted behaviour towards a loyal trainer. 'The Queen has done something I thought was impossible,' observed Woodrow Wyatt, the journalist and broadcaster who was a close friend of the Queen Mother. 'She is turning the Jockey Club and the racing world into republicans.'[36]

Though the matter was eventually resolved to everyone's satisfaction – the Queen eventually countermanded Carnarvon's advice and allowed Hern to stay in his home and continue using the West Ilsley stables as well – it revealed an unexpected side of the Sovereign, that she far too readily took the advice of those she trusted, in this case the 7th Earl of Carnarvon, without question. More galling for Her Majesty, as a competitive racehorse breeder, was the fact that a Hern-trained horse, Nashwan, would gallop to a five-length victory in the 1989 Epsom Derby, the one major event in the racing calendar that the Queen has never won.

These sporting matters faded into the background when, on 2 August 1990, Iraq invaded Kuwait and five months later the first Gulf War began. Before Allied troops went into battle, on 24 February 1991 the Queen gave her first-ever televised address to the nation. It was a low-key, sober talk in which she expressed her hope for a swift resolution of the conflict with minimum loss of life.

As a counterpoint to her address, newspapers continued to focus on the self-absorbed behaviour of other members of the Royal Family. 'This country is at war,' declared *The Sunday Times* editorial, 'though you would never believe it from the shenanigans of some members of Her Majesty's clan.'[37]

The newspaper cited recent occasions of the Duchess of

York skiing, the Prince of Wales pheasant-hunting and the Duke of York golfing, as well as featuring a photo of Lord Linley, the Queen's nephew, at a nightclub on a Caribbean island, wearing red lipstick and standing next to some men in drag. Even though it was pointed out that the picture was taken long before the Gulf War conflict, the damage was done.

Royal expert Harold Brooks-Baker, the publishing director of Burke's Peerage Partnership, commented that the war in the Gulf had only served to crystallize what he described as 'building public resentment over the behaviour of some members of the Royal Family'.[38]

The Queen, stung by accusations that her family were not supportive of the British troops, authorized a statement in her name: 'All members of the Royal Family are behind British forces every inch of the way.'[39] This was followed by a long inventory of the visits and events attended by various royals that highlighted the support being shown to service personnel and their families.

It was time, somewhat belatedly, to take back the narrative, to demonstrate the importance of the monarchy in the life of the nation and remind British citizens that the institution was about service, duty and obligation, not sunshine holidays at the taxpayers' expense.

CHAPTER ELEVEN

ONE'S ANNUS HORRIBILIS

O N THE EVENING OF 6 February 1992, the fortieth anniversary of the Queen's accession to the throne, Britain's electricity grid and water companies experienced an historic and alarming surge. Emergency reserves were tapped to keep up with demand. The reason behind the rush was the screening of a remarkable television documentary that had viewers making a cup of tea or using the bathroom when it ended. Around 30 million people – more than half the population – had tuned in to watch a year in the life of the most famous pensioner and grandmother on the planet, Her Majesty the Queen. As Edward Mirzoeff, the director of *Elizabeth R*, observed: 'At a time when the Queen was rather disregarded, there was a need to remind the nation what she was like.'[1]

For years she had been overshadowed by her children, whose television antics had done little to burnish the Crown. This documentary was different. Mirzoeff, who spent eighteen months filming the Monarch at State banquets, spending time with her grandchildren at Balmoral, meeting world leaders and even having a flutter on the horses, ensured that the Queen was the star of the show. Her husband made a fleeting appearance, but that was it. Her children were nowhere to be seen, unlike the first fly-on-the-wall documentary *Royal Family*, which was broadcast over twenty years earlier.

Mirzoeff focused on her status as the Head of State, a post she held for life. It was a unique and solitary position, one that several portrait artists, notably Pietro Annigoni, had previously tried to capture. Though she was small and unimposing in stature, she exuded a sense of majesty. Staff described encounters with the Sovereign as entering 'the presence'. A presence, though, with a sense of humour, which was a characteristic that Mirzoeff captured at the 1991 Derby. During the race, the viewer glimpsed the almost girlish, wry and knowing individual behind the mask of the Monarch.

She was seen drawing the horses and the guests' names for the Derby sweepstake (picking the stallion Generous for herself), then watching coverage of the race on a television in the royal box. As the horses approached the finish line, she ran to the balcony to see Generous crossing the line first, then cried out excitedly: 'That's my horse ... I've won the sweep!' Her takings were £16 and, despite being one of the world's richest women, she was genuinely thrilled. As she pocketed her winnings, she flashed a confiding grin at the camera.

She later told Mirzoeff that the documentary was the 'only good thing' that had happened to her in that year. In a voiceover for the programme, the Queen gave an unintentional hint about the coming crisis when she reflected on the difficulties faced by the younger members of the Royal Family in terms of getting used to living within an institution governed by tradition and continuity.

This was something of an understatement. In the months leading up to the broadcast, she had a full-scale royal rebellion on her hands. The first signs had come during the Balmoral holiday in August 1991, during which both Diana and Fergie had seemed frustrated and anxious. There was a wildness about their behaviour that did not go unnoticed. One evening they took the Queen Mother's Daimler and a four-wheel-drive estate vehicle out for a spin and raced each other along the private roads. On another occasion, they commandeered a quad bike and went racing over the golf course, in the process churning up the greens. It was a manifestation of the chaos and unhappiness in their lives.

At the time, both women had discussed leaving their marriages and the Royal Family in tandem. At family gatherings, they took the opportunity to speak separately to the Queen about their marital problems. They acted almost like a wrestling tag team, each one taking it turns to bend her ear. A former servant, who described such approaches as 'the kind of chats the Queen had come to dread', also remarked: 'Her big worry was for the grandchildren.'[2]

As well as the Monarch, they consulted with a small army of astrologers and soothsayers for guidance on making their next step. Diana told Princess Anne that Fergie was so disillusioned with married life that the visit in 1991 would probably be the last time she came to Balmoral as a married member of the Royal Family. Her prediction proved to be accurate.

In any case, Fergie was skating on very thin ice. She had embarked upon an affair with Steve Wyatt, the adopted son of a Texan oil tycoon, while five months pregnant with her second daughter, Princess Eugenie. During their relationship, she had arranged for Dr Ramzi Salman, the head of Iraq's State Oil Marketing Organization, to pay a private visit to Buckingham Palace sometime between Iraq's invasion of Kuwait and the start of the first Gulf War. There he enjoyed dinner with the duchess and her American lover, whose family had continuing business ties with the regime of the Iraqi dictator Saddam Hussein.

Once the Queen and her advisers learned of her imprudent behaviour, she was summoned to the office of the Queen's private secretary, Sir Robert Fellowes, for a formal dressing-down. 'You have abused Her Majesty and her kindness,' he told her, emphasizing that he and two colleagues who were also present had the Queen's full authority to speak to her in this manner.[3] The following Sunday, Fergie spoke to the Sovereign at Windsor Castle and asked why she had been given such a tongue-lashing. Rather than confront her daughter-in-law about her behaviour, she feigned ignorance, thus weakening the authority of her Household staff in future confrontations. Her inability to face down members of her extended family, even when they were demonstrably in the wrong, was a quality that quietly enraged her senior officials – and her husband. Philip always knew when his wife had avoided an unpleasant scene as he could see her taking her pack of dogs for a walk.

Even the Duke of Edinburgh was left breathless at the behaviour of the Ferguson family. It transpired that Fergie's lover had also embarked on a relationship with the polo-playing businesswoman Lesley Player, who also happened to be the mistress of Fergie's own father, Major Ronald Ferguson. The major had earlier resigned as Prince Charles's polo manager after allegations were made about his visits to a massage parlour of dubious repute in Marylebone, central London, from which he was photographed leaving. Shortly afterwards, Fergie began another affair with Wyatt's friend and financial adviser, John Bryan.

Though Fergie's marriage was firmly on the rocks, she consoled herself with the notion that her friend, the Princess of Wales, would leave the Royal Family at the same time. The princess, though, had other ideas. Unbeknownst to the duchess, Diana was secretly working on a no-holds-barred biography of her life in which she openly discussed her eating disorders, her half-hearted suicide attempts, or desperate cries for help, as well as her husband's long-running relationship with Camilla Parker Bowles. During this time, Diana's own affair with Army captain James Hewitt, who served in the Gulf War, was petering out.

Even as she worked on her biography, entitled *Diana: Her True Story*, she had not been idle in discussing her marriage with the Queen. While she kept silent about the book, the princess had spoken to her mother-in-law face-to-face on numerous occasions about Charles and his behaviour. Scarred by the bitter divorce between her parents, which left her father, Earl Spencer, winning custody of the four children, Diana had a morbid fear of being blamed for the collapse of her own marriage. Ideally, she wanted the Queen to side with her and condemn her son for his infidelity. This, of course, would have ignored her own conduct.

Between the Sovereign and Diana there was an uncomprehending respect. While Her Majesty recognized the Princess of Wales's popularity and her ability to physically embrace the public, a quality which was not part of her own DNA, she found her tears and tantrums hard to grasp. For her part, Diana admired and respected the Queen because of her unrelenting stoicism, a characteristic that was not part of her personal make-up. On one very hot day in July 1991, for instance, before a garden party at Buckingham Palace, a friend suggested that Diana should bring along a fan to keep cool. Diana wouldn't hear of it. She knew that the Sovereign would be there, heatwave or not, wearing stockings and gloves and carrying a large handbag, a model of dutiful self-control. 'She has dedicated her whole life to Britain,' she told her friend Simone Simmons.[4]

The princess's takeaway from these often unproductive meetings was the Queen's observation that Diana's bulimia was the *cause* rather than the *symptom* of Charles's estrangement. At the same time, Her Majesty confided that she found the direction of her eldest son's life unfocused and that his behaviour could be odd and erratic. It did not escape her notice that he and Diana were equally unhappy and frustrated with their marriage.[5] There were no easy answers to this vexing issue, the Sovereign reduced to offering bromides in the face of Diana's tears.

The Queen's fortieth year as Head of State was not turning into a happy anniversary. Not by any means. In January 1992, Fergie and Andrew finally managed to make an appointment to discuss their failed five-year marriage with her. Even though Andrew was nominally the Monarch's favourite son, it had still taken him three weeks to arrange a summit. It was not a jovial gathering as the couple tried to explain how things had gone wrong and how they had let the Queen down. Fergie confessed that her own behaviour had not been befitting that of a duchess of the realm. For once, though, it was not entirely the fault of the royal system.

During their marriage Andrew, as a serving Navy officer, only spent about eighty days a year on shore leave. For the rest of the time, Fergie was left to her own devices and Andrew was not around to advise and guide her, which resulted in her making blunder after blunder. In her mind, she felt that she had not been given the support she deserved from courtiers, though her own greed combined with her newly elevated position did, in her father's words, 'go to her head': 'She didn't read the rule book properly.'[6]

The Queen, somewhat reluctantly, read the pair the riot act and convinced them to give their marriage another six months. They agreed to her wishes, in part, as Fergie reflected, because they had never seen her looking quite so sad.

Unfortunately, Her Majesty's desire for a reconciliation was thwarted within weeks when a cache of photographs from 1990 of the duchess on a Moroccan holiday with her lover Steve Wyatt and her eldest daughter Beatrice were stolen from a central London apartment and made their way onto the front pages of the tabloids. In March 1992, divorce lawyers were called in and Fergie was effectively banished from royal circles. As the BBC's royal correspondent Paul Reynolds broadcast: 'The knives are out for Fergie in the palace.' A former private secretary, Martin Charteris, described her as 'vulgar, vulgar, vulgar'[7] and Prince Philip made it clear that he never wanted to be in the same room as her again.

As Fergie and Andrew wrestled with their future, in February Diana and Charles flew to India on an official visit which laid bare their marital disconnect. It was symbolized when the princess sat on her own in front of the Taj Mahal in Agra, the temple dedicated to love, while her husband was at a business conference in Bangalore. After a polo match, when Charles was presented with the trophy by his wife, Diana deliberately moved her head when he went to kiss her cheek and his face ended up by her ear. The Queen, who was still at Sandringham, was a concerned viewer of this unhappy scene which was broadcast on news bulletins across the world. Soon enough, Her Majesty became the reluctant referee between the warring parties.

In late March, Diana's father Earl Spencer died suddenly following a heart attack while she, Charles and the boys were on a skiing holiday in Austria. When Diana was told about his death, she refused to return home with her husband, saying that she wanted the right to grieve without going through a hypocritical masquerade. Such was the ice-cold atmosphere in the ski resort of Lech that Charles asked her bodyguard, Inspector Ken Wharfe, to convince her to allow him to accompany her back to England. At first she refused point-blank, only relenting after a phone call with Windsor Castle, during which the Queen insisted that the couple put on a united front. As Diana predicted, the journey home together was purely for the sake of appearances. Once they landed in London, Charles headed to Highgrove while Diana was left alone at Kensington Palace to mourn.

There was more bad news for the Queen when, a few days after Earl Spencer's funeral, the palace announced the divorce of Princess Anne and her husband of more than eighteen years, Captain Mark Philips. Under normal circumstances the break-up would have captured the front pages, but these were not ordinary times as all eyes were on the Prince and Princess of Wales and their troubled relationship.

The dam burst on 16 June 1992 with the publication of the biography *Diana: Her True Story*. What was shocking was the book's depiction of a royal world where the emotional temperature was chilly and the social landscape forbidding. When the book was first serialized in *The Sunday Times* on 7 June under the front-page headline 'Diana driven to five suicide bids by "uncaring" Charles', the response was explosive.

Criticism of the book, which came from all sectors of society, was severe and unrelenting. The Archbishop of Canterbury, the chairman of the Press Complaints Commission, assorted Labour and Conservative Members of Parliament and rival newspaper editors joined together in their condemnation. Various bookshops and supermarkets banned its sale. However, Diana refused to put her name to a statement, to be issued by Buckingham Palace on behalf of the Prince and Princess of Wales, denouncing the book as inaccurate and distorted.

Though Charles's friends were instructed to remain silent, the Queen and Prince Philip could not. The day before the newspaper serialization, Prince Charles met his mother at Windsor Castle to discuss the possibility of seeking a separation. He had already lined up the prominent lawyer Lord Goodman, who had a reputation as a conciliator, to explore the legal and constitutional ramifications of a royal divorce.

On the day of the serialization, the Queen was the guest of honour at a polo match held in Windsor Great Park in which Charles was playing. Her decision to invite Andrew and Camilla Parker Bowles into the royal enclosure, while the nation was reviewing the details of the Waleses' miserable marriage, was seen by Diana and her supporters as a public rebuke of the princess.

As a matter of prudence, Prime Minister John Major was briefed on the marital crisis, as too were the Lord Chancellor, Lord Mackay, and the Archbishop of Canterbury, George Carey. All the mood music suggested that the prospects of a positive resolution were not good. Though the Queen had been painfully aware of the rift for some time, she was unprepared for such a detailed and public exposition. While the palace was searching for a suitable strategy, outwardly it was business as usual. Diana stood beside her mother-in-law on the balcony at Buckingham Palace for the official birthday salute in mid-June and the following week joined the Royal Family at Windsor Castle on the occasion of Royal Ascot.

Behind the scenes, the Queen and her aides tried to manage the unhappy situation. Her private secretary Sir Robert Fellowes asked the princess, his own sister-in-law, point-blank if she had cooperated with the book. She looked him straight in the eye and told him a bald-faced lie: 'No.' When he subsequently learned that she *was* involved he offered his resignation, which the Queen refused to accept.

Instead, she and Philip brokered a meeting with the prince and princess at Windsor Castle. During the conversation, Diana was alarmed when Prince Philip mentioned that there was a tape recording of the princess discussing the serialization, an assertion which puzzled her as she had had nothing to do with negotiations with *The Sunday Times*. While the duke may have been incorrectly briefed by aides, in Diana's eyes it confirmed her long-standing suspicions that her phone calls were regularly monitored by the shadowy security forces.

The central point, during what was a difficult and tetchy meeting, was that the senior royal couple insisted that the Waleses should give their marriage some more time and make a real effort to resolve their differences. According to Diana's account, their wishes conflicted with an earlier decision made between her and Prince Charles, when they had agreed that an amicable separation was the only practical way forward. The princess was horrified when her husband remained silent and agreed with his mother's proposal. Such was the concern of the Queen and Prince Philip that they suggested a date for a second meeting. To their lasting irritation, Diana did not show up.

Nonetheless, Philip continued the conversation by letter, sending the princess a series of missives, ranging from cajoling and pointed to conciliatory, where he asked her to look at her own behaviour and acknowledge that there had been faults on both sides, signing them: 'Affectionately Pa'. While he modestly admitted that he was not a professional marriage guidance counsellor, her father-in-law asked her to think very carefully about her marriage and the implications for herself, her children, her husband and the monarchy. In one blunt note, he implied that the Queen shared his view of Mrs Parker Bowles. He wrote: 'I cannot imagine anyone in their right mind leaving you for Camilla. Such a prospect never even entered our heads.'[8] It remained the popular view for many years to come.

In a dismal summer where calamity followed upon calamity, Fergie was next in the firing line. 'The redhead's in trouble,' Diana told a friend on his pager messenger, then a rudimentary form of texting.[9] It was August 1992 and the 'trouble' in question involved some long-range paparazzi pictures of a topless Duchess of York having her toes sucked by her 'financial adviser', John Bryan, at the side of a swimming pool in the south of France while her daughters looked on. As luck would have it the duchess, by then formally separated from Prince Andrew, had just returned to Balmoral to discuss access arrangements for the children when the story appeared on the front pages.

She may be the Queen and Head of State of Britain and the Commonwealth, but that means nothing to her dorgis and corgis who appear reluctant to follow her lead as she prepares to board an aircraft of the Queen's Flight at Aberdeen Airport, near to her private estate of Balmoral in the Scottish Highlands. Her corgis, a breed which she has had since childhood, are instantly recognizable symbols of her reign.

Above: The Queen in her favourite habitat – the countryside. Here she is chatting away with an unconcerned Highland shepherd at a gun-dog trial in the early 1960s. If she hadn't been the Queen, she wanted to live in the country surrounded by children, horses and dogs.

Above: Photographer Cecil Beaton captures the domesticity of motherhood in the grand setting of Buckingham Palace. The birth of Prince Edward in March 1964 completed her family. Prince Andrew, who was intrigued by his baby brother, looks on.

Above: The Queen tours the site of the mining disaster in the South Wales village of Aberfan, when a colliery spoil tip collapsed and slammed into a school and local houses killing 144, mainly children. Her Majesty always regretted not going earlier.

Above left: Prince Charles pledges his loyalty to the Queen at his investiture as Prince of Wales at Caernarfon Castle, 1 July 1969. The ceremony helped to reignite interest in the monarchy. Above right: In the unlikely setting of a fair in the New Zealand town of Greymouth in March 1970, the Queen made history when she became the first monarch since King Charles II to mingle with her subjects.

Below: The Queen in her study at Windsor Castle in May 1977 as she prepares for her Silver Jubilee celebrations. Note the picture of her father, King George VI, with his grandson, Prince Charles, placed prominently on her desk.

Above: Prince Charles kisses his bride, the newly minted Princess of Wales, after first asking his mother for permission. Their wedding, watched by 750 million people globally, was described by the Archbishop of Canterbury as 'the stuff of which fairy tales are made'.

Left: The Queen had a tricky relationship with Princess Diana, especially as her marriage began to collapse. While Diana respected her, she felt that she should blame her son for their marital breakdown. Here they are at Victoria Station in 1986, preparing for the arrival of a foreign dignitary.

Right: The Queen, accompanied by a young Prince William on the forecourt of Buckingham Palace, bids farewell to the Duke and Duchess of York as they embark on their honeymoon on 23 July 1986.

Above: The Queen, desolate and clearly upset, inspects the damage to her beloved Windsor Castle following a devastating fire in November 1992, the year she described as her 'Annus Horribilis', which saw the separation or divorce of three of her children. Above right: The Queen and Prince Philip survey the mountain of flowers outside Buckingham Palace following the death of Princess Diana in a car crash in a Paris underpass in August 1997.

Left: Her Majesty wipes away a tear during the decommissioning of the Royal Yacht *Britannia* in December 1997. The yacht was the Queen's much-loved home away from home on arduous official tours.

Below: The Queen, together with the rest of the Royal Family, bids a final farewell to the Queen Mother at her funeral on 9 April 2002 at Westminster Abbey.

Left: In 2002 the Queen and Prince Philip ride in the Gold State Coach on their way to St Paul's Cathedral for a Service of Thanksgiving to celebrate the fiftieth anniversary of Her Majesty's succession.

Right: Prince Harry essays a joke with his grandmother as they watch a fly-past over Buckingham Palace during the 2008 Trooping the Colour ceremony. Of all her grandchildren, Harry has often had the Queen's ear and been able to engage her in some of his jaunty schemes.

Below: The Queen took an early interest in Prince William's romance with Catherine Middleton and liked that she loved him for himself not his position. Here they are on their wedding day, 29 April 2011, on the Buckingham Palace balcony.

Left: The Queen and other senior members of the Royal Family watch an armada of water-borne craft as part of the Thames River Pageant to celebrate her Diamond Jubilee in June 2012. One casualty from the constant chilling rain was Prince Philip, who was later taken to hospital with an infection and missed the rest of the festivities.

Right: The future is assured. The Queen and Prince William point out aircraft to Prince George, then aged two, whose arrival pushed Prince Harry down the line of succession. The Duchess of Cambridge and Princess Charlotte look on during the traditional Trooping the Colour tableau in 2016.

Below: Happy families? Prince William cracks wise as the latest recruit to the Royal Family, Meghan Markle, joins in the merriment while the Royal Air Force stages a fly-past in July 2018 to celebrate its centenary. Unity did not last long. Harry and Meghan moved to California after leaving the Royal Family, and later accused the institution of various acts of racism.

Left: At the funeral service for Prince Philip, who died peacefully on 9 April 2021, the Queen was forced to sit on her own due to strict COVID-19 regulations. The sight of Her Majesty, hunched and diminutive, saying her final farewells to her husband of more than 73 years without any member of her family nearby to comfort her, was for many the most poignant moment of a brief but moving ceremony at St George's Chapel, Windsor.

Above: The Queen is in the handshaking and people-meeting business. So, when the pandemic took hold, she was forced to adapt, using modern technology to speak remotely to those she would otherwise see in person. Here she is in her study at Windsor Castle, where she remained for much of the crisis.

Left: Thrilled to be back. In one of her first public engagements since the death of Prince Philip, the Queen attended Royal Ascot week. She genuinely loves the turf, a passion that began when she was a little girl. It was no surprise when, in 2021, she was inducted into the QIPCO British Champions Series Hall of Fame.

As she came down for breakfast, the rest of the Royal Family were studiously examining the tabloid story at the table. It was a moment of excruciating embarrassment, even by her own standards. As she recalled in her autobiography: 'It would be accurate to report that the porridge was getting cold. Eyes wide and mouths ajar, the adults were flipping through the *Daily Mirror* and the rest of the tabloids ... I had been exposed for what I truly was. Worthless. Unfit. A national disgrace.'[10] There was little sense of irony in her final description.

The Queen was furious and summoned Fergie up to her sitting room. In her eyes, even though the disgraced Duchess of York was now separated, she still had a royal title and the appellation 'Her Royal Highness'. Such behaviour had resulted in exposing herself to ridicule and the monarchy to contempt. Her mother-in-law was cold, ice-cold, as she listed her transgressions and the damage she had done to the institution to which the Sovereign had devoted her life. She was also deeply upset on behalf of her son, who, according to one close figure, had been made 'to look such a cuckolded fool before the entire world'.[11] Fergie later recalled: 'Her anger wounded me to the core.'[12]

The almost weekly accumulation of family scandal severely jolted the Queen's habitual equanimity. One senior courtier at Balmoral during this unhappy period described her as looking 'grey and ashen and completely flat. She looked so awful.'[13] As a rather unusual pick-me-up, however, she and Prince Philip decided to go off ferreting, the couple and their gamekeeper using ferrets to catch rabbits and rats on the estate. She drove off with a smile on her face, presumably looking forward to a brief break from the never-ending carousel of bad news.

In a kind of emotional ping-pong, three days later it was Diana's turn to face the music. On 23 August, *The Sun* revealed the existence of a tape recording of her speaking to a long-time admirer, James Gilbey, on her mobile phone. In the early days of these then brick-sized devices, radio hams were able to listen in to other people's conversations and, if they wished, make a recording. Diana's worst phone-tapping fears had come true. Suspicions that she was and had been targeted by her enemies seemed to be borne out by the tape.

The embarrassing twenty-three-minute conversation with Gilbey had been recorded on New Year's Eve 1989, but was not published until almost three years later, and at a most sensitive time in the marriage of the Prince and Princess of Wales. During the late-night chat, Gilbey affectionately referred to Diana as 'Squidgy', which led to this latest scandal being dubbed 'Squidgygate'. In the surreptitiously taped conversation, Diana criticized Prince Charles as well as the Duchess of York and the Queen Mother. She told Gilbey that her husband made her life 'real, real torture'. She also complained that she was not properly appreciated by the Royal Family for her work on their behalf.

Though not as humiliating as the Fergie photos, the Squidgygate tape seriously compromised the princess. Her comments about various royal in-laws were certainly injudicious, but for many, including Diana, the prime takeaway was that the tape's contents had been made public at a crucial moment, as it could weaken her position regarding her future dealings with the Royal Family now that separation and divorce were being spoken of openly. Many thought the tape was a 'set-up', so much so that Stella Rimington, the head of MI5, was forced to formally deny any involvement.

During this fevered summer, the Queen summoned Harry Herbert, the son of her racing manager the Earl of Carnarvon, to Balmoral. He was liked and trusted by both Diana and the Sovereign, who wanted to get a friend's honest opinion on the state of her daughter-in-law's marriage. As they looked out over a 'beautiful' scene of rolling hills and heather, he explained to Her

Majesty that it was a bad time for Diana. 'The light had gone out,' he recalled. 'The Queen wanted to talk to me about it because she was so worried. It was a sad discussion, a sad moment, because that was when everything was at its worst.'[14]

The Monarch had a further sense of how bad the situation had become when the princess declined to accompany her husband on the first-ever royal visit to South Korea. She was impervious to all entreaties, even though she realized that her absence would create a media firestorm. At Balmoral, the Queen implored her to change her mind. Initially, Diana was deaf to reason and it was a sign of her mother-in-law's waning authority over her that a royal command no longer inspired instant obedience. It was only after a concerted campaign by the Queen and Prince Charles that she finally agreed to go.

She shouldn't have bothered, as the tour was a disaster from the moment they landed, the royal couple barely able to raise a smile or a glimmer of enthusiasm. 'We've lost this one,' palace press officer Dickie Arbiter said out loud, as he watched their distant body language as they walked down the aircraft steps.[15] They were dubbed 'The Glums' by the media, who inevitably focused on their disintegrating marriage rather than the purpose of the tour, which was to improve trade and cultural links between the two countries.

During this tumultuous period the monarchy faced an existential crisis. Opinion polls revealed the general public's growing dissatisfaction with the institution. Numerous Church figures castigated the Royal Family for failing to provide a healthy example of family life. Walter Bagehot's 'interesting' notion of 'a family on the throne' no longer seemed so appealing.

At around the same time the Queen's financial lawyer, Sir Matthew Farrer, was deep in negotiations with Downing Street over secret proposals for the Queen to pay tax on her private income. It was considered the minimum needed to stay the slew of criticism.

In the midst of this correspondence, Prince Philip visited Argentina on official business. While he was away, the Queen suffered the greatest physical catastrophe of her reign. On 20 November 1992, which by chance was the day of the couple's forty-fifth wedding anniversary, Windsor Castle caught fire. The inferno began in Queen Victoria's Private Chapel when a faulty spotlight overheated and set a curtain on fire. It quickly engulfed St George's Hall and the chapel. The blaze could be seen for miles and needed over 200 firemen and thirty-nine appliances to bring under control.

It was a devastating event. Ever the pragmatist, the Queen would later remark that the three positive takeaways were that no one was injured, many of the most precious artefacts had already been removed (in advance of planned rewiring work) and it was a still evening so the blaze did not spread as quickly as it might have done. In a further slice of luck, Prince Andrew was on hand to organize the removal of paintings, antique furniture and other works of art, with workers forming a human chain to carry them to safety.

When the Queen, dressed in a green mackintosh and matching hat, came to visit the smouldering ruin, she looked and indeed was utterly devastated, shocked beyond words – and tears. The castle, an icon of Britain's history, had also been her home for most of her life. She retreated to the Royal Lodge and spent the weekend with her mother and sister, almost inconsolable. 'The symbolism of the fire at Windsor Castle was not lost on anyone inside the family,' Diana recalled.

Four days after the blaze, nursing a heavy cold but with her husband now by her side, she addressed the Guildhall in London at an event to mark the fortieth anniversary of her accession. In a voice hoarse with coughing, she spoke sadly about the events of the year. '1992 is not a year on which I shall look back with undiluted pleasure. In the words of one of my more sympathetic correspondents, it has turned out to be an '*Annus Horribilis*'. Or as *The Sun* newspaper, one of the Queen's chief tormentors, translated it: 'One's Bum Year.'

She went on to acknowledge that any institution must expect criticism, but hoped that it was done 'with a touch of gentleness, good humour and understanding'. Sadly, there was little on offer. The initial response to the notion that the taxpayer would pay for the restoration of the castle, it being a national monument, was angrily dismissed by the media and the public. A rancorous debate ensued about who was responsible for footing the bill. Several lawmakers and parts of the media insisted that the Queen should pay, even though Windsor Castle was legally owned by the nation.

As a result, the Queen, who was shocked by the hostile attitude of some of her subjects, eventually agreed that parts of Buckingham Palace could be opened up to the public for the first time to help fund the restoration of Windsor Castle by using monies raised from the entry charge. It was estimated that this would cover around 70 per cent of the repair costs, and so the Sovereign also donated £2 million of her personal wealth to the cause.

Unfortunately for the Queen, the debate over who was responsible for the cost of the castle's refurbishment became conflated with the announcement by the Prime Minister, on 26 November, that the Monarch and the Prince of Wales had agreed to pay tax on their private income from April 1993 onwards, and also that the Civil List, the taxpayers' contribution to the upkeep of the monarchy and all its trappings, was to be reduced. In this sour public mood, many argued that Her Majesty had been forced into this position as a result of the outcry over the Windsor Castle fire rather than, as was the case, that this had been a result of months of earlier discussions. 'The Queen pays tax and it's a victory for people power,' boasted *The Sun*.[16]

In this republican atmosphere it was clear that, whatever she did, the Queen couldn't catch a break. Her earlier invitation to a firm of accountants to look for savings in the workings of the monarchy – she accepted without demur more than 200 recommendations – was seen as too little too late. Her own dry suggestion that members of her Household no longer dot their i's and cross their t's in order to save ink was not received with as much mirth as it would have been in previous times.

The Queen had little to smile about. An irate phone call from Prince Charles capped off a miserable year. He had arranged a shooting party with friends at Sandringham, and William and Harry had been scheduled to join the group; Diana, however, had other plans. Not only did she refuse to go, but she also insisted on taking the boys to Windsor Castle. For the prince it was the final straw and he explained his exasperation to his mother. Once again, as was her policy, she counselled patience, but Charles had reached the end of his tether. In an uncharacteristic outburst, he shouted down the line to her: 'Don't you realize she's mad, mad, mad?' and slammed down the phone.[17]

Everyone, including the Queen, was now coming to accept that a separation – the solution Diana that had been arguing in favour of for months – was the only workable way forward for the warring Waleses. On 25 November, just five days after the Windsor fire, the couple met at Kensington Palace to confirm their agreed course of action and sort out access to the boys and other matters, before passing on their decision to their families and lawyers.

Their decision became public on 9 December, when Prime Minister John Major stood up in the House of Commons and announced 'with regret' the separation of the Prince and Princess of Wales. He went on to say that the split was amicable and that it had no constitutional implications. But he drew puzzled gasps from lawmakers when his carefully worded remarks included the assertion that 'there is no reason why the Princess of Wales should not be crowned Queen in due course'. This made no sense. As MPs and commentators had quickly concluded, the plain facts were that separation was simply a prelude to divorce. Moreover, a divorced princess could not possibly be the Queen of England. The idea of a divorced, or even separated, King and Queen sitting beside one another during their Coronation was grotesque.

In almost sixty years, the Royal Family – and society – had seemingly come full circle. Edward VIII, as Head of the Church of England, abdicated in 1936 in order to marry the twice-divorced American, Wallis Simpson. Now it seemed that there was no hindrance to allowing a divorced Prince of Wales to claim the throne.

The Queen was, according to a friend, at her 'wits' end', wondering aloud when her family and the institution that was her lifeblood would be given some respite. A clergyman who has known the Sovereign for years observed her mood at this difficult time. 'She felt that things were slipping away from her, that so many horrible things were happening, and when would it end? In a sense, she was feeling that she was losing control. It was the cumulative weight of all the personal disasters.'[18] Staff also noticed that her modest consumption of alcohol – she enjoys a dry Martini in the evening – had noticeably increased.

The run-up to Christmas, a traditional time of good cheer, brought little reprieve. Days after the separation announcement, Diana made an appointment to see the Queen at Buckingham Palace. When she entered the Sovereign's suite, Diana burst into floods of tears claiming that everyone was against her.

'The Queen didn't know what to do,' recalled a lady-in-waiting afterwards. 'She has always hated this kind of emotional confrontation and, frankly, has never had to deal with it before or since.'[19]

During their hour-long conversation, which was punctuated by more tears from Diana, the Queen was able to reassure her that, come what may, she would never be challenged regarding custody arrangements for her two boys. This was a profound relief for the princess, who had fretted about this issue long before the actual separation.

Early the following year, William and Harry were away at boarding school when yet another scandal concerning their parents burst into the open. This time it was Prince Charles's feet that were being held to the flames. 'Just when we thought things couldn't get any worse,' the Queen is said to have remarked wearily.[20]

Once again it was a late-night mobile telephone conversation – illicitly recorded by radio hams, who listened into conversations as a form of titillation – which was the cause of the royal embarrassment. In the so-called Camillagate tapes, which were released in January 1993, the prince and his lover Mrs Parker Bowles were recorded having a lovey-dovey chat. During their conversation, which had originally taken place in December 1989, Prince Charles made distasteful references to his desire to be a tampon inside his lover, a sentiment which Diana later described as 'just sick.'[21]

It was clear to listeners that Charles and Camilla had enjoyed a passionate and enduring relationship that had fully justified Diana's long-held suspicions. If they hadn't thought so before, the majority of the public believed that Diana was indeed the wronged wife. As the prince's popularity ratings plummeted, some churchmen and politicians publicly declared that Charles was not fit to be King. The cry arose that the crown should skip a generation and go directly to Prince William. While the Queen was resolutely opposed to any change in the rules of succession, it is not a clamour that has abated much over the ensuing decades.

For the next few years, the 'War of the Waleses' consumed the media and agitated the Queen and the rest of the Royal Family. Everyone tiptoed around Diana, concerned that the unpredictable princess, referred to as a loose cannon, would further damage the already listing institution. Much against the better judgement of her mother and sister, the Queen tried to keep the Princess of Wales within the fold, quietly hopeful that at some point Charles and his wife could effect a reconciliation. During this delicate period, the olive branch was ever present.

The Queen's somewhat forlorn wish for a positive resolution echoed her mindset during the marital convulsions of her sister and Lord Snowdon. Long, long after the couple had accepted that their marriage was dead and buried, the Queen refused to inter the corpse, desperate that things would somehow change for the better.

Her policy fed into her personality as her unwillingness to grasp the nettle would unnecessarily drag out difficult issues, especially those involving the family, though sometimes playing for time did work. She had done so when Margaret fell in love with the married and subsequently divorced Group Captain Peter Townsend at a time when divorce was neither acceptable to the State nor the Church of England. Back then, the Queen had played the long game, which was a strategy that ultimately helped to resolve this vexatious issue.

The Waleses' situation was quite another matter as the drip, drip, drip of bitterness and anger seeping into the media slowly corroded respect for the monarchy. The Sovereign was, though, clinging to the words of Prime Minister Major, who had asserted in the House of Commons that the couple had no plans to divorce. As long as that notion held good, there could still be light at the end of the dark tunnel.

Long after other members of the Royal Family had given up, the Queen always lent a listening ear to the princess, ever concerned about her well-being. She would receive messages as to Diana's state of mind from her private secretary, Sir Robert Fellowes, whose wife Jane was Diana's sister, and occasionally phone her at Kensington Palace to check that she was all right.

In late April 1993, the Queen invited the Princess of Wales to a

State banquet held at Buckingham Palace in honour of President Mário Soares of Portugal. She did so without telling any other members of the Royal Family, including Charles. They were furious when they found out, but the Queen was doing all she could to encourage a truce between the Waleses in their increasingly bitter feud. After all, the separated princess still continued to perform royal duties and even made overseas visits on behalf of the monarchy. She also invited Diana to Sandringham for Christmas that year, when the Waleses had been officially parted for twelve months. The princess stayed overnight on Christmas Eve and went with her sons and the other royals to church, but then left before Christmas Day lunch. Servants recalled that the atmosphere lightened after her departure.

In the end, it was not the hostility of the Royal Family that made Diana ultimately take the decision to step back from formal duties, but rather the behaviour of the tabloid media. In November 1993, a Sunday newspaper published covertly taken pictures of the princess as she exercised in a private gym. The gym owner, Bryce Taylor, had rigged his workout equipment with cameras to snap her during her early-morning routine. Diana was shocked, the Queen horrified. 'Oh my God, no' was her response as she reviewed the Sunday papers over breakfast at Windsor Castle.[22] As a result of this intrusion, Diana decided to retire for a time from public life and gave what was known as her 'Time and Space' speech on 3 December at a charity lunch for Headway, the brain injury association.

She announced that this unwarranted invasion into her private life had forced her to step back and reconsider her public role. While she thanked the Queen and the Duke of Edinburgh for their kindness and support, her husband's name was conspicuously omitted.

As much as the Queen worried about her son and daughter-in-law, her focus, too, was on William and Harry. She would always clear her diary if there was a possibility of Diana bringing them to Buckingham Palace or Windsor Castle for afternoon tea. Such meetings were useful to Diana, too. Her private secretary Patrick Jephson observed: 'The princess also used these opportunities to express loyalty and give assurances about her wish to do no harm either to the institution or to her husband who would inherit it.'[23] Her protestations of loyalty were met with scepticism by both the Queen and Jephson, though they cautiously continued the collaboration.

For her part, and somewhat naively, Diana continued to see her mother-in-law as a family referee with regard to her separation from Prince Charles. She was frustrated that the Monarch had not intervened to end his relationship with Camilla Parker Bowles. Although both the Queen and the Queen Mother had shown their disapproval of this long-running affair by refusing to invite Mrs Parker Bowles to any Court functions, it was, as far as Diana was concerned, not enough. 'My mother-in-law has been totally supportive, but it's so difficult to get a decision out of her,' she observed diplomatically.[24] Essentially, she was playing a waiting game, being prepared to sit on the sidelines until her husband took the initiative and asked for a divorce. She felt that because he had asked her to marry him, so he should be the one to initiate proceedings. It was a view she made clear to the Queen in the hope that she would push her son in the direction of divorce.

After giving her 'Time and Space' speech, Diana was nervously anticipating her husband's authorized book and television documentary about his life and work, which had been two years in the making. So too was his mother. While relations between the Sovereign and heir are historically regarded as difficult – a famous example being Queen Victoria and the Prince of Wales, later Edward VII – in this case and at this moment they were racing towards a head-on collision. Her Majesty and her advisers felt that Charles's decision, encouraged by his private secretary Richard Aylard, to work with broadcaster Jonathan Dimbleby on a 'warts and all' biography was a gross mistake. His strategy of airing his dirty linen in public by confessing his adultery with Mrs Parker Bowles was viewed with horror by the palace.

Charles and his camp argued that only by acknowledging the issue directly could a line be drawn to enable him to move forward. It was by no means a unanimous opinion. Some supporters, including Camilla Parker Bowles herself, thought it a great mistake. His estranged wife felt the same.

The resulting documentary, *Charles: The Private Man, the Public Role*, was broadcast on ITV on 29 June 1994, the same night that Diana had been invited to the *Vanity Fair* fundraising dinner at the Serpentine Gallery in Kensington Gardens. The princess arrived at the venue dressed in a flirty black Christina Stambolian number that was forever known as 'the revenge dress', as it neatly overshadowed Charles's prime-time confessional. Though the programme focused on his good works, it was defined in the public's mind by his strangled admission of adultery. When Dimbleby asked the question, 'Did you try to be faithful and honourable to your wife when you took on the vow of marriage?' the prince answered, 'Yes, until it became irretrievably broken down, us both having tried.'[25]

Neither the television profile nor the confession went down well either inside or outside Buckingham Palace. The Queen's former press secretary Dickie Arbiter observed: 'The programme was a complete whinge, a terrible own goal that not just affected relations between the prince and princess, but between St James's Palace and Buckingham Palace.'[26] That is to say, between the Queen and her eldest son.

If the documentary was divisive, the authorized biography

was, in many ways, so much worse. Not only had his friends and staff been given licence to speak freely, but the prince had also allowed Dimbleby access to official papers. Once this fact had come to the Queen's attention, however, the papers were retrieved and those sections of the book based on confidential State papers were excised.

Her Majesty was fighting a rearguard action to save her son from himself – and from damaging the monarchy. Unfortunately, she could do little about the *Sunday Times* serialization, which coincided precisely with her historic visit to Russia, the first by a British sovereign. Charles was doing to his mother exactly what he had complained that his wife had often done: overshadowing her work through his own behaviour.

This tactless diary clash paled into insignificance when the contents of the biography were made public. Jonathan Dimbleby, with the approval of Prince Charles, described his subject as suffering from a lack of appreciation and affection from either of his parents. His mother was remote, his father was a bully. Thus, the reason for the breakdown of his marriage was forged in the crucible of his childhood, where he wanted for nothing except love and parental warmth. In other words, his marital collapse was not his fault. It was laid at the door of the Queen and Prince Philip. That neatly sidestepped his long-term relationship with Mrs Parker Bowles.

For her part, the Queen was disappointed at the way that Charles had drifted back to Camilla amidst the turmoil of his own marriage. He was taking the easy way out, she thought. What is more, he made himself a hostage to fortune when he stated that Camilla's presence in his life was 'non-negotiable'.[27]

Two absent words run like a river through the recent history of the Royal Family: 'Well done.' During her brief stay within the institution, Meghan Markle complained that she was never praised by anyone in the system. So too did Diana. For Charles, he would have done anything to hear those words from the Queen. But he never did. As one of his circle noted: 'He can't understand the total absence of motherly genes in her. He feels that she doesn't really like him.'[28] Other friends repeated this refrain: 'Charles is absolutely desperate for his mother's approval and knows he'll never really get it. He's the wrong sort of person for her – too needy, too vulnerable, too emotional, too complicated, too self-centred.'[29]

The tragedy of Charles's upbringing, of course, is that he would go on to repeat his memory of his father's behaviour towards him with his own sons. Prince Harry publicly questioned why his father had refused to question the self-imposed hardships of his own life. Instead, he replicated the same actions and attitudes when raising his children. Harry explained in a television interview: 'My father used to say to me when I was younger, "Well, it was like that for me, so it's going to be like that for you". He went on to query the logic of this parental philosophy, saying: 'That doesn't make sense. Just because you suffered, that doesn't mean that your kids have to suffer, in fact quite the opposite.'[30]

If Prince Charles had imagined receiving sympathy from his siblings after the publication of his biography, he was profoundly mistaken. His brothers and sister were furious at this unfair and one-sided portrayal, and told him so. They had very different memories of their upbringing, cherishing the times that their father read to them or made up a story at bedtime, took them swimming in the palace pool and taught them country pursuits. In their eyes, Charles was articulating *his* truth about his childhood, not necessarily *the* truth, or the truth as they remembered it.

Inevitably, because of her unique role as mother, Head of State, Head of the Commonwealth and head of the household, the Queen had had to ration her time, especially during Charles's early years. Though perhaps it could be argued that she had delegated too much parental control to her husband, his bluff, brusque behaviour being considerably at odds with his son's sensitive spirit.

The Sovereign and her husband had no right of reply. By instinct and training, the public confessional was anathema to them. 'We did our best' was all Prince Philip would say about the couple's parenting skills when asked by his biographer Gyles Brandreth.[31] They had no choice but to take their son's critical testimony on the chin. But not so when the Princess of Wales decided to go public as well. At last the Queen was stirred into action over an issue – the separation of the Prince and Princess of Wales – which had been hanging over the monarchy for so long.

On 20 November 1995, Diana appeared on the BBC's long-standing documentary series *Panorama*, and spoke candidly about her loves and her life. Wearing striking black eye makeup that gave her a haunted look, she discussed her eating disorders, her failed marriage, her depression and her husband's adultery. She also talked about her lover James Hewitt, her belief that Charles was not up to the 'top job' of King and her desire to be a 'queen of people's hearts'. She reserved her most devastating zinger for her love rival, Mrs Parker Bowles. When interviewer Martin Bashir asked about Camilla's role in the princess's relationship with the Prince of Wales, she replied sweetly: 'Well, there were three of us in this marriage so it was a bit crowded.'

She shot the devastating interview on a quiet Sunday at Kensington Palace, her only stipulation being that she could inform the Queen about it before the BBC announced its coup. When she spoke to the Queen's private secretary Sir Robert Fellowes, he asked innocently if it was an interview for the popular charity Children in Need. When she told him that it was for the hard-hitting current-affairs show *Panorama*, he visibly blanched. His response of 'Oh' said it all. Despite entreaties from her private secretary, lawyer and others in her dwindling circle, Diana steadfastly refused to divulge the contents.

When it was broadcast, her television confessional was both shocking and, as far as the Royal Family were concerned, unforgiveable. From the perspective of the Queen and other royals, notably Princess Margaret, Diana crossed a line when she spoke of her wish to be a 'queen of people's hearts' and articulated her doubts about Prince Charles's fitness to be King. She told Bashir: 'Because I know the character, I would think that the top job, as I call it, would bring enormous limitations to him, and I don't know whether he could adapt to that.'

At the time, the programme was seen as a devastating riposte to Prince Charles's Dimbleby interview, a fatal ratcheting of the couple's escalating feud that finally prompted decisive action from the Queen. Diana, in the eyes of many, had gone too far. Her behaviour was seen as inexcusable in terms of both questioning Charles's right to be King and challenging the Sovereign herself. There was only one Queen and she had served the nation dutifully for more than forty years.

When the Queen finally watched a recording of the show, she was despairing, her husband apoplectic. Something must be done, not just for the sake of the monarchy, but also for their grandchildren. Having held out the olive branch for so long, Her Majesty was now determined to cut the marital Gordian knot. She spoke to the Prime Minister John Major, the Archbishop of Canterbury George Carey and the historian Lord Blake, who advised the palace on constitutional issues. 'The present situation, in which they seem to be giving a sort of tit-for-tat, running each other down, really has become almost intolerable,' warned the peer.[32]

Once the Queen had made up her mind, matters moved forward quickly. On 18 December 1995, Diana received a handwritten note from the Sovereign delivered by a uniformed courier to Kensington

Palace from Windsor Castle. It was, Diana noted ruefully, the first letter she had ever received from her mother-in-law. In part, the missive said: 'I have consulted with the Archbishop of Canterbury and with the Prime Minister and, of course, with Charles, and we have decided that the best course for you is divorce.'[33]

Shortly afterwards, she received a note from Prince Charles in which he personally requested a divorce. In the letter, which began 'Dearest Diana', the prince described the failure of their relationship as a 'national and personal tragedy'.[34] She duly forwarded both pieces of correspondence to her lawyer, Anthony Julius, and sent holding responses saying that she would need time to reflect and consider her options.

The timing of the Queen's historic letter reflected a genuine sense of crisis and exasperation felt by senior royals and their courtiers. It also exposed the failure of her previous policy of prevarication and conciliation, which had merely served to drag out the marital conflict and cause long-term harm to the Crown. As the historian Sarah Bradford observed: 'The Waleses' divorce was undoubtedly the most damaging event since the abdication. It brought into question the reality of the monarchy and the Queen's personal attributes as a mother and as a monarch.'[35]

Even in this personal crisis, the Queen still invited Diana to stay with the family at Sandringham for Christmas. The princess declined, though, telling friends, 'I would have gone up in my BMW and come out in a coffin'.[36] Instead, she spent Christmas Day alone at Kensington Palace before flying off to the Caribbean for a much-needed break.

The princess's decision to turn down the Sovereign's offer, which would normally have been viewed as a command, marked the nadir of her relationship with her mother-in-law. It was an affront too many. From then on, the Queen was less available to take her phone calls and her invitations to afternoon tea were not as frequent. Their dealings were necessarily more business-like than before as Her Majesty had become one of the interested parties in divorce negotiations.

Discussions with Prince Charles focused on the princess's financial settlement, while the Queen dealt with Diana's future title, her continued residence at Kensington Palace and arrangements for her boys. At a meeting at Buckingham Palace in February 1996, the Sovereign, once again, reassured Diana about the custody and care of William and Harry, and indicated that it was 'highly unlikely' that Charles would ever marry Camilla Parker Bowles.

The princess's title did, though, become a matter of dispute. It was reported that she had decided to become known as Diana, Princess of Wales, and had told friends that she had agreed to drop the 'Her Royal Highness' appellation. But the Queen intervened, making clear that Diana's 'decisions' were still just requests and that she had in no way been pressurized to give up the HRH. 'It is wrong that the Queen or the Prince asked her,' said an official palace spokesman.[37]

After agreeing to an uncontested divorce on 28 February 1996, months of negotiations took place until the decree nisi was granted on 15 July, with the decree absolute following on 28 August. Despite giving up her title, which would mean curtsying to junior royals in the future, the resulting financial agreement – an estimated lump sum of around £17 million – had made her a very rich woman in her own right. As for her title, Prince William told her: 'Don't worry, Mummy, I will give it back to you one day when I am King.'[38]

In the months that followed her divorce, the absence of a royal appellation seemed to help rather than hinder her popularity. She became seen as a strong, independent and glamorous humanitarian in her own right, a feature of her life that had been developing since her separation. As a semi-detached royal, Diana had been courted by the likes of American statesman Henry

Kissinger, former US secretary of state Colin Powell and media queen Barbara Walters. She was also viewed as a global superstar, whose causes and concerns eclipsed those espoused by the House of Windsor.

The Queen always appreciated that the monarchy survived by the consent of the people. She fully recognized that, after a bruising few years, now was the time to regroup.

CHAPTER TWELVE

FLOWERS, FLAGS AND FORTITUDE

I N LATE AUGUST 1997, members of the Royal Family were enjoying their annual summer holiday at Balmoral. William and Harry had just come down from the hills and were playing with their cousin Zara Phillips in the grounds of the castle when the phone rang. It was their mother, who had just landed in Paris. She was due back in London the following day and was keen to touch base with her sons.

Harry was too involved in his game to want to spend much time chatting. Their conversation was short and monosyllabic, the princess suffering the frustration every mother knows when their children would rather be doing something else. 'I can't really necessarily remember what I said,' revealed Harry years later. 'But all I do remember is probably, you know, regretting for the rest of my life how short the phone call was.'[1]

William was a little easier to communicate with as he wanted to speak to his mother about an issue that was on his mind. The prince was worried about a proposed photo call that had been arranged to mark his third year at Eton, his exclusive public school. Harry had been held back a year at Ludgrove preparatory school and William felt that the staged event would overshadow his brother. Diana promised to discuss it with his father when she returned to the UK the following day. She had spent the last few days on an idyllic sunshine cruise with her boyfriend, Dodi Fayed, sailing round the Mediterranean on board *Jonikal,* the yacht owned by Dodi's controversial businessman father, Mohamed Al-Fayed. Now she was looking forward to seeing her boys.

The couple had flown from Sardinia to Paris on a private jet on Saturday 30 August. On arrival in the French capital, they briefly stopped at Villa Windsor, the former home of the Duke and Duchess of Windsor in the Bois de Boulogne, then inspected Dodi's apartment before driving to the Ritz Hotel where they planned to stay for the night. During the journey, they were surrounded by motorbike riders, drivers with cameramen travelling pillion, who were desperately trying to get shots of the couple.

Late into the evening, the paparazzi were still waiting by the front entrance of the Ritz when, in a change of plan, Dodi, Diana, their chauffeur and bodyguard left by the hotel's rear entrance and got in their car, intent on heading to Dodi's apartment. Five minutes later, the hired Mercedes hurtled into the thirteenth pillar of the Place de l'Alma underpass by the River Seine, killing Dodi and driver Henri Paul instantly and leaving Diana and their bodyguard Trevor Rees-Jones grievously injured.

At one o'clock on the morning of 31 August, the Queen's assistant private secretary Robin Janvrin, who was staying on the Balmoral estate, was woken up by a telephone call from the British Ambassador to France, Sir Michael Jay, informing him of the accident. Janvrin was confounded. He hadn't even known that Diana was in Paris. He immediately threw on some clothes and alerted the staff in the 'big house' to wake Her Majesty and other senior royals. By the time he had got there, the whole castle was stirring, the mood one of bewilderment and confusion. 'What is she up to now?' asked the Queen.[2]

In a rare show of affection, the Sovereign and her son physically consoled one another, perhaps sensing that this event was going to be emotionally unprecedented. The Queen ordered a pot of tea but never touched a drop as she, Prince Philip and Prince Charles paced the tartan-carpeted corridor wondering what should be done.

Early reports suggested that Diana had only suffered a broken arm and had walked away from the accident. Her mother-in-law's initial response to the news was extraordinary: 'Someone must have greased the brakes.'[3] Her gnomic reaction shocked and puzzled her staff, who rarely heard her use such colloquial language.

An alternative view was that the Queen was not referring to Diana being the target of such a treacherous act, but to the possibility that one of Mohamed Al-Fayed's many avowed enemies had taken lethal action against his son and that Diana was innocent collateral damage. Sinister schemes, murderous intrigues and cold-hearted conspiracies: anything seemed possible in the uneasy hours before dawn.

As the minutes ticked by the news became ever bleaker. The family were told that paramedics were fighting to keep the princess alive. At that point she was already on artificial respiration, her blood pressure was very low and she had suffered a major cardiac arrest. While Prince Charles arranged to fly to France to be by Diana's side, Ambassador Jay relayed the terrible news that she was dead.

The news triggered all the swirling emotions that the Prince of Wales had hitherto been keeping under control. He wept, saying over and over: 'What have we done to deserve this?' His first instincts were about how the public would blame him for the tragedy, an assumption that was largely accurate. It was an issue that he discussed at length with Camilla, who was at her Wiltshire home, and his London-based aide Mark Bolland. He feared that the world would go mad and it could destroy the monarchy.[4] It was a measure of his character and position, torn between duty and self-interest, that his fears for the future of the monarchy became conflated with his concern and sorrow for his children, who had just lost their mother.

As the respective staffs of the Queen and the Prince of Wales tried to decide the official response to Diana's death, Her Majesty wisely ordered the removal of the radio and television from the boys' nursery. She did not want the princes to hear about the news from anyone but their father. William and Harry were her immediate and continuing priority.

The Queen had also been at Balmoral when Mountbatten was assassinated. Then, after processing the initial shock and disbelief, the Royal Family and their advisers knew that there was a road map for the funeral arrangements. Uncle Dickie had meticulously planned everything, right down to the last medal and insignia. For a disaffected Princess of Wales, who had voluntarily relinquished her formal HRH appellation during the divorce negotiations, everyone, including the Monarch, was entering unknown territory.

Although Diana was the mother of the future king and his brother, since the divorce she was technically no longer a member of the Royal Family. Not only did she spend much of her time in America, but she had also not attended family gatherings for several years. The last time the Queen had seen Diana was at William's confirmation in March, more than five months before. Initially, it was the express wish of the Spencer family that the funeral be a private affair followed by a memorial service. 'When I rang up,' says one ex-courtier who was out of the country, 'there was genuine uncertainty about whether it [the funeral] was going to be public or private. If it had been private, guidance wouldn't have been needed.'[5]

In the meantime, the circumstances surrounding the interment of her boyfriend, Dodi Fayed, had been swift and straightforward. Within hours of a prompt return to the UK, an Islamic funeral was held at Regent's Park Mosque before his body was laid to rest at Brookwood Cemetery near Woking in Surrey.

While discussions continued apace regarding the most appropriate course of action for Diana's funeral, the new Prime Minister, Tony Blair, inevitably became involved. Based at his Sedgefield constituency in County Durham, he immediately appreciated the global implications. He told his press secretary Alastair Campbell: 'This is going to unleash grief like no one has ever seen anywhere in the world.'[6]

After further discussion between the Spencers, the palace and Downing Street, the family accepted that a private funeral was inappropriate for a much-loved public figure. The Queen's private secretary Sir Robert Fellowes was pivotal. As he was married to Diana's sister Jane, he was able to steer the Spencer family towards accepting a more regal and public send-off for the princess.

Back at Balmoral, Prince Charles readied himself to break the tragic news to his sons. At 7.15, he woke fifteen-year-old William and told him of his mother's death. 'I knew something was wrong,' William later recalled. 'I kept waking up all night.'[7] His father explained that he had to fly to Paris and so the boys would stay with their grandparents at Balmoral. 'Thank goodness we're all together,' was the Queen Mother's immediate response. 'We can look after them.'[8] Her mood, according to a courtier, was 'steely'. Like the rest of the family, she was trying to cope with the tragedy by sticking to routine. Fortunately, Princess Anne's son Peter Phillips and the princes' official companion Tiggy Legge-Bourke were guests at the castle, so they could help keep the children occupied.

Before the Queen left for church, she spoke to the Prime Minister. By now the family had released a brief statement saying:

'The Queen and the Prince of Wales are deeply shocked and distressed by the terrible news.'[9] When she spoke to Blair, she made it clear that no further statement would be made, but she had no objection to him making a public tribute that morning.

He later recalled: 'She was most worried about the impact on the boys, obviously sad about Diana, and concerned about the monarchy itself because the Queen has a very strong instinct about public opinion and how it plays out, and, in that first conversation, we agreed to keep closely in touch with it.'[10] He had only been Prime Minister for four months and now had to navigate unknown and treacherous social terrain, namely the tensions between the Spencers and the Windsors, and also between the Prince of Wales and the Queen.

In an emotional tribute made on the morning of Sunday 31 August, Blair captured the national mood of shock and bewilderment at losing such a radiant individual so young. In a telling sentence, he proclaimed: 'She was the people's princess and that's how she will stay, how she will remain in our hearts and in our memories forever.'

Though his words were well intentioned, the phrase 'people's princess' would not be received favourably in certain quarters. As Archbishop Carey watched him speak, he felt that Diana's alternative iconography would be set against the Royal Family. And so it proved. As he recalled: 'These fears were soon realized. There seemed to be mounting hysteria, fuelled by the media's focus on this beautiful but essentially ordinary person.'[11] Political observers believed that the Prime Minister's choice of words was not entirely welcomed by the Queen. It initially led to a degree of strain which, as the week progressed, had largely dissipated.

At the time Prince Harry, then nearly thirteen, was bewildered. He and his elder brother had attended the Sunday morning service at Crathie Church at the Queen's suggestion, but there was no mention of his mother's passing in either the prayers or the sermon. Instead, a visiting minister, Reverend Adrian Varwell, stuck to his prepared notes about moving house and joked about the Scottish comedian Billy Connolly. Little wonder, then, that Harry asked: 'Is it true that Mummy's dead?'[12] While the kirk's minister, Reverend Robert Sloan, explained later that he did not mention the late princess for fear of further upsetting the boys, it played into an emerging narrative that the Royal Family were cool to indifferent about Diana's death.

Certainly not every member of the family felt the princess's passing as keenly as others. Princess Margaret had fallen out badly with Diana after her appearance on *Panorama* when she questioned Charles's fitness to be King and talked of her ambition to be a 'queen of people's hearts'. Not only did Margaret consider these sentiments a betrayal of the Prince of Wales but, as far as she was concerned, there was only one Queen – and it was her sister. From then on, Margaret would have nothing to do with Diana and she expected her children, David and Sarah, to ignore her too. As a result, she was deeply irritated by being obliged to stay at Balmoral in Court mourning instead of flying off to Tuscany where she was looking forward to her annual cultural holiday in the sun.

While complaining about the 'fuss' that Diana had caused, Margaret was, like her sister, very much concerned about the impact on William and Harry. 'Terrible to lose your mother at that age, and with little Harry's birthday only a few days away,' she said.[13]

Just like the young princes, millions of people worldwide were disbelieving of Diana's death. It was only the sight of the BAE 146 of the Queen's Flight, with the princess's coffin on board, making its final approach from Paris to RAF Northolt in West London, that the enormity of her loss began to sink in. Her coffin, draped with her own Royal Standard, was borne in silence across the tarmac by six RAF pall-bearers, watched by the Prime Minister and other government and military dignitaries.

If the Spencer family needed any further convincing that a private ceremony was wholly inappropriate, then the drive into central London along the A40 dual carriageway was further proof. Thousands of people, some openly weeping, lined the roadside or watched from bridges and other vantage points as the cortège drove past, her body taken first to a private mortuary in West London and then to the Chapel Royal at St James's Palace where she lay in state.

The outpouring of grief took everyone, not just the Royal Family in their Scottish castle, by surprise. Early on that fateful Sunday morning, Princess Margaret's chauffeur Dave Griffin was at Kensington Palace, discussing the tragic events with the duty police inspector. According to Griffin, the officer had predicted a handful of bouquets from a few well-wishers, not appreciating for a moment that the woman he waved through the gates every day had touched such a nerve in the global psyche. By late on Sunday afternoon, Kensington Palace was a floating moat of cellophane-wrapped floral tributes, poems, pictures and lighted candles. As Archbishop Carey predicted, the contrasting iconography of Diana and the Royal Family came into play, the perceived warmth, accessibility and normality of the princess conflicting with the cold, indifferent and aloof House of Windsor, whose members used duty and tradition as a shield.

Over the next few days Britain succumbed to flower power, the scent and sight of countless bouquets bearing witness to the love and respect that people felt for a woman whom, they believed, had been scorned during her lifetime by the Establishment. Thousands of people, most of whom had never met the princess, made their way to Kensington Palace to pay homage. In a spontaneous outpouring of feeling, they expressed their grief, their sorrow, their guilt and their regret. Total strangers hugged and comforted one another.

Others prayed. Some mourned Diana with a greater intensity and feeling than they had done for their own lost family members.

While the church service at Crathie – where Diana's name was not mentioned – had jarred with the public, resentment was beginning to build as the palace seemed more interested in maintaining protocol than supporting the needs of the people. At first, the police would not allow the public to place bouquets outside the royal palaces, while those wishing to pay tribute were having to wait up to twelve hours to sign one of a handful of books of condolence. The fact that the flagpole at Buckingham Palace was naked – traditionally, only the Royal Standard is flown and then only when the Sovereign is in residence – soon became a focal point, the absence of a raised flag or one flying at half-mast seen as a sign of the Royal Family's indifference and invisibility.

Britain's monarchy seemed to be retreating from the nation rather than leading them in mourning. People wanted to see the Queen as unifying and consoling rather than watching from the wings. The Sun was typically blunt: 'Where is the Queen when the country needs her? She is 550 miles from London, the focal point of the nation's grief.'

There was a bitter irony in this criticism of the Monarch. In the past, she had been accused of putting duty above motherhood, particularly during the childhoods of Prince Charles and Princess Anne. Now she was being attacked for placing her compassion and concern for her grandchildren above her obligation to the nation. At Balmoral, Her Majesty's priority was to keep the boys occupied, just as she had done in 1979 when she showed Timothy Knatchbull 'unstoppable mothering' as he recovered from the Mountbatten assassination.[14] Prince Philip was a constant presence, reassuring and consoling. He set the boys to work preparing food for barbecue picnics, Princess Anne took Harry out exploring the Balmoral wildlife, while Peter and Zara Phillips and the boys went quad-biking, horse riding, fishing and shooting. In between endless meetings, their father brought out the old family albums to take them on a trip down memory lane. Harry also took solace in the arms of Tiggy Legge-Bourke, the woman who was known to call William and Harry 'my babies'.[15]

During that fateful week, William and Harry valiantly tried to absorb their family's fortitude and stoicism: 'I kept saying to myself that, you know, my mother would not want me to be upset,' William revealed years later. 'She'd not want me to be down. She'd not want me to be like this. I kept myself busy as well – which is good and bad sometimes – but allows you to kind of get through that initial shock phase.'[16]

If they had returned to Kensington Palace, they would have been kicking their heels and listening to the wailing and keening outside the gates. 'Thankfully, we had the privacy to mourn and collect our thoughts and to have that space away from everybody,' William later recalled: 'We had no idea the reaction to her death would be quite so huge.'[17]

At the business end of planning Diana's funeral, the Queen's management team, together with officials from the Prime Minister's office in Downing Street and representatives from the Spencer family, had worked into the early hours of Monday morning to come up with a proposal tailored to remember and celebrate a unique human being. Her Majesty's senior officials – Fellowes, Janvrin and the Lord Chamberlain, the Earl of Airlie – outlined what they considered to be an appropriate commemoration of Diana's life. Working *de novo*, as Lord Airlie put it, there being no precedents, the idea was to create a funeral that neatly meshed the ancient and modern with the traditional and innovative.

Diana's coffin would be pulled on a horse-drawn gun carriage and twelve pall-bearers from the Welsh Guards would accompany it. The standard military procession would be replaced by 500 workers from the princess's charities. Lord Airlie argued: 'It was important to bring a cross section of the public not normally invited to the Abbey – the people Diana associated with.'[18]

Everyone nervously awaited the Sovereign's verdict. Thankfully, she agreed to the proposals and made it clear that the Royal Family were not detached from this major event. 'She was very happy with the charity workers,' courtier Malcom Ross recalled.[19] Blair's press secretary, Alastair Campbell, was impressed by the Queen's flexibility, creativity and even risk-taking – hardly words usually associated with the Head of State. However, there were some elements that she refused to move on, in particular her family's wish to grieve privately in Scotland. She also objected to Earl Spencer's demand that Diana be buried at Althorp rather than Frogmore.

This spikiness between the Houses of Spencer and Windsor continued throughout the week, as Archbishop Carey recalled: 'I had sent a first draft of the prayers I proposed to read at the service to the Dean of Westminster for comments from those directly involved. I was taken aback when the reaction revealed intense bitterness. It was reported to me that the Spencer family did not want any mention of the Royal Family in the prayers, and in retaliation Buckingham Palace had insisted that they must have a separate prayer for the Royal Family, and that the words "people's princess" be removed. While I was saddened by this, I considered it essential to get the prayers right, for everyone's sake. It was a time of exceptional bewilderment, and the strain was affecting everybody.'[20] The Archbishop was also concerned that Earl Spencer had been invited to give the address when, traditionally, only members of the clergy preached at funeral services. Though he contacted Diana's brother and urged him to bring out the Christian message of hope and life evermore in God, he got the impression that the earl had other ideas about what he wanted to say.

There was another conflict brewing, which had the potential to be far more damaging than Windsor versus Spencer, namely the disagreements between Prince Charles's advisers based at St James's Palace and those of Her Majesty at Buckingham Palace. In the early stages, the prince's spin doctors attempted to portray Charles as decisive and democratic while all the Queen's men were dithering, delaying and hiding behind precedent and tradition.

In their misleading narrative, the Sovereign was depicted as having been initially opposed to the use of an aircraft of the Queen's Flight to bring Diana's body home, much to the alleged frustration of her advisors. Indeed, her deputy private secretary Robin Janvrin is said to have asked the Queen: 'What would you rather, Ma'am, that she came back in a Harrods van?' (The department store Harrods was then owned by Mr Al-Fayed.) Journalists were briefed that the Prince of Wales had decisively countermanded the original decision for Diana to remain in a public mortuary in Fulham, West London. Instead, according to his aides, he had ordered that the princess should rest in the Chapel Royal. It seemed that during this traumatic time, certain courtiers allied to Charles were playing an unpleasant game of one-upmanship.

In reality, both the Queen and her private secretary Sir Robert Fellowes had agreed from the very beginning that a plane should be sent to Paris to carry her back to the UK, that she should lie in state at the Chapel Royal and that there should be a full ceremonial funeral.

As an official who was present during that week recalled: 'One of the most dangerous things which took place during those fraught days was that the two palaces were totally at odds with each other.'[21] In short, those in Charles's camp were prepared to throw anyone under the bus in order to protect their man – and that included the Queen and other members of the Royal Family. This conflict would continue long after Diana's burial.

As well as the flag-flying – or lack of it – at Buckingham Palace, the issue of the boys walking behind the funeral cortège was the most contentious. Earl Spencer said that he should be the only one to do this, while representatives of the Royal Family pointed out that traditionally all the close male relatives would accompany the coffin. This tussle was not resolved until the evening before the funeral. The boys became something of a shuttlecock between the different parties.

As one Downing Street aide revealed: 'There was an amazing moment when we were on speaker with [who] we thought was Janvrin alone and Prince Philip came booming over the squawk box. The Spencer side had been saying what the role of the children had to be and Philip suddenly blasted, "Stop telling us what to do with those boys! You're talking about them as if they are commodities. Have you any idea what they are going through!" It was rather wonderful. His voice was full of emotion, a real voice of the grandfather speaking.' During another conference call later in the week, the duke once again made another impromptu contribution. 'Our worry at the moment is William. He's run away up the hill and we can't find him. That's the only thing we are concerned with at the moment.'[22]

Twenty years later, William tried to explain his confused feelings during that difficult time. 'There's nothing like it in the world. There really isn't. It's like an earthquake has just run through the house and through your life and everything. Your mind is completely split. And it took me a while for it to actually sink in.'[23] During this time he found consolation from his grandmother who, as he described later, 'understood some of the more complex issues when you lose a loved one'.[24]

As the boys sought solace with their family, and the senior royals and their officials tried to work out a unique funeral for a unique individual, on the streets of London the mood had turned genuinely nasty. The initial target was the tabloid media for hiring the paparazzi who had apparently chased Diana to her death. Public anger was also directed at the Royal Family, not only for their slow and muted response to the tragedy but also for their indifference to her during her lifetime.

With the crowds on London's streets swelling at a rate of 6,000 an hour, Downing Street officials feared that rioting could break out. People were standing in line for several hours to sign books of condolence. Still no flag flew from Buckingham Palace. 'Where was the Queen?' asked mourners in The Mall. 'Where is our Queen?' chanted the tabloids. 'Show us you care,' they hysterically demanded in ninety-six-point type. Still the Sovereign refused to budge and return to the capital.

Courtiers tried in vain to convince the Queen and Prince Philip to recognize the increasingly precarious situation and fly back to the nation's capital. Tony Blair, sensing matters were genuinely getting out of hand, called Prince Charles to discuss the worrying state of affairs and made it clear that 'the tide of public opinion could not be "turned back, revisited or ignored".[25] In the end, an alliance of the Prince of Wales, the Prime Minister and every royal adviser came together and, over a conference call, managed to persuade the Queen of the magnitude of the situation. Once she was convinced that inaction was harmful to the monarchy, everything changed. She agreed to travel back to London a day sooner than planned, go for a walkabout outside Buckingham Palace on her return, broadcast to the nation and, for the first time in history, allow the Union Flag to fly at half-mast at the palace.

On that final evening at Balmoral, Prince Philip suggested that they should attend the service at Crathie Church the next morning. This time Diana was mentioned in a prayer for the family. On their way back to the castle, the boys were photographed looking at the mounds of flowers and reading the notes outside the gates.[26]

In this highly charged atmosphere, the Queen's departure from Scotland and her decision to give her own public tribute to Diana direct from Buckingham Palace immediately helped to heal the evident dislocation between the Monarch and the people. The Prime Minister advised her to show that she was vulnerable. He said: 'I really do feel for you. There can be nothing more miserable than feeling as you do and having your motives questioned.'[27]

On Friday afternoon, after flying down from Scotland, the Queen and Prince Philip finally made their much-anticipated appearance among the grieving crowds. A momentary expression of anxiety flashed across her face, betraying her uncertainty as to how her people would react. 'We were not confident,' a former courtier stated, 'that when the Queen got out of the car, she would not be hissed and jeered.'[28] But as soon as she walked among her people, the ugly atmosphere evaporated and the crowds erupted into spontaneous if polite applause. When an eleven-year-old girl held out a bouquet of red roses, the Queen asked: 'Would you like me to place them for you?' The girl replied, 'No, Your Majesty, they're for you.'[29]

Back in the palace, the Queen and her husband spent a long time talking about the public mood and what was on people's minds, the royal couple barely able to process what was going on. It was like entering another world. As a senior aide explained: 'At Balmoral, she hadn't taken it in. You never know what it is like until you are actually there. All the remarks and people hugging each other, sobbing – the whole nation seemed to have gone bananas. The Queen and Prince Philip felt utterly bewildered.'[30]

They would have understood the national mood more keenly had they been in London, at Buckingham Palace or Windsor Castle, when the tragedy occurred. It was their fortune – or misfortune, depending on perspective – that they were staying at Balmoral several hundred miles away. Nor did they fully appreciate, along with many others, the impact of Diana's death on the national psyche. 'The world has lost the plot,' wrote commentator Gyles Brandreth at the time.[31] Yet for the public, who had keenly watched the upward trajectory of Diana's life, it was the suddenness of her death that was so difficult to bear. It was an unequal end to everything that had gone before in her life.

The Queen and her family did not see what the public saw. They mourned someone whom they all knew, the family lamenting the flawed individual rather than the saintly icon. Years later, Harry discussed his own confusion. He heard people sobbing when he couldn't bring himself to cry for his late mother. His father felt a similar sense of bafflement, the Prince of Wales recalling: 'I felt an alien in my own country.'[32]

Meanwhile, Her Majesty was preparing for only the second special televised address of her reign – the first was in late February 1991, as Allied troops were preparing to join the first Gulf War. 'She knew it was something she should do,' noted one senior adviser.[33] Her speech was initially drafted by her private secretary, then discussed with the Queen, Prince Philip and other courtiers before being sent to Downing Street for final approval. As Blair and Campbell read the draft, one of the duo suggested that the Sovereign should speak not only as the Queen but also as a grandmother. It was a touch of genius.

She agreed to be filmed live in the Chinese Dining Room in front of a large window overlooking The Mall, which was teaming with flowers and mourners.[34] The speech, which lasted three minutes and nine seconds, was one of the most effective of her reign, her uncomplicated authenticity, clear reading and respect shown towards the late princess meant that there was an immediate 'dissipation of the hostility to the Windsors.'[35]

She spoke of the disbelief, incomprehension and sense of loss: 'We have all felt those emotions in these last few days. So what I say to you now, as your Queen and as a grandmother, I say from my heart. First, I want to pay tribute to Diana myself. She was an exceptional and gifted human being. In good times and bad, she never lost her capacity to smile and laugh, nor to inspire others with her warmth and kindness. I admired and respected her – for her energy and commitment to others, and especially for her devotion to her two boys.'

With a nod to the criticism of herself and her family, she continued: 'I for one believe there are lessons to be drawn from her life and from the extraordinary and moving reaction to her death.'[36]

She had been slow to change direction when it became clear she was out of step with the nation, and although the boys were the focus of the family and her own concerns, there had been nothing to stop a camera crew from filming a similar message at Balmoral several days earlier. This would have stopped criticism of the Royal Family and the monarchy in its tracks.

Her speech, though several days late, had done the trick. Archbishop Carey remarked that 'it showed her compassion and understanding. It went a very long way towards silencing her critics and removing the misunderstanding that had developed.'[37]

At dinner on Friday evening, one final question needed to be answered: would William and Harry walk behind their mother's coffin and follow royal tradition? While the final decision was left to the princes themselves, in the end it was the intervention of their grandfather, Prince Philip, that proved decisive. 'If I walk, will you walk with me?' he asked.[38] When William agreed, Harry followed his lead. 'The boys are very close with their grandparents, adore them,' observed press secretary Dickie Arbiter. 'Significantly, they walked for their grandfather, not their father or uncle.'[39] There was also the fear that if only Prince Charles and Charles Spencer appeared on foot behind the coffin, the future king, who had received numerous threatening letters during the week, could be jeered at or physically attacked by one or more members of the crowd who blamed the prince for Diana's death.

On Saturday 6 September, the day of the funeral, the Queen and her family assembled outside the gates of Buckingham Palace. As the funeral cortège passed the royal party, Her Majesty bowed her head in a moment of obeisance, acknowledging Diana herself but also perhaps what she represented about the changing values of modern Britain.

As other members of the family also lowered their heads as a sign of respect, Princess Margaret remained upright and upstanding, looking as though she would rather be somewhere else. Somewhat bizarrely, while the Queen and Margaret were waiting for the arrival of the cortège, Margaret had been nagging her sister about improving the lavatories at Kensington Palace.[40] It was a moment that symbolized the extent of the estrangement between Margaret and Diana, the two former royal neighbours.[41]

Paradoxically, it was the fact that the boys displayed the traditional royal virtues of stoicism and fortitude amid a sea of tears that lent the funeral such an emotional resonance. They adhered impeccably to the maxim of Princess Alice, Countess of Athlone: 'You don't wear private grief on a public sleeve.'[42] Prince Philip comforted his grandsons on that lengthy walk by quietly pointing out historic landmarks and explaining their background.

Inside Westminster Abbey, an estimated worldwide audience of 2.5 billion watched as Diana's sisters, Jane and Sarah, each read a verse of poetry and Tony Blair read a chapter from the Bible, while Elton John gave an emotional rendition of his hit song 'Candle in the Wind', which he dedicated to the late princess.

It was Charles Spencer who publicly threw down the gauntlet to the Royal Family and the mass media in his funeral oration, implicitly rebuking the former for stripping the princess of her royal appellation – 'She needed no royal title to continue to generate her particular brand of magic' – and for the distant way they raised their children. He pledged to William and Harry that the Spencers, their 'blood family', would 'continue the imaginative way' in which Diana was steering her sons 'so that their souls are not simply immersed by duty and tradition, but can sing openly' as she planned. He also ripped into the popular press, highlighting their seemingly 'permanent quest ... to bring her down'.

In his concluding words, praising his sister as 'the unique, the complex, the extraordinary and irreplaceable Diana, whose beauty, both internal and external, will never be extinguished from our minds', applause rippled from the crowd outside the open doors of Westminster Abbey. Inside the building, after a moment of recognition, the congregation, including William and Harry, also began clapping. It was unclear, however, whether the applause was in acknowledgement of the Earl's assessment of his sister, the mass media or the Royal Family.

The Queen stared ahead, stony-faced, as did her husband. Prince Charles was so incensed that later he had to be restrained from issuing a public statement. As Dickie Arbiter recalled: 'The mood inside the Royal Family was very angry about what he said and the courtiers were apoplectic, shell-shocked.'[43] Her Majesty believed that Earl Spencer should have focused more on Diana's evident Christian qualities, a point the Archbishop of Canterbury had made before the service. It was an opportunity missed, she felt.

After the funeral and Diana's burial at Althorp, the Royal Family returned to Balmoral. The next day, exactly a week after the accident, Tony and Cherie Blair flew to the Queen's Highland home for an abbreviated prime ministerial autumn weekend. During his private audience with her, Blair spoke about the possible lessons to be learned from Diana's death. He recollected that the Sovereign was 'reflecting, considering and adjusting'.[44]

Before she headed off on her delayed Italian holiday, Princess Margaret sent her sister a note of thanks for 'how kindly you arranged everybody's lives after the accident and made life tolerable for the two poor boys. There, always in command, was you, listening to everyone and deciding on all the issues. I just felt you were wonderful.'[45] After such a bruising week, the Monarch appreciated the loyalty and support of a person who knew her so intimately. Brought up not to show emotion in public, Margaret, like the Queen, found the wailing and keening hard to understand.

In another private letter, this time a reply that the Sovereign sent to one of her close aides, Lady Henriette Abel Smith, Her Majesty referred to the negatives and positives that had emerged from the funeral week. In a typed portion she wrote: 'It [Diana's death] was indeed dreadfully sad, and she is a huge loss to the country. But the public reaction to her death, and the service in the Abbey, seem to have united people around the world in a rather inspiring way. William and Harry have been so brave and I am very proud of them.'

In a handwritten paragraph at the end, she added: 'I think your letter was one of the first I opened – emotions still so mixed up but we have all been through a very bad experience!'[46]

Even though the Queen had been on the throne for more than forty-five years, following Diana's death it felt as if the Monarch, or rather the monarchy, was on probation. She had gone head-to-head with her people, and by and large the people had won.

While the mantra from Buckingham Palace was that lessons had been learned, a sceptical nation watched warily – and reserved judgement. It was recognized that the disconnect between Sovereign and society during the tumultuous funeral week would take some healing, although the polls clearly showed that Britons didn't want a republic. They wanted to see a modernized monarchy more in touch with a multicultural UK. An Ipsos poll for *The Mail on Sunday* that was commissioned during the week of the funeral gave the Queen some comfort, as it showed that 45 per cent of the public felt that Britain would be worse off without a monarchy.

For a woman schooled in precedent and tradition, with the unspoken question 'What would my father have done?' always hanging in the air, any reform would be sensible and incremental. She was also stubborn when under threat. In 1957, when Lord Altrincham argued for the abolition of the presentation of debutantes at Buckingham Palace, for example, the Sovereign delayed the decision for a year so as not to give the radical peer the satisfaction of saying: 'I told you so.'

And Britain was changing. While the new Labour Prime Minister Tony Blair praised the Queen as 'the best of British' at a lunch to celebrate her fiftieth wedding anniversary in November 1997, he was on the cusp of overseeing a remodelling of the political landscape, with closer European integration, devolution of powers to Scotland, Wales and Northern Island, an elected Mayor of London and the London Assembly on the horizon, as well as closer integration with European laws and conventions. With a growing movement for Scottish devolution, and the Queen's beloved Commonwealth of Nations something of a political afterthought, the nation was fundamentally evolving – and not in a way that necessarily enhanced the monarchy.

Amid calls for a 'People's Monarchy' to mirror the work of the 'People's Princess', the Queen gradually adjusted her public persona, often with the advice of pollsters, well-connected diplomats and media mavens. Prince Philip was especially interested in the new monarchy website, www.royal.uk, while the inception of the Way Ahead Group, which comprised senior members of the family and their advisers, was designed to give early warning of problems ahead and chart a safe course for the monarchy in the future.

Although the Queen has said 'I don't do stunts', meaning that she won't play up to the camera or the prevailing view, the media pack had become swollen with correspondents looking for signs of the 'Diana effect'. Had Her Majesty truly learned lessons from the princess's life and altered her tone and style accordingly? The omens seemed positive.

When the Sovereign visited a school, she now sat with the children rather than stood with the head teacher. At a drive-through McDonald's in Ellesmere Port in July 1998 she allowed herself to be photographed with excited staff, and on a 1999 visit to the Craigdale housing estate in Glasgow, she joined pensioner Susan McCarron for tea and chocolate biscuits in her neat-as-a-pin home.

During a tour of Malaysia in September 1998, the Queen signed a Manchester United football for supporters. Though she was not an ardent football fan, she was happy for others to relay a story of her reaction during a needle match between England and Argentina in the 1998 World Cup. When England had a goal disallowed, she had thrown her arms up in the air in disgust at the decision and declared, in a parody of her personality: 'One is not amused.' Former Edinburgh provost Eric Milligan, who watched the match on television with Her Majesty at the Palace of Holyroodhouse, recalled that she was so excited that she had to leave the room for the penalty shoot-out which, predictably, England lost.

There were other unexpected sightings of the new-look Sovereign. In a nod to egalitarianism, she regularly took the train to and from King's Lynn in Norfolk when she stayed at Sandringham. Several commuters expressed their shocked delight at walking past her first-class carriage and seeing the Queen quietly looking out as her fellow travellers passed by. As a writer in the *Sunday Telegraph* observed: 'We are not seeing a new Queen. What we are gradually noticing is the same Queen reflecting the changing society around her.'[47]

In a further nod to Diana, the Union Flag was now routinely

raised over unoccupied royal residences. The bare flagpole which had caused so much concern during the funeral week was no more. 'The princess was very good at picking issues,' a palace official reflected, 'and we have to learn from that. She was very good at keeping abreast of topics of public concern. That was one of her strengths and a lesson that could be learned.'[48]

In December 1997, the Royal Yacht *Britannia*, the floating country home and safe haven on overseas visits, was decommissioned in Portsmouth after more than forty-five years of service. Her Majesty was reluctant to say goodbye as the yacht held so many memories of happy times spent together as a family, particularly the annual cruise in the Western Isles that they would take during their summer holidays in Scotland.

Before the formal service, the Royal Family took one last lingering look around the vessel. It was an emotional private farewell, the Queen seen dabbing away tears before retiring for lunch in the State dining room. Later, at the public ceremony on the quayside, the Queen and the Princess Royal both watched tearfully as the Royal Marine Band played the highly evocative 'Highland Cathedral' during the final farewell. It was quickly pointed out by several media pundits that although they never shed a tear for the princess, they cried over a floating piece of metal.

The yacht was then stripped of all its royal memorabilia, which were placed into temporary storage at Windsor while *Britannia* sailed north and was settled into her permanent mooring at Leith harbour in Scotland.

Over at Kensington Palace, a similar operation had been undertaken by the Spencer family. Following Diana's death, everything in her apartment was taken away lest her precious belongings fell into the hands of trophy hunters or members of staff with an eye for the main chance. The carpets, silk wallpaper, plants and even the light bulbs were removed. Her butler Paul

Burrell thought the exercise was excessive, and complained that Diana's mother, Frances Shand Kydd, had even shredded the blotting paper on her daughter's desk.

Within a matter of months, all traces of the princess had been removed from her former royal home.

CHAPTER THIRTEEN

TWO WEDDINGS AND TWO FUNERALS

WHILE DIANA WAS GONE but not forgotten, Camilla Parker Bowles, who had been divorced since 1995, was very much around and Prince Charles made it abundantly clear that she was not going anywhere. His obdurate attitude had placed St James's Palace and Buckingham Palace on a collision course.

The prince had already laid the groundwork for her continuing presence in his life: publicly in his 1994 documentary, when he said that Camilla was a good friend then and would be in the future; and privately in her role as the mistress, albeit a low-profile one, of Highgrove. This did not please the Queen, who had wanted Camilla gone, both before and after Diana's death. Her senior officials, notably her private secretary Sir Robert Fellowes, were in firm agreement. They felt that Charles's desire for self-fulfilment was in danger of jeopardizing the monarchy.

As Camilla's biographer Penny Junor noted: 'It was nothing personal. She had been very fond of Camilla in all the years she had been married to Andrew, but it was Camilla who had been responsible, wittingly or not, for all the disasters that had befallen the prince since his marriage.'[1]

The Queen could be forgiven for thinking that Charles had not spent enough time working on his relationship with Diana before going back to Camilla's soothing ministrations. However difficult the princess had been, and the Sovereign knew all about her wayward behaviour, she had deserved more than the four or so years that he had devoted to married life before going his own way. The now unanswerable question was whether Charles and Diana would have remained together as a couple had Camilla not been on the scene.

Few attending the prince's official fiftieth birthday party, which was held at Buckingham Palace on 13 November 1998, would have sensed the familial tension in the air. An estimated 850 guests, including Prime Minister Tony Blair and former premier Margaret Thatcher, toasted his achievements and life in the presence of the Queen and Prince Philip, while the Monarch praised her son for his 'diligence, compassion and leadership'.[2] It all seemed so friendly and easy-going. Prince Charles referred to the Queen as 'Mummy', a description that always received an amused reaction so he tended to use it often.

Behind the public smiles, though, relations between 'Mummy' and 'Darling' could not have been worse. The first issue concerned the thudding absence of Mrs Parker Bowles, who had deliberately been left off the party invitation list by the Queen. The second was an ITV television documentary, broadcast to coincide with the prince's birthday, which had the fingerprints of his charming but ruthless deputy private secretary, Mark Bolland, all over it. A 'senior royal aide' had apparently briefed the TV producers that Charles wanted a slimmed-down monarchy and would be 'privately delighted' if the Queen abdicated.[3]

When confronted by his mother, the prince apologized and

said the story was untrue. However, this was by no means the end of the matter. A rival BBC documentary team, also well briefed by 'a senior official', emphasized that Charles was irritated with the Sovereign for not stepping back from more of her official duties and letting him take over. To make matters even more awkward, one of her aides anonymously advised the BBC programme on the Monarch's attitude towards Camilla by revealing that the Queen 'has not and will not formally meet with Camilla. She will not even appear at the same social function.'[4] In fact, she had not been on the guest list of either Her Majesty or the Queen Mother for the last fifteen years or so.

There were parallels with the Queen's refusal to meet Princess Margaret's boyfriend Roddy Llewellyn, who came into her life while she was still married, albeit very unhappily. In the court of public opinion Roddy, rightly or wrongly, was seen as the catalyst who exploded her marriage to Lord Snowdon and led to the first royal divorce since Henry VIII. In a comparable situation, at least as far as the Queen and her private secretary were concerned, Charles's continuing association with Mrs Parker Bowles was damaging the monarchy, as the public, again rightly or wrongly, believed that Camilla, being the third wheel in the Waleses' relationship, had precipitated their divorce.

Though Camilla was omitted from the Buckingham Palace list of invitees, she did appear at Highgrove on the actual date of Charles's birthday, 14 November, when she and the prince hosted a party for more than 250 guests, including actors, politicians and comedians. The Queen and Prince Philip turned down the invitation as did his three siblings. However, Princess Margaret was there along with various crowned heads of Europe. As Charles and Camilla greeted everyone, it was clear to fellow partygoers that the couple were together for the long haul.

So too was Charles's public-relations guru and deputy private secretary Mark Bolland, whose brief was to grasp the nettle and make Camilla acceptable to the Queen and the British public. If it meant treading on toes to make the Prince of Wales look good, so be it, even if those toes were firmly ensconced within a pair of size four shoes by Anello & Davide, makers of the Queen's shoes.

He and other supporters of Prince Charles were aware that the 'love her but leave her' attitude of the Queen and Sir Robert Fellowes towards Camilla was not universally accepted by all senior advisers, who felt that an olive branch should be proffered to the couple. The world had moved on since the 1936 abdication and Princess Margaret's renunciation of her lover, Group Captain Peter Townsend, on the issue of divorce.

The Archbishop of Canterbury, George Carey, and his wife Eileen had privately met with Camilla on several occasions, and he came to appreciate the deep and affectionate relationship that existed between her and Prince Charles. 'Subsequent meetings gave us no reason to change our opinion that her future was irrevocably bound up in his,' he recalled.[5]

While the prince was in no rush to remarry, the circumstances could not remain this way indefinitely. Even though the Queen was in robust health, there was no point in tempting fate. A king living with his divorced mistress would not find approval among clerics, churchgoers and those who still carried a torch for the late princess. The strategy, therefore, was to navigate a pathway that would allow Charles to marry Camilla without their union being seen to harm the monarchy. As for the prospect of 'Queen Camilla', that was some way down the road.

Bolland realized that Camilla's rehabilitation would be accelerated if she was recognized in a positive light by Diana's sons. They were her living representatives. If they could accept Camilla, why not the British public who, according to opinion polls, opposed the notion of Camilla becoming Queen by a slim majority.

On a sunny day in June 1998, Camilla would get the chance to find out as William arrived unexpectedly at York House, a wing of St James's Palace, while she was present. She offered to leave but Charles insisted that she stayed to say 'hello' to his eldest son. They were formally introduced and then spoke privately for about thirty minutes. The meeting went well, though afterwards Camilla announced that she needed a gin and tonic to calm her nerves.

The Queen's men, however, were not so easily swayed. Shortly after William had been introduced to Camilla, the Queen's deputy private secretary Sir Robin Janvrin also happened to be in the building. Charles, who felt he was on a regal roll, asked his private secretary Stephen Lamport to organize another meeting, this time between Camilla and Sir Robin. Janvrin refused, saying that he would have to ask Her Majesty first. Sometime later, after Sir Robert Fellowes' retirement in February 1999, the Queen did give Janvrin – who became her new private secretary – leave to have a confidential meeting with Mrs Parker Bowles and take the constitutional temperature.[6]

On 28 January 1999, the temperature outside the Ritz Hotel in central London was freezing when Charles continued his campaign to encourage the public to warm to his companion. That night Charles and Camilla were guests at the fiftieth birthday party of her sister, Annabel Elliot, at the Ritz. The couple arrived separately but later left together, their path to a waiting limousine illuminated by scores of camera flashbulbs. The unofficial photo call was organized by Mark Bolland, whom William and Harry now dubbed 'My Lord Blackadder', after the devious character in a BBC TV comedy.

This was the first of a series of highly orchestrated public moves to introduce Camilla to the nation. Over the next few months, the couple appeared in the audience at West End plays in London, at the Swan Theatre in Stratford-upon-Avon and at a classical music concert at London's Royal Festival Hall, as well as on the hunting fields of East Yorkshire. There was clearly a sign of a thaw from Buckingham Palace.

In January 1999, the engagement of Prince Edward to a public relations executive, Sophie Rhys Jones, was also announced. The couple, who had been together for several years, spent their six-month engagement under the same roof at Buckingham Palace, occupying adjoining rooms with the Queen's consent. The times they were indeed a'changin'.

The following year, in May 2000, Camilla's appearance at the General Assembly of the Church of Scotland in Edinburgh, at which the Prince of Wales gave the keynote address, was a further indication of her wider acceptance. At dinner that evening Camilla told Janis Milligan, the wife of the Lord Provost of Edinburgh, Eric, that her presence at this event was a big moment for her. It was perhaps fitting that the couple should have been invited to attend a gathering hosted by the Church of Scotland, a body that is considered to be more liberal than the Church of England and had been willing to marry the divorced Princess Anne and her second husband, Commander Timothy Laurence, back in December 1992.

Finally, on 3 June 2000 Camilla came face-to-face with the Queen for the first time since 1992. When the Monarch accepted her son's invitation to attend a barbecue lunch at Highgrove – held in honour of Charles's cousin Constantine, the former king of Greece, who was celebrating his sixtieth birthday – she was fully aware of the consequences. She was acknowledging, if not yet accepting, Charles's companion at Court. The Queen smiled, Camilla curtsied and they made brief small talk before retiring to their separate tables.

Though Camilla was now referred to as the prince's 'companion', there was still no place for her at formal royal functions. Later that month at a grand black-tie ball at Windsor Castle, the first since the devastating fire, the Queen hosted a combined birthday party for her mother's hundredth, her sister's seventieth, her daughter's fiftieth, Prince Andrew's fortieth and Prince William's eighteenth. Mrs Parker Bowles, though, was not invited. With public opinion becoming more favourable towards Camilla, the Queen was in danger of looking out of step with her subjects. Even members of her own family, especially the younger generation, felt that Charles's close companion should be formally recognized.

Nonetheless, Camilla was also notably absent from the Queen Mother's official hundredth birthday celebrations, when her beloved grandson, Prince Charles, accompanied her in a horse-drawn carriage on Horse Guards Parade in July 2000 before a cheering crowd.

Acceptance came in increments. In February 2001, both Prince Charles and Prince William attended the tenth anniversary of the Press Complaints Commission at Somerset House. Fifteen minutes later, Camilla joined the prince, leading the ladies and gentlemen of the mass media to conclude that if Mrs Parker Bowles was publicly accepted by William, Diana's earthly torchbearer, then everyone else should follow suit. The Queen Mother was far from ready, though, as Camilla would remain on the sidelines when Charles's grandmother's 101st birthday celebrations took place later that year.

Inadvertently, Prince Edward's wife Sophie, the Countess of Wessex, had indicated the prevailing mood at Court in April 2001, when she was unwittingly trapped in a tabloid sting by the notorious Fake Sheikh, a newspaper reporter impersonating a wealthy Arab. During the secretly taped conversation, the countess described Charles and Camilla as 'possibly number one on the people's unpopular people list' who would only marry after the death of 'the old lady', meaning the Queen Mother.[7]

Terrible events in New York City, Washington DC and Pennsylvania overshadowed all thoughts of 'Queen Camilla', though, when Al-Qaeda terrorists carried out multiple atrocities on 11 September 2001. The Queen, who was in Balmoral, acted with alacrity. Her robust decisions were in sharp contrast to the paralysis that affected the Royal Family following Diana's death. She agreed to the Union Flag flying over Buckingham Palace at half-mast and prepared to fly to London to attend a special service at St Paul's Cathedral to honour the dead, who included sixty-seven Britons. The Queen also approved a suggestion that at the next Changing of the Guard, the band of the Coldstream Guards would play 'The Star-Spangled Banner'. It was a deeply emotional few minutes that left many of the crowd outside the gates of Buckingham Palace in tears. In her message of condolence, which was read out by the British ambassador to the US, Sir Christopher Meyer, at a memorial service in New York, the ringing phrase 'Grief is the price we pay for love', which was penned by Her Majesty's private secretary Sir Robin Janvrin, struck just the right tone.[8]

The Queen perhaps felt the tragedy even more keenly as her great friend and racing manager, Henry 'Porchie' Carnarvon, died of a heart attack on the very same day. He had been watching television coverage of the strikes on the World Trade Center when he suffered what proved to be a fatal episode. It was all the more devastating as it was so sudden. Porchie and the Queen had been friends since their younger days, and at one point he was considered as a possible romantic partner. Besides her immediate family, he had been one of only a handful of people who would be put through by the Buckingham Palace operator to speak to her directly by phone, notably to relay news from her stables and share gossip from the equine world. His death was a real blow to both the Queen and the world of racing.

As well as grieving the loss of her old friend, the Queen had a great deal to worry about regarding her two dearest relatives. The health of both the Queen Mother and Princess Margaret was deteriorating quite severely, so much so that they were brought by helicopter to spend the 2001 festive season at Sandringham. Both were confined to wheelchairs: the Queen Mother had previously broken her hip in a fall, while Margaret had suffered several strokes that had left her visually impaired. Though the Queen encouraged her sister to try walking rather than rely on her wheelchair, her jaunty attempts at cajoling had fallen on deaf ears.

For the most part Margaret retired to her room and listened to the radio, a sad shell of the vibrant, glamorous woman who had graced nightclubs and featured on glossy magazine covers. The Monarch tried her best to encourage her sister to join the family throng but she 'looked so awful' that she declined. It was seen as a minor triumph when the princess's lady-in-waiting, Lady Glenconner, successfully enticed her to eat a jam tart. At one point, Margaret complained to her maid: 'If only I were a dog, I could be put down.'[9]

On 8 February 2002, the seventy-one-year-old princess suffered yet another stroke and died early the next morning at King Edward VII's Hospital in London with her children by her bedside. 'We four' were now 'we two', the Queen losing another member of the family quartet whom she had been able to trust and rely upon completely. Her mischievous little sister had proved a loyal and dutiful adviser who enjoyed an instinctive bond of blood and shared experience. Now she was gone.

The funeral ceremony took place at St George's Chapel, Windsor, on 15 February. The Queen Mother was flown over from Sandringham by helicopter and taken to the service in a wheelchair. After the ceremony, as the coffin was borne out of the chapel, with great difficulty the Queen Mother struggled to her feet in a final sad acknowledgement of her youngest daughter. The

Queen too appeared overwhelmed by her sister's loss, someone to whom she spoke almost every day by phone.

As the coffin was laid in the hearse, bound for Slough Crematorium, the Queen gripped the hand of her niece, Sarah Chatto, and with her other hand she brushed away a tear. Princess Margaret's ashes were later interred in the King George VI Memorial Chapel within St George's Chapel, next to her father – to fulfil her long-held wishes.

There was little respite for the Queen. It was her Golden Jubilee year and she was touring extensively. After bidding a sad farewell to Margaret, later in February she and Prince Philip went on official visits to Jamaica, New Zealand and Australia. During the two-week tour, the Sovereign telephoned her mother every day and as soon as she arrived back at Heathrow Airport in early March, she drove immediately to Royal Lodge in Windsor to check on her well-being. She discovered that although the Queen Mother was eating little, she was still seeing people, drinking champagne and telephoning old friends and associates in a long, last goodbye.

Later that month, Her Majesty was out riding in Windsor Great Park when her groom had word from the castle on his radio that the Queen Mother was fading quickly. Immediately, she headed over to Royal Lodge where she found her mother, her eyes closed, seated in a chair, her dresser and a local nurse by her side.

In between the comings and goings of medical personnel, Canon John Ovenden, the parish priest of St George's Chapel, Windsor, arrived. He held her hand and recited a Highland lament. Later, the Queen Mother was put to bed. By her bedside were the Queen, Princess Margaret's children David Linley and Sarah Chatto, as well as Lady Margaret Rhodes, who was always considered the Queen Mother's third daughter. Canon Ovenden returned to the room later and uttered a poignant word of prayer: 'Now lettest thou thy servant depart in peace.' The Queen Mother died at 3.15 p.m. on 30 March 2002. 'We all had tears in our eyes and to this day I cannot hear that being said without wanting to cry,' recalled Margaret Rhodes.[10]

Her death was the signal for Operation Tay Bridge – the code name for the Queen Mother's funeral arrangements – to be put into action. On Friday 5 April, an estimated quarter of a million people lined the streets as the Queen Mother's oak coffin was taken from St James's Palace to lie in state at Westminster Hall. On top of the coffin, which was draped in her personal standard, lay her Coronation crown and a wreath, with a card that read: 'In Loving Memory, Lilibet.'

Following a brief ceremony, as the Queen was being driven back to Buckingham Palace, the crowds outside burst into spontaneous applause, a gesture that stirred her profoundly. The Queen Mother's official biographer William Shawcross recalled that Her Majesty 'was visibly moved and she said to one of those with her that this moment was one of the most touching things that had ever happened to her'.[11]

In only her third special television address to the nation, on the night before the funeral the Queen reflected on that particular experience and singled out the mourners whose 'kindness and respect' had given her great comfort: 'This is what my mother would have understood, because it was the warmth and affection of people everywhere which inspired her resolve, dedication and enthusiasm for life.'[12] She later told friends that if she had had to speak about the loss of her sister as well she would not have been able to maintain her composure.

The next day, 9 April 2002, the Queen Mother's coffin was placed on a gun carriage and taken on the short journey from Westminster Hall to Westminster Abbey for the funeral. Following the solemn service, her body was driven to St George's Chapel to lie forever beside her husband, George VI. The ashes of the recently departed Princess Margaret were also placed within the royal tomb. 'We four' were now reduced to one.

With the Queen Mother laid to rest with due pomp and dignity, the auguries seemed propitious for the Queen's Golden Jubilee. Any remaining doubts over whether this wasn't going to be an impressive national celebration were stilled during a busy criss-crossing of the country between May and July.

The enthusiasm was infectious. Women were seen running out of hairdressers, their hair in curlers, in order to catch a glimpse of the Queen as she passed by. At one point, she tapped on the glass ceiling of her limousine and told her chauffeur to slow down as she wanted to savour the atmosphere for a little longer.[13]

On 3 June 2002, after a weekend of street parties and pageantry, the highlight of the celebrations was the 'Party at the Palace', a pop/rock music event held in the gardens of Buckingham Palace. Guitarist Brian May – appropriately from the rock band Queen – opened the proceedings from the roof of the palace with an iconic rendition of 'God Save the Queen'. Pop aristocracy, including Paul McCartney, Elton John, Annie Lennox and Ray Davies, played to the largest audience – estimated to be over 1 million – since Live Aid in 1985, with 12,000 in the palace grounds and the rest watching on screens in the royal parks. When Ozzy Osbourne was introduced to the Queen, he was so nervous he referred to her as: 'Your worship, your holiness.'

Prince Charles got the biggest cheer when he began his speech of appreciation by saying: 'Your Majesty ... Mummy.' He went on to praise her for embodying continuity in the lives of the nation. 'You have been a beacon of tradition and stability in the midst of profound, sometimes perilous change,' he said.[14]

At the first major royal event since the death of the Queen Mother, Camilla was at last included with the royal party, seated in the row behind Princes Charles, William and Harry. She sang along to the Phil Collins song 'You Can't Hurry Love', which features lyrics that, as columnist Caitlin Moran observed, must have been of great comfort to her over the years.[15] At the end of the show, she joined the Queen and the rest of the family in a celebratory dinner at the Ritz Hotel.

Of wider import was the decision in July by the Church of England to allow divorced couples to marry in church even if a former spouse were still alive in 'exceptional circumstances'. Modern domestic realities combined with greater tolerance was changing the landscape regarding divorce and remarriage. Two of the beneficiaries seemed set to be the Prince of Wales and his companion.

There was also a step change in the Queen's manner. Those who had known her for some time remarked on how she seemed more relaxed, more approachable and at ease now that she was no longer having to second-guess what her mother might say or think. She was now the undisputed matriarch of the family, free to carve out her own path. As historian Hugo Vickers observed: 'After the Queen Mother's death, suddenly the Queen did blossom, there is no doubt about it.'[16]

Peace was also breaking out between the various royal palaces following the departure of contentious courtiers who had polarized opinions inside the royal court. With the passing of the Queen Mother, the Prince of Wales would take over her London home, Clarence House, as well as Birkhall in Scotland.

Before he could move into Clarence House, however, extensive renovations of both a structural and decorative nature were needed. To achieve the latter he had hired interior designer Robert Kime, who had previously restored Highgrove, to enhance a suite of rooms for Camilla as well as guest quarters for her father Bruce Shand. It was clear that the prince intended to live there with his companion.

Work was still ongoing in Charles's new home in October 2002 when the ghost of Diana came to haunt the Royal Family once more. This time the Queen was centre stage, the Monarch involved in a high-profile court case at the Old Bailey in London, which revolved around Paul Burrell, Diana's former butler, who was accused of stealing property belonging to the late princess, her sons and Prince Charles. Numbering over 300 separate articles, the items allegedly stolen included signed pictures and letters, designer clothes and other personal memorabilia. When he was arrested almost two years earlier, he insisted that he had only taken the possessions, valued at £6 million, for safekeeping. He was eventually charged with theft in August 2001.

After several days of evidence had been heard at the famous Court No. 1, there was an extraordinary twist that defied even the script contortions of a Hollywood movie. Just before Burrell was due to take the stand, the trial was halted. Enter Her Majesty the Queen.

On 25 October 2002, while travelling to a memorial service at St Paul's Cathedral for victims of the Bali bombing, the Queen, Prince Philip and Prince Charles were discussing the case when the Sovereign recalled a lengthy audience with Paul Burrell five years previously, in which he had referred to safekeeping some of Diana's documents. She had not considered this relevant as they formed only a small proportion of the large amount of allegedly stolen items that he had in his possession. However, this revelation seriously undermined the prosecution's case that Burrell had never told anyone that he was taking Diana's things for safekeeping. Now it seemed he had.

When the Queen was further questioned by Prince Charles's new private secretary, Sir Michael Peat, she confirmed that Burrell was going to look after Diana's papers as he was concerned that her mother, Frances Shand Kydd, was shredding important documents relating to the princess's life and legacy.

While the Queen's timely recollections added to the surreal nature of the trial, equally bizarre was the fact that, in the twenty months since his arrest, Burrell had not once mentioned to his lawyers this conversation with the Queen, even though the thrust of the prosecution case against him was that he told no one that he had taken some of Diana's belongings. Once the new information was brought to the attention of the police and then passed on to the prosecution team, it became clear that the trial was no longer viable, having proceeded on a false premise.

On 1 November, the court case was duly halted and all charges were dropped. As he left the court in relieved triumph, Burrell told the milling throng: 'The Queen has come through for me.'[17] Commentators immediately seized on the fact that the trial had concluded just before the former butler had been due to take the stand, in order to ensure his silence. During his testimony, he had been widely expected to reveal potentially embarrassing details about the late princess, Prince Charles and the dark side of the monarchy. As the Royal Family had had numerous opportunities to resolve this matter before it came to trial, there was naturally a great deal of intrigue surrounding the unprecedented outcome.

What was intriguing, though, was Burrell's assertion that he had enjoyed a ninety-minute conversation with the Queen in her private apartments, when they had discussed everything from Diana's personality and her relationship with Dodi Fayed to Burrell's concerns about the behaviour of the Spencer family in destroying Diana's artefacts. During their lengthy chat, the Queen had apparently issued a somewhat melodramatic warning: 'Be careful, Paul. No one has been as close to a member of my family as you have. There are powers at work in this country about which we have no knowledge. Do you understand?'[18] She then ended the conversation by saying: 'I must take the dogs for a walk.'

While Burrell did not explain nor know what 'powers' may have posed a threat to him, it was all of a piece with Diana's suspicions about her personal safety when she was alive. She had her apartments swept for listening devices on several occasions. While the Queen did not jump at shadows, in the early 1990s she too had been unnerved by the rash of illicit tape recordings of private conversations made by members of her family. Burrell later told the *Daily Mirror*: 'She made sure I knew she was being deadly serious. I had no idea who she was talking about. There were many things she could have been referring to. But she was clearly warning me to be vigilant.'[19]

A year later, in October 2003, Burrell had his moment in the sun when he released his biography, *A Royal Duty*, which revisited the turbulent life of the princess and her relationship with the Royal Family. One of the more contentious issues was the publication of a letter from Prince Philip to Diana, concerning Prince Charles's affair with Mrs Parker Bowles. The duke wrote: 'Charles was silly to risk everything with Camilla for a man in his position. We never dreamed he might feel like leaving you for her. I cannot imagine anyone in their right mind would leave you for Camilla. Such a prospect never even entered our heads.'[20]

Written in the 1990s, it neatly encapsulated the Queen's objections to her son's choice of partner and also made sense of Camilla's subsequent uphill struggle to be accepted both inside and outside the Royal Family. Her undefined status continued to cause embarrassment and offence as members of society took their cues from the Queen.

The 2004 marriage of Lady Tamara Grosvenor and Edward van Cutsem, the son of Charles's long-time friend and prominent Catholic Hugh van Cutsem, proved to be a turning point. It was the society wedding of the year with a guest list that included the Queen and Prince Philip as well as Prince Charles, who was

Edward's godfather, and also Camilla Parker Bowles. As the big day approached, the groom's mother Emilie van Cutsem informed Camilla, who was her friend, that to avoid giving offence to the Queen she would be seated separately from Charles, who would be sitting in the front pews with other members of the Royal Family. In addition, she would be obliged to travel separately from the prince.[21] Charles was furious at what he interpreted as a snub and withdrew their acceptance of the wedding invitation. Instead, he visited his regiment, the Black Watch, meeting families of soldiers at a barracks in Wiltshire, while Camilla spent the day at home, doubtless pondering when this social uncertainty would finally be resolved. It would not be long.

Aside from the niceties of etiquette at social events such as weddings, there were serious constitutional matters to consider. It wasn't just a question of becoming man and wife, but also King and Queen. What would Camilla's status be if Charles succeeded and they were still unmarried?

Though Prince Charles wanted a church wedding, the new Archbishop of Canterbury, Dr Rowan Williams, argued against. He felt that a church wedding would offend many Anglican priests and parishioners. Instead, a compromise was reached: the couple could marry in a civil ceremony and have a service of prayers and a blessing in church afterwards.

Once the ecumenical matters were resolved, it was a matter of formally asking the Queen, under the Royal Marriages Act of 1772, for permission to marry. He received her blessing and those of his sons at Sandringham during Christmas 2004. Finally, over New Year at Birkhall, a rather more grown-up setting than the nursery at Windsor where he had asked Lady Diana Spencer to marry him, the Prince of Wales got down on one knee and asked Camilla to be his bride. He presented her with an art-deco-style diamond ring that he had inherited from the Queen Mother.

It was almost the end of a long, uncertain march, with the prospect of a happy future together now beckoning. After publicly announcing their engagement in February 2005, the couple set a date in April for their civil ceremony wedding at the Guildhall in Windsor.

On the morning of her big day, Saturday 9 April, Camilla was so nervous that it took four people to coax her out of bed and help her into her Anna Valentine dress. Once suitably attired, she was driven to the Guildhall in the Queen's maroon Rolls-Royce.

When she emerged from the car she looked pensive, perhaps worried that she might be heckled by someone in the crowd. But everyone was very much on her side, the many onlookers applauding as she and Prince Charles went indoors to meet their close friends and relatives, in front of whom they exchanged their vows and their rings of Welsh gold.

The Queen did not attend, though her grandsons and other family members did; in fact, Prince William was a witness alongside Camilla's son Tom. As Head of the Church of England, it was not the Sovereign's practice to ever attend civil ceremonies. While some interpreted her absence as a snub, it was predicated on her decision to put her duty before any family feelings. She did not want to set a precedent that could compromise her position as the Supreme Governor of the Church of England. She was present at the service of dedication inside St George's Chapel, however, which was conducted by Archbishop Williams. As a further gesture of goodwill, she hosted and paid for the wedding reception.

After the service of dedication, it was a very relaxed party that walked to the historic Waterloo Chamber in Windsor Castle where the Queen had organized celebrations for the 700 guests. In a deft and witty speech Her Majesty, who had a horse running at the Grand National at Aintree that day, told the rowdy throng that she had two announcements. The first was that Hedgehunter had won the National and the second was that she was delighted to be welcoming her son and his bride into 'the winners' enclosure'.

'They have overcome Becher's Brook and The Chair [two famous jumps at the Grand National] and all kinds of other terrible obstacles. They have come through and I'm very proud and wish them well. My son is home and dry with the woman he loves.'[22] Though the newest member of the Royal Family could have taken the title 'Princess of Wales', out of deference to Diana's memory Camilla was granted the title 'Duchess of Cornwall', along with the appellation 'Her Royal Highness'.

It was late afternoon when Charles's Bentley, festooned with 'Just Married' signs, drove away from the castle, a honeymoon at Birkhall firmly in the couple's sights. It was the end of a historic day that had finally seen the resolution of an issue that had blighted the Queen's reign for more than a decade.

—·—

It was a moment of unadulterated joy and celebration. Red, white and blue ticker tape showered the cheering crowd in Trafalgar Square while the Red Arrows aerial display team screamed past overhead, leaving a red, white and blue vapour trail of triumph. Even Prime Minister Tony Blair admitted to dancing a jig of excitement. After years of planning, presentations and private arm-twisting, for the first time since 1948 London was chosen to host the Olympic Games in 2012. The next day, however, jubilation turned to horror when, on 7 July 2005, four suicide bombers detonated explosives during the morning rush hour in London – three on the Underground and one on a bus – killing fifty-two people, themselves and injuring hundreds.

The Queen was quick to respond. The following day she visited the Royal London Hospital in Whitechapel and met emergency responders and nursing staff, as well as some of the injured. Then she made an unusually 'forthright' speech in the informal setting of the hospital canteen, where she praised Londoners for being 'calmly determined' to resume their normal everyday lives. 'Atrocities such as these simply reinforce our sense of community, our humanity and our trust in the rule of law. That is the clear message from us all.'[23]

She referred to the outrage again during commemoration services marking the sixtieth anniversary of the end of the Second World War. As with the 9/11 atrocity in 2001, she ordered the flag at Buckingham Palace to fly at half-mast. In times of national crisis, the Queen had become much more proactive than she had been earlier in her reign. With her mother no longer around to remind her of precedent and tradition, Her Majesty relied a great deal more on her own judgement. In the past it had been her habit to sit on the sidelines, most notably after the Aberfan disaster. Now she was far more willing to adopt the role of grandmother to the nation, the consoler-in-chief during times of national calamity. She clearly felt at ease in her position as royal matriarch.

As she approached her eightieth birthday, she looked younger, more relaxed and much more stylish. 'She's reached a stage in her life where she has complete confidence in who she is,' said her designer, Stewart Parvin. 'The Queen looks squarely in the mirror and she likes what she sees. She has a confidence that transcends beauty – that's the most fascinating thing with her.'[24]

Largely responsible for that transformation was haute couture designer Angela Kelly, the daughter of a Liverpool dock worker, who joined the Queen's staff as assistant dresser in 1994. She encouraged the cautious Sovereign to take chances, and it paid off. The Queen went from occupying a place on a list of the 'Worst Dressed' people to being voted one of British *Vogue* magazine's

'Most Glamorous Women' in late 2007, included in the same company as supermodels Naomi Campbell, Kate Moss and the actor Helen Mirren, who played the Monarch in the 2006 film *The Queen*.

Understated elegance and attention to detail were her recipe for late-blooming fashion success. When the Queen agreed, after some hesitation, to wear a monochrome black-and-white outfit for meeting American President George W. Bush at the White House in 2007, the striking ensemble, which was designed by Angela Kelly and Alison Pordum, earned widespread praise.

While Kelly could never take the place of Bobo MacDonald (the Queen's childhood maid and later her dresser) in the Sovereign's life, over the years they forged a close bond. 'We could be sisters,' Her Majesty once said to her.[25] It was a remarkably relaxed and intimate comment, even to a long-serving senior official.

Those who saw this double act in action pointed out that Kelly was never servile, she made the Queen laugh and, perhaps most importantly, filled in a lot of the lonely time, the waiting hours, in her life. She brought her solutions, not problems. When the Monarch forgot to buy a birthday present for her eldest son, for example, it was her dresser who offered to fix it. Such was her influence that before the Queen's long-haul flight to Australia to open the Commonwealth Games in March 2006, Her Majesty accepted Kelly's advice about resting for thirty-six hours beforehand. Unusually, she also granted her permission to write two books about her life as the Queen's dresser, and even posed for exclusive photographs to illustrate them. As a general rule, those who worked for the Royal Family were legally obliged to a vow of silence about their royal relationships. This was a sign of the Sovereign's confidence in the woman whom she chose to guard her jewellery – and her burgeoning fashion reputation.

The confluence of the Queen's eightieth and Prince Philip's

eighty-fifth birthday in 2006 led to speculation that the royal couple would choose this moment to abdicate or retire. Her lifelong friend and cousin, Margaret Rhodes, quickly stifled this talk: 'I am sure that she will never abdicate. She believes that would be a dereliction of her Coronation vow to serve her country for life. I'm perfectly certain she will never retire as such.'[26]

Her Majesty, in her own subtle way, endorsed her friend's ringing statement when she allowed herself to be photographed out riding with her groom, Terry Pendry, in Windsor Great Park. By the age of eighty, she was mainly riding smaller Fell ponies and, in spite of advancing years, she resolutely refused to wear proper head protection. As they joked at the palace, the only thing standing between Prince Charles and his destiny was a Hermès scarf.

Elizabeth II was a picture of health in comparison to the other two octogenarian British monarchs, George III and Victoria, who were both physically frail during their eighties. She made light-hearted reference to her age at an eightieth birthday celebration lunch held at Mansion House in London, stealing a line from Groucho Marx: 'Anyone can get old – all you have to do is to live long enough.'[27]

In a televised appreciation, Prince Charles remembered how, when he was very young, she would tuck him up in bed at night while she practised wearing her Coronation crown to get used to the weight. He praised her steadfast nature, describing her as 'an example to so many of service, duty and devotion in a world of sometimes bewildering change and disorientation.'[28]

As the Queen and Prince Philip's diamond wedding anniversary approached in November 2007, those who had known the prince for a number of years noticed that old age had mellowed him. Never an easy man, friends noted that he had aged 'benignly'. His mind remained sharp, his bearing erect, and he seemed closer and more supportive of his wife than in the past. He was always fiercely protective of her, a one-man ice-breaker forever on hand to ensure that she was conversationally comfortable. At the endless receptions they attended, they were an effective double act, the duke confident that he could get a reaction, normally laughter, within a few seconds of meeting a member of the public. He remained provocative and challenging; behaviour that some considered rudeness was often his way of putting someone on their mettle to see if they could rise to the challenge.

She still told him to 'shut up' if he overstepped the mark, while he mocked her use of her dogs to avoid serious discussion. For all his rattiness she relied heavily on his judgement, particularly with regard to family matters. As Lady Penn, widow of Sir Eric, the Queen's former comptroller, observed: 'They've always leaned on each other. How else do you think she managed to cope so incredibly well through such tough times?[29] They are very good friends and that is their secret. The Queen has had a lot to contend with. The fact she has coped so wonderfully is largely due to the support he has given her over the years.'[30]

Even after a long marriage, there was still a spark between them, still a glint in the eye. As a former lady-in-waiting observed: 'I was watching them teasing each other and giggling just the other day and I thought how lucky they are to have each other. They've always been different – he's sharp, decisive, bold, and she's cautious and slow to make up her mind – and they don't always like the same things but they fit like hand in glove.'[31] British television presenter Carol Vorderman, who dined privately with the couple, felt a similar chemistry, remembering how the couple were 'flirting with each other madly and laughing' during the meal.[32]

Along with her faith and her family, the Queen's relationship with the Duke of Edinburgh has been at the core of her life. In short, Prince Philip has been the only man in the world to treat her like a normal human being, a quality that she truly valued.

Appropriately, on the day of their sixtieth wedding anniversary they paid a brief visit to Malta, the island they called home for a while when they were a young married couple.

Since becoming grandparents and great-grandparents, they have enjoyed a close relationship with their grandchildren and great-grandchildren, joining them for afternoon tea or sitting on the sofa and watching Mickey Mouse and other Disney cartoons. The palace switchboard has always known to patch the youngsters through to Her Majesty wherever she might be in the world.

While paying special attention to Harry after he lost his mother at such a young age, the Sovereign also carefully monitored the development and well-being of her eventual heir, Prince William. Their relationship blossomed when he was a boarder at Eton, just a short walk from Windsor Castle. Every Sunday he would join the Queen and Prince Philip for lunch or afternoon tea. Once they had finished the meal, the duke would make a discreet exit so that grandmother and grandson could talk further. In between chit-chat about his schoolwork, their meetings were an early chance to impress upon the thoughtful teenager the need to protect and sustain his birthright: the monarchy.

As Her Majesty's friend and cousin Lady Elizabeth Anson once observed: 'The Queen spent a huge amount of time with William. They are exceptionally close and the Queen has been a wonderful mentor for William over the years.'[33] Her thoughtful conduct was reminiscent of the way her own father, George VI, gradually inducted his eldest daughter into the family 'Firm'.

She and the Duke of Edinburgh always ensured that their diaries were free in order to watch William mark the major milestones in his life. They were present at St Andrew's University on the north-east coast of Scotland on 23 June 2005 when, at the formal graduation ceremony, he was awarded an upper-second-class degree in geography. His girlfriend, Catherine Middleton, earned the same grade for her subject, the history of art. Though she and her parents were introduced to the Queen and Prince Philip that day, few palace insiders expected the romance to last long after college. But Catherine had other ideas and continued to stick around, much to the surprise of the media and various courtiers.

Such was the hysteria surrounding the possibility of an engagement announcement on Catherine's twenty-fifth birthday that, on 9 January 2007, the young woman was mobbed by paparazzi as she left her Chelsea flat to walk to her car before driving off to work. A seething Prince William, astonished that the paparazzi had learned nothing from his mother's untimely death, issued a statement condemning the harassment.

The incident was a turning point. William was so concerned that Catherine did not truly understand what she was letting herself in for that, in April 2007, he ended the relationship. He later explained: 'I wanted to give her a chance to see and to back out if she needed to, before it all got too much. I'm trying to learn from … the past. I just wanted to give her the best chance to settle in and to see what happens [on] the other side.'[34]

After the well-publicized break-up, Catherine simply kept smiling and carried on having a good time. It was not long before William realized his mistake and renewed their relationship. This time he was back for good.

The Queen kept a watchful but benign eye on the burgeoning romance, her attention growing when Catherine represented William, who was abroad, at Peter Phillips' wedding to Autumn Kelly at St George's Chapel in May 2008. The following month, when William was appointed as a Royal Knight Companion of the Most Noble Order of the Garter at a ceremony at St George's Chapel, Her Majesty invited her to watch the pageant from the Galilee porch. She also suggested that Catherine affiliate herself with a charity, and so the young woman became involved in raising funds for Starlight Children's Foundation, a charity for seriously and terminally ill youngsters.

It seemed that Her Majesty was taking a particularly close interest in the woman who might one day become Queen Consort. And the mood music was almost entirely favourable. There were reports that the Queen had invited the couple for a quiet dinner at Windsor Castle, while a lady-in-waiting gave her the thumbs-up. She reported: 'The Queen has taken genuine delight in Kate Middleton. She sees in Kate a young woman who has no interest in being royal but loves William for himself. The Queen is very positive about the match. She sees in them two young people who are capable of capturing the affection of the people.'[35]

When William trained as a search-and-rescue pilot based at RAF Valley Station on Anglesey, off the north-west coast of Wales, the Queen gave her approval for Catherine to live with him in a rented cottage. This courtship was so very different from that of his father. Charles only had a few weeks of romancing Lady Diana Spencer before proposing. His eldest son was much more circumspect. William followed his mother's advice, which was to 'marry your best friend'. He had spent years with Catherine before he finally asked her to marry him after a fishing expedition while on holiday in Kenya in October 2010. Shortly after the engagement announcement on 16 November, he was calling his grandmother for advice.

At the first meeting with palace officials, he was presented with a list of 777 candidates for consideration as wedding guests. He had never heard of most of them, let alone met them. The prince and his bride-to-be wanted to organize their nuptials their way. Noticeably he went to the Queen rather than his father for advice. She suggested that he scrap the first list and begin by writing down the names of those with whom he and Catherine actually wanted to share their special moment, then work from there.

The wedding day itself, on 29 April 2011, was a splendid confluence of pomp, pageantry and family intimacy. Catherine looked stunning in her Sarah Burton satin-and-lace gown, while William seemed nervous as he watched his bride make her way down the aisle in Westminster Abbey. Following the ceremony, the obligatory balcony appearance at Buckingham Palace and their wedding breakfast, the couple's drive to Clarence House in Prince Charles's vintage Aston Martin was a brilliant *coup de théâtre*.

The Queen was positively playful on the day of her grandson's nuptials, 'practically skipping' according to one observer, absolutely thrilled at the way the public had reacted to the royal newly-weds.[36] She had a sense that the future of the Royal Family, her family, was now secure. The monarchy was once again held in admiration and affection by the masses. Prince Edward reflected on her feelings sometime later, revealing how surprised she was by how well the happy couple had been received: 'I don't think my mother ever expected the public's response or thought people would come out in such support of her family as they did during William and Catherine's wedding. It was wonderful. My mother really cares about the British people and their welfare. It was wonderful to see the warm and heartfelt support.'[37]

Clear skies, however, rarely lasted long over the House of Windsor. The build-up to the wedding had overshadowed an embarrassing family matter. Prince Andrew had come under intense scrutiny over his position as the UK special representative for international trade and investment. Concerns were raised about the costs of his extensive travel and the people he was linked with, including Saif Gaddafi, the son of the Libyan dictator Colonel Gaddafi, and another Libyan associate who was described as a gun smuggler. Most damning was his continued relationship with the millionaire sex offender Jeffrey Epstein. Even though Epstein was convicted in 2008 for procuring a child for prostitution, after his release from prison the prince and Epstein were photographed together in New York's Central Park in December 2010.

Much as the Queen indulged her second son, both financially and emotionally, the media and political criticism was unrelenting. It went up a gear when it was learned that Fergie, the Duchess of York, had accepted a loan from the sex offender to help pay off some debts. Shortly after a difficult hour-long conversation with his mother, Andrew resigned from his position as trade envoy. His surrender was 'inevitable' noted BBC royal correspondent Peter Hunt. This was a classic example of a witless royal falling prey to the generosity of wealthy friends of dubious provenance.

Meanwhile, as the brooding scandal was developing on the home front, William and Catherine were 5,000 miles away enjoying their honeymoon on an island in the Seychelles in the Indian Ocean. The prince spent time on his computer trying to find out about a visit that had the Queen, a veteran of dozens of royal tours, filled with eager anticipation. For the first time since 1911, when George V visited Dublin during its days as part of the British Empire, a reigning monarch was about to set foot on Irish soil.

The long history of animosity, resistance and revolution between these two neighbouring islands had previously made an official royal tour unthinkable – until now. After months of back and forth, the two countries agreed an agenda that placed the emphasis on peace and reconciliation, which had been a key element of the Good Friday Agreement of 1998.

As Prince William told writer Robert Hardman: 'She was so excited about it and really looking forward to it. It was quite sweet.'[38] From the moment the Queen stepped off the aircraft wearing an emerald coat, dress and hat, Irish eyes were smiling, cooing at the compliment paid to the Irish nation in her choice of colour scheme.

During the four-day State visit in May, the Queen and Prince Philip visited Trinity College Library in Dublin where they saw the ninth-century Book of Kells, one of the world's most ancient volumes, laid a wreath at the Garden of Remembrance which is dedicated to the memory of all those who died in the cause of Irish freedom, visited a trio of stud farms – and watched a pint of Guinness being carefully poured. At the State banquet, Her Majesty began her speech in Gaelic, which earned warm applause from President Mary McAleese and other dignitaries.

In a careful and well-judged address, the Queen acknowledged the 'sad and regrettable reality' of Britain's troubled relationship with Ireland, referring to the 'heartache, turbulence and loss' of the past. 'We can all see things which we would wish had been done differently or not at all.'[39] Prime Minister David Cameron described her visit as a 'game-changer'[40] that heralded a new era of Anglo-Irish relations, the official tour helping to embed the peace process between the peoples of the Republic of Ireland and Northern Ireland.

Indeed, the Queen would continue to play her part when, in June 2014, she visited Belfast and shook the hand of Martin McGuinness, Deputy First Minister of Northern Ireland and former hard man of the Provisional IRA. It was one of the most symbolic gestures of her reign. Her handshake was seen as a sign of forgiveness and reconciliation with a man whose terrorist organization had killed Lord Mountbatten and many others. This simple but significant act demonstrated how far the peace process had come.

Later in 2011, there was constitutional housekeeping taking place much nearer to home. As the Diamond Jubilee of the Queen's reign approached, she agreed to sweeping but long overdue reforms to the royal succession. In October, at the Commonwealth Heads of Government meeting in Perth, Western Australia, British Prime Minister David Cameron put forward proposals, unanimously agreed by the other fifteen leaders of Commonwealth realms, to change the law so that first-born girls could become Queen. This would mean that if William and Catherine were to have a girl and then later a boy, their first child, a daughter, would be the Sovereign.

The leaders unanimously agreed to reform the 1701 Act of Settlement and also repeal the Royal Marriages Act of 1772. The changes would introduce absolute primogeniture for individuals in the line of succession born after 28 October 2011, allow the Monarch to marry a Roman Catholic, and also remove the requirement for all those in line to the throne, apart from the first six, from obtaining permission to marry from the Sovereign. These changes were eventually made law under the Succession to the Crown Act (2013).

Not only did these constitutional updates bring the House of Windsor into the twenty-first century, they also deliberately coincided with a radical adjustment in the funding of the monarchy. Under the Sovereign Grant Act of 2011, the age-old Civil List was replaced by a single annual grant, the running of the institution now subsidized by a percentage from the profits of the Crown Estate, the independent corporation which is owned by the Sovereign but is not his or her private property. These much-needed reforms effectively wiped the constitutional slate clean for the Queen's immediate heir, Prince Charles, who for some years had been a firm advocate of a supple, slimmed-down monarchy.

During the Diamond Jubilee celebrations in June 2012, the future direction of travel for the Royal Family was on full display. When the Queen and Prince Philip stood on the deck of the lavishly decorated royal barge, *Spirit of Chartwell*, to review the stunning 1,000-boat flotilla on the River Thames in central London, they were joined only by the Duke and Duchess of Cambridge, the Duke and Duchess of Cornwall and Prince Harry. The remaining senior royals, Prince Andrew, Prince Edward and Princess Anne, were assigned to other boats for the pageant.

It was noticeable too that the Duchess of Cornwall, for so long a royal outsider, was now on easy and convivial terms with the Queen and every other member of the Royal Family. As the royal barge approached the National Theatre, Her Majesty nudged her daughter-in-law to point out Joey, the puppet realization of Michael Morpurgo's *War Horse*, which had reared up in greeting as the barge travelled along the South Bank. Her Majesty was a fan of the production, having seen the original play in London and having also hosted a special screening of the movie at Windsor Castle earlier in the year for members of the Household, an event that was also attended by the film's director, Steven Spielberg.

The one casualty of the four-hour Thames River Pageant, which took place in chilling June rain and wind, was Prince Philip, who was subsequently hospitalized with a bladder infection. He never really fully recovered. He missed the spectacular three-hour firework concert outside Buckingham Palace on 4 June, featuring performances from, among others, Elton John, Paul McCartney and Kylie Minogue. In a symbolic moment, the band Madness played their hit 'Our House' from the roof of the palace, a clever light show turning its frontage into a varied range of properties, such as a row of terraced houses and a huge doll's house.

In a touching speech to his mother, Prince Charles paid tribute to the Queen's selfless duty, service and 'for making us proud to be British'. The grand finale of the celebration was the reappearance on the Buckingham Palace balcony of the Magnificent Seven (minus Prince Philip). The signal was clear – the succession was assured.

'An incredible day, absolutely wonderful,'[41] the Queen said to her eldest son on the palace balcony as they watched a fly-past by the Red Arrows display team and Second World War fighter planes on the final day of the Diamond Jubilee celebrations. The commemorations had been, she said in a short broadcast of thanks, 'a humbling experience'.[42]

The festivities not only marked the Queen's magnificent sixty years on the throne, but also the beginning of a new era for the British Royal Family.

CHAPTER FOURTEEN

GOOD EVENING,
MR BOND

O N A BALMY SUMMER'S NIGHT in July 2012, the eighty-six-year-old Queen gave herself a licence to thrill and surprise a worldwide audience that was eager to watch the opening ceremony of the London 2012 Olympic Games.

Wearing a peach dress and pearls, 'Her Majesty' leapt from a hovering helicopter, her Union Flag parachute illuminated in the night sky as she fell safely to earth, somewhere offstage. The next shot was of her in the same-coloured outfit and fascinator, walking to her seat at the specially built Olympic Stadium in Stratford, East London, to formally open the international sporting event.

There were many among the watching millions who genuinely thought that the real Monarch had made the most daring and dangerous entrance of her reign. Former Health Secretary Jeremy Hunt later told the Sovereign that he had read about a Japanese tourist who had said how wonderful it was for the Queen to be involved in the Olympics in such a daring manner, as back home they would never get their emperor to jump out of a plane. She was not amused.[1]

In the beginning, there were some inside Buckingham Palace who never thought that the Queen would agree to becoming the highest-profile 'Bond girl' ever and, for good measure, to utter the immortal line: 'Good evening, Mr Bond.' Yet the longer she reigned, the more willing she seemed to kick back and take a chance. British film-maker Danny Boyle, who had the daunting task of creating and directing the content of the opening ceremony for London 2012, wondered if she would take a chance on him.

Some months before, he had the idea of using the Monarch in a short promotional film to be broadcast just before the start of the event. She was to be rescued from some unseen threat by 007 himself. James Bond, in black tie, would meet her at Buckingham Palace and escort her to a helicopter where 'the Queen' would fly over and under various London landmarks, such as Tower Bridge and the Houses of Parliament, before dramatically jumping out of the helicopter into the night sky. Would the idea fly with Her Majesty?

Initially, Boyle put the scheme to Lord Coe, the London 2012 chief, who in turn spoke to Princess Anne. In her matter-of-fact manner, she replied simply: 'Why don't you ask her?'[2]

Within days, Boyle was inside Buckingham Palace sketching out the scenario to the Queen's deputy private secretary Edward Young and her dresser Angela Kelly. Kelly loved the idea and went upstairs to speak to the Sovereign in person. It found immediate royal approval, but with one proviso: she had to speak the iconic – and much-parodied – line 'Good evening, Mr Bond' while actor Daniel Craig, who played the evergreen hero, stood to attention as he waited for her to finish some paperwork at her desk. Then the Queen, her corgis and her page, followed by Commander Bond, would walk through the palace to a waiting helicopter, which Her Majesty and 007 both boarded to take a ride over London, before ending with that iconic parachute jump in an evening gown.

Not only was the sketch one of the highlights of a memorable Olympic Games, but it revealed a daring, almost mischievous, side to the Queen's personality which came to the surface from time to time.

During that Olympic year, she confided in her dresser that ever since she was young she had harboured a secret wish. As a child her elders, especially Queen Mary, had insisted that she always kept her hands out of her pockets. And, just to make sure, all the pockets in all her clothes were sewn up. For years she had wanted to make a childhood dream come true and to be photographed more informally, with her hands in her pockets, despite the fact that the Queen Mother and her advisers had always suggested it was not an appropriate look for the Sovereign. Then, as with so many things, she had given in to their arguments. But not this time.

Kelly brought in photographer Barry Jeffery, who shot Her Majesty as she mimicked the poses of a professional model – with and without her hands in the pockets of her white dress. For several years the pictures remained private. Officials from the Royal Collection argued, according to Kelly, that these more candid informal photographs of the Queen could bring down the monarchy and therefore were not suitable for the public.[3] However, in 2019 the whole set of photographs was released – and the sky did not fall in on the institution.

Though the dead hand of protocol and proper form was an ever-present element in Her Majesty's life, occasionally she was able to show flashes of a very different Head of State, such as the time that she entertained US President Barack Obama and First Lady Michelle at a Buckingham Palace reception in 2009. It seemed like a routine meet-and-greet until the Queen reached over and slipped her arm around the waist of Michelle Obama who, at 5 feet 11 inches tall, towered over the diminutive Monarch. In turn, the

First Lady placed her arm around the Sovereign's shoulder telling her: 'I really enjoyed our meeting.'[4] Later, Mrs Obama explained that they had bonded over their sore feet.

As the traditional image of Queen Elizabeth II was of someone who discouraged intimacy, who was usually seen holding her oversized handbag in front of her like a shield, this show of amiable familiarity was startling. In the past, acres of newsprint had been spilled in baying disapproval when a host had so much as touched the Monarch's back to help guide her through a throng.

Her willingness to take a risk was rewarded when, in April 2013, the British Academy of Film and Television Arts conferred an honorary BAFTA on the Queen for her 'sensational' appearance at the opening ceremony of the Olympics, as well as for her support of the world of arts and entertainment. Actor Kenneth Branagh, who made the presentation at Windsor Castle, joked that several colleagues were so impressed by her performance at the Olympics that they had further scripts ready for her perusal.

At the time of the BAFTA event, actor Helen Mirren – who played the Queen in Peter Morgan's eponymous movie – was reprising her regal role once more in Morgan's new play, *The Audience*, in London's West End and so missed the royal engagement. Her depiction of the Sovereign as imperious, no-nonsense and drily witty was so realistic that when Prince William presented Mirren with the BAFTA Fellowship Award the following year, he described her as 'an extremely talented British actress whom I should probably call "Granny"'.

In turn, Mirren admitted that although she had performed as the Monarch both on stage and film, she experienced a 'lesson in embarrassment' when she joined the Queen and Prince Philip for afternoon tea at Buckingham Palace. She found herself reduced to speaking 'gobbledegook'. When asked for her thoughts on being introduced to Her Majesty, she duly acknowledged her nerves:

'You're thinking "It's the Queen, it's the Queen"!'[5] In a cute inversion of roles, Mirren admitted that she was now even more starstruck when meeting the woman she had played so successfully. 'I am genuinely always astounded by her aura, her twinkle, her presence. It never fails to surprise me.'[6]

The fact that so many people – even Oscar-winning actors – were reduced to talking 'gobbledegook' in 'the presence' helped to explain her lifelong love of horses and racing. As the novelist Jilly Cooper observed: 'A horse wouldn't know she was the Queen; a horse would just treat her like any other human. She would have had to earn a horse's love and respect, not expect it as a given. That must have been such a release for her.'[7]

More than a hobby, breeding and racing horses was her refuge from the endless problems that passed across her desk. It was positively relaxing to spend a few minutes with the comforting columns of the *Racing Post* or to talk about horses, discussing the personalities, auctions and pedigrees, with knowledgeable experts. It was a world in which she felt utterly at home. Horses were her hinterland, an engrossing place that provided an enriching alternative to the day-to-day royal world.

So while she was pleased with her honorary BAFTA, there was no mistaking the sheer unadulterated excitement on the Queen's face two months later, in June 2013, when she and her racing manager John Warren cheered on Estimate as she ran to victory in the Gold Cup at Royal Ascot. With this win, Her Majesty became the first reigning monarch in the race's 207-year history to take the prize. Her lifelong passion had yielded her biggest triumph since 1977. A few years later, it came as no surprise to the racing community when she was inducted into the QIPCO British Champions Series Hall of Fame, the first to gain membership within the 'special contributor' category.[8]

In 2015, the Queen celebrated another unique milestone when

on 9 September she toppled Queen Victoria's record of 63 years 216 days on the British throne. She became the longest-reigning female monarch in world history, although she treated the historic moment as just another day in the office when she opened the new Borders Railway in Scotland connecting Edinburgh to Tweedbank. Her lengthy service was, as the Princess Royal observed, a double-edged sword: 'People tend to forget, when she passed the longest-reigning monarch that was only because her father died so young. So for her that's a very mixed blessing and it's a record that she would much rather not have been able to pass.'⁹

Though Prince Philip had talked about retiring when he reached the ripe old age of ninety, he was by her side when she reached her own date with destiny. A three-day visit to Malta in November 2015, where the couple had spent part of their early married life, brought back many pleasant memories. Her Majesty was visiting in her capacity as Head of the Commonwealth Heads of Government Meeting and though she and the prince no longer undertook long-haul flights, the three-hour trip from London was deemed acceptable.

For the Queen, Prince Philip and those who knew them in the 1940s, this was truly a trip down memory lane. During a tour of the island, the couple made time to visit the polo field where Philip and Dickie Mountbatten had played. As they looked around, the Sovereign spotted Elizabeth Pulé, the daughter of her former housekeeper Jessie Grech, in the crowd. Another familiar face was Freddie Mizzi, a clarinet player with the Jimmy Dowling Band that used to play their favourite tunes from the musical *Oklahoma!* at the Phoenicia Hotel. When she told her audience that she spent some of the happiest years of her life there, she was not exaggerating. She genuinely remembered those who worked for her, and kept up with current affairs on the Mediterranean island with a regular delivery of the *Times of Malta* newspaper.

The Queen has always been interested in and appreciative of her former staff. From the palace to Parliament, Balmoral, Sandringham and the Commonwealth beyond, she likes to keep her finger on the pulse. As the former Lord Provost of Edinburgh Eric Milligan observed: 'She knows what is going on and cares for the people who have cared for her.'[10]

Her extensive knowledge of the social scene has also impressed Prince Andrew: 'Her intelligence network – of who's done what, what's happened, who's ill, who's died, who's had a birth – is extraordinary. How she finds out is a mystery.'[11]

Of course, her own brood mattered most as she demonstrated on her ninetieth birthday, when American photographer Annie Leibovitz was invited to take a family portrait of the Queen, Prince Philip, her two youngest grandchildren and all of her great-grandchildren at Windsor Castle. Leibovitz also had time to fit in some shots of the Queen on her own with her corgis and dorgis. This time, in one of the photos, the Sovereign's left hand was placed resolutely in her cardigan pocket.

Though her great-grandchildren were not fazed in her presence, at a certain age they came to realize who they were dealing with. Elton John watched the Queen in action at one party when she asked Princess Margaret's son David Linley to check on his sister Sarah, who had fallen ill and gone to her room to recover. When he tried to wriggle out of doing his duty, his aunt playfully slapped him across the face saying: 'Don't' – SLAP – 'argue' – SLAP – 'with' – SLAP – 'me' – SLAP – 'I' – SLAP – 'am' – SLAP – 'THE QUEEN!' When she noticed Elton John observing this family scenario, she gave him a wink and walked off.[12]

During their childhoods and teenage years, William, Harry and her other grandchildren viewed the Queen as a wise woman, at times slightly forbidding but always there to offer help and advice. In their eyes, she was a brisk, no-nonsense figure who commanded respect and never treated them with kid gloves. William remembered the day on the Balmoral estate when he received the 'most mighty bollocking' from his grandmother after he and Peter Phillips, while riding on a quad bike, chased his cousin Zara, who was driving a go-kart, into a lamp post which then fell down and nearly squashed her.[13] Her Majesty, dressed in her kilt, was the first person out of the house and she ran across the lawn to help her shocked granddaughter before delivering a severe tongue-lashing to the boys.

The somewhat safer activity of horse riding is a Royal Family pastime that has been passed down from generation to generation. The Queen herself was given her first Shetland pony at the age of four, and her daughter Anne and granddaughter Zara both went on to compete in the Olympics on horseback. Following in the footsteps of her grandfather, Prince Edward's daughter Lady Louise Windsor has taken up competitive carriage driving.

On gentler occasions, Princess Eugenie recalled picking raspberries with Granny and then finding their haul turned into jam for afternoon tea. As the Duke of York explained: 'She's been a fantastic grandmother to Beatrice and Eugenie – and probably revels in that more than being a mother, to some extent; always interested and concerned for what the girls are up to.'[14]

In July 2013, the Duke and Duchess of Cambridge welcomed their first child into the world with the birth of George Alexander Louis. Almost two years later, in May 2015, his sister Charlotte Elizabeth Diana was born. The arrival of the prince and princess ensured the stability of the dynasty, an often unstated but crucial feature of the Monarch's role. 'The Queen can see continuity with William, Catherine, George and Charlotte,' said her friend Lady Elizabeth Anson. 'That has changed her life.'[15]

As the nation celebrated the Sovereign's ninetieth birthday, a jaunty Prince Harry managed to inveigle his way into her sitting room at Windsor Castle and get her to take part in a stunt to publicize the Invictus Games – an international sporting event for 'wounded, injured or sick' former servicemen and women – of which he was patron.

Her Majesty had a genuine soft spot for Harry, the grandchild who seemingly had the knack of being able to jump the line to see her – much to the frustration of royal officials. This time, in a video that went viral, Harry invited the birthday girl to watch a message that popped up on his smart phone from American President Obama and his wife Michelle, ahead of the Games that were due to be held in Orlando, Florida in May 2016.

A stern-faced First Lady pinged into view alongside her husband, with three US service personnel in the background, and challenged Harry over the inter-service rivalry between America and Britain by saying 'Remember when you told us to "Bring it" at the Invictus Games?' The President then chipped in with 'Careful what you wish for' as the service personnel joked around in the background and one said, 'Boom!' accompanied by a mic drop gesture.

With a glint in her eye, the Queen looked unimpressed, remarking: 'Oh, really. Please.' A red-faced Harry then looked at the camera and repeated rather sheepishly: 'Boom.'[16]

Beneath the grandmotherly levity and the confetti of souvenir newspaper editions celebrating the Queen's milestone year, there was a growing sense of transition. It was a change that Harry wanted to be part of. The following summer, in June 2017, Prince Harry told writer Angela Levin that he was eager to 'get on with' an overhaul of the monarchy. 'We are involved in modernizing the British monarchy. We are not doing this for ourselves but for the greater good of the people.'[17]

A reminder of just why the institution still mattered came in the days following the terrible Grenfell tower-block fire in West

London on 14 June, which left seventy-two dead and hundreds homeless. The Queen and Prince William were quick to visit the survivors and first responders, the Monarch there as a listening ear and a comforting presence during a national calamity.

'The Queen looked at me. There was compassion, it was – caring and sincere,' concluded one survivor, after outlining her own ordeal in a face-to-face meeting with the Queen.[18] Here was the nation's grandmother in action, bringing comfort and acknowledgement of loss.

Elizabeth had always made it crystal clear, in spite of years of speculation, that she would reign as long as she had her health and strength. As she told the Archbishop of Canterbury George Carey upon his retirement: 'That's something I can't do. I'm going to carry on to the end.'[19] But that did not prevent thinking and planning with regard to the inevitable change of reign.

Her private secretary Sir Christopher Geidt earned a second knighthood as early as January 2014 for his key contribution to this issue. His citation for the honour of Knight Commander of the Order of the Bath read: 'for a new approach to constitutional matters … [and] preparation for the transition to a change of reign.'[20]

There were other straws in the wind. In 2016, the Queen elevated Camilla to the Privy Council, the Monarch's most senior advisory body, which meant that she was entitled to be present at the Accession Council to hear the future proclamation of the new Sovereign. As for the Prince of Wales, he now routinely received despatch boxes on a read-only basis, so that he was fully up to speed with government policy. Although there were those who believed the Queen was still as sprightly and as energetic as she had been in her middle years, the truth was that she was slowing down and spending much more time at Windsor Castle and rather less at Buckingham Palace.

While Her Majesty had no intention of abdicating, she recognized that it was time for her husband, almost five years her senior, to step down. His eyesight, hearing and memory were failing to the point where it was only his legendary stubbornness that kept him going. In early May 2017, he told the family of his intentions and in August he conducted his final solo public engagement on the forecourt of Buckingham Palace, meeting a group of marines involved in the 1664 Global Challenge fundraising endeavour in his capacity at Captain General of the Royal Marines.

Prince Philip deserved his rest. During his royal career he had shaken hundreds of thousands of hands, given thousands of speeches covering personal interests, including science, the environment and religion, and, since 1952, he had attended some 22,219 engagements in his own right. At an Order of Merit reception at St James's Palace shortly after the duke's upcoming retirement was made public, eminent mathematician Sir Michael Atiyah, himself eighty-eight, said to the prince, 'I'm sorry to hear you're standing down.' In typically humorous fashion, Philip replied, 'Well, I can't stand up much longer.'[21]

He retired to Wood Farm, the spacious but modestly furnished cottage on the Sandringham estate, where the ninety-six-year-old patriarch spent his days reading, painting watercolours, writing letters, and having friends and family to stay and sample his cooking – he liked to make recipes that he had spotted on TV cooking shows. An old friend observed: 'He is enjoying reading things he's always wanted to read and gets up to what he wants without an equerry telling him he has to be elsewhere or a camera following him around.'[22]

The move came entirely with the Queen's blessing, even though she recognized that it would mean they would see much less of one another. They spoke on the phone daily and she visited Sandringham more frequently. She was initially alarmed when he was involved in a collision with another vehicle while behind the wheel of his Land Rover in January 2019, but was grateful that the incident forced him to give up his driving licence. In her view, he had always driven too fast – his motoring habits a source of decades-long conflict and sharp words.

With the family's enforcer out to pasture, it fell to the Queen's private secretary, Sir Christopher Geidt, to propose changes for the future monarchy. He promoted the policy of centralizing its structure so that Buckingham Palace would take the lead, supported by Clarence House, Prince Charles's London home, and Kensington Palace, the residence of Prince William and Prince Harry. However, his command-and-control proposals did not find favour with the princes, who wanted the autonomy to 'do their own thing' rather than have to constantly defer to Buckingham Palace. Each Household wanted to operate from its own silo, thus weakening the authority at the centre. Charles, William, Andrew and Harry favoured a collegiate system, and so they decisively rejected the Geidt plan for centralization.

Although he had intended to step down at some point in the near future, having served the Queen for ten years, Geidt decided to leave early rather than fight it out with the Queen's children and grandchildren, and announced his decision in July 2017. 'This summertime bloodless palace coup means Prince Charles can now exercise more control over the monarchy's direction of travel,' noted BBC royal correspondent Peter Hunt.[23]

Part of the argument marshalled by the royal princes was that Prince Charles, rather than the Queen, should be responsible for shaping the modern monarchy. There were unconfirmed proposals that he wanted Buckingham Palace to be open to visitors all year-round, while the new King would live in an apartment in the palace, similar to the Prime Minister's flat above Downing Street. Charles's main home would be Highgrove in the West Country, while William and Catherine would move from Kensington Palace to Windsor Castle. Balmoral Castle would be turned into a museum, though the Prince of Wales would still keep nearby Birkhall Lodge.

While the consequences of the behind-the-scenes power struggle were not immediately apparent, it was clear that the Queen's authority had been diluted and that the princes had a freer hand to shape their own future vision of the monarchy. While her institutional authority was diminished, she was still held in considerable respect, not to say awe, by her family and staff.

Although there were tensions between the Households, there was cooperation elsewhere, no more so than with the Queen's beloved Commonwealth, an organization that she had nurtured and supported throughout her reign. At a London gathering of the Commonwealth Heads of Government Meeting in 2018, she spoke of her 'sincere wish' that one day the Prince of Wales should carry on the important work started by her father in 1949.[24] Before the conference ended, the leaders gathered and unanimously agreed to accept her recommendation for Charles to be the next Head of the Commonwealth. It was a welcome success for the House of Windsor.

The diversity of race, creed and colour, which was the cornerstone of the Commonwealth, came closer to home with the warm acceptance into the Royal Family of Prince Harry's girlfriend, Meghan Markle, a divorced, dual-heritage American actor. During the run-up to the May 2018 wedding, she thoughtfully recognized how much the Commonwealth mattered to the Queen when she came up with the idea of having the national flowers of the fifty-three nations of the organization embroidered into her bridal veil. It was a gesture that the Sovereign much appreciated, in the same way that she was pleased by Meghan's decision to be baptized into the national faith, the Church of England, before her wedding day.

As she watched Meghan, from a different country, colour and culture, walk down the aisle of St George's Chapel, she was witnessing history in the making. At a stroke, their marriage made the monarchy seem more relevant and inclusive in an ever-changing world. As it transpired, however, their brief journey at the heart of the institution would ultimately test the patience of the Queen, expose her familial indulgence, and stretch and strain the bonds of blood and sinew.

At first all seemed well. A month after the wedding, the Queen invited Meghan on the royal train for a day's engagements in Cheshire in the north-west of England. On the journey there, Her Majesty presented the Duchess of Sussex (as she had become known since her nuptials) with a beautiful pearl necklace and matching earrings. 'I really love being in her company,' Meghan said later, comparing the Monarch's warmth and welcoming nature with that of her own grandmother, Jeanette.[25]

To ensure that the duchess was properly briefed for future events, the Queen had assigned her own experienced assistant private secretary Samantha Cohen to Meghan's office, to provide her with insight into the workings of the monarchy and the Commonwealth. She appointed Harry as a Commonwealth youth ambassador, while months later Meghan became patron of the Association of Commonwealth Universities. These appointments would give the couple an international role and leave the domestic scene largely to the Duke and Duchess of Cambridge. As participants in a YouGov poll in autumn 2018 voted Prince Harry the most popular member of the Royal Family, just ahead of the Queen, it seemed a shrewd strategy to ensure that the future King was not overshadowed by his younger brother.

Harry seemed determined to carve out a role very different from that of his brother, having developed a mindset that would put them on conflicting paths, but despite the distance growing between the two princes the younger man still had the ear of his grandmother. A story in *The Times* newspaper in November 2018, shortly after Meghan and Harry had returned from a successful first tour of Australia, Fiji, Tonga and New Zealand, gave an intimate flavour of the relationship between the prince and his Sovereign.

It revolved around the tiara, held under lock and key in the vaults of Buckingham Palace, which Her Majesty had loaned to Meghan before the wedding. The story stated that prior to the royal nuptials, Harry was angry when the precious item was not immediately made available for a hair fitting with Meghan's hairdresser, Serge Normant, who had flown in specially from New York. The Queen's dresser, the redoubtable Angela Kelly, who is also guardian of her private jewellery collection, explained that certain security protocols had to be adhered to in order to access the priceless piece. Harry would have none of it and angrily told staff: 'What Meghan wants Meghan gets.'[26] In the end, he went to see his grandmother, who agreed to grant access to the tiara for the purpose of the fitting.

Although the media focus was on Meghan's alleged prima-donna behaviour, the most telling takeaway from the 'tiara tantrum' story was the way that Harry was able to go over the head of a trusted royal aide directly to the Queen and convince her to do his bidding. In an organization within which it can take weeks to gain an appointment with the Monarch, this access was remarkable. Family came first. It was both a strength and a flaw. As an aide later observed: 'It has to be remembered that this is a family and a court, not a corporation.'[27]

A family in which position not popularity ultimately mattered most. Meghan joined the institution at a time when it was under-going gradual but nonetheless seismic change, which inevitably comes with the passing of the crown from one generation to the next. As popular as they were, Meghan and Harry would in time slide down the royal totem pole, just like Prince Andrew who, from once being second in line to the throne, was now a member of the supporting cast. The royal couple wanted to shape an alternative future for themselves, which would eventually place them in direct conflict with the existing order.

As the rifts inside the Royal Family, particularly between Harry and William, became ever more pronounced, the Queen's theme for 2019 – mutual respect and conciliation – seemed as appropriate for her warring family as for a Britain still licking its wounds following the fractious referendum over leaving the European Union. In fact, it was a theme that she returned to often during the year: in a speech to the Women's Institute; during US President Donald Trump's visit to Britain; and at the twentieth anniversary of the opening of the Scottish Parliament. She saw it as her role to try to cool political passions and soothe the brow of a nation turning in on itself.

Her wisdom and judgement were soon needed much closer to home. Ever since 'her strength and stay' Prince Philip had retired, her second son Prince Andrew had done his best to make up for his father's absence. He accompanied his mother to church on Sundays and ensured that his daughters, Beatrice and Eugenie, kept in contact.

In her eyes, Andrew had, in times of crisis, shown qualities of courage and leadership, notably during the Falklands conflict and the Windsor Castle fire. Though he had a reputation for being arrogant, his loyalty to the Sovereign was unswerving. She appreciated his dogged support, even if his judgement was somewhat simplistic. During the week of Diana's funeral, for instance, when passions were running hot inside Balmoral about how to deal with the situation, the prince declared to a roomful of warring palace advisers, 'The Queen is the Queen. You can't speak to her like that!'[28] meaning that her view should be accepted without question.

Though he had become a reassuring and welcome presence, distracting his mother from her two grandsons at war, his own issues soon dominated the royal agenda. Try as he might, he could not lay to rest his association with the banker and convicted paedophile Jeffrey Epstein. Matters became much worse when, in August 2019, while awaiting trial on sex trafficking charges, Epstein committed suicide in a cell at the Metropolitan Correctional Center in Manhattan.

One of his most prominent and persistent accusers was Virginia Roberts Giuffre, who alleged that when she was seventeen years old Epstein had forced her to have sex with his friends, including Prince Andrew on three separate occasions. As proof of having met him, she released a photograph that showed a smiling prince with his arm around her at Ghislaine Maxwell's London home. While the Duke of York denied having had any sexual contact with Giuffre, the negative headlines continued.

In November 2019, following discussions with his lawyers and private secretary Amanda Thirsk, Andrew decided to consider giving an extended interview to the BBC presenter Emily Maitlis on a specially recorded edition of *Newsnight*, the popular current-affairs programme. When the *Newsnight* team came to the palace to make their final pitch, Andrew stated that he must 'seek approval from higher up'.[29]

The final decision was to be taken by the Queen and Prince Charles, who were both nervous about the possible fallout. His mother knew from past experience with her family, notably Prince Charles's prime-time confession of adultery in *Charles: The Private Man, the Public Role* and Diana's appearance on *Panorama*, that royalty did not fare well on TV. However, following internal communications, the Queen and the Prince of Wales were sufficiently reassured to give the interview the go-ahead.

After the fifty-minute grilling by Maitlis, Andrew thought the conversation, which had taken place in a ballroom at Buckingham Palace, had gone well and called the Queen to tell her: 'Mission accomplished.' He imagined it to be such a success that, after filming, he took the *Newsnight* team on a tour of the palace.

The cacophony of criticism that immediately followed the broadcast soon stilled that wrong-headed belief. Andrew's public cross-examination was deemed a disaster; 'Car crash TV' was one of the kinder descriptions.[30] The prince didn't appear to regret his relationship with Epstein nor did he express any sympathy for the disgraced banker's victims, even though he was given ample opportunity to do so. Although the Queen was said to be horrified, for once she too came into the firing line for allowing Andrew to proceed with an interview that not only wrecked his reputation but also damaged the standing of the monarchy. 'Prince Andrew's TV calamity suggests Queen is losing her grip on "the firm"' was the headline in *The Times*, the Establishment's paper of record.[31]

Her advanced age, the absence of Prince Philip – the family 'enforcer' – from the fray and the Queen's fondness for Andrew were suggested as factors contributing to the debacle. However, the fact that the prince had not been able to provide a convincing reason for his continued friendship with the millionaire paedophile, or explain away the photo that showed his arm around Giuffre's waist after he stated that he could not remember meeting her, proved damning. Moreover, his breezy responses and unreflective manner suggested a man totally out of touch with the #MeToo generation.

As charities, colleges, businesses and other organizations with associations to the prince began to wash their hands of him, within days of the November broadcast the Duke of York became the first member of the Royal Family in history to be forced to retire from royal duties. He made the decision following crisis talks with the Queen and Prince Charles, who was consulted during a tour of New Zealand.

As far as the Queen was concerned, those last few days had compelled her to choose between the demands of her family and the institution they served. Andrew's historic statement announcing his departure was released just a few minutes before the Monarch arrived at Chatham House, where she was to present her friend Sir David Attenborough with an international award regarding his work highlighting plastic pollution in the world's oceans.

Nothing in her demeanour suggested anything other than delight at honouring the distinguished naturalist and broadcaster. She smiled broadly and as she signed the visitors' book she mischievously asked for the date. It was 20 November, her seventy-second wedding anniversary. 'Oh, I knew that,' she deadpanned.[32] No one present would have had an inkling that just a few minutes before, she had been party to ousting her son from the front ranks of the Royal Family.

She demonstrated that she remained ruthless when necessary in order to protect the institution to which she had sacrificed her whole life. Andrew was a problem, and she and her eldest son had moved swiftly to exorcize him from the public realm. Andrew now had the rest of his life to reflect on his folly. Though he expressed regret for his 'ill-judged association' with Epstein in his statement, and declared 'I deeply sympathize with everyone who has been affected', it was all too little too late.[33]

Matters only got worse for the disgraced duke. After a month-long trial in December 2021, his friend Ghislaine Maxwell was found guilty of sex trafficking, while in January 2022 he lost his bid to have Virginia Giuffre's case against him thrown out. Days later he was, with the Queen's 'approval and agreement', stripped of his royal patronages and military titles, leaving him to fight the court case as a private person. The case was promptly settled out of court.

Within days of dealing with her second son's folly, the Queen was plunged into a crisis at the opposite end of the scale. Whereas

Prince Andrew was desperate to hang on to the trappings of royalty and was devastated by his abrupt relegation, Prince Harry was making it abundantly clear that he would like to resign from the family 'Firm'.

Harry had always been a reluctant royal. Ever since the death of Diana, he found public appearances a trial, breaking into a nervous sweat when faced with camera flashes. He would much rather have continued his career in the Army than spend his days shaking hands with well-wishers at royal engagements. The problem was that he was a natural, the public seeing in him shades of his much-loved, much-missed mother. As the BBC's royal correspondent Jonny Dymond noted: 'To watch Prince Harry ... is to observe a man who comes alive with crowds, with love, with those who need him. But also to see a man entirely unhappy with his lot. A man who desperately wants to get away from cameras, observers, outsiders, looking and filming and exploiting him.'[34] He had, at his brother's suggestion, gone for psychological counselling to help him cope. The Queen had kept a weather eye on him, as far as time allowed, and he was always welcome to see her.

Although the arrival of Meghan Markle in his life was looked upon by some rather doubtfully, including Prince William, there were others who hoped she would bring Harry to safe harbour. History was not on their side, however, as evidenced by the abdication of Edward VIII and his relationship with the twice-divorced American Wallis Simpson.

While Harry and Meghan's royal life together had started brightly, it soon began to unravel and they began crafting a road map for their future that ran parallel to that of the Royal Family rather than being directly part of it. The Windsors and their officials had been aware of the couple's discussions about living in both North America and Britain, being financially independent and focusing on their own humanitarian mission from around May 2019.

During the summer and autumn of that year, it became even more apparent that Harry and Meghan were unhappy with the unrelenting media criticism and what they considered to be a lack of support from inside the institution. With no change on the horizon, Prince Harry had spoken to the Queen and his father about stepping back as senior royals and raising funds privately so that they would not need the Sovereign Grant nor monies from the Duchy of Cornwall, Prince Charles's estate, to subsidize their lifestyle. As private citizens, they would not be beholden to the media but would still be able to serve the monarchy, albeit in a limited capacity. The Queen's initial reaction to this idea was that it was almost impossible to be half in and half out of the Royal Family. It was akin to being 'slightly' pregnant.

The couple, who spent Christmas 2019 at a borrowed Canadian mansion on Vancouver Island, watched the smoke signals emerging from Buckingham Palace and realized that the message did not include them. First came the Queen's Christmas message, when there was clearly no photograph of Harry, Meghan and Archie Harrison Mountbatten-Windsor – her most recent great-grandchild who was born in May 2019 – visible on her desk alongside the other members of her family. Then, in early January, an official royal photograph was released. Taken at Buckingham Palace, it featured the reigning Monarch and her direct heirs in the line of succession: Charles, William and George. It was only the second time the existing and future Sovereigns had been pictured together.

Prince Harry, notoriously thin-skinned at the best of times, interpreted this in the most conspiratorial way possible, that they were no longer part of the Royal Family. It all fed into the couple's decision-making as they carefully worked out their future. On 8 January 2020, Harry and Meghan announced on Instagram, giving minimal notice to the Queen, Prince Charles and Prince

William, that they were indeed 'stepping back' from royal duties and dividing their time between Britain and North America. Their official statement, which was issued against the Queen's express wishes, read in part: 'After many months of reflection and internal discussions, we have chosen to make a transition this year in starting to carve out a progressive new role within this institution. We intend to step back as "senior" members of the Royal Family and work to become financially independent, while continuing to fully support Her Majesty the Queen.'

They aimed to 'collaborate' with the Queen and the rest of their family to make this happen. This choice of wording clearly demonstrated how weakened the Queen's position had become. The idea of a junior member of the Royal Family 'collaborating' with the Head of State on an equal footing left historians, royal officials and commentators aghast. If it was anything, the Royal Family was a clearly defined hierarchy, not a republic of equals.

The couple's declaration of independence, some 244 years after the US original, was met with disbelief by the rest of the family and their officials. A new front in the War of the Windsors was about to break out. Though increasingly incapacitated, Prince Philip's indignant and mystified response summed up the feelings of many inside and outside the institution: 'What the hell are they playing at?'[35] The idea of a royal not wanting to be a royal any more nor willing to accept the Queen's authority without question was simply incomprehensible, particularly to a man who had sacrificed his whole life in supporting the Queen and upholding the monarchy.

The Sovereign agreed to a meeting at Sandringham a few days later with herself, Charles, William, Harry and their senior staff. Officials were told to work 'at pace'.[36] For once she was not prepared to let this matter drag on as she had with her sister's marital separation and the damaging War of the Waleses that had erupted when Charles and Diana separated in December 1992.

Nor was there any 'ostriching', that is to say her habit of avoiding unpleasant realities.

From the off, it was clear that the Queen wanted to carve a workable solution to accommodate the Sussexes while maintaining the integrity of the monarchy, especially in regard to finances. The idea that Meghan and Harry could monetize their royal brand 'Sussex Royal', for example, was a non-starter. Subsequently, however, they were able to craft deals for themselves as individuals, the couple going on to surprise the family and the wider world by quickly snagging multi-million-dollar agreements with the likes of Netflix, Spotify and other media outlets.

In a warm and friendly statement issued after the initial talks, the Queen conveyed the following sentiments: 'My family and I are entirely supportive of Harry and Meghan's desire to create a new life as a young family. Although we would have preferred them to remain full-time working members of the Royal Family, we respect and understand their wish to live a more independent life as a family while remaining a valued part of my family.'

It was clear from the start of negotiations that if they wanted freedom, they had to give up their royal privileges. After much back and forth, the couple agreed to pay for the renovations of Frogmore Cottage at Windsor (the home they had moved into after their marriage), underwrite their own security, abandon the 'Sussex Royal' brand and relinquish Harry's honorary military patronages, notably his position as Captain General of the Royal Marines, a post he had held since taking over from his grandfather in 2017.

On 18 January, just ten days after Meghan and Harry's stepping-back announcement, the way forward was mapped out, drawn up and agreed. Though Charles and William had doubtless pushed matters along, in the end it was still the Queen who issued the statement about the departing royal duo. While she hoped that the young couple would 'start building a happy and peaceful new life', not everyone was so fulsome.

The awkwardness and tension between the Cambridges and the Sussexes, the quartet once dubbed 'the Fab Four' after The Beatles pop group, was very much on public display at the televised Commonwealth Day service at Westminster Abbey on 9 March 2020. The brothers barely exchanged a word. Shortly afterwards, Meghan and Harry flew back across the Atlantic and returned to their Canadian retreat, keeping out of sight at a waterside mansion on Vancouver Island.

In fact, once they had made their great escape, they had a secret weapon already primed. Just a few months after their wedding, in December 2018, Harry had held secret discussions in a London hotel with talk-show queen Oprah Winfrey, who had been a guest at their nuptials, about the possibility of an interview. When they flew to Canada for the winter, the media deal was already in the bag.

Then the term COVID-19 was on everybody's lips. And nothing was ever the same again. Just two days after the Commonwealth Day service, the World Health Organization formally declared a pandemic because of a coronavirus that was sweeping across the globe. This resulted in the shutting down of schools, retail stores, pubs and restaurants, public gatherings, while all except vital travel was discouraged. Within two weeks the UK had been placed in lockdown, and the royal drama was suddenly forgotten in the midst of a life-or-death struggle that the British nation had not seen since the Second World War.

In the days before an effective vaccine had been developed, the staggering numbers of those dying from COVID-19 in the UK's capital were higher than they had been in the worst week of the Blitz in 1940, when Nazi bombers rained down death and destruction on London, killing more than 4,000 in a week. Frontline National Health Service doctors, nurses and others, some of whom ended up losing their lives in the line of duty, were compared to the heroic Spitfire pilots who thwarted the Nazi invasion. Thursday nights at eight o'clock became a regular time for the people of Britain to show their appreciation by standing on their doorsteps to applaud NHS staff and other carers.

For the Queen, who had lived through the Blitz, it was a moment to remind the country of what its citizens were made of. With her son and heir self-isolating up at Birkhall in Scotland while suffering from the illness, and her Prime Minister Boris Johnson admitted to St Thomas's Hospital in central London, where he ended up fighting for his life in intensive care, the Monarch made a televised speech to a deeply anxious and nervous nation, albeit one that was united in the face of a common enemy.

While the Queen may have been in the autumn of her reign, she was perfectly positioned to speak to the British people with knowledge and empathy. Her evening address on Sunday 5 April 2020 may only have lasted four minutes, but the impact was long-lasting as she successfully evoked Britain's wartime stoicism, quiet courage and ability to meet deadly calamity with a smile.

The Sovereign, who wrote the evocative speech together with her private secretary Sir Edward Young, began by saying: 'I am speaking to you at what I know is an increasingly challenging time. A time of disruption in the life of our country: a disruption that has brought grief to some, financial difficulties to many and enormous changes to the daily lives of us all.'

After thanking those on the front line, she continued: 'I hope in the years to come everyone will be able to take pride in how they responded to this challenge. And those who come after us will say the Britons of this generation were as strong as any. That the attributes of self-discipline, of quiet good-humoured resolve and of fellow-feeling still characterize this country. The pride in who we are is not a part of our past, it defines our present and our future.'

She finished on a note of encouraging positivity: 'We should take comfort that while we may have more still to endure, better days will return: we will be with our friends again; we will be with our families again; we will meet again.'

Many of the estimated 24 million people who had tuned into the fifth non-festive special address in Her Majesty's sixty-eight-year reign admitted that they had a lump in their throat and tears in their eyes as she echoed the famous words of wartime favourite Dame Vera Lynn: 'We will meet again.' It was a speech of hope, consolation, inspiration – and steely resolve. Her long experience with crises and dramas gave her words a resonance and authority that a younger voice would not have had. She was the right person with the right speech at the right time. In that moment, the Queen was truly the grandmother to the nation.

From then on, she and Prince Philip, who had returned from his Sandringham cottage, lived together in a protective bubble at Windsor Castle. Though they had a staff of twenty-two, the couple found themselves spending as much time together as they had in their first days of marriage.

The pandemic tested everyone's ingenuity – including that of the Queen and the Royal Family. Throughout her life she had been in the waving and hand-shaking business. As she has been known to say: 'I have to be seen to be believed.'[37] Not any more. The Sovereign and the rest of the family had to adapt to a world of video calls and talking to a computer or television screen. This was the new normal. The Monarch was able to keep in touch with her subjects via the very medium she had once opposed. Besides her April 2020 speech, she used television to deliver her Easter message and to commemorate the seventy-fifth anniversary of Victory in Europe or VE Day.

At Easter she called for hope and light in a darkened world. 'We know that Coronavirus will not overcome us. As dark as death can be – particularly for those suffering with grief – light and life are greater. May the living flame of the Easter hope be a steady guide as we face the future.'

She looked back fondly on VE Day as the nation, under lockdown, remembered those who had laid down their lives in the cause of freedom: 'Today it may seem hard that we cannot mark this special anniversary as we would wish. Instead, we remember from our homes and our doorsteps. But our streets are not empty; they are filled with the love and the care that we have for each other. And when I look at our country today, and see what we are willing to do to protect and support one another, I say with pride that we are still a nation those brave soldiers, sailors and airmen would recognize and admire.'

Her grandson Prince Harry, himself hardened by warfare in Afghanistan, had another battle to fight. It concerned what he considered to be the unfair treatment meted out to Meghan and himself by his family and their officials. After several fraught conversations with members of the Royal Family and their advisers, he had concluded that he could never resolve his complaints privately. Waiting in the wings was Oprah Winfrey, eager to discuss on television their royal experiences.

Broadcast in March 2021, the ninety-minute conversation for once lived up to the billing. The couple dropped bombshell after bombshell, accusing the Royal Family of racism as well as indifferent and callous treatment in the face of Meghan's mental health struggles, isolation and 'imprisonment'. Many of their claims, such as suggesting they were formally married three days before the televised wedding ceremony, were subsequently shown to be false or exaggerations.

It was hurtful for the Queen, who had shown continuing good faith in her support of Harry, both before and after his marriage. She was, as a friend of Diana's observed, 'disappointed' by his behaviour. Her formal response in the statement issued by

Buckingham Palace after the UK broadcast was classic HMQ – modulated, loving but firm – while her phrase 'some recollections may vary' spoke volumes about the accuracy of some of Meghan and Harry's assertions. Her Majesty's decision to investigate the allegations of racism in private indicated her preferred direction of travel. Once again television proved that it was a fairweather friend: marvellous for royal spectacle, highly damaging for the monarchy once one of its members clipped on a microphone.

COVID-19, though, constrained everything. Like Mountbatten, Prince Philip had painstakingly planned his funeral right down to the colour of the Land Rover designed to carry his coffin. When he died on the morning of 9 April 2021, just weeks short of his one-hundredth birthday, his elaborate plans had to be severely scaled back. His passing was described as 'gentle and peaceful'. Prince Edward's wife Sophie, the Countess of Wessex, revealed: 'It was just like somebody took him by the hand and off he went.'[38] While Prince Andrew remarked that his father's death left the Queen with 'a huge void' in her life.[39]

The Duke of Edinburgh's funeral at St George's Chapel was, due to COVID-19 regulations, a limited celebration of his life. Only thirty members of the family could take part in the service on 17 April, which saw the Queen, a diminutive lonely figure in black, sitting apart from everyone else as she made her final goodbyes. 'To see Her Majesty on her own,' said the Countess of Wessex, 'it was very poignant.'[40] The service was brisk and to the point like the man himself. 'Just get on with it,' he would doubtless have said.

Despite her personal sadness, the Sovereign continued fulfilling her royal duties in a way that would have made her husband rightly proud, attending an engagement just four days after his death. In the days following the funeral, she was phlegmatic and reflective but was never left alone. Senior members of the Royal Family, particularly Sophie Wessex, were regular visitors to Windsor Castle.

The arrival of Lilibet Diana Mountbatten-Windsor, the daughter of Meghan and Harry, on 4 June was a welcome addition to the clan, demonstrating once again that in death there is also life, especially a new baby who bore the Monarch's childhood nickname. Using technology to which she had become accustomed during the pandemic, the Queen had to make do with Zoom shots of the baby rather than seeing her in person.

By contrast, her trusted and loyal ladies-in-waiting were a constant physical presence. On the journey to bid farewell to Prince Philip, it was Lady Susan Hussey – who joined Court circles in 1960 – who accompanied Her Majesty to the service in the State Bentley. Her ladies-in-waiting were not just unpaid helpers, but genuine friends who had experienced marital bereavement themselves. The Queen proved herself remarkably stoical and, as the Countess of Wessex noted, was always 'thinking of others before herself'.[41]

A similar comment was made about her many years before in a tone of some wonderment by her father's gruff private secretary, Tommy Lascelles, during the famous tour of South Africa in 1947. He described her as having 'an astonishing solicitude for other people's comfort';[42] he had been used to members of the Royal Family putting themselves before others. Not Elizabeth Alexandra Mary Windsor.

She became a young adult in wartime, witnessing at first hand the many guises of bravery. During those dark days of hardship and sacrifice, her steadfast Christian faith lit the way. Her quiet conviction sustained her through the many challenges she faced, often at a young age. Her own memories of VE Day, dancing with strangers in the crowd, have stayed with her throughout her life, as have her days living as a Navy wife in Malta with the hope and expectation of a normal life stretching out before her.

Normal is a word she has embraced. Her life has been uniquely privileged but uniquely constrained, always on the inside looking out. She has never allowed her heart to rule her head and yet, ironically, it has been matters of the heart that have defined her reign. Protocol and tradition have been her safety net – and at times proved her undoing, most notably after the death of Diana, Princess of Wales. Her initial instinct was to clam up and retreat, though in later life she is far more her own person, more relaxed and willing to let her hair down, her wit as dry as her evening Martinis. The older she has become, the more her capacity to surprise.

Throughout her life she has put up with excessive amounts of praise and equally excessive criticism, though she is an instinctive conciliator, a follower of the middle way, an apostle of tolerance. She is wise, shrewd and in her own way, beneath the brittle façade, rather soft-hearted.

Though she too has suffered health issues, her 'business as usual' attitude has always shone through. The prospect of becoming the first-ever British Monarch to celebrate her platinum anniversary in 2022, after seventy years on the throne, gave her an undoubted sense of achievement.

To mark the seventieth anniversary of the Accession, 6 February 2022, the Queen issued an official statement expressing her 'sincere wish' that Camilla be crowned Queen Consort when Prince Charles becomes King. It was the most public indication of Her Majesty's wish to ensure a smooth, orderly and uncontroversial transition of reign.

Queen Victoria earned herself the title grandmother of Europe, while Queen Elizabeth II has become grandmother to the United Kingdom and the Commonwealth. The longest-serving female monarch in history has devoted herself to her family and the wider family of nations. Through the many shocks and surprises that have studded her record-breaking reign, she has stood for service and dedication, patiently watching the passing

REFERENCES

INTRODUCTION

1   *Prince Philip: The Royal Family Remembers* (UK: Oxford Films, 22 September 2021), BBC One.

2   Kiron K. Skinner, Annelise Anderson and Martin Anderson (eds.), *Reagan: A Life in Letters* (New York: Free Press, 2003), 48.

3   Joan Goulding, 'Queen Elizabeth II left her luxury yacht today', *UPI Archives*, 5 March 1983.

4   Henry Samuel, 'Teetotal Sarkozy uses Dutch courage to grill Queen', *The Independent*, 7 October 2010.

5   'Obituary: Sir Kenneth Scott', *The Times*, 2 March 2018.

CHAPTER ONE

1   Marion Crawford, 'The day the Queen threw a tantrum and tipped a pot of ink over her own head', *Daily Mail*, 18 May 2012.

2   Anne Edwards, *Royal Sisters: Queen Elizabeth II and Princess Margaret* (Guilford, CT: Lyons Press, 1990), 11.

3   Duchess of Windsor, *The Heart has its Reasons* (London: Michael Joseph, 1956), 225.

4   Matthew Dennison, *The Queen* (London: Head of Zeus, 2021), 100.

5   Jane Dismore, *Princess: The Early Life of Queen Elizabeth II* (Guilford, CT: Lyons Press, 2018), 104.

6   'A young Princess Elizabeth: the early years', *The Australian Women's Weekly*, 5 September 2015.

7   Margaret Rhodes, 'The day the Queen did a conga into the Palace', *Daily Mail*, 18 June 2011.

8   Eliana Dockterman, 'Elizabeth didn't expect to be Queen. Here's how it happened', *Time*, 1 June 2018.

9   William Safire (ed.), *Lend Me Your Ears: Great Speeches in History – Updated and Expanded* (New York: W. W. Norton & Company, 2004), 422.

10　Ann Morrow, *The Queen* (New York: William Morrow and Company, Inc., 1983), 15.

11　Marion Crawford, *The Little Princesses* (New York: St Martin's Griffin, 2020; orig. pub. 1950), 63.

12　Lydia Starbuck, 'The Queen's birth: what the papers said', *Royal Central*, 21 April 2021.

13　William Shawcross, *The Queen Mother: The Official Biography* (New York: Knopf, 2009), 257.

14　Ben Pimlott, *The Queen: Elizabeth II and the Monarchy* (London: HarperCollins, 1996), 3.

15　Shawcross, *The Queen Mother*, 307.

16　Ibid., 302.

17　'Featured document: letter from Princess Elizabeth to WSC', *International Churchill Society*, 5 June 2018.

18　Jennifer Ellis (ed.), *Thatched with Gold: The Memoirs of Mabell, Countess of Airlie* (London: Ulverscroft, 1992), 180.

19　Richard Kay and Geoffrey Levy, 'The Queen of mischief', *Daily Mail*, 16 March 2016.

20　Ian Lloyd, 'Revealed: the little girl the Queen chose to be her best friend', *Daily Mail*, 25 July 2014.

21　Dismore, *Princess*, 91.

22　Shawcross, *The Queen Mother*, 316.

23　Ibid., 320.

24　Edward Owens, '"This is the Day of the People": the 1937 Coronation', *The Family Firm: Monarchy, Mass Media and the British Public, 1932–53* (University of London Press, 2019), 133–98. www.jstor.org/stable/j.ctvkjb3sr.9.

25　Crawford, *The Little Princesses*, 22.

26　Margaret Rhodes, 'The day the Queen did a conga into the Palace', *Daily Mail*, 18 June 2011.

27　'Visit to MTB (Motor Torpedo Boat) in July 1946', page 4, in 'Crawford, Marion (re: *The Little Princesses*, 1949)', Box 6, File 30, Bruce and Beatrice Blackmar Gould Correspondence, Rare Books and Special Collections, Firestone Library, Princeton University, Princeton, NJ.

28　Ibid, page 5.

29 Pimlott, *The Queen*, 28.

30 Crawford, *The Little Princesses*, 26.

31 Maria Coole, 'The Queen's ruined childhood and why she won't let Prince George suffer the same heartbreak', *Marie Claire*, 25 December 2019.

32 Crawford, *The Little Princesses*, 19.

33 Untitled, Box 6, Folder 32, Bruce and Beatrice Blackmar Gould Correspondence, Rare Books and Special Collections, Firestone Library, Princeton University, Princeton, NJ.

34 Crawford, *The Little Princesses*, 28.

35 Ibid., 21.

36 Ibid., 72.

37 Royal Collection Trust, RCIN 1080431.

38 Dismore, *Princess*, 110.

39 Crawford, *The Little Princesses*, 84.

40 Ibid., 79.

41 Ibid., 102.

42 Gyles Brandreth, *Philip and Elizabeth: Portrait of a Royal Marriage* (London: W. W. Norton & Company, 2004), 68.

43 Crawford, *The Little Princesses*, 103,

CHAPTER TWO

1 Henry Holloway, 'Nazi plot to kill Winston Churchill with spy parachuted into Britain to win WW2', *Daily Star*, 3 July 2017.

2 Richard M. Langworth, 'How many assassination attempts on Winston Churchill? Ask Walter Thompson', *The Churchill Project: Hillsdale College*, 18 September 2019.

3 Comer Clarke, 'Kidnap the Royal Family', *Sunday Pictorial*, 22 March 1959.

4 Andrew Stewart, *The King's Private Army: Protecting the British Royal Family During the Second World War* (Solihull: Helion & Company, 2015), 124.

5 Hannah Furness, 'Queen Mother learned to shoot Buckingham Palace rats in case Nazis tried to kidnap Royal family', *Daily Telegraph*, 30 April 2015.

6 William Shawcross (ed.), *Counting One's Blessings: The Selected*

Letters of Queen Elizabeth the Queen Mother (New York: Farrar, Straus and Giroux, 2012), 277.

7   Stewart, *The King's Private Army*, 127.

8   Elizabeth Longford, *The Queen Mother* (New York: W. Morrow, 1981), 80.

9   Stewart, *The King's Private Army*, 126.

10   John W. Wheeler-Bennett, *King George VI: His Life and Reign* (London: Macmillan, 1958), 464.

11   Ibid., 468.

12   Caroline Davies, 'How the Luftwaffe bombed the palace, in the Queen Mother's own words', *The Guardian*, 12 September 2009.

13   Shawcross (ed.), *Counting One's Blessings*, 296.

14   Julia Labianca, '17 wild secrets you never knew about Windsor Castle', *Reader's Digest Canada*, 31 May 2021.

15   Alathea Fitzalan Howard and Celestria Noel (ed.), *The Windsor Diaries, 1940–45* (London: Hodder & Stoughton, 2020), 35.

16   Shawcross, *The Queen Mother*, 586.

17   'Wartime broadcast, 1940', royal.uk website, published 13 October 1940.

18   Anne Glenconner, *Lady in Waiting: My Extraordinary Life in the Shadow of the Crown* (London: Hodder & Stoughton, 2019), 18.

19   Duff Hart-Davis (ed.), *King's Counsellor: Abdication and War: The Diaries of Sir Alan Lascelles* (London: Orion Publishing, 2006), 208.

20   'Obituary: Sir Geoffrey de Bellaigue', *Daily Telegraph*, 8 January 2013.

21   Gill Swain, 'My picnics with the Queen', *Daily Mirror*, 19 September 1998.

22   Stewart, *The King's Private Army*, 63–64.

23   Shawcross (ed.), *Counting One's Blessings*, 361.

24   Ibid., 354.

25   Harry Wallop, 'Her REAL highness', *Daily Mail*, 4 February 2018.

26   Crawford, *The Little Princesses*, 134.

27   Ibid., 126.

28   Fitzalan Howard and Noel (ed.), *The Windsor Diaries*, 100.

29   'ER's Press Conference in Canterbury, England, 18 November 1942',

reprinted in Maurine Beasley (ed.), *White House Press Conferences of Eleanor Roosevelt* (New York: Garland, 1983).

30 F. J. Corbitt, *My Twenty Years in Buckingham Palace: A Book of Intimate Memoirs* (New York: David McKay Company, Inc., 1956), 188.

31 Shawcross (ed.), *Counting One's Blessings*, 366.

32 Veronica Maclean, *Crowned Heads: Kings, Emperors and Sultans: A Royal Quest* (London: Hodder & Stoughton, 1993), 32.

33 'Queen Mum falters on memory lane: writer accused of ill table manners in reporting anecdote', *Los Angeles Times*, 11 July 1990.

34 Hart-Davis (ed.), *King's Counsellor*, 85.

35 Tim Heald, 'A very contrary Princess – why did the charming Margaret turn into the most unpopular royal?', *Daily Mail*, 29 June 2007.

36 Gyles Brandreth, *Philip: The Final Portrait: Elizabeth, Their Marriage and Their Dynasty* (London: Coronet, 2021), 171.

37 Fitzalan Howard and Noel (ed.), *The Windsor Diaries*, 131.

38 Margaret Rhodes, *The Final Curtsey: A Royal Memoir by the Queen's Cousin* (London: Umbria Press, 2012), 87.

39 Dismore, *Princess*, 193.

40 Ibid., 145.

41 Ibid., 194.

42 Philip Eade, 'The romances of young Prince Philip', *The Daily Telegraph*, 5 May 2017.

43 Ingrid Seward, *Prince Philip Revealed: A Man of His Century* (London: Simon and Schuster, 2020), 66.

44 Annie Bullen, *His Royal Highness The Prince Philip, Duke of Edinburgh (1921–2021): A Commemoration* (London: Pitkin Publishing, 2021), 23.

45 Seward, *Prince Philip Revealed*, 69.

46 Crawford, *The Little Princesses*, 150.

47 Fitzalan Howard and Noel (ed.), *The Windsor Diaries*, 217.

48 Ibid., 282.

49 Valentine Low, 'VE Day: Queen recalls joining the party with Margaret', *The Times*, 9 May 2020.

50 Chris Pleasance, 'Don't look now, Your Majesty!', *Daily Mail*, 17 March 2014.

51   Valentine Low, 'VE Day: Queen recalls joining the party with
     Margaret', *The Times*, 9 May 2020.
52   *The Way We Were*, BBC Radio 4, 24 December 1985.

CHAPTER THREE

1   Sarah Bradford, *George VI* (New York: Viking, 2011), 346.
2   D. R. Thorpe (ed.), *Who Loses, Who Wins: The Journals of Kenneth
     Rose, Volume Two, 1979–2014* (London: Weidenfeld and Nicolson,
     2019), 177.
3   *Prince Philip: The Plot to Make a King* (UK: Blakeway Productions,
     30 July 2015), Channel Four.
4   Seward, *Prince Philip Revealed*, 75.
5   Andrew Hornery, 'Happy 99th birthday to Philip', *The Sydney
     Morning Herald*, 14 June 2020.
6   Michael Thornton, 'Was Philip really a philanderer?', *Daily Mail*,
     18 March 2017.
7   Dismore, *Princess*, 195.
8   Maclean, *Crowned Heads*, 34.
9   Thorpe (ed.), *Who Loses, Who Wins*, 319.
10   Seward, *Prince Philip Revealed*, 73.
11   Dismore, *Princess*, 244.
12   Corbitt, *My Twenty Years in Buckingham Palace*, 204.
13   Ingrid Seward, *My Husband and I: The Inside Story of 70 Years of
     the Royal Marriage* (New York: Simon & Schuster, 2017), 70.
14   Tom Utley, 'Grandad's words made Churchill and the Queen cry',
     Daily Mail, 7 June 2012.
15   Graham Viney, *The Last Hurrah: South Africa and the Royal Tour of
     1947 Royal Tour* (Johannesburg: Jonathan Ball Publishers, 2018), 274.
16   Ibid., 270.
17   'A speech by the Queen on her 21st birthday, 1947', royal.uk
     website, published 21 April 1947.
18   Viney, *The Last Hurrah*, 275.
19   Ibid., 273.
20   Ibid.
21   '95 Years, 95 Jewels: Part 2 (March–April 1947)', *The Court Jeweller*,
     29 March 2021.

22 Viney, *The Last Hurrah*, 153.

23 *Prince Philip: The Plot to Make a King* (UK: Blakeway Productions, 30 July 2015), Channel Four.

24 Peter Townsend, *Time and Chance: An Autobiography* (London: Collins, 1978), 147.

25 Glenconner, *Lady in Waiting*, 275.

26 Dermot Morrah, *The Royal Family in Africa* (London: Hutchinson, 1947). See also Edwards, *Royal Sisters*, 160.

27 *Prince Philip: The Plot to Make a King* (UK: Blakeway Productions, 30 July 2015), Channel Four.

28 Reiss Smith, 'The Crown: why did King George call Queen Elizabeth his pride and Margaret his joy?', *Daily Express*, 7 December 2016.

29 Shawcross, *The Queen Mother*, 629.

30 Shawcross, *The Queen Mother*, 626.

31 Steph Cockroft, 'How Prince Philip curtsied to King George VI', *Daily Mail*, 31 July 2015.

32 *Prince Philip: The Plot to Make a King* (UK: Blakeway Productions, 30 July 2015), Channel Four.

33 Seward, *Prince Philip Revealed*, 82.

34 Ingrid Seward, 'So what is the truth about Philip and those "affairs"?', *Daily Mail*, 15 November 2017.

35 Jonathan Mayo, 'Minute by mesmerizing minute, relive the Queen's most joyous day', *Daily Mail*, 10 November 2017.

36 Ibid.

37 Pamela Hicks, 'Philip's risqué party trick and my mischievous friend Lilibet', *Daily Mail*, 14 December 2012.

38 Elizabeth Grice, 'Royal Wedding: a marriage made in history', *The Daily Telegraph*, 25 March 2011. See also '"Alles sal reg kom": Churchill on the Royal Wedding', Richard M. Langworth website, 29 April 2011.

39 Erin Hill, '"I lost something very precious": read King George VI's touching letter to daughter Elizabeth on her wedding day', *People*, 20 November 2015.

40 Kate Nicholson, 'The heart-warming speeches Prince Philip and the Queen gave on their wedding day revealed', *Daily Mirror*, 20 November 2019.

41　Shawcross, *The Queen Mother*, 631.

42　Rhodes, *The Final Curtsey*, 44.

CHAPTER FOUR

1　*The Private Lives of the Windsors* (UK: Renegade Pictures, 7 October 2019), Smithsonian Channel.

2　Seward, *Prince Philip Revealed*, 95.

3　Vanessa Thorpe, 'Queen Mother was "ruthless" to royal nanny', *The Guardian*, 24 June 2020.

4　Sarah Bradford, *Elizabeth: A Biography of Her Majesty the Queen* (London: Penguin Books, 1996), 151.

5　Vicky Spavin, 'Was Crawfie victim of royal conspiracy?', *Scottish Daily Record*, 24 June 2000.

6　Pimlott, *The Queen*, 159.

7　Chloe Foussianes, 'New letters by Princess Margaret reveal love for her "heavenly nephew", Prince Charles', *Town and Country*, 13 March 2019.

8　Queen Mother to Mabel Strickland, 7 February 1972, Private Papers, Estate of Robert Hornyold-Strickland, Malta, GC.

9　Joan Alexander, *The Life of Mabel Strickland* (Malta: Progress Press Co., 1996), 194.

10　Janet Morgan, *Edwina Mountbatten: A Life of Her Own* (London: HarperCollins, 1991), 444.

11　Richard Kay and Geoffrey Levy, 'The surprising truth about the Queen's very amorous marriage', *Scottish Daily Mail*, 8 March 2016.

12　Philip Ziegler, *Mountbatten: The Official Biography* (London: William Collins & Sons, 1985), 492.

13　Morgan, *Edwina Mountbatten*, 444.

14　Miles Jebb (ed.), *The Diaries of Cynthia Gladwyn* (London: Constable, 1995), 92.

15　Dismore, *Princess*, 256.

16　Camilla Tominey and Phil Dampier, '"Forget protocol, darling!"', *Daily Express*, 18 November 2012.

17　Princess Elizabeth memo to Jessie Grech, 15 September 1950, author collection.

18 Fr Geoffrey Attard, 'Queen Elizabeth II's connection to Gozo', *Times of Malta*, 23 November 2015.

19 Queen Elizabeth II to Mabel Strickland, 5 January 1975, Private Papers, Estate of Robert Hornyold-Strickland, Malta, GC.

20 Seward, *My Husband and I*, 82.

21 Graham Turner, *Elizabeth: The Woman and The Queen* (London: Macmillan, 2002), 5.

22 Seward, *My Husband and I*, 85.

23 Ibid., 84.

24 John Hartley, *Accession: The Making of a Queen* (London: Quartet Books, 1992), 128–29.

25 Ibid., 113.

26 Ibid., 128.

27 Ibid., 130.

28 Ibid., 131.

29 Ibid., 131–32.

30 Pimlott, *The Queen*, 179.

31 Hartley, *Accession*, 131–32.

32 Ibid., 136.

33 *Queen and Country* (UK: Crux Productions, 1 May 2002), BBC One.

34 Holly Evans, 'Queen responded with brutal swipe after Royal Family tragedy', *Daily Express*, 19 May 2021.

CHAPTER FIVE

1 Sir John Wheeler-Bennett, *Friends, Enemies and Sovereigns: The Final Volume of His Autobiography*, (London: Macmillan, 1976), 133.

2 Sally Bedell Smith, *Elizabeth the Queen: The Life of a Modern Monarch* (London: Random House, 2012), 66.

3 Ibid., 66–67.

4 Pimlott, *The Queen*, 176.

5 Andrew Roberts, *Churchill: Walking with Destiny* (New York: Penguin, 2018), 929.

6 Kate Williams, *Young Elizabeth: The Making of the Queen* (Berkeley: Pegasus Books, 2015), 47.

7   Shawcross, *The Queen Mother*, 658.

8   Ibid.

9   Pimlott, *The Queen*, 199.

10 Box 314, Sir Fitzroy Maclean Papers, MSS 11487, Albert and Shirley Small, Special Collections Library, University of Virginia, Charlottesville, Virginia.

11 Ingrid Seward, 'So what is the truth about Philip and those "affairs"?', *Daily Mail*, 15 November 2017.

12 Author interview with anonymous source, June 2019.

13 Michael Bloch, *The Secret File of the Duke of Windsor* (New York: HarperCollins, 1988), 264.

14 Robert Lacey, *Monarch: The Life and Reign of Elizabeth II* (New York: Free Press, 2003), 175.

15 Jonathan Dimbleby, *The Prince of Wales: A Biography* (New York: William Morrow and Company, Inc., 1994), 18.

16 'His people's day', *The Courier-Mail*, 11 February 1952.

17 Charles Drazin (ed.), *The Journals/John Fowles: Volume One, 1949–1965* (Evanston, IL: Northwestern University Press, 2003), 172.

18 Laura Connor, 'How last Victoria Cross holder "Big Bill" hurled rocks and beer cans to keep the North Korean army at bay', *Daily Mirror*, 22 June 2018.

19 Bedell Smith, *Elizabeth the Queen*, 73–74.

20 Robert Lacey, *The Crown: The Official Companion, Volume 1: Elizabeth II, Winston Churchill and the Making of a Young Queen (1947–1955)* (New York: Crown Archetype, 2017), 76.

21 Elizabeth Longford, *Elizabeth R: A Biography* (London: Hodder & Stoughton, 1984), 238.

22 Bradford, *Elizabeth*, 220.

23 Bedell Smith, *Elizabeth the Queen*, 93.

24 Edwards, *Royal Sisters*, 246.

25 Ibid., 247.

26 Pimlott, *The Queen*, 185.

27 Bradford, *Elizabeth*, 170–71.

28 Deborah Hart Strober and Gerald Strober, *The Monarchy: An Oral Biography of Elizabeth II* (New York: Broadway Books, 2002), 80.

29 Williams, *Young Elizabeth*, 275.

30 Seward, *My Husband and I*, 89.

31 Brandreth, *Philip and Elizabeth*, 254.

32 Longford, *Elizabeth R*, 192.

33 Adil Najam, 'How a British royal's monumental errors made India's partition more painful', *The Conversation*, 16 August 2016.

34 *Prince Philip: The Plot to Make a King* (UK: Blakeway Productions, 30 July 2015), Channel Four.

35 Untitled, *Daily Express*, 20 October 1952.

36 *Elizabeth: Our Queen* (UK: ITN Productions, 6 February 2018), Channel Five.

37 Townsend, *Time and Chance*, 198.

38 Bedell Smith, *Elizabeth the Queen*, 81–82.

39 Edwards, *Royal Sisters*, 257.

40 Dominic Midgley, 'The Coronation of Queen Elizabeth II: how the *Daily Express* reported it 61 years ago', *Daily Express*, 18 September 2014.

41 Bedell Smith, *Elizabeth the Queen*, 67.

42 Pimlott, *The Queen*, 209.

43 Katy Winter, 'The Queen asked, "Ready girls?"', *Daily Mail*, 16 April 2013.

44 Bedell Smith, *Elizabeth the Queen*, 85.

45 Lacey, *The Crown*, 125.

46 Glenconner, *Lady in Waiting*, 74.

47 Maclean, *Crowned Heads*, 40.

48 Ellen Castelow, 'The Coronation 1953', Historic UK website, undated.

49 Brandreth, *Philip: The Final Portrait*, 282.

50 Glenconner, *Lady in Waiting*, 77.

CHAPTER SIX

1 Townsend, *Time and Chance*, 188.

2 Shawcross, *The Queen Mother*, 684.

3 Christopher Warwick, *Princess Margaret: A Life of Contrasts* (London: André Deutsch, 2000), 190; Williams, *Young Elizabeth*, 293.

4 Pimlott, *The Queen*, 219.

5   Christopher Warwick, 'Princess Margaret letter changes how we view her life', *The Daily Telegraph*, 7 November 2009.

6   Karen Kissane, 'It happens even in royal marriages', *The Sydney Morning Herald*, 28 September 2011.

7   Robert Hardman, *Our Queen* (London: Hutchinson, 2011), 195.

8   Warwick, *Princess Margaret*, 197.

9   Roya Nikkhah, 'Princess Margaret recently unearthed letter sheds new light on decision not to marry', *The Daily Telegraph*, 7 November 2009.

10 Katie Sewell, 'Princess Margaret: unearthed letter reveals Peter Townsend split not all as it seemed', *Daily Express*, 4 January 2021.

11 Sarah Pulliam Bailey, 'Fact checking "The Crown": Queen Elizabeth's faith and her close relationship with preacher Billy Graham', *The Washington Post*, 9 January 2018.

12 Marshall Frady, *Billy Graham: A Parable of American Righteousness*, (Boston: Little, Brown, 1979), 372.

13 Paul Reynolds, 'Did the Queen stop Princess Margaret marrying Peter Townsend?', *BBC News*, 19 November 2016.

14 Townsend, *Time and Chance*, 234.

15 Seward, *Prince Philip Revealed*, 135.

16 Townsend, *Time and Chance*, 236.

17 Maclean, *Crowned Heads*, 42.

18 Seward, *My Husband and I*, 139.

19 Bradford, *Elizabeth*, 264.

20 Seward, *Prince Philip Revealed*, 256.

21 Bradford, *Elizabeth*, 268.

22 Seward, *My Husband and I*, 137.

23 Andrew Pierce and Richard Kay, 'Princess Margaret's very private correspondence', *Daily Mail*, 20 February 2015.

24 Jebb (ed.), *The Diaries of Cynthia Gladwyn*, 207.

25 Bradford, *Elizabeth*, 240.

26 Ibid.

27 Bedell Smith, *Elizabeth the Queen*, 128.

28 Untitled, Box 6, Folder 32, Bruce and Beatrice Blackmar Gould Correspondence, Rare Books and Special Collections, Firestone Library, Princeton University, Princeton, NJ.

29 'Christmas broadcast 1947', royal.uk website, published 25 December 1947.

CHAPTER SEVEN

1   Seward, *Prince Philip Revealed*, 150.
2   Ibid., 145.
3   Dennison, *The Queen*, 240.
4   *Prince Philip: The Royal Family Remembers* (UK: Oxford Films, 22 September 2021), BBC One.
5   Bradford, *Elizabeth*, 282.
6   Christopher Wilson, 'Punched as he slept, friends tortured with pliers', *Daily Mail*, 1 February 2013.
7   Bradford, *Elizabeth*, 276.
8   James Pope-Hennessy and Hugo Vickers (ed.), *The Quest for Queen Mary* (London: Hodder & Stoughton, 2018), 222.
9   Bedell Smith, *Elizabeth the Queen*, 188.
10 Abbie Llewelyn, 'Prince Philip's staggering confession about Prince Andrew exposed', *Daily Express*, 4 August 2020.
11 Bedell Smith, *Elizabeth the Queen*, 146.
12 Seward, *My Husband and I*, 144.
13 Tim Heald, *Princess Margaret: A Life Unravelled* (London: Weidenfeld & Nicolson, London, 2007), 121.
14 D. R. Thorpe (ed.), *Who's In, Who's Out: The Journals of Kenneth Rose, Volume One, 1944–1979* (London: Weidenfeld & Nicolson, 2019), 160.
15 Dennison, *The Queen*, 311.
16 Ibid.
17 'Watch: Queen Elizabeth II's 1961 visit to Ghana', *British Heritage Travel*, 3 December 2021. See also Dennison, *The Queen*, 307–308.
18 Dennison, *The Queen*, 307.
19 Valentine Low, Hugo Vickers and Alice Foster, 'Queen dancing in Ghana: the story behind her iconic visit to save the Commonwealth', *The Times*, 26 March 2018.
20 Tom Parfitt, 'Yuri Gagarin's brush with royalty revealed in new biography', *The Guardian*, 12 April 2011.
21 Craig Brown, *Ninety-Nine Glimpses of Princess Margaret* (New

York: Farrar, Straus and Giroux, 2017), 7.

22　Andrew Glass, 'Jackie Kennedy adopts Sardar, 23 March 1962', *Politico*, 23 March 2011.

23　Jack Whatley, 'Remembering The Beatles' 1963 Royal Variety Performance', *Far Out*, 4 November 2019.

24　Queen Elizabeth II to Mabel Strickland, March 1964, Private Papers, Estate of Robert Hornyold-Strickland, Malta, GC.

25　Bradford, *Elizabeth*, 308.

26　Miranda Carter, *Anthony Blunt: His Lives* (New York: Farrar, Straus and Giroux, 2001), 376.

27　Turner, *Elizabeth*, 57.

28　Ibid.

29　'How many prime ministers has the Queen had in her reign?', inews.co.uk website, 13 December 2019. See also Andrew Marr, *The Real Elizabeth: An Intimate Portrait of Queen Elizabeth II* (New York: Henry Holt and Company, 2012), 158.

30　Hardman, *Our Queen*, 205.

31　Marcia Falkender, *Inside Number 10* (London: New English Library, 1975), 17.

32　Matthew Francis, 'Harold Wilson's "white heat of technology" speech 50 years on', *The Guardian*, 19 September 2013.

33　Nicole Stinson, 'Revealed: Queen broke protocol for Winston Churchill by bestowing rare honour on prime minister', *Daily Express*, 22 February 2018.

34　Reiss Smith, 'The Crown: who is John Lithgow, the American actor playing Winston Churchill on Netflix?', *Daily Express*, 7 December 2016.

CHAPTER EIGHT

1　Pimlott, *The Queen*, 371.

2　Ibid.

3　Author interview with Grania Forbes, February 2015.

4　Abbie Llewelyn, 'Princess Anne loathed Royal Family documentary: "It was a rotten idea"', *Daily Express*, 29 January 2021.

5　Dennison, *The Queen*, 332.

6   Bradford, *Elizabeth*, 353.

7   Sally Bedell Smith, *Prince Charles: The Passions and Paradoxes of an Improbable Life* (New York: Random House, 2017), 43.

8   Anne de Courcy, *Snowdon: The Biography* (London: Phoenix, 2008), 192.

9   Bradford, *Elizabeth*, 397.

10 Lacey, *Monarch*, 238.

11 Turner, *Elizabeth*, 91.

12 Ibid.

13 Ibid., 97.

14 Ibid., 95.

15 Bradford, *Elizabeth*, 412.

16 Bedell Smith, *Prince Charles*, 63.

17 Bradford, *Elizabeth*, 415.

18 Katie Frost, 'The Queen and Prince Philip's best quotes on married life', *Harper's Bazaar*, 9 April 2021.

19 Hardman, *Our Queen*, 270.

20 Turner, *Elizabeth*, 110.

21 Ibid., 111.

22 Sheila Langan, 'The Irish Lord who captured Queen Elizabeth's heart', *British Heritage Travel*, 6 July 2021.

23 Pimlott, *The Queen*, 441.

24 Lisa Waller Rogers, 'Princess Margaret and her guttersnipe life', Lisa's History Room website, unknown date.

25 Sean Smith, 'Will she finally be Elizabeth the first?', *Daily Mail*, 16 May 2011.

26 Ibid.

27 Author interview with Sean Smith, October 2021.

28 Theo Aronson, *Princess Margaret: A Biography* (London: Thistle Publishing, 2013), 276.

29 De Courcy, *Snowdon*, 230.

30 Ibid., 234.

31 *Elizabeth and Margaret: Love and Loyalty* (UK: Outpost Facilities, 26 September 2020), Channel Five.

32 Shawcross, *The Queen Mother*, 850.

33 R. W. Apple Jr, 'Northern Ireland, awaiting Jubilee visit by the

Queen, erupts in violence fatal to two', *The New York Times*, 10 August 1977.

34 David McKittrick, 'Northern Ireland: memories of 1977 and a "terribly tense" royal visitor', *The Independent*, 28 June 2012.

35 Turner, *Elizabeth*, 117.

36 Dimbleby, *The Prince of Wales*, 205.

37 Ibid., 260.

38 Sally Bedell Smith, '"A sympathetic ear and a goofy sense of humour"', *Daily Mail*, 2 April 2017.

39 Ben Pimlott, *The Queen: Elizabeth II and the Monarchy* (London: Harper Press, 2012; paperback version), 470.

40 Dimbleby, *The Prince of Wales*, 267.

41 Dennison, *The Queen*, 384.

CHAPTER NINE

1 Jimmy Carter, *White House Diary* (New York: Farrar, Straus and Giroux, 2010), 49.

2 Dennison, *The Queen*, 415–16.

3 Catherine Armecin, 'Queen Elizabeth reportedly loves "good gossip" about "immoral Balmoral"', biographer says', *International Business Times*, 24 February 2019.

4 Horace Smith, *A Horseman Through Six Reigns: Reminiscences of a Royal Riding Master* (London: Odhams, 1955), 144. See also Carolly Erickson, *Lilibet: An Intimate Portrait of Elizabeth II* (New York: St Martin's Press, 2004), 58.

5 Author interview with Eric Milligan, February 2019.

6 Anne Glenconner, 'Princess Margaret, her lover and me', *Daily Mail*, 27 September 2019.

7 Ibid.

8 Ibid.

9 Ingrid Seward, *The Queen and Di: The Untold Story* (London: HarperCollins, 2000), 41.

10 Ibid., 47.

11 Author interview with anonymous source.

12 Rhodes, *The Final Curtsey*, 114.

13 Seward, *My Husband and I*, 165.

14 Andrew Morton, *Diana: Her True Story – In Her Own Words* (New York: Simon & Schuster, 2017; 25th anniversary edition; orig. 1992), 56.

15 'Another round in Prince Charles's matrimonial sweepstakes', *UPI Archives*, 22 November 1980.

16 Joel Day, 'Princess Anne's brutal assessment of Diana amid relationship tensions', *Daily Express*, 14 July 2021.

17 Seward, *The Queen and Di*, 46.

18 Ibid., 63.

19 Paul Riddell, 'MI5 blamed BP for security lapse before IRA bomb attack on Queen at Sullom Voe', *The Shetland Times*, 27 October 2009.

20 Graham Strachan, 'The IRA plot to bomb The Queen in Shetland following the death of Bobby Sands', *The Press and Journal Evening Express*, 7 May 2021.

21 *Elizabeth at 90: A Family Tribute* (UK: Crux Productions, 21 April 2016), BBC One.

22 Stephanie Linning, 'The Queen steps out in her third headscarf in as many days', *Daily Mail*, 12 May 2017.

23 Seward, *The Queen and Di*, 52.

24 Morton, *Diana: Her True Story*, 82.

25 Bedell Smith, *Elizabeth the Queen*, 303.

26 Hugo Vickers, *Elizabeth the Queen Mother* (London: Hutchinson, 2005), 424.

27 Seward, *The Queen and Di*, 59.

28 Morton, *Diana: Her True Story*, 184.

29 Ibid., 67.

30 Seward, *The Queen and Di*, 65.

CHAPTER TEN

1 Morton, *Diana: Her True Story*, 72.

2 Bedell Smith, *Elizabeth the Queen*, 306.

3 Ibid.

4 'The Princess and the Press: Interview Ken Lennox', *PBS Frontline*, undated.

5 Morton, *Diana: Her True Story*, 71.

6   Andrew Morton and Mick Seamark, *Andrew: The Playboy Prince* (London: Corgi, 1983), 88.

7   'Queen praying for troops in Falklands', *UPI Archives*, 26 May 1982.

8   Erickson, *Lilibet*, 266.

9   Talia Shadwell, 'Royal baby: Queen cracked this "mean joke" when she met another new arrival', *Daily Mirror*, 9 May 2019.

10 Andrew Morton, *Inside Buckingham Palace* (New York: Summit Books, 1991), 28.

11 'A Talk with the Queen', *The Washington Post*, undated.

12 Morton, *Inside Buckingham Palace*, 84.

13 Brandreth, *Philip: The Final Portrait*, 226–27.

14 Michael Dennigan, 'Queen's former bodyguard cleared of charges', *UPI Archives*, 24 November 1982.

15 Victoria Murphy, '60 amazing facts you never knew about the Queen', *Daily Mirror*, 1 February 2012.

16 Seward, *The Queen and Di*, 103.

17 Ibid., 103–104.

18 'Andrew and Koo reported back on track', *UPI Archives*, 2 May 1983.

19 Monica Greep and Chloe Morgan, 'Prince Andrew ex-girlfriend Koo Stark', *Daily Mail*, 28 May 2021.

20 Morton, *Diana: Her True Story*, 219.

21 Dennison, *The Queen*, 410.

22 Seward, *The Queen and Di*, 7.

23 Morton, *Diana: Her True Story*, 229.

24 Shawcross (ed.), *Counting One's Blessings*, 589.

25 Morton, *Diana: Her True Story*, 367.

26 Camille Heimbrod, 'Prince Philip saw Sarah Ferguson as "great asset" to Prince Andrew', *International Business Times*, 11 August 2019.

27 Seward, *The Queen and Di*, 166.

28 Morton, *Diana: Her True Story*, 221.

29 Brandreth, *Philip: The Final Portrait*, 375.

30 Turner, *Elizabeth*, 90.

31 'Thatcher declines to answer questions on Queen', *United Press*

International/LA Times Archives, 23 July 1989.

32   Charles Moore, *Margaret Thatcher: From Grantham to the Falklands* (New York: Vintage Books, 2015).

33   Brandreth, *Philip: The Final Portrait*, 15.

34   Anna Kretschmer, 'Queen heartbreak: greatest regrets of Her Majesty's reign revealed', *Daily Express*, 14 December 2019.

35   Andrew Neil, *Full Disclosure* (London: Pan Macmillan, 1996), 276.

36   Bedell Smith, *Elizabeth the Queen*, 350.

37   William E. Schmidt, 'Far from Gulf, British royalty is under fire', *The New York Times*, 12 February 1991.

38   Ibid.

39   Ibid.

CHAPTER ELEVEN

1   Alex Zatman, 'Filmmaker Edward's right royal legacy', *Jewish Telegraph*, 2012.

2   Richard Kay and Geoffrey Levy, 'How Diana broke the Queen's heart', *Daily Mail*, 6 March 2016.

3   Ingrid Seward, *The Queen and Di*, 193.

4   Author interview with Simone Simmons, August 2021.

5   Morton, *Diana: Her True Story*, 298.

6   Seward, *The Queen and Di*, 168.

7   Rachel Borrill, 'No shock as "vulgarian" Fergie leaves the royal fold', *The Irish Times*, 18 April 1996.

8   Britta Zeltmann, 'Pen Papa' *The US Sun*, 15 April 2021.

9   Richard Kay, 'The night Diana told me "the redhead's in trouble"', *Daily Mail*, 31 October 2014.

10   Sue Leeman, 'Scarlet hussey or persecuted flop?', *AP News*, 7 November 1996.

11   Richard Kay and Geoffrey Levy, 'How Diana broke the Queen's heart', *Daily Mail*, 6 March 2016.

12   Anna Kretschmer, 'Royal rage: how Sarah Ferguson faced Queen's fury at Balmoral', *Daily Express*, 1 November 2019.

13   Turner, *Elizabeth*, 9.

14   *Diana, Our Mother: Her Life and Legacy* (UK: Oxford Film and Television, 24 July 2017), ITV.

15 Dickie Arbiter, 'Diana and Charles's ex-press chief reveals advice he gave', *Daily Mail*, 21 September 2014.

16 Pimlott, *The Queen*, 558.

17 Seward, *The Queen and Di*, 203.

18 Richard Kay and Geoffrey Levy, 'How Diana broke the Queen's heart', *Daily Mail*, 6 March 2016.

19 Ibid.

20 Dennison, *The Queen*, 437.

21 Ken Wharfe with Robert Jobson, *Guarding Diana: Protecting the Princess Around the World* (London: King's Road Publishing, 2017).

22 Andrew Morton, *Diana: In Pursuit of Love* (London: Michael O'Mara Books, 2004), 87.

23 Ibid., 107.

24 Ibid., 109.

25 John Darnton, 'Prince Charles, in TV documentary, admits to infidelity', *The New York Times*, 30 June 1994.

26 Morton, *Diana: In Pursuit of Love*, 137.

27 Robert Jobson, 'Charles: Camilla is central to my life', *Evening Standard*, 12 April 2012.

28 Turner, *Elizabeth*, 169.

29 Ibid., 169–170.

30 Andrew Morton, *Meghan: A Hollywood Princess* (New York: Grand Central Publishing, 2021; paperback version), 319.

31 Brandreth, *Philip and Elizabeth*, 225.

32 Morton, *Diana: In Pursuit of Love*, 209.

33 Jennifer Newton, 'Queen's letter to "furious" Princess Diana that finally ended marriage to Charles', *Daily Mirror*, 28 June 2021.

34 Morton, *Diana: In Pursuit of Love*, 211.

35 Ibid., 210.

36 Ibid., 213.

37 Bedell Smith, *Elizabeth the Queen*, 387.

38 Matthew Kirkham, 'Prince William's promise to Princess Diana revealed', *Daily Express*, 15 February 2019.

CHAPTER TWELVE

1   Naomi Gordon, 'Prince William and Prince Harry speak of their regret at "rushed" last call with Princess Diana', *Harper's Bazaar*, 23 July 2017.

2   Seward, *The Queen and Di*, 12.

3   Ibid., 14.

4   Penny Junor, *The Duchess: Camilla Parker Bowles and the Love Affair that Rocked the Crown* (New York: HarperCollins, 2017), 150.

5   Pimlott, *The Queen* (2012 paperback), 609.

6   Deirdre Fernand, 'Diana, the Queen and a final royal family reckoning', *The Times*, 17 September 2006.

7   Beth Whitehouse, 'The lives of "the heir and the spare", with and without Diana', *Los Angeles Times*, 22 August 2001.

8   Pimlott, *The Queen* (2012 paperback), 615.

9   Robert Seeley, 'Britain shocked by Princess Diana's death', *AP News*, 31 August 1997.

10 *Diana: 7 Days* (UK: Sandpaper Films, 27 August 2017), BBC One.

11 George Carey, *Know the Truth: A Memoir* (New York: HarperCollins, 2004), 407.

12 Siofra Brennan, '"Is it true that Mummy's dead?"', *Daily Mail*, 30 May 2017.

13 Warwick, *Princess Margaret*, 285.

14 Frances Hardy, 'My twin brother was dead', *Daily Mail*, 6 August 2010.

15 Isaac Bickerstaff, 'Who was Prince William and Prince Harry's nanny, Tiggy Legge-Bourke?', *Tatler*, 30 November 2020.

16 *Diana, Our Mother: Her Life and Legacy* (UK: Oxford Film and Television, 24 July 2017), ITV.

17 *Diana: 7 Days* (UK: Sandpaper Films, 27 August 2017), BBC One.

18 Bedell Smith, *Elizabeth the Queen*, 397.

19 Ibid.

20 Carey, *Know the Truth*, 409.

21 Turner, *Elizabeth*, 159.

22 Tina Brown, *The Diana Chronicles* (New York: Penguin Random House, 2007), 472.

23 *Diana, Our Mother: Her Life and Legacy* (UK: Oxford Film and Television, 24 July 2017), ITV.

24 'The Queen starts celebrations for her 90th', *Sky News*, 20 April 2016.

25 'Princess Diana's death was "global event" says Blair', *BBC News*, 1 September 2010.

26 Bedell Smith, *Elizabeth the Queen*, 402.

27 Ibid., 401.

28 Pimlott, *The Queen* (2012 paperback), 623.

29 Bedell Smith, *Elizabeth the Queen*, 403.

30 Pimlott, *The Queen*, 623.

31 Dennison, *The Queen*, 453.

32 Ann Leslie, '"So tell me, ma'am, why do you always look so grumpy?"', *Daily Mail*, 17 September 2008.

33 Bedell Smith, *Elizabeth the Queen*, 403.

34 Ibid., 404.

35 Pimlott, *The Queen* (2012 paperback), 624.

36 Bedell Smith, *Elizabeth the Queen*, 404–405.

37 Ibid., 405.

38 Ibid., 406.

39 Author interview with Dickie Arbiter, January 2019.

40 Petronella Wyatt, 'Taking sides in the battle royal', *Daily Mail*, 29 June 2019.

41 Andrew Morton, 'Destroyed: the letters that fuelled a royal feud', *The Daily Telegraph*, 20 September 2009.

42 Brown, *The Diana Chronicles*, 471.

43 Morton, *Diana: In Pursuit of Love*, 272.

44 Bedell Smith, *Elizabeth the Queen*, 408.

45 Camille Heimbrod, 'Princess Margaret wrote "secret" letter to Queen Elizabeth after Princess Diana's death', *International Business Times*, 24 October 2018.

46 Andrew Pierce, '"We have all been through a very bad experience"', *Daily Mail*, 12 August 2017.

47 Editorial, *Sunday Telegraph*, 24 September 1998.

48 Pimlott, *The Queen*, 663.

CHAPTER THIRTEEN

1   Junor, *The Duchess*, 157.

2   Bedell Smith, *Prince Charles*, 345.

3   John Davison and Kathy Marks, 'Prince's charm offensive backfires', *The Independent*, 10 November 1998.

4   *Prince Charles at 50: Heir to Sadness* (UK: Imagicians Television, 12 October 1998).

5   Carey, *Know the Truth*, 412.

6   Anna Kretschmer, 'Royal bombshell: what the Queen "hates above all things" revealed', *Daily Express*, 21 April 2019.

7   Penny Junor, *The Firm: The Troubled Life of the House of Windsor* (London: HarperCollins, 2005), 363.

8   Bedell Smith, *Elizabeth the Queen*, 432.

9   Thorpe (ed.), *Who Loses, Who Wins*, 363.

10   Rhodes, *The Final Curtsey*, 5.

11   Shawcross, *The Queen Mother*, 935.

12   'Queen thanks nation "for their love"', *The Guardian*, 8 April 2002.

13   'The Queen tells driver to slow down', YouTube, 31 July 2012.

14   Bedell Smith, *Elizabeth the Queen*, 446–47.

15   Caitlin Moran, 'The best bit was seeing reactions in the Royal Box; Golden Jubilee', *The Times*, 4 June 2002.

16   Gerrard Kaonga, 'Queen "blossomed" as she "heralded new era" of the monarchy after Royal Family death', *Daily Express*, 14 January 2021.

17   Caroline Davies, 'The Queen came through for me', *The Daily Telegraph*, 2 November 2002.

18   'What the butler Paul Burrell said about the Queen, Prince Philip, Charles ... and himself', *Daily Mail*, 15 January 2008.

19   Steve Bird and Sam Lister, 'The Queen "warned butler to beware of dark forces at work"', *The Times*, 6 November 2002.

20   Bronwen Weatherby, 'Diana's letters from Prince Philip reveal he and the Queen "never dreamed" Charles would leave her for Camilla', *Daily Mirror*, 8 September 2018.

21   Richard Kay, 'War of the Wedding', *Daily Mail*, 4 November 2004.

22   Bedell Smith, *Prince Charles*, 400.

23   'Queen condemns bombing "outrage"', *BBC News*, 8 July 2005.

24 Liz Jones, 'Queen Elizabeth looks in the mirror and likes what she sees', *Daily Mail*, 26 May 2012.

25 Richard Kay, 'Angela, we could be sisters', *Daily Mail*, 29 October 2019.

26 Rebecca English, 'The Queen will never consider abdicating', *Daily Mail*, 20 April 2006.

27 'A speech made by The Queen at Mansion House for Her Majesty's 80th Birthday', royal.uk website, published 15 June 2006.

28 Poppy Danby, 'A birthday like no other', *Daily Mirror*, 21 April 2021.

29 Geoffrey Levy and Richard Kay, 'His Royal Grumpiness', *Daily Mail*, 10 November 2007.

30 Valentine Low, 'What now for the Queen without Prince Philip at her side?', *The Times*, 9 April 2021.

31 Geoffrey Levy and Richard Kay, 'His Royal Grumpiness', *Daily Mail*, 10 November 2007.

32 Holly Fleet, 'Carol Vorderman describes spark between Queen and Philip', *Daily Express*, 9 April 2021.

33 Nicholl, *William and Harry*, 61.

34 Kate Nicholson, 'Kate Middleton heartbreak: real reason William waited so long to propose revealed', *Daily Express*, 10 October 2019.

35 'Focus: the girl who would be Queen', *The Sunday Times*, 31 December 2006.

36 Kate Nicholson, 'How Queen was "practically skipping" on William and Kate's wedding day', *Daily Express*, 29 April 2020.

37 Sunday People, 'Queen will protect Kate Middleton says Prince Edward', *Daily Mirror*, 25 March 2012.

38 Hardman, *Our Queen*, 53.

39 Alan Cowell, 'In Ireland, Queen Elizabeth offers "deep sympathy" for past', *The New York Times*, 19 May 2011.

40 'PM says Queen's visit to Ireland was a "game-changer"', *BBC News*, 27 December 2011.

41 David Collins, '"An incredible day … absolutely wonderful": what Queen told Prince Charles on balcony as a million well-wishers cheer', *Daily Mirror*, 6 June 2012.

42 Ibid.

CHAPTER FOURTEEN

1   Tom Sykes, 'Jeremy Hunt jokes with Queen, Queen not amused', *The Daily Beast*, 17 October 2012.

2   Anne Pukas, 'Transformed into our merry monarch: how the Queen never seemed so informal and relaxed', *Daily Express*, 19 July 2013.

3   Angela Kelly, *The Other Side of the Coin: The Queen, the Dresser and the Wardrobe* (New York: HarperCollins, 2019), 186.

4   Murray Wardrop, 'Michelle Obama hugs the Queen', *The Daily Telegraph*, 2 April 2009.

5   Rebecca English, '"And I told Wills"', *Daily Mail*, 17 February 2014.

6   'The Queen welcomes A-list actors at palace celebration', *BBC News*, 18 February 2014.

7   Jilly Cooper, 'That's the end of the ride, ma'am', *Daily Telegraph*, 8 March 2011.

8   Jack Haynes, '"She loves the sport so much" – the Queen inducted into racing's Hall of Fame', *Racing Post*, 12 October 2021.

9   *Elizabeth at 90: A Family Tribute* (UK: Crux Productions, 21 April 2016), BBC One.

10 Author interview with Eric Milligan, July 2019.

11 *Our Queen at 90* (UK: Oxford Film and Television, 27 March 2016), ITV.

12 Carly Ledbetter, 'Elton John reveals he once saw Queen Elizabeth jokingly slap her nephew', *Huffpost*, 10 July 2019.

13 Nina Massey, 'Prince William recalls moment the Queen gave him an "absolute b*****king"', *The Independent*, 20 April 2016.

14 *Elizabeth: Queen, Wife, Mother* (UK: ITN Productions, 1 June 2012), ITV.

15 Bedell Smith, *Prince Charles*, 492.

16 Dan Roberts, 'Obamas, Prince Harry and the Queen trade mic drops in comedy sketch', *The Guardian*, 26 April 2016.

17 Angela Levin, 'Exclusive: Prince Harry on chaos after Diana's death and why the world needs "the magic" of the Royal Family', *Newsweek*, 21 June 2017.

18 Oliver Harvey and Emma Lake, 'Queen of Hurts', *The Sun*, 16 June 2017.

19 Dennison, *The Queen*, 481.

20 Elizabeth Sanderson and Katie Nicholl, 'Buckingham Palace reshuffles key personnel in "first step to bringing Prince Charles to the throne"', *Daily Mail*, 18 January 2014.

21 Martin Robinson and Amie Gordon, 'Prince Philip seals his "standing down" announcement', *Daily Mail*, 4 May 2017.

22 Richard Kay and Geoffrey Levy, 'Prince Philip downsizes for retirement', *Daily Mail*, 3 November 2017.

23 'Buckingham Palace plays down "power struggle" claims', *BBC News*, 16 September 2017.

24 Laura Smith-Spark, 'Britain's Queen hopes Prince Charles will "one day" lead Commonwealth', *CNN*, 19 April 2018.

25 Rachel Brodsky, 'Meghan Markle says Queen Elizabeth was "always wonderful"', *The Independent*, 8 March 2021.

26 Luke May, 'Queen DID slap down Meghan Markle over her choice of wedding day tiara', *Daily Mail*, 29 July 2020.

27 Sean O'Neill, 'Prince Andrew's TV calamity suggests Queen is losing her grip on "the firm"', *The Times*, 18 November 2019.

28 Seward, *My Husband and I*, 210.

29 Mark Landler, 'In Prince Andrew scandal, Prince Charles emerges as monarch-in-waiting', *The New York Times*, 1 December 2019.

30 Rebecca English, 'Prince Andrew's regret over "car crash" TV interview', *Daily Mail*, 17 November 2019.

31 Sean O'Neill, 'Prince Andrew's TV calamity suggests Queen is losing her grip on "the firm"', *The Times*, 18 November 2019.

32 Valentine Low, 'Prince Andrew interview: Queen does her duty despite disgrace of "favourite son"', *The Times*, 21 November 2019.

33 'A statement by His Royal Highness The Duke of York', royal.uk website, published 20 November 2019.

34 Jonny Dymond, 'Harry and Meghan: the royal couple are looking for the exit', *BBC News*, 13 January 2020.

35 Jemma Carr, 'Fuming Prince Philip was left in "disbelief" at the lack of respect shown to the Queen by his grandson Prince Harry and Meghan Markle', *Daily Mail*, 11 January 2020.

36 Caroline Davies, 'The royal showdown: everything you need to know', *The Guardian*, 13 January 2020.

37 Bedell Smith, *Elizabeth the Queen*, 494.

38 Victoria Ward and Jessica Carpani, '"It was like somebody took him by the hand and off he went," says Countess of Wessex of Prince Philip's last moments', *The Daily Telegraph*, 11 April 2021.

39 Daniel Uria, 'Prince Andrew: Queen Elizabeth II feels "void" after Prince Philip's death', *UPI Archives*, 11 April 2021.

40 Naledi Ushe, 'Prince Edward's wife Sophie shares emotional moment "when everything stopped" during Prince Philip's funeral', *People*, 4 June 2021.

41 Naomi Adedokun, 'Sophie Wessex "proven to be Queen's most reliable" aide as monarch copes with Philip death', *Daily Express*, 13 April 2021.

42 Pimlott, *The Queen*, 119.

ACKNOWLEDGEMENTS

For more than forty years I have been, along with other subjects, reporting on and writing about the British monarchy. During that time, I have met with members of the Royal Family, with varying degrees of brevity, as well as their managerial staff, popularly known as courtiers, and their 'downstairs' employees – the valets, chauffeurs, bodyguards, chefs, gardeners, maids and others who keep the wheels of this ancient institution turning. On the way some have become friends, others have remained acquaintances. They have one thing in common – a story to tell, often about the woman the late Diana, Princess of Wales referred to as the 'chief lady', Her Majesty the Queen, the longest-reigning monarch in British history. In reviewing her life and times, some have preferred to remain in the background but others are happy to be acknowledged for their contribution to this biography of a remarkable woman.

I would like to thank Dickie Arbiter, Sarah Bradford, Phil Dampier, Grania Forbes, Dave Griffin, Patrick Jephson, Richard Kay, Ken Lennox, Eric Milligan, former Lord Provost of Edinburgh, Katie Nicholl, Professor Jonathan Petropoulos, Dr Frank Prochaska, Paul Reynolds, Ingrid Seward, Professor Andrew Stewart, Noreen Taylor, Ken Wharfe and Christopher Wilson.

In Malta, my thanks to Charles Azzopardi, General Manager, Phoenicia hotel, Michael Bonello, Carmen Glenville, Tony Grech, the late Dr Joseph Micallef Stafrace, Robert and Dee Hornyold-

Strickland as well as Marisa Xuereb for her splendid organization.

I would like to thank my agent Steve Troha as well as researchers Claudia Taylor, Camille J. Thomas and Andrina Tran for their sterling efforts during the pandemic. Thanks too to Gretchen Young, my editor at Grand Central in New York, for bringing a fresh and perceptive focus to the project. My appreciation too to assistant editor Haley Weaver and copy editor Laura Jorstad at Grand Central, and my editor Louise Dixon, copy editor Helen Cumberbatch, proofreader Meredith MacArdle and picture researcher Judith Palmer at Michael O'Mara Books in London.

In this marathon pandemic, I have much appreciated the patience and forbearance of my wife Carolyn.

PHOTO CREDITS

Page 1: George Elam/*Daily Mail*/Shutterstock.

Page 2: Shutterstock (top); Design Pics Inc/Shutterstock (centre and bottom).

Page 3: *Daily Mail*/Shutterstock (top); Richard Gardener/ Shutterstock (bottom).

Page 4: Design Pics Inc/Shutterstock (top); Shutterstock (centre); AP/Shutterstock (bottom).

Page 5: Eddie Worth/AP/Shutterstock (top); AP/Shutterstock (centre); Everett/Shutterstock (bottom).

Page 6: AP/Shutterstock (all).

Page 7: Everett/Shutterstock (top); AP/Shutterstock (centre); Shutterstock (bottom).

Page 8: *Daily Mail*/Shutterstock.

Page 9: Photo courtesy of Ken Lennox.

Page 10: Photo courtesy of Ken Lennox (top); AP/Shutterstock (bottom left); *Evening Standard*/Hulton Archive/Getty Images (bottom right).

Page 11: Reginald Davis/Shutterstock (top left); Central Press/ Hulton Archive/Getty Images (top right); AP/Shutterstock (bottom).

Page 12: Mike Lawn/Shutterstock (top); Shutterstock (centre); Mike Forster/ANL/Shutterstock (bottom).

Page 13: Gillian Allen/AP/Shutterstock (top left); AP/Shutterstock (top right); Shutterstock (bottom left); Santiago Lyon/AP/ Shutterstock (bottom right).

SELECT BIBLIOGRAPHY

Airlie, Mabell, Countess of. *Thatched with Gold.* Edited by
  Jennifer Ellis. London: Hutchinson, 1962.

Barry, Stephen. *Royal Secrets: The View from Downstairs.*
  London: Random House, 1985.

Bradford, Sarah. *Elizabeth: A Biography of Her Majesty the
  Queen.* London: Penguin Books, 1996.

Brandreth, Gyles. *Philip and Elizabeth: Portrait of a Royal
  Marriage.* London: W.W. Norton & Company, 2004.

_____. *Philip: The Final Portrait.* London: Coronet, 2021; updated
  from 2004 version *Philip and Elizabeth.*

Brown, Tina. *The Diana Chronicles.* New York: Penguin Random
  House, 2007

Corbitt, F.J. *My Twenty Years in Buckingham Palace.* New York:
  David McKay, 1956.

Crawford, Marion *The Little Princesses.* New York: St. Martin's
  Griffin, 2020; orig. 1950.

Dennison, Matthew. *The Queen.* London: Head of Zeus, 2021.

Dimbleby, Jonathan. *The Prince of Wales: A Biography.* New York:
  William Morrow and Company, Inc., 1994.

Dismore, Jane. *Princess: The Early Life of Queen Elizabeth II.*
  Guilford, Connecticut: Lyons Press, 2018.

Duncan, Andrew. *The Reality of Monarchy.* London: Pan Books,
  1973.

Edwards, Anne. *Royal Sisters: Queen Elizabeth II and Princess
  Margaret.* Guilford, Connecticut: Lyons Press, 1990.

Erickson, Carolly. *Lilibet: An Intimate Portrait of Elizabeth II.*
New York: St. Martin's Press, 2004.

Flamini, Roland. *Sovereign: Elizabeth II and the Windsor Dynasty.* London: Bantam Press, 1991.

Glenconner, Anne. *Lady in Waiting: My Extraordinary Life in the Shadow of the Crown.* London: Hodder & Stoughton, 2019.

Harris, Kenneth. *The Queen.* New York: St. Martin's Press, 1995.

Hartley, John. *Accession: The Making of a Queen.* London: Quartet Books, 1992.

Hoey, Brian. *At Home with the Queen.* London: HarperCollins Publishers, 2002.

Howard, Alathea Fitzalan. *The Windsor Diaries: 1940–1945.* London: Hodder & Stoughton, 2020.

Jay, Antony. *Elizabeth R.* London: BBC Books, 1992.

Jebb, Miles, ed. *The Diaries of Cynthia Gladwyn.* London: Constable, 1995.

Keay, Douglas. *Elizabeth II: Portrait of a Monarch.* London: Ebury Press, 1991.

Kelly, Angela. *The Other Side of the Coin: The Queen, the Dresser, and the Wardrobe.* New York: HarperCollins, 2019.

Lacey, Robert. *The Crown: The Official Companion, Volume 1: Elizabeth II, Winston Churchill, and the Making of a Young Queen (1947–1955).* New York: Crown Archetype, 2017.

_____. *Monarch: The Life and Reign of Elizabeth II.* New York: Free Press, 2003.

Longford, Elizabeth. *Elizabeth R: A Biography.* London: Hodder & Stoughton, 1984.

_____. *The Queen Mother.* New York: W. Morrow, 1981.

Maclean, Veronica. *Crowned Heads: Kings, Emperors, and Sultans – A Royal Quest.* London: Hodder & Stoughton, 1993.

Marr, Andrew. *The Real Elizabeth: An Intimate Portrait of Queen Elizabeth II.* New York: Henry Holt and Company, 2012.

Morgan, Janet. *Edwina Mountbatten, A Life of her Own*. London: HarperCollins, 1991.

Morrow, Ann. *The Queen*. New York: William Morrow and Company, Inc., 1983.

Noel, Celestria. ed. *The Windsor Diaries 1940-45*. London: Hodder and Stoughton, 2020.

Pimlott, Ben. *The Queen: Elizabeth II and the Monarchy*. London: HarperCollins Publishers, 1996.

Rhodes, Margaret. *The Final Curtsey: A Royal Memoir by the Queen's Cousin*. London: Umbria Press, 2012.

Seward, Ingrid. *My Husband and I*. New York: Simon and Schuster, 2017.

_____. *Prince Philip Revealed: A Man of His Century*. London: Simon and Schuster, 2020.

_____. *The Queen and Di: The Untold Story*. London: HarperCollins, 2000.

Shawcross, William ed. *Counting One's Blessings: The Selected Letters of Queen Elizabeth the Queen Mother*. New York: Farrar, Straus, & Giroux, 2012.

Shawcross, William. *The Queen Mother: The Official Biography*. New York: Knopf, 2009.

Smith, Sally Bedell. *Elizabeth the Queen: The Life of a Modern Monarch*. New York: Random House, 2012.

_____. *Prince Charles: The Passions and Paradoxes of an Improbable Life*. New York: Random House, 2017.

Smith, Horace. *A Horseman Through Six Reigns: Reminiscences of a Royal Riding Master*. London: Odhams, 1955.

Stewart, Andrew. *The King's Private Army: Protecting the Royal Family during the Second World War*. Warwick: Helion & Company, 2015.

Strober, Deborah Hart and Gerald S. Strober, *The Monarchy: An Oral Biography of Elizabeth II*. New York: Broadway Books, 2002.

Thorpe, D. R, ed. *Who's In, Who's Out: The Journals of Kenneth Rose, Volume One:, 1944-1979.* London: Weidenfeld & Nicolson, 2019.

_____. *Who Loses, Who Wins: The Journals of Kenneth Rose, Volume Two: 1979-2014.* London: Weidenfeld & Nicolson, 2019.

Turner, Graham. *Elizabeth: The Woman and the Queen.* London: Macmillan, 2002.

Vickers, Hugo. *Elizabeth the Queen Mother.* London: Hutchinson, 2005.

Viney, Graham. *The Last Hurrah: South Africa and the Royal Tour of 1947.* Johannesburg: Jonathan Ball Publishers, 2018.

Wheeler-Bennett, Sir John. *Friends, Enemies and Sovereigns.* London: MacMillan, 1976.

Williams, Kate. *Young Elizabeth: The Making of the Queen.* Berkeley: Pegasus Books, 2015.

Windsor, Duchess of. *The Heart has its Reasons.* London: Michael Joseph, 1956.

INDEX